CON
THE DEMOCRAT

SEAN RORISON
UPDATED BY GILLIAN GLOYER

www.bradtguides.com

Bradt Guides Ltd, UK
The Globe Pequot Press Inc, USA

Bradt GUIDES

TRAVEL TAKEN SERIOUSLY

The River Congo is a lifeline for the deep interior of central Africa
page 3

Adventurous travellers can seek out traditional handicrafts, thronged markets and pulsating nightlife in Kinshasa
page 90

Discover historic towns and mangrove forests where the River Congo meets the Atlantic Ocean in Kongo-Central province
page 110

Salonga National Park is home to rare species such as the bonobo, giant pangolin and slender-snouted crocodile
page 127

CAMEROON

EQUATORIAL GUINEA

GABON

REPUBLIC OF THE CONGO

C.A.R.

Zongo
Gbadolite
Libenge
Businga
Gemena
Lisala
Basankusu
Mbandaka
Lake Tumba
Salonga North National Park
Lake Mai-Ndombe
Salonga South National Park
Dekese
Bandundu
Ilebo
Mweka
Luebo
KINSHASA
Kenge
Kikwit
Kana
Gungu
Tshikapa
Cabinda (Angola)
Boma
Mbanza-Ngungu
Muanda
Matadi
Tembo Falls

ATLANTIC OCEAN

ANGOLA

Di

KEY

■	Capital city
●	Main town
○	Other town
✈	Airport
═	Main road
─	Other road
▤	Railway
–·–	International boundary
––––	National park/reserve

N

Bradt

| 0 | 200km |
| 0 | 100 miles |

Watch Wagenia fishermen securing their catch with conical baskets suspended from wooden frames across the river near Kisangani page 175

Although difficult to access, Garamba National Park rewards the determined visitor with wildlife including giraffes and white rhinos page 178

Virunga National Park has two of the world's most active volcanoes and the largest remaining population of mountain gorillas page 208

Kahuzi-Biega National Park is the only place in the world where eastern lowland gorillas can be tracked page 199

Perhaps the country's most picturesque town, Bukavu overlooks Lake Kivu page 194

The marshlands of Kundelungu and Upemba national parks have beautiful waterfalls and shelter rich wildlife and birdlife page 156

Old colonial façades abound in the relaxed town of Lubumbashi page 142

SOUTH SUDAN

Garamba National Park

Bondo
Niangara
Faradje
Watsa
Titule
Mungbere
Buta
Aketi
Tsiro
Bunia

UGANDA

Basako
Nia-Nia
Beni
Yangambi
Bafwasende
Butembo
Kisangani
Stanley Falls
Virunga National Park
Ubundu
Opala
Lubutu
Lake Edward

DEMOCRATIC REPUBLIC OF THE CONGO

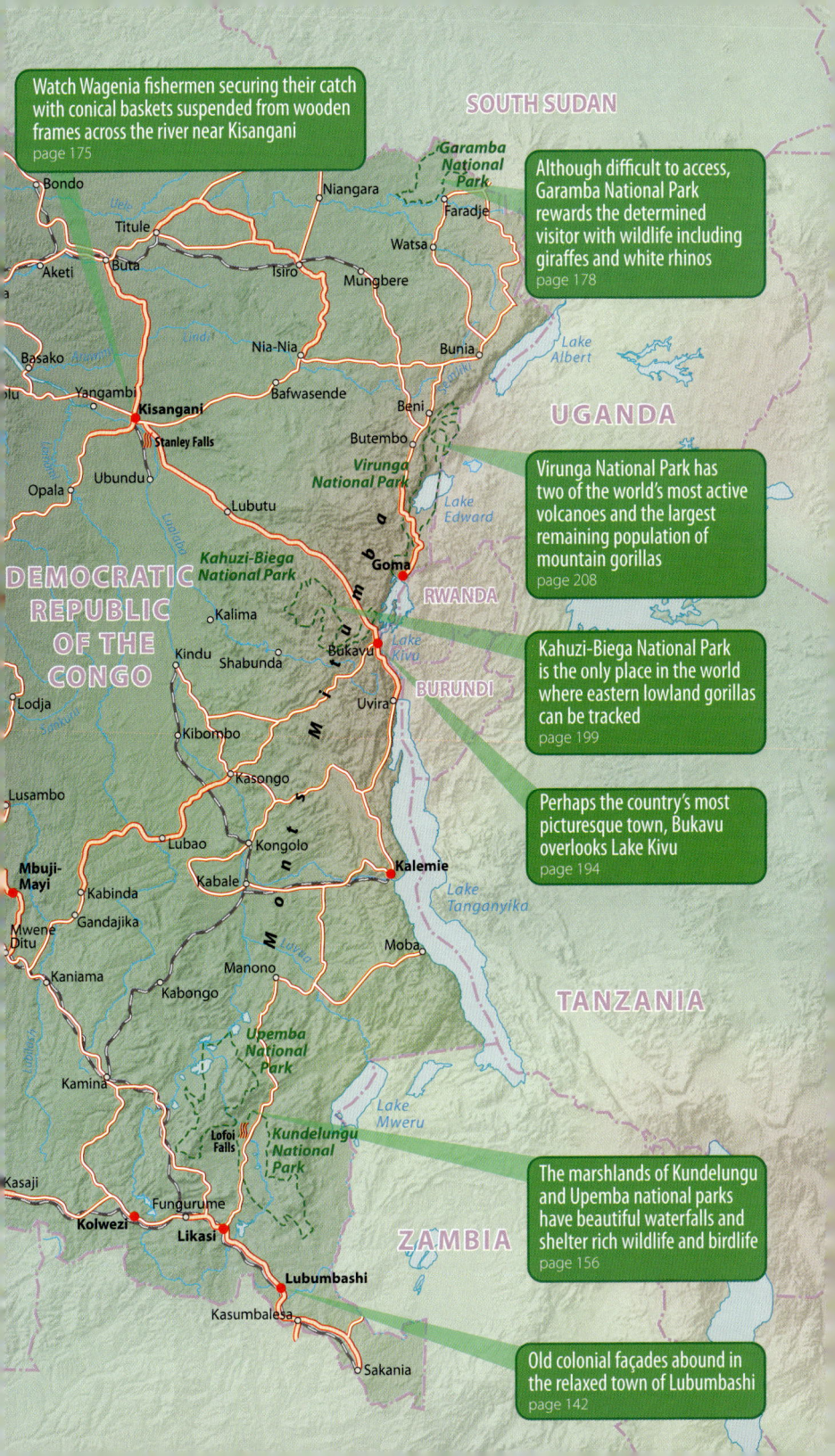

Kahuzi-Biega National Park
Goma
RWANDA
Kalima
Bukavu
Lake Kivu
Kindu
Shabunda
BURUNDI
Uvira

Lodja
Kibombo

Lusambo
Kasongo

Mbuji-Mayi
Lubao
Kongolo
Kabale
Kalemie
Kabinda
Gandajika
Mwene-Ditu
Lake Tanganyika
Kaniama
Moba

TANZANIA

Manono
Kabongo

Kamina

Upemba National Park

Lake Mweru

Lofoi Falls
Kundelungu National Park

Kasaji

ZAMBIA

Fungurume
Kolwezi
Likasi
Lubumbashi

Kasumbalesa

Sakania

Monts Mitumba
Lake Albert

CONGO:
THE DEMOCRATIC REPUBLIC
DON'T MISS...

LOFOI FALLS
The dramatic Lofoi Falls in Kundelungu National Park pour straight down a 300m cliff-face PAGE 156
(SR)

RIVER CONGO
Deep, powerful and rich in wildlife, the River Congo is an artery for transporting people and goods through the country PAGE 3
(SS)

KAHUZI-BIEGA NATIONAL PARK
Kahuzi-Biega National Park is the only place in the world where visitors can track eastern lowland gorillas PAGE 199
(EV/S)

WAGENIA FISHERMEN
The fishermen at the Boyoma Falls have developed a unique method of fishing in the rapids, with baskets suspended from wooden structures PAGE 175
(SS)

BONOBOS
Peaceful and sociable, bonobos are closely related to humans and are found only in the DRC PAGE 123
(FoB/LH)

CONGO:
THE DEMOCRATIC REPUBLIC
IN COLOUR

above
(IK/S)

Brazzaville and Kinshasa face each other across the River Congo, the two closest capital cities in the world PAGE 94

below
(SS)

Kinshasa's cathedral, Our Lady of the Congo, dates from 1947 PAGE 106

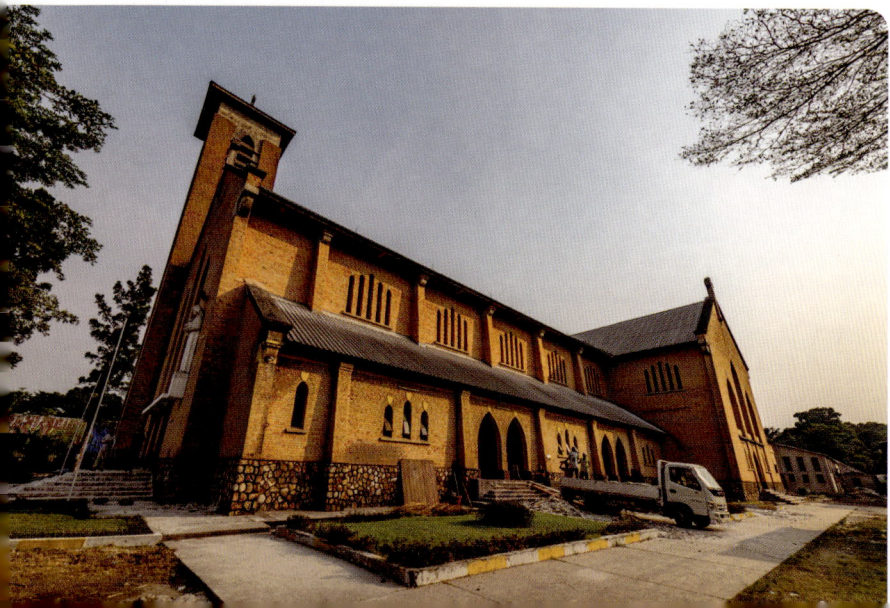

The bustle of Kinshasa's streets is what the city is all about PAGE 103

top
(PAI/A)

Fruit and vegetable markets offer a bewildering variety of delicious fresh food PAGE 76

above left
(EM/S)

The huge range of bread and patisserie in Kinshasa's bakeries is a legacy of Belgian colonial rule PAGE 99

above right
(AT/S)

Lac Ma Vallée is a remnant of tropical rainforest only a few miles outside Kinshasa PAGE 109

below
(NNK/S)

AUTHOR

Sean Rorison is a writer from Vancouver, British Columbia, who has made his way to over 90 countries. His range of travel interests is broad, including some of the most contentious regions of the world – from Afghanistan to Iraq, Colombia to Somalia; he has also indulged his love for more mainstream destinations like Liechtenstein, Malta and Japan. He has written numerous articles on the political and social situations in Somalia, Algeria, Pakistan and the DRC. In 2002, he helped start the popular travel journal site Polo's Bastards, which focuses primarily on difficult destinations. While his readers revel in his journeys to the Congos, they still haven't warmed up to his visits to Malta.

UPDATER

Gillian Gloyer is the author of Bradt's guide to Albania. When she is not supporting democracy in places like the Democratic Republic of the Congo, she divides her time between the bright lights of Edinburgh and the power cuts of a village in southern Albania. She speaks fluent French (as well as Albanian and Spanish) but, despite great intentions, failed to make any progress with Swahili while in the DRC.

AUTHOR'S STORY

It may come as a surprise to some observers that the DRC is improving – in fits and starts, and certainly not in a uniform fashion, but economic development and new opportunity are rampant. The fact that one can travel around with a credit card, and pull out fresh US dollar bills from bank machines in major cities, is a telling example of the DRC becoming reintegrated into the wider world.

New roads, shiny new towers and new businesses galore have appeared since I wrote the first Bradt guide to the Congo, covering both the Republic of the Congo and the DRC. Tourists are arriving in increasing numbers, and of course the ubiquitous business traveller has become ever-present in regions that were once completely off-limits to outsiders.

This means that, more than ever, the DRC is a place open for tourism and business in a way that it has never been before. Indeed, on my first visit to the Democratic Republic of the Congo officials laughed at me when I said I was a tourist – what a ridiculous notion! But these days, even in the most sensitive regions of the country, no-one blinks twice.

This is still not the easiest destination in the world – prices are high and corruption remains a problem. But the signs of improvement are there, and should make anyone optimistic for the future.

A note on this book The contents of this book are adapted from the Bradt Guide to the Congo (2nd edition, 2012), which covered both the Democratic Republic of the Congo and Republic of the Congo.

First edition published April 2025
Bradt Travel Guides Ltd
31a High Street, Chesham, Buckinghamshire, HP5 1BW, England
www.bradtguides.com
Print edition published in the USA by The Globe Pequot Press Inc,
PO Box 480, Guilford, Connecticut 06437–0480

ISBN: 9781804692608

British Library Cataloguing in Publication Data
A catalogue record for this book is available from the British Library

Photographs African Parks: Kate Wilson (KW/AP), Marcus Westberg (MW/AP), Martin van Rooyen (MvR/AP), Ruth Westrick (RW/AP); Alamy Stock Photos: imageBROKER.com GmbH & Co. KG (IB/A), PA Images (PAI/A), Xinhua (X/A); Dreamstime.com: Jiri Hrebicek (JH/D); Friends of Bonobos, photo by Leon Haberkorn (FoB/LH); Gillian Gloyer (GG); Joris de Nocker (JdN); Naturepl.com: Fiona Rogers (FR/NPL); Sean Rorison (SR); Shutterstock. com: Alexandra Tyukavina (AT/S), Biandudi Rene Biar (BRB/S), David Havel (DH/S), Denys. Kutsevalov (DK/S), Eric Valenne geostory (EV/S), Ernesto Martin (EM/S), Issa Kashala (IK/S), Michal Varga (MV/S), Nolda NSEKA KIKO (NNK/S), Omri Eliyahu (OE/S), Ondrej Prosicky (OP/S), Paola Mermati (PM/S), The Road Provides (TRP/S), Thomas Markert (TM/S), Wirestock Creators (WC/S); SuperStock (SS)

Front cover Young male bonobo, Lola Ya Bonobo (FR/NPL)
Back cover, clockwise from top left Countryside around Bukavu (WC/S); fishing on Lake Kivu (OE/S); okapi (JH/D); Congolese masks (PM/S)
Title page, clockwise from top left Our Lady of the Congo cathedral, Kinshasa (SS); Garamba National Park (MW/AP); hippos (SS); Liberian banana frog (SS)

Maps David McCutcheon FBCart.S. FRGS, assisted by Pearl Geo Solutions

Typeset by Ian Spick, Bradt Guides, and BBR Design, Sheffield
Production managed by Imprint Press; printed in India
Digital conversion by www.dataworks.co.in

Acknowledgements

Guidebooks are never written alone, and a great number of people turned out to help with the previous incarnation of this book as a joint guide to the DRC and the Republic of the Congo. In fact, I'd wager that tourism in both Congos is doing better than ever and the number of passionate people who took time out to help are a great indication of this.

First a great thanks to Sarah Trice for her help in expanding and improving the Lubumbashi section, and for all her efforts in helping me while visiting Katanga. Its robustness is a testament to her passion for helping improve tourism in the Congo!

Many thanks to Erin Levi and her contacts in the DRC, especially Dirk Druet for his help in Bukavu, Kate Rougvie in Mbuji-Mayi, and Hugo Warner in Kinshasa. Nuria Ortega at Garamba National Park deserves great thanks for communicating the status of this remote region, and I wish her all the best in the challenge of bringing the park back to its former glory. Thanks to Andrew Fowler for updating me on the excellent progress that has been made in the Lomako-Yokokala Faunal Reserve, and thanks to Christopher Imbsen at Eos-Visions for help in updating the situation in Kahuzi-Biega. Thanks to Michel Van Roten of Go Congo and his associates for helping to update the listings in Goma and Kisangani. Thanks to Philip Briggs for helping to round out the section on Virunga National Park.

Also thanks to those who used the first edition of the guide and took time to write in with updates, most especially Bert Schönfeld and Anton Van Boxtel. And thanks to others: Mathieu Mills and Augustin Nduwa Kakwata.

GILLIAN GLOYER It was thanks to The Carter Center that I spent almost three months in the Democratic Republic of the Congo, as a Long-Term Observer of the December 2023 elections. Several of my colleagues on that mission gathered information for me in their own operational areas. I am especially grateful to Diana Putman, Simon Vall-llosera and Khalil Zerargui for their research in Kalemie, Kananga and Kisangani. Thanks also to Virginie Adala, Allaoua Chelbi and Serge Possiti. Emilio Noorani readily answered my questions about Kinshasa; his blog, w emilioincongo.com, was a source of inspiration as well as information. Professor Francis Lelo Nzuzi kindly fact-checked the Education section in Chapter 1.

Finally, thanks to the readers of the second edition of Bradt's guide to the Congo (which covered both the DRC and the Republic of the Congo), who took the trouble to contact Bradt with updates or corrections. The detailed notes sent by Alejandro Gámez were particularly useful.

Contents

LIST OF MAPS

HOW TO USE THIS GUIDE

PRICE CODES Throughout this guide we have used price codes to indicate the cost of those places to stay and eat listed in the guide. For a key to these price codes, see page 75 for accommodation and page 78 for restaurants.

MAPS
Keys and symbols Maps include alphabetical keys covering the locations of those places to stay, eat or drink that are featured in the book. Note that regional maps may not show all hotels and restaurants in the area: other establishments may be located in towns shown on the map.

Grids and grid references Several maps use gridlines to allow easy location of sites. Map grid references are listed in square brackets after the name of the place or site of interest in the text, with page number followed by grid number, eg: [92 C3].

Introduction

The Democratic Republic of the Congo (DRC) is almost twice the size of the entire European Union and only slightly smaller in area than the South of the United States. Its huge size means it has around 20 different ecosystems: among them tropical rainforest, volcanic mountains, great lakes and savannah plateaux. What unites the country, as well as dividing it, is the River Congo. The Congo rises in the south (as the River Lualaba) and, gathering further tributaries along its way, runs for 4,700km, curving to and fro across the Equator, until it reaches the Atlantic Ocean. The rainforests of the Congo Basin are the second largest carbon-sink in the world, after the Amazon, and are home to the great apes which, for many visitors, will be the main reason to venture to the DRC.

It's the only country in the world with two subspecies of gorilla (mountain and eastern lowland gorillas), and it's the only country in the world that's home to the peaceful, sociable bonobo. Other endemic species include the okapi, a creature related to the giraffe, but with a shorter neck and unmistakable striped hindquarters. Over a thousand distinct species of birds have been recorded in the DRC, the highest count for any single African country. In addition to its amazing wildlife, the DRC's attractions include its world-famous music – *musique congolaise* – and its art.

Much of the country is now relatively safe to visit, although travelling by road remains a challenge, particularly in the rainy season. Internal flights are the easiest way to cover the vast distances involved. This book covers all nine of the country's national parks and many of its other protected areas. It also gives practical information about the cities and major towns, including those that serve as access points for the national parks, and about some out-of-the-way places too, although you should make sure you have the appropriate contacts and permits before wandering around the interior. Many aspects of the DRC's history and culture are also included.

It is hard to say whether one can really know Africa without knowing the DRC. It is so easily overlooked by travellers because of its problems, but those who make the effort to visit will be pleasantly surprised. The scenery is spectacular, the wildlife is fascinating, and the people are resilient and adaptable. Optimism is easy to find, and travellers arriving with the same attitude will not be disappointed. An increase in tourism can only help the country and its people; it is our hope that, for those of you who are thinking of visiting, this book will point you in the right direction.

Part One

GENERAL INFORMATION

DEMOCRATIC REPUBLIC OF THE CONGO AT A GLANCE

Location Central Africa – from the Atlantic coast eastward to the Great Lakes of East Africa

Neighbouring countries Angola, Burundi, Central African Republic, Republic of the Congo, Rwanda, South Sudan, Tanzania, Uganda, Zambia

Size 2,344,858km^2

Climate Equatorial near the Equator; tropical north and south of the Equator; oceanic on Atlantic coast; cooler in southern and eastern highlands

Population 115,403,027 million (2024 estimate)

Life expectancy 62.6 years (2024 estimate)

Capital Kinshasa: population between 11 and 17 million (estimate)

Other major cities Lubumbashi, Kisangani, Goma, Mbuji-Mayi

Languages French (official), Lingala, Kikongo, Tshiluba, Swahili (national)

Religion Christianity, Islam, Kimbanguism, traditional beliefs

Currency Congolese franc (Fc); trades as CDF: £1=Fc3,456; €1=Fc2,902; US$1=Fc2,841 (January 2025)

International airports Kinshasa Ndjili (FIH), Lubumbashi (FBM), Goma (GOM)

International telephone code +243

Time GMT+1 from the Atlantic coast to Bumba/Kikwit; GMT+2 from Kisangani eastward, including Katanga

Electrical voltage 220V

Flag Bright blue with a five-pointed star in the upper left-hand corner, and a wide red stripe with yellow lining running diagonally from bottom left to top right

National sport Football (soccer)

Public holidays 1 January (New Year), 4 January (Martyrs' Day), 6 April (Kimbangu Day), 1 May (Labour Day), 17 May (Liberation Day), 30 June (Independence Day), 25 December (Christmas Day). See also page 78.

1

Background Information

GEOGRAPHY

The Democratic Republic of the Congo (DRC) is the second-largest country in Africa (after Algeria); it is the size of western Europe and about a quarter of the size of the continental United States. Its area of 2,344,858km² includes 77,810km² of water. The DRC is named after and defined by the river that runs through it. Joseph Conrad described the **River Congo** as 'resembling an immense snake uncoiled, with its head in the sea, its body at rest curving afar over a vast country, and its tail lost in the depths of the land'. Indeed, the River Congo (with its main tributary) is 4,700km long – the second-longest river in Africa after the Nile – and crosses the Equator twice. From its banks spreads the Congo rainforest, second in size only to the Amazon rainforest. Because it is fed by tributaries north and south of the Equator, and because the rainy season is different on each side of the Equator, the Congo's flow is stable throughout the year. From the South Atlantic, it is navigable only as far as the port of Matadi, the ending point of the Livingstone Falls, a 350km series of rapids that begins just downstream from Kinshasa. Navigation becomes possible again upstream from Kinshasa, at the Pool Malebo (whose colonial name was the Stanley Pool), as far as the next set of rapids at Kisangani.

The River Congo's sources are in the **mountains and lakes** of the East African Rift. This is the DRC's eastern frontier, marked by volcanoes and highlands, interspersed with fertile rolling grassland. The Rwenzori range, on the border between the DRC and Uganda, has some of Africa's highest mountains; the tallest summit, Pic Marguerite on Mont Ngaliema (Mount Stanley), is 5,109m above sea level. The Virunga Mountains are a chain of volcanoes, of which two are active. Mount Nyiragongo erupts fairly regularly, most recently in May 2021, causing devastation and deaths in the city of Goma. The DRC's border is also marked with a chain of Africa's Great Lakes. Lakes Tanganyika, Kivu and Mweru drain into the Congo's tributaries; lakes Edward and Albert, further north, are part of the complex system of the Upper Nile.

Further south, the equatorial jungles give way to the rolling plains that are more typical of southern Africa. Fertile **savannah** grasslands, with hot summers and a short rainy season, create a much drier atmosphere than the rainforests to their north. And being situated on a high plateau easing slowly downward into the Congo Basin, they have less humidity than the deep jungle. The plateau has fertile land and, below it, vast deposits of mineral wealth.

CLIMATE

The DRC is such a large country that it has several different climatic zones. Near the Equator, for example at Kisangani, the climate is **equatorial**, with high temperatures and humidity throughout the year. On either side of the Equator is the **tropical** zone, with two seasons: dry and rainy (or 'wet'). To the north of the Equator, the rains fall from April to October; to its south, the rainy season runs from November to March. It is thanks to this difference in the rainfall pattern that the River Congo's flow is constant throughout the year. The eastern highlands, including the Virunga and Rwenzori mountains, are cooler, but wetter, than lower-lying regions. The southern plateau (Katanga) has a shorter rainy season, from December to March, and once it reaches the altitude of Lubumbashi, the temperatures are somewhat cooler than they are closer to the River Congo; in the rainy season, nights in Lubumbashi can actually be cold, down to single figures (centigrade). The short stretch of Atlantic coast has an **oceanic** climate, with less rain and lower temperatures than elsewhere in the country.

When it rains, it really rains. The downpours do not usually last more than a couple of hours, but they are torrential, flooding city streets and unpaved roads. Getting around the country is even more of a challenge in the rainy season than in the dry season.

NATURAL HISTORY AND CONSERVATION

What is now the Democratic Republic of the Congo has had protected areas for longer than any other part of Africa. King Léopold II created the first African nature reserves in 1889, concerned for the long-term survival of the elephant. While his Belgian officials were ruthlessly destroying whole communities to increase the volume of rubber extracted from the Congo Free State, the king would be paying more attention to the well-being of elephants across his private nation.

The first official park that still exists was created in 1925 by King Albert and, unsurprisingly, called Albert National Park. After independence, it was renamed Virunga National Park. Other parks and reserves would follow: Kagera in 1934 (now Kahuzi-Biega), Garamba in 1938, Kundelungu in 1939. The Belgian administration managed the parks separately from the rest of the colony, and they were well protected during the colonial period. Mobutu Sese Seko added more protected areas: Salonga, Upemba and Maiko national parks, plus the Okapi Wildlife Reserve.

The DRC now has nine national parks, which are managed by the Congolese Institute for the Conservation of Nature (ICCN). Increasingly, the parks are co-managed by ICCN and an international partner; this co-management model has come from the reluctance of foreign donors to fund protected areas managed by ICCN alone. In 1979, Virunga National Park was designated as a UNESCO World Heritage Site. Since then, UNESCO has added four more protected areas in the DRC to its World Heritage list: Garamba and Kahuzi-Biega in 1980, Salonga in 1984 and the Okapi Wildlife Reserve in 1996. The DRC also has two Biosphere Reserves, both created in 1976: Luki in Kongo-Central province and Yangambi in Tshopo province, downriver from Kisangani. Biosphere Reserves are places for studying the interactions between social and ecological systems. They are nominated by national governments and designated by UNESCO's Man and the Biosphere Programme.

Despite the protected status of the national parks and reserves, wildlife and habitats alike are extremely vulnerable. Poaching, mainly for bushmeat but also for ivory, has been made worse by decades of conflict, with soldiers who are hiding in the forests killing animals for food. Former ICCN directors were allegedly involved in trafficking protected wildlife, including primates and okapi, in return for bribes. Forest burning, for charcoal and by the mining industry, is as bad as it is in the Amazon rainforest, but much less well known. Anti-poaching patrols, park rangers and international partners do their best to protect these vulnerable parks, but hundreds of rangers have been killed in the line of duty.

See the relevant chapters for more information about all these protected areas.

WILDLIFE GUIDE with Mike Unwin

Mammals
Mammals as a class (Mammalia) are distinguished by having hairy bodies, among other anatomical traits, and by their habit of suckling their young. The DRC is especially rich in mammals, with upwards of 400 species. These range from such 'megafauna' as gorillas and elephants, to a multitude of lesser known rodents, bats and other smaller creatures of the night.

Ungulates and other herbivores
Ungulates, or hoofed mammals, can be divided into two principal groups: the even-toed ungulates (order Artiodactyla), which have two or four toes, and include antelope, cattle, pigs, giraffes and hippos; and the odd-toed ungulates (order Perissodactyla), which have one or three toes, and include horses and rhinos. All ungulates are herbivores, grazing or browsing on a wide range of shrubs, grass and herbs across their range. Other large herbivores include elephants, which belong to a separate order: Proboscidae.

Antelope The antelope family (Bovidae) is well represented in the DRC, with a wide variety of species, each of which occupies a different habitat niche in the region. **Duikers** (*Cephalophus* spp), are small to medium-sized antelope with short horns and rounded backs. Approximately 17 species occur in the region. The majority are adapted to forest habitats, where they take refuge in thick undergrowth when disturbed, though most common is the **bush duiker**, which – as its name suggests – is also common in savannah. The larger **reedbuck** (*Redunca arundinum*) has short, forward-curving horns, a sandy coat and prefers long-grass habitats. In the same family is the **Nile lechwe** (*Kobus megaceros*), which has long lyre-shaped horns and prefers moist regions. The **hartebeest** (*Alcelaphus buselaphus*) belongs to a different antelope tribe. It has short twisted horns, a long narrow snout and long legs that allow a loping, energy-efficient gait.

The spiral-horned antelope (*Tragelaphini* spp) are more closely related to cattle than to other antelope. The **bongo** (*Tragelaphus euryceros*) is a forest species, with a stocky, chestnut body emblazoned with white stripes, and sturdy, twisted horns. The similar but smaller **bushbuck** (*Tragelaphus scriptus*) is much more common, and can be distinguished by the white spotting along its flanks. The **sitatunga** (*Tragelaphus spekeii*) has shaggier fur and longer horns than a bushbuck and is restricted to marshy habitats, where its unusually long, splayed hooves are an adaptation for moving across wet ground. The **greater kudu** (*Tragelaphus strepsiceros*) is a tall, elegant species of dry bush country, with spectacular spiral horns in the male that can reach a length of over 1.5m. Even larger is **Derby's eland** (*Taurotragus derbianus*), which has a square, ox-like build, straight horns and a prominent dewlap, and can reach a weight of nearly 1,000kg. It is the only member of this group in which the female, as well as the male, carries horns.

African buffalo (*Syncerus caffer*) The buffalo belongs to the same family as the antelope and is Africa's only true ox. Two races inhabit the DRC, with the forest race being redder in colour than the savannah race. These sociable animals may gather in herds of hundreds or even thousands. Both sexes carry impressive horns, though the larger males can be distinguished from females by the heavier 'boss' or bony plate on top of the head.

Wild pigs (Suidae) The **warthog** (*Phacocherus africanus*) is the best known of Africa's wild pigs. It prefers lightly wooded country, where it is easily identified by its bare, grey skin and large curling tusks. More common in woodland and forested areas is the hairier, shorter-tusked **bush pig** (*Potamochoerus larvatus*), which is strictly nocturnal, and digs for roots and tubers along forest trails. The **red river hog** (*Potamochoerus porcus*) is a rainforest species, and has a rich red coat, bold white face markings and long tasselled ears. The **giant forest hog** is the largest of the family, with males sometimes exceeding 250kg. This rare species has a long black coat, stout tusks and occurs patchily in forests at up to 3,800m.

Hippopotamus (*Hippopotamus amphibius*) Hippos are unmistakable, with their great size, rotund body, huge teeth and, most of all, their habit – unique among ungulates – of spending the daylight hours submerged in water. They frequent shallow lakes, rivers and swamplands, emerging at night to graze on waterside grassland. An adult may weigh over 2,000kg and requires about 60kg of food per night.

Okapi (*Okapia johnstoni*) The okapi is a member of the giraffe family (Giraffidae), and has been a curiosity since it was first discovered at the beginning of the 20th century. This bizarre-looking animal has a longish neck, long ears, short horns and an exceptionally long tongue, used for plucking leaves from overhead branches. Its chocolate to purplish-brown coat is patterned with white face markings and white zebra-like stripes on the legs. Okapis are extremely shy, living only in deep rainforests, where they prefer low river valleys but migrate to higher ground in the rainy season. Giraffes themselves are only found in the far northeast of the DRC.

White rhinoceros (*Ceratotherium simun*) Rhinos (Rhinocerotidae) are odd-toed ungulates, closely related to horses. These massive, thick-skinned animals have stout legs with three toes on each foot, and two distinctive horns. Two species occur in Africa, of which only the larger white rhino remains in the DRC and is now reduced to a handful of reintroduced individuals in Garamba National Park. This animal can exceed 2,500kg in weight, making it the second-largest African mammal after the elephant, and prefers open woodland and grassland habitats. It is distinguished from the smaller black rhino (*Diceros bicornis*) by a hump on its neck, as well as by its longer head and broader mouth, the latter an adaptation for grazing.

Common zebra (*Equus zebra*) The zebra is a member of the horse family, also an odd-toed ungulate, and is rendered quite unmistakable by its pattern of black and white stripes. It travels in small family groups of up to 30, preferring open plains with good grazing and easy access to water. In the DRC, zebras are found only in Upemba and Kundelungu national parks.

African elephant (*Loxodonta africana*) The African elephant is the largest land mammal on the planet. It is divided into two subspecies, the forest elephant (*L. a. cyclotis*) and bush elephant (*L. a. africana*), now considered by many authorities to be separate species. Forest elephants are the smaller of the two and distinguished by their downward-pointing tusks. They are the more widespread race in the DRC. Elephants are highly gregarious creatures with complex social structures and a sophisticated range of communication techniques. They tend to move in family groups, led by a dominant older female, or matriarch, but may form larger herds in times of migration and drought.

Carnivores A wide spectrum of carnivores (order Carnivora) is found in the DRC, including cats, dogs and hyenas, as well as several smaller groups. Carnivores are specialised meat-eaters, with teeth and claws adapted to their predatory way of life. A few species, however, also include some plant matter in their diet.

Cats (Felidae) Cats are perhaps the most specialised of all carnivores. Most species are solitary and nocturnal, and have retractile claws with which to capture and despatch prey.

Lion (*Panthera leo*) The lion is both Africa's largest feline and its largest carnivore, famous for its far-carrying roar and the flowing mane of hair carried by adult males. It hunts medium-sized to large game up to the size of buffalo, but will take smaller prey if nothing else is available. Lions are the most sociable of all cats, with groups – known as 'prides' – numbering anything from five to more than 30 individuals, depending upon the availability of prey. They are primarily nocturnal and prefer open bush, though they have been found in all habitats except deep equatorial rainforest. Lions occur in the eastern half of the DRC.

Leopard (*Panthera pardus*) The leopard is about half the weight of a lion, and its distinctive coat of black spots on a tawny to yellow background provides excellent camouflage. It is a secretive, solitary hunter, and uses stealth and cover to ambush its prey. Leopards are extremely versatile, occurring in all habitats from rainforest to desert, and are the national animal of the DRC. They feed on anything from medium-sized antelopes to small mammals, frogs and birds.

Cheetah (*Acinonyx jubatus*) The cheetah is the fastest of all land mammals. It is the size of a leopard, but slimmer, with a smaller head, longer legs and small solid spots rather than rosettes. Cheetahs need open country in which to hunt their medium-sized to small antelope prey, running them down at exceptional speeds of up to 112km/h. They are threatened throughout Africa and rare in the DRC.

Smaller cats Smaller cats include the **golden cat** (*Felis aurata*), a powerful forest dweller that ambushes prey up to the size of duiker, and the long-legged, spotted **serval** (*Felis serval*), which uses expert hearing to locate its rodent prey in long grass and marshlands.

Other carnivores The **spotted hyena** (*Crocuta crocuta*) is the largest member of the hyena family (Hyenidae). This sociable predator is not only an expert scavenger, with powerful, bone-crunching jaws, but also a proficient hunter capable of tackling prey as large as zebra. It prefers open habitats and is absent from deep forest. The **side-striped jackal** (*Canis adustus*) is the most abundant member of the dog family in the DRC, and flourishes around villages and small towns. Its omnivorous diet includes anything from small antelope to berries.

Lower down the carnivore scale, the weasel family (Mustelidae) is represented by a variety of species, varying from the widespread **honey badger** (*Mellivora capensis*), a specialist raider of bee nests, to the **swamp otter** (*Aonyx congica*), one of three otter species that use their excellent swimming skills to catch fish in the region's lakes and rivers. The genet and civet family (Viverridae) comprises a number of long-tailed, low-slung species, most of which are arboreal, including the **central African linsang** (*Poiana leightoni*), which has a lithe, spotted body

1

and hunts small prey in the tree canopy, and the **African palm civet** (*Nandinia binotata*), which feeds primarily on fruit and often frequents cultivated areas. The closely related mongooses (family Herpestidae) are small to medium-sized, short-legged carnivores. Some, such as the crab-eating **marsh mongoose** (*Atalix paludinosus*), are largely solitary and nocturnal; others, such as the smaller **banded mongoose** (*Mungos mungo*), are sociable and forage by daylight.

Primates The Congo region, with its huge tracts of forest, has the greatest variety of primate species (order Primates) in Africa. These fall into two main subdivisions: the apes and Old World monkeys (Catarrhini); and the more primitive bushbabies and pottos (Strepsirrhini), collectively known as prosimians.

Apes Apes are our closest living relatives. They are distinguished from monkeys by, among other things, their lack of a tail.

Gorilla (*Gorilla gorilla*) The gorilla is the world's largest primate. Scientists currently recognise three main subspecies: the western lowland gorilla (*Gorilla gorilla gorilla*), eastern lowland gorilla (*Gorilla beringei graueri*) and mountain gorilla (*Gorilla beringei beringei*). Further research may add more, specifically the gorillas of Mount Tshiaberimu (*Gorilla gorilla tshiaberimuensis*). By far the most numerous is the western lowland race. The eastern lowland race has slightly shorter fur and is the largest of the three. The mountain gorilla is easily recognisable by its long black fur, an adaptation to its cold, high-altitude habitat. Gorillas are herbivores and forage within their range during the day for leaves, bamboo shoots and other plant matter. They form groups of ten to 30, presided over by a dominant male identified by his saddle of grey fur and known, consequently, as a silverback.

Chimpanzees (*Pan troglodytes*) Chimpanzees are smaller than gorillas but are more closely related to humans. They inhabit deep rainforests, where they feed largely on fruit in the canopy of large trees, but may also frequent low mountain forests and savannah. Their omnivorous diet includes meat, and they are capable hunters, sometimes using organised ambushes to capture monkeys or small antelope. Chimpanzee groups may number up to 120 and are strongly territorial. Individuals build nests in trees with twigs and branches, preferring areas as high as possible from the ground.

Bonobo (*Pan paniscus*) The bonobo, once thought to be a subspecies of chimpanzee, has a complex social system, in which sexuality plays a prominent role. It is also known for its habit of often walking nearly upright. Its hair is shorter than that of the other apes, and it has an entirely hairless face and usually a bare chest. Bonobos are confined to the DRC, where they frequent swampy habitats and jungle, and seldom travel far from their home range. They eat mostly plant matter and fruit, and, like chimps, may use items as tools to retrieve their food.

Monkeys Monkeys are generally smaller than apes. Most species have long tails and dextrous limbs, allowing them great agility among the branches.

Baboons (*Papio* spp) Baboons are large, sociable monkeys that feed mostly on the ground and roost in trees. They have distinctly bushy hair, and a long dog-like muzzle – most pronounced in the male. The two subspecies found in the DRC are the olive baboon (*Papio anubis*) and the yellow baboon (*Papio cynocephalus*), the latter being distinguished by its darker, thicker fur, including a heavy mane around the neck. Baboons are quite adaptable to human settlements and often become a nuisance in farmlands by raiding crops. They inhabit mostly bush and savannah regions, and are among the most abundant and approachable animals in many game parks, where they occur in large groups, dominated by one or more adult males.

Colobus monkeys (family Colobinae) Several species of colobus occur in the DRC. These long-legged, arboreal monkeys feed on leaves and are found mostly in rainforest, where they make spectacular leaps through the canopy. Most abundant is the **Tshuapa red colobus** (*Piliocolobus tholloni*), which has red-brown fur and a long face. The similar but larger **central African red colobus** (*Piliocolobus foai*) has a more easterly range and distinctly thicker fur. The **Angola pied colobus** (*Colobus angolensis*) has thick ruffs of white fur on the face, shoulders and tail, which contrast with its otherwise all-black coat. The similar **guereza colobus** (*Colobus guereza*) has a longer white cape and tends to occur at higher elevations.

Other monkeys Other monkeys found in the DRC include the **grey-cheeked mangabey** (*Lophocebus albigena*), which has long limbs, a ragged tail and frequents swamp forest; the common and versatile **tantalus monkey** (*Cercopithecus aethiops tantalus*), which has a distinct white trim around its dark face and is commonly found in cultivated areas; and **De Brazza's monkey** (*Cercopithecus neglectus*), which is a shy inhabitant of riverine forest and sports a distinctive combination of orange brow and white beard.

Prosimians Several small, primitive primates, known collectively as prosimians, inhabit the forests of the DRC. These only come out at night, so are seldom seen, although a spotlight might pick up their eyes in the tree canopy. **Bushbabies** (*Galago* spp) are squirrel-sized, agile little creatures, with big ears, saucer eyes and piercing cries – hence the name. The slightly larger **potto** (*Perodicticus potto*) is a slower-moving, sloth-like primate that spends the night foraging upside down from branches.

Other mammals In addition to the better-known mammals described on page 5, the DRC is home to a great many others, most of which are small, nocturnal and seldom seen by the average visitor. These include such prolific groups as bats (Chiroptera), rodents (Rodentia) and insectivores (Insectivora), as well as oddities such as pangolins and hyraxes. A few species warrant a brief mention here.

The **giant pangolin** (*Manis gigantea*) has a scaly body, resembling a giant pine cone, set off by a long tail and long, narrow snout. Unlike other pangolins in the region it feeds primarily on the ground, where it uses powerful claws to break into termite mounds. The **hammer bat** (*Hypsignathus monstrosus*), the largest of the region's many fruit bats, forms large roosts in lowland forests and is identified by its bizarre, hammer-shaped head. The **African giant squirrel** (*Protoxerus stangeri*) is the largest squirrel in the region, with a distinctive ringed tail, and feeds on fruits high in the rainforest canopy. **Lord Derby's anomalure** (*Anomalurus derbianus*) is a fine-furred, nocturnal rodent that makes prodigious glides from tree to tree using a thin membrane stretched between its extended limbs. The **brush-tailed porcupine** (*Atherurus africanus*) is a rainforest porcupine, with a low-slung body and sharp quills along its back and tail. The **giant otter shrew** (*Potamogale velox*) is an aquatic insectivore closely related to the tenrecs of Madagascar, which uses its flattened tail for swimming and its bristly snout to capture prey such as crabs and frogs. The **western tree hyrax** (*Dendrohyrax dorsalis*) has evolutionary affinities with elephants, despite looking like a fat furry rodent, and inhabits evergreen forests, where its eerie wailing calls carry some distance at night.

Also known as a sea cow, the **African manatee** (*Trichechus senegalensis*) is a large aquatic mammal, with seal-like front flippers and a broad paddle-like tail. It lives in warm, shallow coastal waters and mangroves, where it moves slowly across the sea bed, grazing on algae and seagrass, as well as the leaves of mangroves.

Birds The Congo region has Africa's greatest variety of birds, with an amazing 1,150-plus species recorded in the DRC – the highest count for any single African country. It is impossible here to do justice to this staggering richness. The following brief account mentions a few of the better-known and more obvious species to look out for, and lists the endemic and near-endemic birds – ie: those species found only or almost only in the DRC – which are of particular interest to serious birdwatchers.

Waterbirds Lakes and other water bodies often hold a wealth of waterbirds. **Pink-backed pelicans** (*Pelecanus rufescens*) are expert fish catchers, as is the dagger-beaked **African darter** (*Anhinga melanogaster*), which has a characteristic habit of swimming with only its neck protruding above the surface. Among a variety of herons are the enormous **goliath heron** (*Ardea goliath*) and much smaller **black egret** (*Egretta ardesiaca*), the latter making a shady canopy with its wings to lure unsuspecting fish. Storks include the stately **saddle-billed stork** (*Ephippiorhynchus senegalensis*), with its bold red-and-yellow beak, and the massive, carrion-eating **marabou stork** (*Lepotilos crumeniferus*). Among others are the unique **hamerkop** (*Scopus umbretta*), which builds an enormous nest in an overhanging waterside branch; the **African spoonbill** (*Platalea alba*), which sweeps the shallows with its spatulate beak to filter out aquatic invertebrates; and the **sacred ibis** (*Threskiornis aethiopica*), which probes swampy ground with its long curved bill. Meanwhile the attractive **African jacana** (*Actophilornis africana*) explores the swampy vegetation of lake fringes on its huge toes.

Ground birds Among a variety of game birds are the partridge-like **francolins** (*Francolinus* spp) and the ubiquitous **helmeted guineafowl** (*Numida meleagris*), all of which have raucous ear-splitting calls. Open grassland habitats are home to a variety of other ground-nesting birds, including the striking **crowned lapwing** (*Vanellus coronatus*), the elegant **black-bellied bustard** (*Lissotis melanogaster*) and – in more moist areas – the **grey crowned crane** (*Balearica regulorum*), with its beautiful golden crest.

Birds of prey An abundance of prey ensures plenty of raptors: the formidable **crowned eagle** (*Stephanoaetus coronatus*) is the nemesis of monkeys in the rainforest canopy; the **long-crested eagle** (*Lophaetus occpitalis*) watches for rodents from its roadside perches; and the striking **African fish eagle** (*Haliaetus vocifer*) stakes out lakes and rivers for its fishy prey. Vultures range from the huge **lappet-faced vulture** (*Aegypius tracheliotos*) to the smaller **hooded vulture** (*Necrosyrtes monachus*), the latter often found around settlements, and even includes one vegetarian species, the widespread **palmnut vulture** (*Gypohierax angolensis*). Other raptors include the imperious **secretary bird** (*Sagittarius serpentarius*), which stalks grasslands for reptiles and small mammals, the scavenging and migratory **black kite** (*Milvus migrans*) and the **African harrier hawk** (*Polyboroides typus*), which winkles out prey from tree holes using double-jointed legs. When darkness falls, the owls take over, ranging in size from the giant **Verreaux's eagle owl** (*Bubo lacteus*) to the diminutive **pearl-spotted owlet** (*Glaucidium perlatum*), and including the impressive ochre-coloured **Pel's fishing owl** (*Scotopelia peli*), which hunts like a nocturnal fish eagle.

Fruit-eaters and hole-nesters Fruiting forest trees draw a variety of colourful fruit-eaters. These include turacos, such as the huge **great blue turaco** (*Corythaeola cristata*); hornbills, such as the massive-beaked **black-and-white casqued hornbill** (*Bycanistes brevis*); parrots, such as the vociferous **African grey parrot** (*Psittacus erithacus*); and barbets, such as the boldly patterned **double-toothed barbet** (*Lybius bidentatus*). The **African green pigeon** (*Treron calva*), a striking member of the region's large pigeon family, has also adapted to a fruit diet.

Other colourful birds include a variety of bee-eaters, such as the stunning **red-throated bee-eater** (*Merops bulocki*), and rollers, such as the **broad-billed roller** (*Eurostymos glaucurus*), which flashes dazzling azure wings in its display flight. These birds, like hornbills, nest in holes, as do members of the kingfisher family, such as the jewel-like **malachite kingfisher** (*Alcedo criststa*), found in waterside vegetation, or the crow-sized **giant kingfisher** (*Mageceryle maxima*), fond of quiet backwaters.

Passerines The largest order of birds is the passerines (Passeriformes), also known as perching birds. This diverse assemblage comprises about half the species in the region, including such families as the jewel-like **sunbirds** (*Nectariania* spp), whose curved bills are adapted to sipping nectar from flowers; the industrious **weavers** (*Ploceus* spp), which fashion an extraordinary variety of hanging nests; and the exquisite **waxbills** (*Estrilda* spp), which feed on or near the ground in small twittering parties. Many passerines, including numerous similar cisticolas, babblers, greenbuls and other 'small brown jobs', defy identification by any but the most experienced birdwatcher. But more striking and obvious species include the melodious **white-browed robin-chat** (*Cossypha heugleni*), the dazzling **African paradise flycatcher** (*Tersiphone viridis*), the brilliant **black-headed gonolek** (*Lanarius erythogaster*), the ubiquitous **common bulbul** (*Pycnonotus barbatus*) and the spirited **fork-tailed drongo** (*Dicrurus absimiis*).

Endemic birds The following species are found only in the DRC. Many have evolved in isolation in such hotspots of endemism as the Albertine Rift or Itombwe Mountains. The **Congo peafowl** (*Afropavo congensis*) inhabits the deep Congo rainforests, around Maiko and Salonga. It is a colourful, green-winged member of the guinea-fowl family that feeds on the forest floor, although little research has been done on this species. The **Bedford's paradise flycatcher** (*Terpsiphone bedfordi*) is the only all-grey member of the paradise flycatcher family and, at 20cm, the largest. It prefers low-lying rainforest and can be seen in Kahuzi-Biega Park and Mount Hoyo Reserve. The **golden-naped weaver** (*Ploceus aureonucha*) is a medium-sized weaver, almost entirely black except for a red-brown patch on its head and bright orange-yellow collar with yellow along the spine. It is found only in Ituri, if at all. The **Congo bay owl** (*Phodilus prigoginei*) is a small owl found only in the Albertine Rift, with a smooth facial area and dark brown wings. The **Neumann's coucal** (*Centropus leucogaster neumanni*) is distinguished from most other coucals by its black throat and smaller size. It prefers vines on forest edges and is found near rivers in the north of the country. The **Prigogine's nightjar** (*Caprimulgus prigoginei*)

1

is an extremely rare variation of the nightjar from the Itombwe Mountains. It's smaller than other nightjars, with all-brown plumage and small spots. The **Scarce swift** (*Schoutedenapus myoptilus*) and **Schouteden's swift** (*S. schoutedeni*) are both typical swifts, dark in colour with curved, pointed wings. Schouteden's swift has a more distinctly forked tail. The **yellow-crested helmetshrike** (*Prionops alberti*) is a dark-brown to black bird, easily recognised by its bright yellow crown.

Near-endemic birds The following species occur only in the DRC and in the nearby surrounding regions. The **Hartlaub's duck** (*Pteronetta hartlaubii*) is the only truly forest-dwelling African duck and it can be found anywhere north of Katanga. It has a brown body, blue-grey wings and some white on the male's head. The **long-tailed hawk** (*Urotriorchis macrourus*) is Africa's largest hawk. It has a long V-shaped tail with black-and-white markings, and a spotted or white belly. The **bare-cheeked trogon** (*Apaloderma aequatoriale*) has bright yellow patches of skin near its beak, a bright green rump and a red to yellow belly. The **chocolate-backed kingfisher** (*Halcyon badia*) has a bright red bill, brown head, and blue on its wings and tail. Its call is loud and distinctive and it can be found anywhere north of Katanga. The **red-fronted antpecker** (*Parmoptila rubrifrons*) is found in equatorial forests. The male has a bright red patch on its crown and a bright-brown belly, with a more common white belly on the female. It is often confused with the red-headed antpecker, which has a red face but brown crown. The **Rockefeller's sunbird** (*Cinnyris rockefelleri*) has a broad red band across the breast with a small purple band above it. Its bill is longer than most sunbirds. It can be found among the Itombwe Mountains.

Apalises **Kabobo apalis** (*Apalis kaboboensis*), **chestnut-throated apalis** (*Apalis porphyrolaema*), **Kungwe apalis** (*Apalis argentea*) and **buff-throated apalis** (*Apalis rufogularis*) are all small birds with a white belly, a red or dark brown neck and black wings. Range: Albertine Rift, common in Virunga.

Mountain babblers **Chapin's mountain babbler** (*Kupeornis chapini*) has smooth brown plumage all over, whereas the **red-collared mountain babbler** (*Kupeornis rufocinctus*) has bright orange markings on the neck and near the tail. Range: Albertine Rift.

Crombecs **Green crombec** (*Sylvietta virens*), **white-browed crombec** (*Sylvietta leucophrys*) and **Chapin's crombec** (*Sylvietta leucophrys chapini*) are all tiny birds with a brown crown, white belly and green wings. Range: Albertine Rift.

Waxbills Most widespread is the **orange-cheeked waxbill** (*Estrilda melpoda*), which has a bright orange face. The **black-faced waxbill** (*Estrilda nigriloris*) has a black face and black-and-white plumage, and occurs only in the Albertine Rift.

Reptiles and amphibians The DRC is home to some 300 species of reptile and 200 of amphibian. The former, which include snakes, lizards, crocodiles and turtles, are distinguished from the latter by their dry scaly skin. There is no space here to do justice to the many species of frog that dominate the region's amphibian fauna, but the visitor will not be able to avoid their ubiquitous night-time chorus.

Snakes The DRC has a number of venomous snakes whose fearsome reputation precedes them. These include several species of cobra, such as the **forest cobra** (*Naja melanoleuca*), which rear and spread a hood when threatened, and mambas, such as **Jameson's mamba** (*Dendroaspis jamesoni*), which are swift hunters of birds and other prey in the tree canopy. In reality, however, the danger of snakebite is greatly exaggerated and even these impressive-looking species will avoid people if at all possible. More of a danger is the sluggish but quick-striking **puff adder** (*Bitis arietans*), of open country, which has a fat body and distinctive camouflage pattern. Even better camouflaged is the beautiful **gabon viper** (*Bitis gabonica*), a forest-floor resident, which has the longest fangs of any snake. Many more snakes are non-venomous. These include the **African rock python** (*Python sebae*), Africa's longest snake, which can capture and swallow prey up to the size of small antelope. Also notable are the remarkable **egg-eaters** (*Dasypeltis* spp), which can unhinge their jaws wide enough to swallow a hen's egg several times larger than their own head.

Lizards Largest among the lizards are the giant **monitor lizards** (*Varanus* spp). These powerful predators may exceed 2m in length, and are often seen scrambling noisily for the water when disturbed along a riverside path. Other lizards commonly encountered include smooth-bodied, long-tailed **skinks** (*Mabuya* spp), often seen sunning themselves around buildings; **tropical house geckos** (*Hemidactylus* spp), which use adhesive pads on their toes to clamber around ceilings at night in search of insect prey; and **agamas** (*Agama* spp), which have rough, spiny bodies and nod their big colourful heads in striking courtship displays. Most bizarre, however, are the many species of **chameleon** (family Chamaeleonidae), which camouflage themselves among leaves and capture insects by striking with a tongue longer than their own body.

Other reptiles Three other reptiles deserve a mention. The **Nile crocodile** (*Crocodylus niloticus*) is the largest of the three crocodiles found in the DRC. This massive animal can exceed 5m in length and live for over 100 years. It is the supreme predator in most low-lying freshwater systems, capable of capturing prey as large as buffalo, but has declined considerably in the face of relentless persecution. The smallest is the Congo dwarf crocodile (*Osteolaemus tetraspis osborni*) which lives only in the equatorial forests of the DRC. It is very rare and has been little studied. On the Atlantic coastline, the **leatherback turtle** (*Dermochelys coriacea*) hauls ashore to lay its eggs. This species is the largest of the world's sea turtles, reaching over 800kg in weight, and feeds primarily on jellyfish. It spends most of its life far out to sea.

Insects and other invertebrates
The Congo rainforests shelter an incalculable abundance of insect and other invertebrate life, with many species yet to be described by science. It includes well over 1,000 species of butterfly and moth, among which the **swallowtail butterflies** (Papilionidae) and **emperor moths** (Saturniidae) are among the larger and more spectacular. Even more numerous in terms of species are the beetles, with the enormous **goliath beetles** (*Goliathus* spp) being the bulkiest insects on earth. Other notable insects include the many species of predatory **preying mantis** and herbivorous **stick insect** and **leaf insect**, which have evolved an uncanny likeness to the plants on which they live, and the columns of **driver ants** (Dorylinae) that march inexorably through the forest undergrowth, devouring anything edible in their path. Common **termites** (Termitidae family) leave impressive monuments to their industry in the form of towering termite mounds (termitaria) scattered across grasslands, while the ***Anopheles*** mosquito continues to have a deadly and debilitating impact on human populations by transmitting the parasite that causes malaria.

Among other invertebrates to look out for are some impressive spiders, including the **golden orb-web spiders** (*Nephila* spp), whose tiny males are dwarfed by the large females as they sit in the middle of a remarkably robust web strung across a clearing; giant **African land snails** (*Achatina* spp), whose fist-sized shells are often found in the bush; and **millipedes** (order Juliformia), often seen trundling along after rains on their forest of twinkling legs.

HISTORY

The history of the Congo, as the point where the continent converges, is inextricably tied to that of central Africa and even beyond; it can initially be overwhelming due to its numerous interacting elements. Tribal politics and mass migration into the region formed nation-states long before the arrival of Europeans; the middle centuries of the 2nd millennium CE would be marked by the interaction between these kingdoms and European traders. Early European historical texts focused on a primitive and decentralised group of tribes that were encountered in the area, though the explorers and traders themselves would disagree with this notion, as they were in regular contact with what were royalty of the region. However, this attitude would persist for centuries, almost until the present day, and would further justify partitioning of the continent by colonial powers.

EARLIEST HISTORY The first arrivals to the central African landscape were Pygmy communities who settled in the area – they arrived there over 60,000 years ago and lived as hunter-gatherers from the resources of the rainforests (page 180). There are some historical records of these first human inhabitants of this part of Africa – reliefs of Pygmy people can be found on the tombs in Sakkara's pyramid at Giza, which indicates that the Egyptians had contact with them. In the 5th century BCE, the Greek historian Herodotus relates the first contact of ancient civilisations with what are believed to be Pygmy peoples:

> After journeying for many days over a wide extent of sand, they came at last to a plain where they observed trees growing; approaching them, and seeing fruit on them, they proceeded to gather it. While they were thus engaged, there came upon them some dwarfish men, under the middle height, who seized them and carried them off. The Nasamonians could not understand a word of their language, nor had they any acquaintance with the language of the Nasamonians. They were led across extensive marshes, and finally came to a town, where all the men were of the height of their conductors, and black-complexioned. A great river flowed by the town, running from west to east, and containing crocodiles.
>
> The *Histories of Herodotus*, written 440BCE,
> translated by George Rawlinson, 1858

Herodotus goes on to speculate that the city they had encountered beyond the sand was a 'nation of sorcerers' and was near the source of the Nile.

Meanwhile, from about 2000BCE, the so-called 'Bantu expansion' began, with waves of migrations of people from west central Africa to the south and east, including along the River Congo and its tributaries. In the equatorial rainforests, they came into contact, initially limited, with the Pygmy peoples, with whom they would be at odds ever after.

Numerous fracturings occurred in the 1st millennium CE as villages and smaller kingdoms emerged. These settlements displaced proto-Khoisan hunter-foragers who had migrated north from southern Africa and settled in the savannahs of what is modern-day Katanga and points further south.

Complex societies formed across central Africa during this time, with various trade routes slowly established. Nations had arisen by the end of the 1st millennium, and central Africa was dominated by the Kongo, Loango and Ndongo kingdoms along the Atlantic coast, as well as the Luba and Lunda kingdoms deeper inland. These were sophisticated organisations with clear hierarchies of royalty, tradespeople, farmers and enslaved people.

THE LOANGO KINGDOM Loango was founded around the 12th century CE with its full establishment sometime in the mid 14th century. It had a very pronounced monarchy in its capital city of Loango, a town slightly inland from the Atlantic coast and quite near to present-day Pointe Noire, in the Republic of the Congo. They also had a large trading centre at the mouth of the River Congo – then known as the Nzadi. The city was a meeting point for tradespeople and artisans, a large market that tied the regions of the kingdom together. The King of Loango, the Maloango, lived here and made appearances in the centre of the city when fields were being cultivated or when vassals would pay tribute. Loango was itself a vassal state of its larger neighbour Kongo, and would answer to their rule throughout its existence.

The kingdom had a structure of provinces with governors, with a governor succeeding the king upon his death. The governor was then rotated so that the next province in line would see its governor promoted to king in succession.

The kingdom was also a gatherer of ivory and enslaved people for export, which was a principal source of its prosperity upon contact with Europeans in the 17th century. Taxes and duties were excised on European traders arriving in the area, and Loango merchants were very active in exploring the deeper regions of central Africa for people to enslave and other resources to sell to Europeans.

Once the practice of slavery was abolished, the power and influence of the Loango Kingdom waned as one of its principal exports was no longer in demand. Another theory of the decline of the Loango Kingdom is that its highly decentralised power structure created an oligarchy of nobles, and as the higher figure of the Maloango was no longer needed, it was thus unable to hold the various Loango provinces together as a nation.

THE NDONGO KINGDOM The region south of the River Nzadi formed the Ndongo Kingdom, sometimes known as the Mbundu Kingdom as its members were of the Mbundu tribe. It too had a monarchy, with a line of kings known as Ngolas.

The earliest history of the Ndongo speculates that they migrated west to the sea from deeper inland, somewhere near the Luba and Lunda kingdoms, and settled throughout the coastal region. Contact with other tribes introduced their society, which had existed in a hunter-gatherer state, to techniques in blacksmithing and pottery.

The larger and more powerful Kingdom of Kongo to the north stated initially to Europeans that Ndongo was a vassal state under their control; however, in practice this could never be confirmed, and Ndongo had no real interaction with the Kongo Kingdom on a regular basis.

With the arrival of Europeans, Ndongo and Kongo became at odds with each other. Portuguese slave traders established another port of call at Luanda, and the loss of Kongo's monopoly on slave exports in the region put the two nations at war. A critical battle at Caxito, along the Dande River, effectively severed ties between the two kingdoms in 1556. This would remain their border until the eventual dissolution of both states.

THE LUBA AND LUNDA KINGDOMS Discovering where the Luba and Lunda kingdoms divide, merge and divide again is something inexact, but we do know their histories are intertwined.

Coalescing as a people in the 1st millennium CE, the Lunda and Luba peoples lived in almost the middle of the continent. They had already established trade routes east to the Indian Ocean and were working metals for many centuries before merging together in the 16th century to create the Luba and Lunda kingdoms.

Luba's ruler would be appointed by spiritual leaders, the Balopwe, who would speak to ancestors for guidance on whom to appoint to Mulopwe, King of the Luba. Because of his appointment by spiritual leaders, the Mulopwe held significant power over lesser governing subjects in the Luba hierarchy.

The Luba Kingdom was divided among governors as well as village leaders, all of whom belonged to a secret society named Bambudye, and the Luba king was the head of this society. The kingdom expanded quickly from its formation and established mines for copper, organised fishing operations and extracted oil from palm trees.

The Lunda had consolidated power by treaty across village chiefs in the region between the Luba to the north and Kongo to the west, and managed trade caravans throughout the area. Their knowledge of nation-building is usually attributed to a Luba king being married to a Lunda chief, which created enormous disdain among Lunda peoples – who then migrated outside their traditional regions and expanded Lunda territory significantly, but also established a very similar social order in the Lunda nation-state. Lunda were considered a sort of vassal state of the Luba, though this is not entirely accurate either – they were separate states, with the Luba being the stronger and more organised of the two.

THE KONGO KINGDOM Of largest importance to the western region of central Africa is the Kongo Kingdom. It was, in its time, an economic and cultural powerhouse, and the first nation to have regular contact with European explorers, meaning that there is more history known as to its existence than other African nations of the time.

Its beginnings stretch back to around 1100CE, north of the River Nzadi in a kingdom called Bungu, with the marauding son of a local leader, Motinobene. Motinobene used his men to charge tolls along the river to traders, attacked local villages and forced their populations into speaking the Kongo language. Motinobene's men married the daughters of local chiefs, and in this way began to spread their culture and ethnicity. Eventually Motinobene settled in an area near present-day Matadi in the Kwilu Valley, founding a town called Mpemba Ksai. A line of rulers would be buried in the valley, and Kongo tradition would remember this place as an area of sacred beginnings for the Kongo Kingdom. With Motinobene marrying the daughter of a spiritual leader named Manikabunga, he set in place a line of dynastic succession; a subsequent treaty with his neighbours called the Mbata set up a line of royalty. All of his successors would marry the daughters of Mbata, and in this way the royal line of Kongo was born – the ruler of the Kongo Kingdom would be known as the Manikongo.

The Manikongo moved his capital south to a densely populated region called Mbanza Kongo, though Mpemba Ksai would remain a sacred burial ground for royalty. Mbanza Kongo was a large town settled in a fertile area, and had a highly centralised political structure. Further trade and political alliances put the neighbouring kingdoms of Loango and Ndongo under the Manikongo as vassal states, and upon first contact with Europeans, Kongo was a formidable nation in its own right.

It was under this established monarchy that first contact with Portuguese explorers would occur in 1482, when the renowned navigator Diogo Cão arrived at the mouth of a massive river.

ARRIVAL OF THE EUROPEANS The reign of King John II of Portugal saw numerous changes in the monarchy and aristocracy in the seafaring European country, and one of the king's central interests was reigniting the oceanic explorations that would further expand the trade routes and influence of Portugal. With the blessing of King John II, the explorer Diogo Cão set out to chart the southern Atlantic coasts of Africa. Hoping to find a fast shipping route to Asia, he was known to have stopped at the Gold Coast (modern-day Ghana). Further south he eventually encountered the mouth of a massive river. In 1482, he set anchor in the bay of Loango (present-day Cabinda) and asked local people what the name of the river was. They said 'Nzadi', but he misunderstood them and recorded the river's name as 'Zaire'.

Cão and his men erected a stone pillar in honour of St George on the southern banks of the Zaire River and sailed upriver for a while before deciding to send some local messengers out on foot in search of a ruler, and then continuing south along the African coast. Upon returning to pick up his messengers, Cão found they were still absent, and so instead took four prominent local men and returned to Portugal. He was ennobled for his discoveries and would make further explorations along the southern African coast.

It was not until his second voyage southward in 1485, returning with the same local men, that contact with the Kongo's leader occurred. Nzinga Nkuwu was Manikongo at the time and welcomed contact with the Portuguese explorer, and being sufficiently impressed by his culture, permitted Catholic missionaries to arrive six years later. Nzinga himself took a European name after this contact, calling himself John after the Portuguese king of the time. John's successor as Manikongo was even more enamoured with the Catholic religion: he was baptised, given the European name of Alfonso, and began creating a tax structure to support the Church. The Kongo Church incorporated European religious ceremonies with local animist ones, and would remain an important part of the kingdom's culture for the remainder of its existence.

INTERCONTINENTAL TRADE AND THE FIRST EUROPEAN COLONIES Slavery was a practice that had existed for quite some time in the Kongo Kingdom, usually with captured prisoners of war being sold or traded. European missionaries helped establish schools and churches in the kingdom, and the successor to Manikongo Alfonso, Manikongo Alvaro, enacted further Westernisation of his upper classes by assigning European titles such as Duke and Marquis to their names. Kongo also established embassies in several European nations as relations developed between the two continents.

European contact, though, would be overshadowed by the slave trade. Portugal's king was looking for labour to be used at farms in nearby São Tomé, and Kongo was willing to trade them. The Portuguese presence in the region was also growing: they had settled in Luanda after a conflict with the Ndongo Kingdom in 1579, managing this with partial help from the Kongo, and would create a larger footprint of foreigners on the continent. Further agitation was created when the King of Portugal won the right to nominate bishops to a new cathedral in Mbanza Kongo, renamed to São Salvador.

THE DECLINE OF THE KONGO KINGDOM Enslaved people were being exported at increasing rates throughout the 16th century while other Portuguese governors, now with a foothold in Luanda, began to hire mercenaries to conduct raids deeper into the territories of both Kongo and Ndongo. The Imbangala were a barbaric group of local Africans who kidnapped children to serve in their army and engaged in cannibalism, and were sent forth by the Governor of Portuguese Angola to invade the southern provinces of Kongo in 1622. Kongo and Portugal from this point on, then, became enemies with each other – though their trading relationship continued as more people were captured from deeper inside the African interior and shipped out for slavery.

Tension continued between Kongo and Portuguese Angola for nearly 50 years. Kongo itself was being torn apart by internal rivalries. Luanda was captured by the Dutch and recaptured by Portugal during this period, and a fracturing of the Kongo Kingdom saw the vassal state of Mbwila sign a treaty with Portugal acceding its authority to them. Kongo sent an army into Mbwila to take back what they thought was rightfully theirs, and Portugal met Kongo's army in Ulanga, Mbwila's capital.

The Battle of Ambuila in 1556 was a critical moment in the downfall of the Kongo Kingdom. The Manikongo of the time, Antonio I, was killed along with many other Kongo nobles. With no clear leadership plan in place Kongo became further fractured, and civil war ensued. São Salvador was razed in 1678 and its population fled into the hills, where rival factions built fortresses and lived in solitude.

Continued battles between groups in this region, along with the constant export of enslaved people, had depleted the kingdom of a cohesive authority. Portuguese Angola still existed as a colonial power along the coast, though, and agitated the actions of local rulers throughout this period. They also commissioned the Lunda Kingdom to raid the eastern edges of the former Kongo, all but eliminating their authority as a singular nation in the mid 18th century. However, the Kongo Kingdom continued to exist in various incarnations until the European nations formally divided the African continent among themselves in the late 19th century. During this period, the lack of a centralised authority helped European trading interests, pulling more people out of the jungles and into enslavement, then on to boats headed for farms and plantations in Brazil and São Tomé.

Other kingdoms began to emerge from the disintegrating ancient territories of Kongo and Luba: enslaved people who had managed to flee from Portuguese traders began forming a society inland from the coast in 1568, giving rise to the Kuba Kingdom. The Lubas as a whole were being whittled away, and in 1858

The last gasp of a unified Kongo Kingdom occurred in 1700; peasants across its former empire lived under constant threat of war and combat, yet were still inundated with the preachings of European missionaries. This created a situation ideal for one woman, who in 1702 would proclaim herself to be the new embodiment of St Anthony. The Kongolese would call her Kimpa Vita, while European texts would call her Dona Beatriz, also referred to as the 'Kongolese Joan of Arc'.

Her claims of direct contact with the spiritual world were believed by the peasants. Born of noble blood some 25 years earlier, Kimpa Vita already had experience in the religious cult of *isimbi* early in her life. This gave her knowledge of how to operate a religious sect, and she would use this knowledge to its full potential. Telling her followers to cast off the Christian practices of marriage, confession and baptism, she was already gaining ire among European missionaries. Then, she stated that the Holy Cross was fetishism and ordered them all burned. She said she died every Friday, travelled to the heavens to communicate with the spirits there, and returned on Monday to convey their message. She also proclaimed herself the religious leader that would reunify the Kongo Kingdom, and implored the nobles scattered across the land's territory to allow her to appoint a new king.

São Salvador had been sacked by the Portuguese and armies loyal to them some decades before. Kimpa Vita requested that the old capital be reoccupied. Kongo noble Pedro IV had already arrived in the former town, and she appointed him the new ruler of Kongo. It was her leadership that brought several splintered factions together under the Kongo banner and under Pedro IV specifically, allowing the kingdom to gel into a nominally cohesive force for a few more decades.

Kimpa Vita, though, would meet an unfortunate fate. Claiming to have possession of a papal bull (a charter from the Vatican Church), she travelled between the strongholds of nobility hoping to get them rallying under Pedro IV; but her boasting of having a papal bull in her possession, and refusing to show it to anyone, resulted in her being arrested. King Pedro IV and the European Church were not kind to her: they declared her a heretic, and in 1706 she was burned at the stake.

For further information, consult *The Kongolese Saint Anthony: Dona Beatriz Kimpa Vita and the Antonian Movement, 1684–1706* by John K Thornton.

Ngelengwa Msiri would form the Kingdom of Garengaze along the western shores of Lake Tanganyika. He would eventually settle in the town of Bunkeya (page 157), and run an important nation there until 1892.

RENEWED EUROPEAN INTEREST By the 19th century, European missionaries had long since departed any establishments inland, and their presence was almost non-existent aside from port towns along the coast. Central Africa was an impenetrable rainforest, and European traders relied upon the merchants of local tribes to bring them the enslaved people and ivory they desired.

One brave British man would change all of this, though. James Kingston Tuckey, a sailor and explorer born in Ireland, had the first steam-powered sloop on his side. Christened the HMS *Congo*, it was destined to finally navigate into the heart of central Africa with its state-of-the-art paddlewheels, swivelling guns, and 30-tonne steam engine bearing the power of 20 horses. Tuckey wanted to prove that the Congo and Niger rivers linked up, thereby opening the heart of the continent to the new technology of paddlewheelers, and to discover what lurked deep inside the jungles of the continent.

Tuckey's luck was not good. The steam engine did not work properly, and the crew had to resort to using backup sails to arrive at the mouth of the River Congo in 1816. They persisted upriver from there, but malaria and yellow fever were wearing down his crew. His mighty vessel then reached impassable rapids. They continued on foot, trying to find the end of the rapids and what lay ahead; the terrain was mountainous and difficult to navigate, and Tuckey continued to lose men to diseases they had not encountered before. On 9 September 1816, he would reach his furthest point:

> We perceived the river winding again to the SE but our view did not extend above three miles of the reach; the water clear of rocks, and, according to the information of all the people, there is no impediment whatever, as far as they know, above this place.

He would turn back and die of exhaustion on the Atlantic coast, near modern-day Moanda, later that same year, with three-quarters of his expedition crew having perished on the journey. Little did he know that the river was actually navigable inland from this seemingly impenetrable point. It would not be for several decades until another European returned to make an attempt at continuing this journey.

Tuckey's diaries and observations would prove to be a catalyst for major change in Africa, and especially the Congos. He had a book published posthumously, *Narrative of an Expedition to Explore the River Zaire*, that provided valuable insight to European explorers of what lay further inland into what was still an empty spot on the map.

Tuckey revelled in the magnitude of the River Congo, as all other explorers who came after him would also do:

> The river now, for the first time, bore a majestic appearance, having the land on each side moderately elevated, with little hills of lime-stone further back, but still almost without wood.

FURTHER EFFORTS AT MAPPING THE RIVER Increased exploration across the continent persisted in the following decades. In 1826, English Captain William F W Owen commandeered two ships, the *Leven* and *Barracouta*, to create the most detailed survey yet of the River Congo, from its mouth to 25 miles inward, halfway between Moanda and Boma. A French captain would be next, Jean-Baptiste Douville, who from 1828 to 1830 made several attempts at navigating up the river – though he did not realise until late in his journey that he was navigating the River Cuanza in Angola. His proclamation of navigating the Congo (or 'Fleuve Couango dit Zaïre' on his maps) to 25°E, as published in *Atlas du voyage au Congo et dans l'intérieur de l'Afrique équinoxiale* in 1832, made the mystery of the River Congo all the more intriguing for future exploration.

Doctor David Livingstone set off from Luanda, in present-day Angola, in 1854, on a journey that would take him across the African continent. He made countless adjustments to previous maps of the rivers and their drainage patterns in southern and central Africa. He debunked Douville's claims of the 'Couango' river, mapped most of the course of the River Zambezi, and won fame across the world for his explorations.

In 1855, James Hunt, commander of the steam sloop *Alecto*, attempted to succeed where Tuckey had failed, but could not ascend the falls. Sir Richard Francis Burton in 1863 followed Tuckey's maps and ascended to the same point on the rapids, but could go no further. Three years later David Livingstone returned to southern Africa, searching – ultimately unsuccessfully – for the source of the Nile. In 1867 he reached Lake Mweru and discovered the River Lualaba, which is fed by the Mweru and Tanganyika lakes. At first he thought it might be the upper waters of the Nile, but he realised that in fact it flowed into the River Congo. This information would remain buried for an extended period of time, though, as the outside world lost contact with Livingstone and his expedition.

The continued mysteries of the River Congo, the disappearance of Livingstone and intense public curiosity about what had happened to him, and growing European interest in the recolonisation of the continent brought a whole new cast of characters to the region in the 1870s. A Belgian monarch, a journalist for an American newspaper, and an eager Italian-cum-Frenchman would begin to write a new chapter in the history of central Africa.

THE ARRIVAL OF TIPPU TIP Trade routes had been developed over the centuries by Swahili traders from their ports on the Indian Ocean into the Congo basin – they had established their first fort in eastern Congo in 1860 at Nyangwe, on the banks of the River Lualaba. Contact with the Portuguese had also opened up trading along the Atlantic coast, and the Luba Kingdom was heavily active in managing a flow of goods into and out of their region. The Lubas had also seen their territory shrink as a result of Garengaze expanding on its eastern edge, and its decentralised system of power sharing had reduced its influence across the region. With new African kingdoms emerging and slavery picking away at the most able bodied, the population was slowly being drained as the power of European and Arab slave traders increased.

Tippu Tip was a businessman and landowner who was employed by sultans in Zanzibar, and heavily involved in establishing trade routes from East Africa to the Indian Ocean coast. Half Arab and half African, he was already active in ivory and slave trading by the age of 18 and was a governor under the Zanzibari sultans early on in his life. His commercial exploits went from strength to strength as he moved further inland with a massive army (nearly 50,000 at its peak), searching for more resources to expand his own estate and those he worked for. Eventually Tippu Tip's army would collide with the Luba Kingdom, though only marginally at first, and some accounts state that they lived side by side for a period of time. Tippu Tip, though, was relentless in his business interests and conducted continuous raids throughout the region for more enslaved people and ivory. In 1875, he established a headquarters in the region at Kasongo, which would be the beginning of his own state within eastern Congo – called the Sultanate of Utetera, or Tippu Tip's State, though his claim on the region was, until 1887, made on behalf of the Sultan of Zanzibar as well as his own.

Tippu Tip's State, at its height, stretched from the northern shores of Lake Tanganyika to the northeast corner of the River Congo. It was fully in his control only briefly, between 1884 and 1887, though his power and influence would linger throughout the region for decades. It was during this peak that he would encounter a curious, and somewhat belligerent, Welsh-American explorer.

STANLEY'S VOYAGE A Welsh orphan who emigrated to the USA, Henry Morton Stanley became a journalist later in life and served as the overseas correspondent for the *New York Herald*. There was great interest in what had happened to the Scottish explorer David Livingstone, who had disappeared into the interior of central Africa in the late 1860s. In 1871, funded by the *New York Herald*'s publisher as a publicity stunt for the newspaper, Stanley travelled to Zanzibar in search of Livingstone. With over a hundred porters, Stanley started moving west into the deeper stretches of African wilderness. He found Livingstone at Ujiji, on the eastern shore of Lake Tanganyika, and (allegedly) uttered the words that became famous: 'Dr Livingstone, I presume?'. Livingstone died two years later; Stanley continued the explorations he had begun.

Stanley was the prototypical 19th-century adventurer, high on himself and his exploits with low opinions of local people and their cultures. His new-found fame brought his name to the steps of the *Daily Telegraph* in Britain, which joined the *New York Herald* in commissioning him to trace the River Congo from its source to the sea.

In July 1876, Stanley moved westward from Lake Tanganyika and deep into the unknown, and it was during this time that he met with Tippu Tip. Tippu Tip had not used the Congo as a navigable route before Stanley's arrival in the

GRANDY'S EXPEDITION TO RESCUE LIVINGSTONE

The discovery of David Livingstone on the shores of Lake Tanganyika was a triumph for Henry Stanley, and also a call for action from Livingstone's friends and supporters back in England. No sooner had the *New York Herald* published its account of their meeting in Ujiji, than Livingstone's compatriots began to plan expeditions to get him out of the dangerous corner of the dark continent that he had found himself in.

Two expeditions from the west and east coasts of Africa set out to rescue Livingstone. Sir Henry Rawlinson funded the expedition from the west coast entirely from his own pocket and employed Lieutenant W J Grandy to lead it. They set out from the town of Ambriz, just north of Luanda; Grandy had planned to locate the River Congo from there, based on Henry Morton Stanley's new mapping of the route, and arrive at the closest possible point to Ujiji.

Even at the outset, there was doubt as to whether the river would bring them close enough to Livingstone, but the urgency for rescuing the doctor was intense among English dignitaries, and so Grandy's expedition went ahead. It finally set out in 1874, far too late to find Livingstone who had died the previous year.

Grandy and his men pushed forward into unexplored and barely mapped territory inside the African continent. They wandered in circles looking for the River Congo – too far south and lacking any real maps or directions for where the river might be, the expedition became lost regularly. Finally a message was received from the Royal Geographical Society in London – Livingstone was confirmed dead, and the eastern expedition was nearing his last-known position. Grandy was ordered to turn back.

Grandy would not make it back, though – he fell ill from malaria or yellow fever, and died somewhere east of Luanda. The expedition was not an entire waste, however – the general mapping of the region was helped extensively due to Grandy's sacrifice. The relationship between the mouth of the River Congo and Luanda was confirmed.

region and he considered Stanley an interesting character who might be of some use to him. Stanley navigated the River Lualaba to its confluence and then traced the River Congo all the way to the Portuguese port of Boma; he was the first to document the river in its full length, including its pitfalls. The River Congo has two notorious sections of rapids, around which the expedition's boats and canoes had to be transported overland: Stanley Falls (now called Boyoma Falls), near the town founded by Stanley that is now called Kisangani; and the Livingstone Falls, 350km of rapids stretching from Malebo Pool – where James Kingston Tuckey had turned back 60 years earlier – to Matadi. Stanley's journey from Nyangwe to Boma took 999 days and confirmed that the river could be used for large ships between the two sections of rapids. In 1878 he published his account of this expedition, the two-volume book *Through the Dark Continent*.

KING LÉOPOLD II European interest in Africa was growing once again and, after centuries of continued trading along coastal outposts, conflicting claims between European powers of territory on the continent were increasing. Léopold II, King of the Belgians, saw his small kingdom as requiring a colony of some sort to secure its position of power in the world, and made several initial attempts in more traditional methods of creating a Belgian colony abroad. The lack of success at these brought him to reconsider his approach at a government-to-colony solution, and instead moved in a different direction – he created a private holding company, the Association Internationale Africaine, or AIA, and sought to acquire territory as private property for his new enterprise.

The AIA was originally heralded as a humanitarian project aimed at shared learning, shared exploration, and the betterment of the African continent as a whole. Founded in 1876, Léopold invited several dozen geographers, explorers and other experts to a conference in Brussels to form the association. Léopold from the beginning had engineered the AIA in such a way that it would benefit him and his imperial goals, and centred the organisation primarily on the formation of a central African state. However the other members of the association also had similar goals, and what had originally (though perhaps not honestly) emerged as a method for furthering European knowledge of the continent had turned into a front for imperialist powers to further secure their own interests in Africa.

In 1878, Léopold began funding another organisation, the International Congo Society, or Comité d'Études du Haut-Congo (CEHC). In collaboration with a British shipping tycoon and Belgian banker, their interest was primarily in the colonisation of Congo. Other European nations, especially France and Portugal, were not so keen on seeing the colonisation of Congo by the Belgians and protested at their alleged expansion and exploration into the region. By 1881, Pierre Savorgnan de Brazza had already made an expedition from the Atlantic to the rapids at Stanley Pool and founded Brazzaville, and Léopold's dream of a Congo colony was quickly losing ground.

In 1879, Léopold contacted Henry Morton Stanley regarding his returning to the River Congo under the auspices of exploration for the Belgian king. Stanley agreed, and the relationship between the two would inform the creation of the Belgian Congo. The CEHC was renamed the Association Internationale du Congo, or AIC.

While the front of the AIC was that of a humanitarian mission, its true intents were relayed to Stanley: he was requested by Léopold to secure treaties, purchase land, resources, and anything else that he could get his hands on in the Congo region. Any treaties signed were required to cede all power and authority over to the AIC. Léopold's method was unique in a way, in that he was acquiring personal property on his own behalf and removing his nation of Belgium from the situation entirely. He was also commissioning other expeditions from the east coast of Africa to the interior, though they were far less successful.

Léopold's public explanation of his exploits focused on how the AIC was to build hospitals and schools across the territory and enrich the lives of African people. As Stanley continued his own mission to secure the resources and territories of King Léopold II in central Africa, all suspicions were assuaged by these public explanations. Belgium itself and Léopold, having little history of imperialist atrocities, would be seen as an ideal neutral party that could bring civilisation to the African hinterlands. Aristocrats and philanthropists across Europe even donated to his cause, lauding his humanitarian interests in the region.

By 1884, Stanley had secured a massive stretch of land in the middle of the African continent in the name of King Léopold and the AIC. This was not Belgian territory, nor any other nation. Léopold was astute, though, and had made an agreement with the US president of the time to recognise his Congo colony as Belgian territory. President Chester Arthur was impressed by the noble-sounding goals of the Congo territory, and Léopold's emissary to Arthur compared the project to the United States's own amicable goals in Liberia of freeing enslaved people to their home continent to improve their lives. With his territory formally recognised, Léopold was in a solid position to make a case for its continued existence as a unique and separate colony at the Berlin Conference of 1884.

THE CONGO FREE STATE Increased interest in the African continent saw a month-long meeting of European nations at the Berlin Conference of 1884, as decisions were made on how exactly to divide up the continent of Africa to satisfy everyone's interests. Léopold II and his emissaries were active behind the scenes, convincing the larger colonial powers of France and Germany of the importance of free trade zones across Africa: the River Congo would remain free for shipping, though this would rarely be useful as it could not be navigated far inland. With the support of the United States, Léopold's pitch for a Belgian colony at the centre of the continent was well received. The Congo state itself would be considered a unique bastion among African colonies, and remain in possession of the AIC. It would be considered a free trade zone, a sort of middle point to keep colonial powers in check, where businesses could operate without crippling tariffs or other governmental intrusion. All of this was presented as a good thing.

In April 1885, the Belgian Parliament appointed King Léopold as the head of the state 'founded by the AIC' – an exclusively personal authority, in which neither the Belgian Parliament nor Government had any role. Léopold had no more need of the fig-leaf of the AIC and, in July 1885, the British vice-administrator of the AIC announced the foundation of the Congo Free State and Léopold as its sovereign. The new state stretched from the mouth of the River Congo all the way east to Lake Tanganyika. Tippu Tip had agreed to cede his territory to the Belgian king in exchange for acting as a governor of the eastern region, and from this point onward worked under Léopold II until 1890, when one of his sons took over the rule of the territory.

THE RUBBER TRADE A new invention changed the fortunes of the Congolese for ever – the pneumatic tyre. Demand for new inflatable rubber tyres in the 1890s was insatiable, and so was the demand for rubber to make them. While the rest of the world was trying to increase the capacity of rubber, Léopold's Congo was discovered to have a very valuable resource – vines (Landolphia spp) which could be tapped for their latex.

The Belgians had begun ruling the Congo Free State with little regard for the local population, and the demand for rubber saw an entirely new method of resource extraction. The rubber vines were buried deep in the jungle; local men were threatened with death or mutilation to go into the forest and extract rubber from the trees into buckets. Tales of exploitation were many during this period, but it went generally unreported due to the inaccessibility of the Congo Free State. When death was no longer a significant motivator for local men to collect rubber for export, Belgian forces began holding families hostage and cutting off hands. A heavy leather whip, the *chicotte*, was used regularly against those who dared to oppose their overseers.

Léopold, famously, never set foot in the Congo himself. The actions against local populations were taken by the mercenary Force Publique, Belgian officials and Africans recruited into a military system that was heavily regimented and as harsh as the terrain in which it operated. They were notoriously cruel, and interested strictly in profiting from whatever they could in the Congo Free State. What happened to their labourers was mostly regarded as collateral damage.

While these deeds were not unique to the Congo Free State at the time, the scale of the operation and the damage done to the local population was enormous. Léopold and his Congo Free State could get away with it in all cases, thanks to the nation being a piece of private property, a free trade zone, with no significant infrastructure or authority over it. For much of the 1890s the rubber boom sent profits right back into Léopold's personal bank account, not even the reserves of the country of Belgium. It would take the journeys of two African Americans into the Congo to discover what was going on, and report it to the world.

THE HUMANITARIAN DISASTER George Washington Williams was a historian who was born and raised in the United States. A journalist by trade, he had a large interest in the originating continent of people freed from enslavement. He founded an African-American newspaper, and wrote the first history of African Americans in the 19th century. He would also be the first person to notice that something was deeply wrong in Léopold's Congo.

With several interests surrounding his desire to visit the Congo Free State, he was granted an audience with Léopold in 1889 and received permission, and indeed Léopold's blessing, for his visit. He departed soon after for the new settlement of Léopoldville, on the bank of the Stanley Pool, and began witnessing what had been hidden to the world. His six months in the Congo, travelling by steamboat from Léopoldville upriver to Stanleyville, allowed him to witness the atrocities inflicted on the Congolese as they were forced into labour.

This prompted him to write his famous 'Open Letter' to King Léopold, addressing to him all that he had seen in the Congo Free State, and demanding (though in the formal tone of the letter, closer to requesting) that something be done about continued abuses. The letter was published, and distributed as a pamphlet in both the USA and Europe. He would also write *A Report upon the Congo-State and Country to the President of the United States of America*, which further documented what was occurring.

There had been increasing friction between Léopold's Congo and businesspeople around the world as they had effectively been shut out of doing any work in the so-called 'Free Trade Zone' of Africa. This disaster of epic proportions served their purposes well, by highlighting the Congo Free State's failure to live up to its original proposed intent.

As George Washington Williams was departing from the Congo another African American arrived, William Henry Sheppard. Arriving as a Presbyterian missionary, he had similar interests as Williams in African-American history and saw contact with Africa as a chance to escape the deep racial divisions inherent in the USA. He picked up where George Washington Williams left off – he was not in the Congo for a brief period as a journalist, but spent two decades there. It was his persistence in bringing to light the continued atrocities that would finally prompt the world to action.

CONGO REFORM ASSOCIATION Inspired by George Washington Williams's 'Open Letter' and continued lobbying from William Henry Sheppard as he wrote countless articles and letters of protest to highlight the atrocities taking place, the Congo Reform Association was formed in 1904. Founded by two Englishmen, Edmund Dene Morel and Roger Casement, their cause was backed by many famous writers of the time including Joseph Conrad – who had travelled down the River Congo in 1890 and enshrined for ever the madness that was occurring, in his novel *Heart of Darkness*. The Congo Reform Association was, in effect, the first human rights organisation the world had ever known and would be a precursor to future human rights groups the world over. Their actions yielded success, with the creation of a Commission of Inquiry, which travelled to the Congo to see if the allegations of abuse were accurate. The resulting 150-page report confirmed everything that had been said by Casement and Morel, Williams and Sheppard, and countless others who had travelled to the Congo Free State over the previous 15 years. As this report became public and the Belgians' opinion of their king began to slip, Léopold's Congo Free State would soon see some transformations.

FROM THE CONGO FREE STATE TO THE BELGIAN CONGO The Commission of Inquiry was the death knell for Léopold's Congo Free State. The king was 70 years old at the time of its publication and, faced with overwhelming opposition in the private sphere and international pressure, he blinked. There were also local problems: several rebellions were occurring simultaneously across the Congo's interior. The authority of the Force Publique had always been nominal far away from European outposts, but in the early 1900s the Shi, Luba and Katanga kingdoms, among others, rebelled and formed their own small states within the Congo. These rebellions would not be quelled until World War I.

As the inquiry moved forward, and as Léopold's popularity plummeted in his advancing years, he agreed to cede the state from his AIC organisation to the Belgian government. However, Léopold did not simply hand the state over to Belgium: he sold it, and spent two years negotiating his price for the colony. In 1906, a major company was founded after initial research revealed vast amounts of underground wealth in the Congo: the Union Minière du Haut Katanga (UMHK), Belgian-owned with a British minority share, was allocated a 20,000km^2 concession in Katanga to mine for copper and other minerals. The demand for minerals would be equal to, if not greater than, the demand for rubber, and the UMHK had quasi-governmental power in Katanga.

In 1908, with the negotiations complete, the Congo Free State became the Belgian Congo. Belgium assumed the debts of the Congo Free State as well as paying King Léopold a massive sum for the colony. Belgium would complete several of Léopold's building projects, assume various loans that he had drawn for 'infrastructure improvements' in Belgium, and pay 50 million francs to the king personally. Not only did Léopold take nearly every shred of profit that the Congo Free State made during its existence, but even after he had parted with it came out far ahead of the game.

A ceremony in Boma in 1908 made the change official, though the effects of this would be, in many ways, nominal. There was continued international interest in how the Congolese people were faring and other Europeans, among them Wilfred Thesiger, visited the Belgian Congo to ensure that reforms were taking place. Others were madly extracting rubber for as long as they could, until whenever they were stopped and requested to leave. Missionaries continued to keep a close eye on what transpired in their regions of the Congo. And in 1909, King Léopold II of Belgium died at the Royal Palace at Laeken, after a 44-year reign. His assets and the vast sums of wealth gained from exploiting the Congo Free State would remain within the possession of his family. The Congo Reform Association, content with the outcomes of what had transpired in the Congo, dissolved in 1913.

THE BELGIAN CONGO AND THE WORLD WARS Since Léopold II had taken the brunt of international pressure for abuses in Africa, the Belgian regime that emerged after his rule could only make matters better. And yet, only slightly – forced labour was still a fact of life, though the most insidious acts of the Léopold era such as corporal punishment and kidnapping were banned. The authority of the Belgian Parliament improved matters, but not greatly, and life in the Belgian Congo would remain similar to what it had been in the Congo Free State.

The Congolese were conscripted into the Belgian military, and in World War I were tasked with fighting the German troops in German East Africa, including participating in the Battle of Tabora in 1916. Those who stayed in eastern Congo were all engaged in the war effort in some way, and with this mobilisation several local rebellions were quelled.

The years after World War I were some of the best that the Congo state had known for decades – though still punctuated by poor working conditions and a merciless set of European companies, the Congolese were no longer stuck in a circle of forced labour and exploitation – or perhaps, not as harsh. UMHK expanded its operations and made them more sophisticated for the time being, creating large mining towns across the southern and eastern regions of the country and employing large numbers of the population. Léopoldville had expanded into a decent-sized town.

Yet anti-colonial attitudes were prominent and with the growing rights of locals, their empowerment led them to more bold displays of dissent. Hundreds of thousands in the west of the Congo joined a religious cult called Kimbanguism, and its founder, Simon Kimbangu, was imprisoned as a result – the unified numbers scared the Belgian authorities and Kimbanguism was quickly banned. Strikes were occurring across numerous mines in Katanga, and UMHK on occasion used deadly force to quell them. The Belgian Congo was still little more than a free trade zone with resource-based companies coming in and using local labour for extraction. Anything resembling a cohesive state, or national identity, was still far away.

During World War II, the Belgian Congo's resources would prove useful to the Allies in the manufacture of their weapons. Famously, the US bought uranium from the Congo for use in the atomic bombs dropped on Hiroshima and Nagasaki. World War II saw several social changes in the Congo as migration moved large populations away from their rural lives and into cities; urbanisation and the notion of a national identity were beginning to form.

INDEPENDENCE FOR THE BELGIAN CONGO In the early 1950s the Congolese finally became citizens: they were allowed to own land, were put on equal ground with Europeans and were given access to public services, including the same courts used by foreigners. They were also given the right to vote at a local level, although their country remained a colony of Belgium. Nonetheless there were rewards for becoming less African and more European with a programme of 'matriculation'. These *évolués* were heralded by the Belgian government for their personal advancements to becoming more 'sophisticated' per se, and given jobs in the public sector. While segregation by race was dwindling, segregation due to cultural assimilation was rising.

Attitudes like this were the catalyst for organisations calling for outright independence from Belgium; this was also the era of other African states lobbying for their own independence, and inspiration for one Joseph Kasa-Vubu to form the political party of ABAKO, or Alliance des Bakongo. The Belgians as well were considering the notion of an independent Congolese state, though some 30 years into the future. ABAKO famously demanded immediate independence – and might have been more careful for what they wished.

ABAKO gained instant popularity among voters across the Congo and did well in the first open local elections in 1957. Kasa-Vubu was elected as mayor of the Dendale district of Léopoldville, and began to make speeches demanding independence for the Congo. On 4 January 1959, an ABAKO rally turned violent and sparked off riots across Léopoldville. Kasa-Vubu was arrested and imprisoned, but the riots led to negotiations in Brussels to agree the terms for the Congo's independence.

There was one other national political party aside from ABAKO, the Mouvement National Congolais or MNC, headed by Patrice Lumumba. The mention of Belgium's government planning independence paved the way for several revolts and secessions in 1959: in Kasai, Luba and Baluba tribes fought each other, while in Stanleyville another riot resulted in the arrest of Lumumba and his subsequent imprisonment. The MNC would experience numerous fractures and Lumumba would remain in prison until he was released to participate in the Brussels conference.

After several months of negotiations, the date of 30 June 1960 was set for the Congo's independence, with elections to be held the previous month. The newly independent country would be known as the Republic of the Congo, with its capital remaining at Léopoldville. In the May elections, the MNC won the most seats in the new parliament. A coalition government was agreed, with Kasa-Vubu as president and Lumumba as prime minister. The independence ceremony on 30 June was addressed by King Baudouin and, in a fiery speech, by Lumumba. Belgium was at last free of its colonial obligations. For the new Republic of the Congo (Congo-Léopoldville), though, its difficulties were just beginning.

FROM INDEPENDENCE TO CHAOS Less than a week after the Republic of the Congo became its own nation, it began tearing itself apart. A mutiny in the Force Publique on 5 July 1960 pitted its European officers against its African soldiers and rumbled on for several days. Lumumba responded by Africanising the army, renaming it the National Congolese Army (ANC) and appointing a new commander-in-chief and a new chief of staff (the latter was a former soldier called Joseph Désiré Mobutu). The mutiny spread across the whole country; Europeans sought refuge in Katanga; and, on 11 July, Belgium evacuated its citizens from Matadi and then bombarded the city. Belgian forces moved to occupy various cities, including Léopoldville. The mineral-rich state of Katanga, under its regional president, Moïse Tshombe, declared its independence from the Republic of the Congo; Tshombe was supported by the Belgian government and the UMHK. Kasa-Vubu and Lumumba appealed to the United Nations for intervention in their country, and the UN called for the withdrawal of Belgian forces and the deployment of UN peacekeepers. By 15 July, UN troops were in the Congo and attempting to restore order.

South Kasai Province seceded as well and, although the Congolese army quelled the rebellion, they did so with violence, massacring Luba civilians. Katanga was a more difficult nut to crack, however. It had the majority of Belgium's UMHK-owned mining operations, a large number of Belgian expats, and plenty of money to keep alive the dream of independence. Katanga's government, led by Tshombe, also hired white mercenaries to defend the province against the Congo and UN soldiers.

Meanwhile, at the top of the Congo's new government were divides as well: Prime Minister Lumumba tried unsuccessfully to get military support from other African governments and threatened to ask the Soviet Union for help if the UN peacekeepers would not assist. On 5 September 1960, President Kasa-Vubu made a radio announcement that he had dismissed Lumumba and six government ministers. Patrice Lumumba responded, again over the radio, that his dismissal was legally invalid and that he was deposing Kasa-Vubu. Several days of parliamentary manoeuvres followed, annulling both men's declarations of dismissal and culminating in granting emergency powers to the prime minister. The following day, 14 September, the army chief of staff, Joseph Désiré Mobutu, led a coup d'état and, within a week, he had appointed a new 'technocratic' government.

Lumumba managed to escape from Léopoldville and was heading for Stanleyville, where he had popular support, but was captured on his way by ANC soldiers and imprisoned, with two of his political allies, in a military barracks at Thysville. Belgium's long arms intervened again and demanded the three prisoners be taken to separatist Katanga, and Mobutu complied. They were flown to Katanga on 17 January 1961, where they were beaten and tortured by Katangese officers. Later that night, they were taken to an isolated spot north of Élisabethville and, one by one, executed by firing squad. It is likely that the executions were carried out by Belgian mercenaries on the orders of the Katangan leadership, allowing foreign governments to appear uninvolved. The three bodies were later dissolved in sulphuric acid, so that there would never be graves where Lumbumba's supporters could gather. (See page 155 for information about the memorial park at the assassination site.)

THE UN IN CONGO: TAKE ONE ONUC, or Opération des Nations Unies au Congo, was the largest UN operation undertaken since its inception, with nearly 20,000 personnel at its peak, and as a result the UN became a major player in gluing together the fractured bits of the Congo and tackling the continued problem of secessionist Katanga. A rival national government had formed in Stanleyville in November 1960 under the leadership of Antoine Gizenga, with Cyrille Adoula as his second in command, drawing from the popular support of Patrice Lumumba. Speculation exists that this government was being funded by communist entities hoping to establish a government in the Congo sympathetic to the USSR. Their party would be instrumental in calling together a UN summit on resolving the continued conflicts across the nation, and in July 1961 plans for a reunified Congo were established. Kasa-Vubu would remain president while Gizenga and Adoula would be given positions in his new government. South Kasai would end its secession, and Cyrille Adoula would be appointed as new prime minister in August.

Katanga, though, would continue to rebel against any Congolese government. In September 1961, ONUC and Katangan forces engaged in eight days of fighting, with military and civilian deaths. The UN secretary-general, Dag Hammarskjöld, headed to Rhodesia to negotiate peace talks between the Congolese and separatist governments. His plane crashed at Ndola, just across the Zambian border from

Katanga; Hammarskjöld was killed, along with everyone else on the plane. The cause of the crash has never been conclusively determined.

Tshombe was well equipped to combat highly trained UN soldiers from Sweden, Ireland, the Philippines, and others. An air war also ensued during this time against Avikat, Katanga's own air force. Receiving side support from the Belgians, along with Tshombe's private mercenaries, combat across Katanga was frequent during this time. Large battles occurred almost continuously between UN troops and aircraft, against Katangese fighter planes and soldiers, for over two years.

Tshombe's power began to slip, however, and after a final fierce month of combat at the beginning of 1963 he conceded defeat to the UN forces. Tshombe fled to Zambia and then Spain, and then, in 1964, he returned to the Congo to participate in a new government. ONUC officially came to an end in 1964, five years after arriving in the Congo, and its actions were heralded as a job well done. A new age of internationalist intervention would arrive, using the Congo as proof of the UN's relevance as a stabilising body in the world – though how it was done, with international troops engaging in open combat, would be debated for decades.

THE RISE OF MOBUTU Rebellions persisted across the Congo between 1964 and 1965, and the ANC had their hands full; yet more importantly, Mobutu's army was expanding its zones of control across the entire nation and creating a level of authority that the Congo had never previously seen. Moïse Tshombe had been instituted as prime minister in 1964 by Joseph Kasa-Vubu and elections were planned for 1965. Belgian paratroopers and mercenaries were being used against leftist rebels active in Stanleyville, and Tshombe's experience in operating mercenary companies would prove invaluable to Kasa-Vubu as he tried to bring his country under control. Rebels loyal to the assassinated Patrice Lumumba were by far the most significant threat to the government at this time, and a small front in the Cold War between Soviet- and Cuban-backed Lumumbist rebels and the US-backed government in Léopoldville was being fought out in the far reaches of eastern Congo.

There were further rifts, though, between Kasa-Vubu and Tshombe. Tshombe himself was gaining in popularity, perhaps too much so, and his attitudes towards maintaining white mercenaries in the Congo led to disagreements between the two men over the Congo's direction in the world: Kasa-Vubu was local in his focus while Tshombe seemed to be firm in his opinion that Western forces should remain in the Congo.

May 1965 saw the last multi-party elections the Congo would know for over 40 years. Moïse Tshombe's coalition won the most seats, but President Kasa-Vubu appointed one of his former allies as prime minister. This appointment led to Mobutu's second coup d'état, on 24 November. He banned political parties and, a few months later, suspended Parliament and assumed almost absolute power. Four government ministers were publicly hanged in May 1966.

Mobutu's life was slowly re-engineered as a legend, and he was popular in his early years. In 1966, he began to change the names of colonial towns: Léopoldville to Kinshasa, Stanleyville to Kisangani, and Élisabethville to Lubumbashi. Katanga Province would be known as Shaba. He nationalised the UMHK, which became Gécamines. He also introduced a new flag to replace the old flag that had remained essentially the same since King Léopold created his massive private colony of the Congo Free State.

A new constitution was created, allowing the President of Congo to rule almost uninhibited by any internal dissent. Uprisings which occurred were put down quickly, and the authority of the ANC remained firm. New elections were to take place in November 1970, and Mobutu was in a solid position to win them, since the party he had created was the only one allowed to nominate candidates.

FROM THE CONGO TO ZAIRE There was little doubt as to who would win the Congo's presidential election in 1970: Mobutu was the only candidate. Not only did he control the army, he also had the support of the West – given eastern Congo's history of leftist uprisings which could potentially bring about a communist-friendly government in the Congo, Mobutu's strong-arm tactics of keeping the country on the capitalist side of the Iron Curtain were undoubtedly welcome to Western governments.

Mobutu's authority over the Congo was complete. During this time his first order of business was 'authenticity', building on the earlier re-naming of Congolese towns and cities, to completely thrust off the colonial past of his nation: from October 1971 onward, the Republic of the Congo would be known as the Republic of Zaire. The Armée Nationale Congolaise became the Forces Armées Zaïroises, or FAZ. He ordered people to change their European names to African ones, and set the example by changing his own name to become Mobutu Sese Seko. Belgium's old plan of promoting *les évolués* had turned 180° to a nearly total elimination of European influences in the country.

It would go further, though. In 1973–74, all foreign-owned businesses were nationalised and handed over to Zairians, mostly Mobutu's relatives and close associates. A good percentage of their profits would then be channelled into his personal bank accounts. Alarming as this may have been for Western businesses, the Cold War meant that their governments overlooked Mobutu's activities. The pro-Soviet governments that were operating on the other side of the River Congo – in Congo-Brazzaville and Angola – were much more disconcerting to governments that feared the domino effect of communist revolution across Africa. In particular, after Angola's war of independence from Portugal (1974–75), Mobutu supported the Bakongo-based FNLA against the Cuba-backed MPLA. In 1975, Zaire sent its troops across the border to support the FNLA and UNITA, who were backed by apartheid South Africa. Thousands of Cuban soldiers defeated the FNLA and drove UNITA and the South Africans out of the provinces they had captured.

Retaliation against Zaire's support for the FNLA came in 1977, when the MPLA supported anti-Mobutu dissidents to invade Shaba from eastern Angola. To Mobutu's chagrin, he had to seek military help, first from the Organisation of African Unity and then from France, to defeat the rebels. They were driven back across the border but invaded again the following year and captured the city of Kolwezi. This time, Mobutu got assistance from the USA as well as France and Belgium; further details of the occupation of Kolwezi can be found on page 162. US-mediated negotiations led in 1979 to a peace accord between Zaire, Zambia and the MPLA. However, Mobutu encouraged the presence of UNITA and the FNLA in the border areas around Shaba, as a buffer against further incursions by the MPLA-backed rebels.

ELECTORAL REFORMS AND THE DECLINE OF MOBUTU Mobutu held further single-candidate 'elections' in 1977 and 1984 and remained Zaire's head of state. A coup plot was unearthed in the military and heads of the army were executed. Intervention in Shaba would give the West some more leverage in adjusting Zaire to their liking, though, and parliamentarians requested that Mobutu institute electoral reforms. In 1982, an opposition party was founded, the Union for Democracy and Social Progress (UDPS). Its co-founder was Étienne Tshisekedi, a politician who had been active in the MPR, Mobutu's vehicle 'party', until relations between the two men broke down around 1980. With the formation of the UDPS, Tshisekedi became the main voice of the opposition to Mobutu. Throughout the 1980s there was continuing pressure on Mobutu to institute some kind of adjustments to his one-party state. Tshisekedi organised a mass protest in Kinshasa in 1988, and student protests in 1989 were repressed with violence from the police forces.

The collapse of the Soviet Union was an important point in Zaire's history. Mobutu must have seen the writing on the wall for his less than stellar methods of running his country and, without the fear of communist influence in Zaire, the West could put more pressure on him to reform the nation. With his support evaporating from the West, he put his well-honed survival skills to work. In April 1990, Mobutu promised to end single-party rule and reintroduce democracy, convening a national assembly, the Sovereign National Conference, to create a new constitution for Zaire. A month later, his FAZ killed hundreds of students in Lubumbashi. His popularity as head of state was taking a beating. He appointed Tshisekedi prime minister on three separate occasions, with his longest period in office only for seven months. Protests and clashes continued into 1991. Unpaid soldiers staged mutinies in Kinshasa and began a full-scale riot in the city: it would be the capital's first major riot in decades, and far from its last. French and Belgian soldiers were called in again to stabilise the city, but rioting would continue across Zaire for two months. There were protests in Kinshasa to reconvene the Sovereign National Conference, which were put down violently by the FAZ, although it did restart several months later.

Mobutu, though, managed to obstruct the conference and shut out Tshisekedi's ministers – his political machinations were expert, having played his own game in Zaire for decades, and it would not be so simple to remove the reins on Mobutu's power. Tshisekedi resigned as prime minister in disgust in 1993 and the conference was suspended indefinitely.

Civil unrest continued across Zaire in spurts, started mostly by soldiers, as Mobutu's grip on his country was slowly slipping. Other parliamentary reforms were run through government, accelerating an excruciatingly slow process towards change. The process, though, would be accelerated enormously as a result of a catastrophe occurring in a much smaller neighbour.

FROM MOBUTU'S ZAIRE TO KABILA'S DEMOCRATIC REPUBLIC OF THE CONGO

A critical moment in the history of East Africa was in 1994 with the Rwandan genocide. This event did not occur in a vacuum, and as could only be expected, its implications for the region as a whole were vast. With the failure of the UN in Rwanda to halt the mass killing of Tutsis by Hutus, refugees flowed from Rwanda into the Congo at the onset of the genocide.

However, this would not be the catalyst for major change in Mobutu's Zaire. The rebel army in Rwanda, the Rwandan Patriotic Army (RPA), eventually halted the genocide and drove Hutu militias – the Interahamwe, extremist Hutus who were primarily responsible for the massacre – into Zaire. While no longer having a presence in Rwanda, the Interahamwe continued their attacks on the Tutsis in Rwanda and began to attack Tutsis resident in Sud-Kivu Province, also referred to as Banyamulenge. While ethnically the same as Rwandan Tutsis, they considered themselves Zairian, first and foremost. Yet the Interahamwe did not differentiate between Banyamulenge and Rwandan Tutsis – the Tutsi group as a whole was being targeted.

The Vice-Governor of Sud-Kivu, witnessing further massacres in his province, issued an edict in 1996 calling for all Banyamulenge to leave the province. Rebellion ensued, and while chaos reigned in the province the government of Rwanda found a chance to spearhead its own incursion into Sud-Kivu under the figure of Laurent-Désiré Kabila, who had long opposed the regime of Mobutu and fought against his forces during popular uprisings of the mid 1960s. Several rebel groups operating within Sud-Kivu were merged under his leadership into the 'Alliance of Democratic Forces for the Liberation of Congo-Zaire', or AFDL. Backed by Rwanda and Uganda, Kabila and his coalition began a march west from the Rwandan border to Kinshasa.

This was begun under the pretence of ousting the Interahamwe from Sud-Kivu to eliminate attacks on Rwandan Tutsis. Uganda had its own rebels, the Allied Democratic Forces (ADF), who had been hiding out in eastern Zaire; their presence there was enough of a reason for their own armies to march into a much larger neighbour. The ulterior motive here was the vast resources of Zaire, and an aim at territorial expansion. Using the pretext of hunting down rebel groups placated international concern, and no intervention from any Western power was forthcoming to stop what had become, in effect, a full-scale invasion of eastern Zaire.

Kabila's long march to Kinshasa saw very little opposition, though several skirmishes were fought across the country as they moved west. Mobutu was in ill health, his power was at its nadir and, during his final days in the country, his formerly formidable network of officials and army generals were as much opposed to his rule as Kabila was. Already rioting against bad pay for years, the FAZ were primarily responsible for much of the looting that occurred while Kabila moved west – while his army was disciplined and focused, the FAZ were in disarray and used a chaos of their own making to further personal gains.

Kabila's arrival in Kinshasa in May 1997 ushered in a new era for Zaire, now to be called the Democratic Republic of the Congo. Mobutu fled to Morocco, where the former strongman died a few months later and was buried in Rabat. Kabila's succession as the head of state was only the beginning of a long and protracted conflict that would be the largest, most complicated and deadliest war the world had seen in half a century.

THE SECOND CONGO WAR: AFRICA'S 'WORLD WAR' The installation of Laurent Kabila as head of state in the now Democratic Republic of the Congo was far less of a drastic change than many had hoped – he immediately began setting up a network of cronies and strongmen who answered to him in much the way that Mobutu ran the nation before him. More importantly for Kabila was that the nations who had engineered his march into Kinshasa, Rwanda and Uganda, no longer saw him as being beneficial to their greater cause of partition and plunder in the eastern regions of the country. And therefore almost as quickly as Kabila was put into power, a plan was formed to take him out.

A new rebel group, the Rally for Congolese Democracy (Rassemblement Congolais pour la Démocratie, RCD), emerged in the east. Again backed by Rwanda and Uganda, the group was portrayed as a strictly home-grown affair that was seeking the overthrow of Kabila – while it was called a civil war, Rwanda and Uganda could use this veneer to divert attention away from their goals of establishing spheres of influence in their much larger neighbour. The group had internal rivalries, though, and split into two: RCD-Goma, Rwanda's rebel wing, and RCD-Kisangani, Uganda's rebel wing. The two groups met in battle several times in Kisangani, between 1999 and 2000 when the Kisangani faction retreated to Bunia and another split occurred, with the new group (RCD-ML) taking control of Ituri.

These groups were mostly at odds with each other, but broadly speaking fighting for the same goal, of again marching on Kinshasa to install a new head of state. Yet Kabila had his own allies, fighting for their own interests: Angola, Zimbabwe,

Namibia and Chad all sent troops in support of Kabila and would prove critical in ensuring that Kinshasa stayed in power.

Of course, ulterior motives for these nations were all ever-present in their decisions to send troops: Angola most especially saw this as an opportunity to cut supply lines to the long-running rebellion in their own country from UNITA, who maintained bases across the border in the Democratic Republic of the Congo. Furthermore oil interests in Cabinda would be threatened if Rwanda and Uganda shared the DRC's vast resources among themselves, operating outside the scope of international law – conflict along the Atlantic coast could cause all sorts of disruptions to the prosperous petroleum industry in the region. Namibia and Zimbabwe's ruling elites both had significant mining interests in the DRC and saw their mission as not only to protect those assets but perhaps also to expand them. Furthermore, Robert Mugabe, Zimbabwe's long-running head of state, could not fail to be concerned over rebellions sponsored by neighbouring states aimed at toppling unelected leaders. Finally, Chad sent 1,000 troops to support Kabila's regime, sponsored by France (and Gabon) out of a sense of guilt at failing to halt the Rwandan genocide until far too late.

With tens of thousands of international troops within the DRC and rebel factions backed by other nations scattered across the east, this war was fought wholly within the borders of the former Zaire and with complete disregard for its citizens. It was a war primarily fought by neighbours hoping to divide the DRC's vast resources among themselves, aimed at protecting their economic interests, and territorial expansion. Perhaps most critical was the fact that with all of these troops present within the country, very little army-to-army combat occurred – yet over 5 million people perished, most of them civilians. Wholesale massacres of women, children and unarmed men occurred throughout the country. It is estimated that 70% of those killed did not perish due to violence but due to inhospitable terrain and disease as millions were displaced and forced to live in foul conditions throughout the vast jungles of the DRC. While a massive war was being fought for the rights to the country's huge resource wealth, its people again suffered. As the 20th century had begun under Belgian rule, it ended in much the same manner.

Diplomatic efforts led, in July 1999 after two years of fighting, to the Lusaka Peace Accord. The six countries involved in the war agreed to track and disarm all armed groups in the DRC. However, there were few concrete provisions for disarming the militias and violent incidents continued. The so-called 'Six-Day War' broke out in Kisangani in August, with Ugandan and Rwandan forces exchanging heavy fire throughout most of the city. RCD continued in the east, with its various factions fighting among each other as well as the local population and the Kinshasa government. Furthermore, new rebel factions were emerging among the jungles of eastern Congo, especially Ituri Province. The war that was supposed to have finished in 1999 would continue well into the next decade, with the arrival of another large presence of troops – though this time under the United Nations, returning 40 years after its first mission in the former Republic of the Congo, and this time called MONUC.

THE UN IN CONGO: TAKE TWO The creation of MONUC (Mission de l'Organisation des Nations Unies en République Démocratique du Congo) followed a familiar tale: it was the largest UN operation yet, comprising a multi-national force that would rotate periodically, and was spread out across the country. While the UN's previous mandate included taking down the well-organised armies of Katanga, its new mission would be far more grey and open-ended: what was occurring in the DRC at the turn of the millennium was not so clear-cut as before, as tribal warfare and fractured rebel groups attacked primarily civilians. However, originally the UN was set up simply to monitor the activities of foreign-government forces in the nation and make sure they complied with the Lusaka Peace Accord and departed. Its major bases were in seven towns across the DRC: Kinshasa, Mbandaka, Kisangani, Kananga, Kalemie, Kindu and Bunia. It developed its own extensive air network, creating an infrastructure amid the chaos that had never existed while the country was standing on its own two feet.

Initially fewer than a hundred UN liaison officers were in the country, but the operation quickly expanded. The first soldiers, so-called 'Blue Helmets', were deployed to join the military observers in early 2001 and, by July, there were over 2,000 UN troops in the DRC. They were there only to protect MONUC sites; they did not have a UN mandate to protect the civilian population, which led to some criticism for this policy. Their presence, however, was a stabilising force. As the DRC entered the new millennium, perhaps MONUC stopped it from slipping further down the precipice.

ENTER JOSEPH Laurent-Désiré Kabila was not a vast improvement on the previous head of state, and in fact was on occasion labelled as a 'mini-Mobutu' by his detractors. He had appointed Étienne Tshisekedi as prime minister once again, though he kicked him out of that position almost as fast as he arrived. His desire for power and lack of interest in genuine reforms were one thing; how he treated members of his inner circle were another.

Laurent Kabila was known to have used child soldiers, as did most of the combatant forces in the Second Congo War, and he kept on some young men as his closest bodyguards. It was one of these youths who shot and killed Laurent Kabila on 16 January 2001. The motive may have been dissatisfaction by the former child soldiers at their poor treatment, or there may have been external machinations. His assassin was killed as well: chased down and shot. What exactly occurred on that day is still unclear, though there was no mistake that Laurent Kabila's death ended his rule before it became too entrenched for change.

Laurent's son moved swiftly to take power. Joseph Kabila had fought alongside his father during the Second Congo War and departed shortly after the AFDL's victory for military training in China. Kabila spoke English, providing a window away from the Francophone world and perhaps a different direction for the DRC. He was just 29 when he assumed the presidency, and few believed that he would last in power as long as he did.

Despite his youth and inexperience, Joseph Kabila succeeded in bringing an end to the Second Congo War. In 2002, peace talks held in South Africa led to the signing of a series of peace treaties. The Sun City Agreement provided a timeline for multi-party elections to be held, two to three years in the future, with Joseph Kabila as interim president and MLC leader Jean-Pierre Bemba as prime minister. South African President Thabo Mbeki hosted the summit, along with the heads of state of Zimbabwe, Zambia, Namibia and Botswana. The Pretoria Accord and Luanda Agreement committed Rwanda and Uganda to withdraw their soldiers from the DRC. Finally, in December 2002, the 'Global and Inclusive Transitional Accord' was signed by all the main Congolese belligerents; it committed them to power-sharing, with civil society and the political opposition, during a transition period of up to three years.

All of this sounded great in principle, though in practice it was harder to implement. Joseph Kabila and Jean-Pierre Bemba set about laying the groundwork for the transition, as MONUC expanded its mandate and, by 2003, had doubled the number of Blue Helmets in the DRC. Rebellions continued across the east with factions of the RCD in Kivu and Kisangani at odds with each other – irregular militias called Mai-Mai were continuously fighting against Interahamwe and anyone else they saw fit, and riots erupted occasionally in Kinshasa. All of this may have been par for the course in the DRC at the time, but the most insidious acts were taking place in a remote northeastern district that had rarely made the news before.

THE ITURI CONFLICT Tribal warfare came to the fore in Ituri, though as a sideshow to what was occurring across the DRC in the late 1990s; as the rest of the country stabilised, Ituri slid deeper into conflict. It originated out of the Hema and Lendu tribes at odds with each other, stretching back decades to a 1973 change in property laws that allowed others to purchase land and force the original owners off it. Animosity began to boil, and conflict occurred between the two groups sporadically for the next few decades. However, Ituri's difficulties would not hit fever pitch until the arrival of Uganda in the Second Congo War.

Uganda had occupied Ituri by 1998 and, in 1999, their local commander declared it as a new province; under Congolese law it was a district within the larger Orientale province. It is unclear whether or not Uganda believed Ituri to be Ugandan or Congolese territory – more than likely it kept it grey to keep international bodies guessing – but the announcement led the Lendu to think that Uganda was favouring the Hema. Extremist Lendus began killing Hema and destroying entire villages. While massacres had been seen before in the DRC, Ituri brought the nation's troubles to a new level by wiping whole villages off the map.

Uganda's army attempted to restore order and keep the two tribes away from each other, all the while extracting goods from Ituri's farms and mines to be siphoned back to their own nation. They would receive criticism of aiding the Hema in their war against the Lendu. Mass migrations occurred as killing continued, sending refugees into Ituri's thick rainforests and spawning large refugee camps. As the Lusaka Peace Accord was signed, Uganda armed both the Hema and Lendu as the majority of their forces departed from the region – giving both tribes the means to attack each other by leaving arms caches behind, and a general lack of authority to keep both sides apart.

As the Second Congo War waned, the Ugandan army kept a minimal presence in Ituri until the arrival of MONUC in the region in 2001. In early 2003, 800 UN soldiers were deployed to Bunia, which had the largest refugee camps. The UN Security Council authorised the deployment of an Interim Multinational Emergency Force, to secure the airport and protect civilians. This was known as Operation Artemis. Led by France, it included EU and non-EU personnel; on their arrival in Bunia, the town was nearly deserted as all business owners had either fled or been killed. Operation Artemis managed to stabilise the situation over the next three months and handed responsibility for security back to the UN in September 2003.

MONUC would conduct an observatory role while trying to keep the two sides away from each other, at least initially – a change in their mandate in 2004 required them to protect civilians who were at risk of violence. This would be a noted adjustment to their role in the DRC as they would now be responsible for protecting innocent people against ethnic conflict, rather than simply acting as observers. It would make their role more relevant, but far more difficult.

While encountering little resistance across other parts of the country, the Blue Helmets would encounter fierce resistance from Hema and Lendu tribes in Ituri. In the worst loss of peacekeepers since Rwanda, nine of them were killed in February 2005 by extremist Lendus. UN soldiers finally responded with authority – a subsequent attack on a Lendu militia base killed 50. MONUC would begin mass arrests across the province. No longer simply observers, they became incredibly active in moderating the Ituri conflict and separating the enemies from each other. MONUC continued its disarmament programme in Ituri and made some progress at removing the threat of militias, but the violence has re-erupted at intervals. Since 2017, both Lendu and Hema villages have been burned and hundreds of civilians killed.

The chaos in Ituri has also led to unmonitored extraction of resources, including gold, by unknown groups across the province. Human rights groups have found evidence that multi-national companies were involved in the conflict between the Hema and Lendu. Gold was smuggled across the border into Uganda and the proceeds were shared between the companies and the militias: amid chaos, business can continue without prying eyes.

POLITICAL PROGRESS The transition period agreed in the December 2002 Accord began officially with the swearing-in of the transitional government on 30 June 2003. A constitutional referendum was held in December 2003, the country's first genuinely democratic process for four decades. The new constitution came into force in February 2006. The South African President Thabo Mbeki and African Union President Denis Sassou Nguesso presided over the ceremony. The new constitution allowed for a president to be elected for a maximum of two five-year terms, and to share power with an elected prime minister. It also foresaw a restructuring of local government – the country's 26 districts would become provinces, replacing the existing 11 provinces – although this was not implemented until 2015. A new flag was introduced, retaining the star of King Léopold but adding three diagonal stripes across its centre.

A general election was held on 30 July 2006, to elect a new president and the members of a new National Assembly (the lower house of parliament). A second round of the presidential election took place in October, between Joseph Kabila and Jean-Pierre Bemba, the two highest-placed candidates. While the country awaited the results of the first round, supporters of those two candidates had confronted each other in the streets of Kinshasa, with artillery and machine-guns being used. The violence went on for three days and 23 people were confirmed to have been killed. There were also clashes in the east of the country. The result of the second round was announced in November; Bemba unsuccessfully challenged the result in the Supreme Court and Kabila was sworn in as president.

In March 2007, the Palais du Peuple, or national assembly, was opened for the first time in over a decade; this reopening was seen by many as a positive step that the 'Third Republic', as the newly elected government would be popularly called, was decidedly different from what had transpired in the past. However, a familiar pattern quickly emerged – in the middle of March an assassination attempt on Jean-Pierre Bemba resulted in open combat in Kinshasa, leaving hundreds dead. Factions loyal to Jean-Pierre Bemba were accused of agitating a difficult situation. Bemba took refuge in the embassy of South Africa with his family, urging his men to stand down. The Kabila government issued a warrant for Bemba's arrest, accusing him of high treason. Bemba was eventually given safe passage to Portugal for treatment at a hospital there. With their leader in Portugal, the MLC withdrew from parliament, citing their own safety concerns – accusations of Kabila's ruling party engaging in practices of intimidation and harassment of MLC senators emerged. The MLC ended their boycott of the parliament at the end of April, but at the end of July, Bemba remained in Portugal. Kabila's government continued its reconstruction programme, and MONUC tightened its grip on remaining pockets of instability in the east. Jean-Pierre Bemba eventually remained in Portugal, and a warrant was issued for his arrest; he was arrested near Brussels in May 2008, and was handed over to the International Criminal Court (ICC) on charges related to the Central African Republic. His trial lasted four years; he was sentenced, he appealed and, after ten years in prison in The Hague, his appeal was upheld, his convictions were quashed and he returned to Kinshasa.

MONUC's full-scale mission in the DRC ended in the middle of 2010. The mission was renamed as MONUSCO, the S standing for 'stabilisation', and it was intended to slowly wind down from an active peacekeeping force into a monitoring mission, as had been intended in the late 1990s.

After months of delays, the DRC held a further presidential election in November 2011. Dozens were killed and several voting stations were burned to the ground. International observers considered the whole electoral process as a step backwards, which could only deepen the crisis of legitimacy of the country's political institutions. To nobody's surprise, Joseph Kabila was once again declared president of the republic.

Étienne Tshisekedi, Kabila's main opponent, rejected the result and declared himself the winner of the election and the legitimate president. In a national speech, he ordered the armed forces to obey his orders and arrest Kabila. In December 2011, effectively under house arrest, he staged a private inauguration inside his own home in Kinshasa. He left the DRC in 2014 for medical treatment in Brussels.

In January 2015, the National Assembly agreed to changes in the electoral law that would allow Kabila to stay in power until a national census had been held, postponing the election due in 2016. Opposition parties called on their supporters to protest outside the Palais du Peuple; the protest was dispersed with tear gas and live ammunition. After several days of violence in Kinshasa and the east, Parliament removed the controversial provision from the legislation. However, the elections did not take place as scheduled; it would be December 2018 before voters could go to the polls. The intervening years saw further protests and outbreaks of violence. Militia activity and tribal conflicts were increasing (page 40).

The 2018 election resulted in the DRC's first ever transfer of presidential power from one party to another. Kabila was ineligible to stand, after serving two terms in office. His party, the PPRD, supported Emmanuel Shadary's candidacy. The two other main candidates were Félix Tshisekedi, son of the veteran opposition leader Étienne who had died in 2017, and Martin Fayulu, a former oil executive. Tshisekedi was declared the winner, with 38.6% of the vote to Fayulu's 34.8%. Kabila's coalition had won a landslide majority in the National Assembly and large majorities in most of the provincial parliaments. Fayulu claimed that Tshisekedi and Kabila had made a deal and challenged the presidential result in the Constitutional Court. Doubts were also cast on the elections by national observers and some international media (international observers had been refused accreditation). Fayulu's appeal was rejected and, after some hesitation, regional and international governments recognised Tshisekedi as president. Martin Fayulu never accepted the Constitutional Court's decision and continued to refer to himself as the DRC's elected president until the subsequent presidential election, in 2023.

The deal between Tshisekedi and Kabila did not last long. It took five months for the two allies to agree on a prime minister. Disagreements continued and, in late 2020, Tshisekedi dissolved the coalition between his small parliamentary party and the large pro-Kabila bloc. He went about luring members of the latter bloc across the floor to his new coalition, the Sacred Union of the Nation (Union Sacrée de la Nation, USN), which also included the parliamentary groups of the opposition heavyweights Jean-Pierre Bemba and Moïse Katumbi, the former governor of Katanga, who had been prevented from standing in the 2018 presidential election. Tshisekedi appointed his new government, without pro-Kabila ministers, in April 2021.

GOVERNMENT AND POLITICS

The Democratic Republic of the Congo is governed by a president, to be elected every five years and eligible to stand for a maximum of two terms; a bi-cameral Parliament, with a lower house (l'Assemblée Nationale) of 500 members, again elected every five years with no restriction on the number of times they can stand, and an upper house (Senate) of 108 members, with four senators for each province and eight for the city-province of Kinshasa; and provincial parliaments, one for each of the country's 26 provinces including Kinshasa. Provincial governors and vice-governors are elected by their respective provincial parliaments. There are also municipal councils and 'conseils de chefferie', councils for sectors in rural areas. The most recent general elections took place in December 2023; gubernatorial elections were held in April and May 2024.

DEMOCRATIC REPUBLIC OF THE CONGO PROVINCES

The 2023 presidential elections offered a choice of 21 candidates. They included the incumbent Félix Tshisekedi, his 2018 rival Martin Fayulu, and Moïse Katumbi, who had withdrawn from the USN in late 2022. Denis Mukwege, a gynaecologist who won the Nobel Peace Prize in 2018 for his work with survivors of rape as a weapon of war, was another prominent candidate. Jean-Pierre Bemba supported Tshisekedi, who had appointed him as Defence Minister. Joseph Kabila and the parties that support him boycotted the 2023 elections, on the grounds that they had no confidence in the national election commission or the Constitutional Court. Tshisekedi was declared to have received 73% of the votes; his own party, the UDPS, and its allies had a large majority in Parliament. Katumbi, who had obtained 18.3% of the votes, and Fayulu, with 4.9%, disputed the results but did not challenge them in court.

An attempted coup d'état took place in May 2024, with the presidential palace and the residence of the Economy Minister being attacked by heavily armed assailants. A gun battle also took place at the parliament building, the Palais de la Nation. The coup leader, Christian Malanga, was killed during the assault. The rest of the 51 alleged coup participants were court-martialled; they included US citizens and a 'naturalised British subject'.

SECURITY Just as Kabila began his first term of office in 2006, a general who had come into the integrated national army from the RCD-Goma faction, Laurent Nkunda, rebelled and began to create problems in the hills near Rutshuru – further aggravating the delicate situation in Nord-Kivu. Nkunda, a Congolese Tutsi, was upset that the new government was not doing enough to oust Interahamwe militias from their last remaining strongholds in eastern DRC. His new rebel movement was called National Congress for the Defence of the People (CNDP). Virunga National Park's gorilla mountains and Rwindi Plains were shut down for two months, and 6,000 of his soldiers were stationed on the outskirts of Goma.

The political and security environment in the DRC has remained unstable since 2011 as new politico-military movements emerged. In April 2012, a new movement called the Movement of March 23 (**M23**) was founded in the province of Nord-Kivu. M23 included rebels from Nkunda's CNDP and was led by General Bosco Ntaganda, who was convicted of war crimes by the ICC in 2021 and is currently in detention in The Hague. After relentless combat, M23 managed to defeat the national army, supported by United Nations peacekeepers, and briefly took control of Goma. In 2013, a Mai-Mai (irregular militia) group operating in northern Katanga briefly invaded the city of Lubumbashi. Both of these invasions were brought to an end by UN peacekeepers, but both groups have continued to operate and are still active at the time of writing. In 2022, the head of MONUSCO warned that M23's firepower and long-range equipment was reaching a sophistication that went beyond the capabilities of the Congolese army and MONUSCO. In May 2024, M23 attacked two refugee camps in the outskirts of Goma, killing at least a dozen people.

There are over a hundred armed groups active in eastern and northern DRC. Inter-communal violence continues in **Ituri** (page 36). An association of various Lendu militias called CODECO has emerged as one of the most violent groups, accused by the UN of massacres 'akin to crimes against humanity'. In 2022, CODECO fighters left 62 people dead in a refugee camp; in 2023, UN peacekeepers discovered a mass grave of 42 civilians, including women and children, alleged to have been killed by CODECO, in a village about 30km east of Bunia. The **Lord's Resistance Army**, originally a Ugandan militia, moved into the DRC in 2005 and set up its camps within Garamba National Park; it continues to smuggle ivory, wildlife and weapons across the border. The **FLDR**, which emerged from the Hutu

Interahamwe, was held responsible for the 2023 murder of the Italian ambassador and his escort on their way to visit a World Food Programme project in Rutshuru.

In 2021, President Tshisekedi declared a 'state of siege' in the provinces of Nord-Kivu and Ituri. This means that the civil authorities in these provinces are suspended and military authorities have taken over the maintenance of order. It also means that Virunga National Park is closed to visitors (page 208) until such time as the state of siege is lifted. The 2023 general elections were not held in three districts due to the armed conflict there.

There are perhaps hundreds of small **Mai-Mai** groups across the DRC, not only in the east. Mai-Mai are defined as community-based militia groups. This sounds very innocuous and indeed some Mai-Mai really are groups of villagers, under the leadership of their traditional elders, trying to defend their territory against better-armed and more lethal militias such as M23. Other Mai-Mai are led by warlords and have been responsible for murdering, kidnapping and raping civilians. Dozens, perhaps hundreds, of national park rangers have been killed by Mai-Mai and other militias; over just ten days in June 2023, seven rangers in Virunga died at Mai-Mai hands. Foreigners have been kidnapped for ransom. About 7 million Congolese have been displaced as they have fled violence; many have found shelter of a kind in huge refugee camps, but many others survive in the forests as best they can, far from any kind of international aid.

In 2023, the DRC government informed MONUSCO that its mission in the country would end. The plan is to replace the UN peacekeepers with forces contributed by other African countries. A 'gradual, responsible and sustainable withdrawal' was agreed between MONUSCO and the government, starting with Sud-Kivu. By mid-2024, UN military and police forces were present only in Nord-Kivu and Ituri, although a residual team remained in Sud-Kivu to ensure a smooth transition. MONUSCO's bases and assets are being handed over to the Congolese army and government.

ECONOMY

The Democratic Republic of the Congo has exceptional natural resources, including minerals, hydropower potential, significant arable land and the world's second-largest rainforest. But this potential wealth has not improved the lives of locals – the DRC is one of the five poorest nations on earth. The World Bank estimates that nearly 75% of Congolese people live on less than US$2.15 a day (2023 estimate). The **agriculture** sector employs over 60% of the workforce, making the economy very vulnerable to climate change – notably floods and droughts. Palm oil, bananas, rubber, coffee and sugar are all cultivated and exported on a medium scale.

The country's mineral wealth includes copper and cobalt (mostly in Katanga), diamonds (mostly in Kasai), gold (mostly in the east and northeast) and the minerals used to make coltan (mostly in the east). The Katanga mines were opened up by the Belgians early in the 20th century; many of Katanga's towns would not exist if not for mining. Most of the large industrial **copper and cobalt** mines are joint ventures between Gécamines, the national mining company, and foreign companies. Over the last decade, Chinese companies have taken over practically all of the industrial mines in Katanga. In addition, there are around 40,000 artisan miners – around twice as many as are employed in the industrial sector – supporting perhaps a million people. The Shinkolobwe Mine near Likasi was where the USA bought uranium for the two atomic bombs detonated in World War II.

Further north, the Kasai region was once known as the world's major producer of industrial **diamonds**, though now output has been severely reduced. In the

1

early 2000s, the DRC exported 33 million carats of diamonds; by 2017 it was about half that. Almost all diamond mining in the DRC is artisan, with villagers panning river-gravel and diving for earth from the river-bottom. A joint venture between the DRC government and China's Anhui group is the largest of a handful of industrial diamond mines, producing about 85% of industrial diamond output in 2016. There have been continued accusations that licence-holders prefer to allow informal exploitation on their concessions and keep the revenue from diamond sales, without anything going back into the country's economy.

The Kibali **gold** mine in Haut-Uélé was first exploited in the early 20th century and is now owned by a multi-national conglomerate; in 2019, it produced 814,000 ounces of gold. There are also many artisan gold-miners. Gold from the DRC is often a conflict mineral, smuggled across the border to Uganda to fund rebel groups. The minerals used to make **coltan** – columbite and tantalite – are mostly produced by artisan miners, working in unsafe conditions for minimal pay, and are similarly conflict minerals. The income from these minerals is also often diverted to fund some of the many armed militias in the eastern provinces.

Mobutu Sese Seko built the Inga **hydro-electric** scheme along the River Congo near Matadi. The dams' output has been at reduced capacity for years due to lack of maintenance. There are regular reports of plans to improve the structure, most recently a reported agreement in 2021 for the Canadian company Ivanhoe Mines to rehabilitate one of the Inga II turbines. There are also plans to create a third Inga dam, Grand Inga, which, if it is ever completed, would be the largest hydro-electric plant in the world, with double the generating capacity of the Three Gorges Dam in China. The potential is massive – Grand Inga could potentially generate enough hydro-electric power to provide electricity to all of central Africa. Although the project has drawn criticism from international river conservation organisations, the DRC has a clear need for more electricity generation. Blackouts are still frequent across even major cities like Lubumbashi and Kinshasa and 84% of Congolese people have no access to mains electricity at all; in many villages, local entrepreneurs or international donors have installed small solar panels where the villagers can at least charge their phones. On the Atlantic coast, the **ports** of Matadi and Boma will soon be complemented by the country's first deepwater port at Banana. This US$1.2 billion development, being built by the Dubai-based logistics behemoth DP World, is expected to be completed in 2025 and to process over 300,000 containers a year. It is controversial because of the port's proximity to Mangroves National Park (page 120). Some oil reserves exist in the DRC's coastal territory, but its output in this arena is far overshadowed by the larger reserves of its neighbours Angola, Congo-Brazzaville and Gabon.

All of this comes down to potential – if the Democratic Republic of the Congo could sort its problems out, and create a political system that was not so easily swayed by corruption and nepotism, its citizens would be some of the richest on the continent. Yet that is still only a dream – unemployment is high, education is low, movement of goods is either expensive or restricted or both. Highly educated Congolese have a hard time getting permission to leave, the government fearing that their brightest would never come back if given the chance to spend time abroad. Unfortunately, that may be the case until further notice.

PEOPLE

With over 115 million inhabitants, the Democratic Republic of the Congo is the most populous nation in central Africa. However, this figure is merely an estimate

– the DRC has not held a population census since 1984. There has been little serious study of the rate at which refugees have poured across the country's borders, and the full level of devastation from the nation's recent conflicts has not been fully measured. While huge numbers live in urban areas such as Kinshasa, Lubumbashi and Goma, the vast majority still live in small villages scattered throughout dense equatorial jungle.

Several hundred tribes make up the population, all of whom are descendants of Bantu lineage – with the exception of the indigenous Pygmy peoples (page 180), who live primarily in the deep rainforests of northern DRC. Small communities of European, Asian and African immigrants have settled in major towns, but not in large numbers – the country lacks the full-blown international diversity of Congo-Brazzaville, its smaller neighbour across the river. Which is not to say it isn't a diverse place; it is inherently diverse from its hundreds of different Bantu tribes.

LANGUAGE

The official language of the Democratic Republic of the Congo is **French** – it is the world's most populous Francophone country. Everyone with any education at all speaks at least some of the language; many speak it extremely well. Travellers will find that even a little French makes it far easier to get around in the DRC; once off the beaten track, a reasonable command of the language will be practically essential.

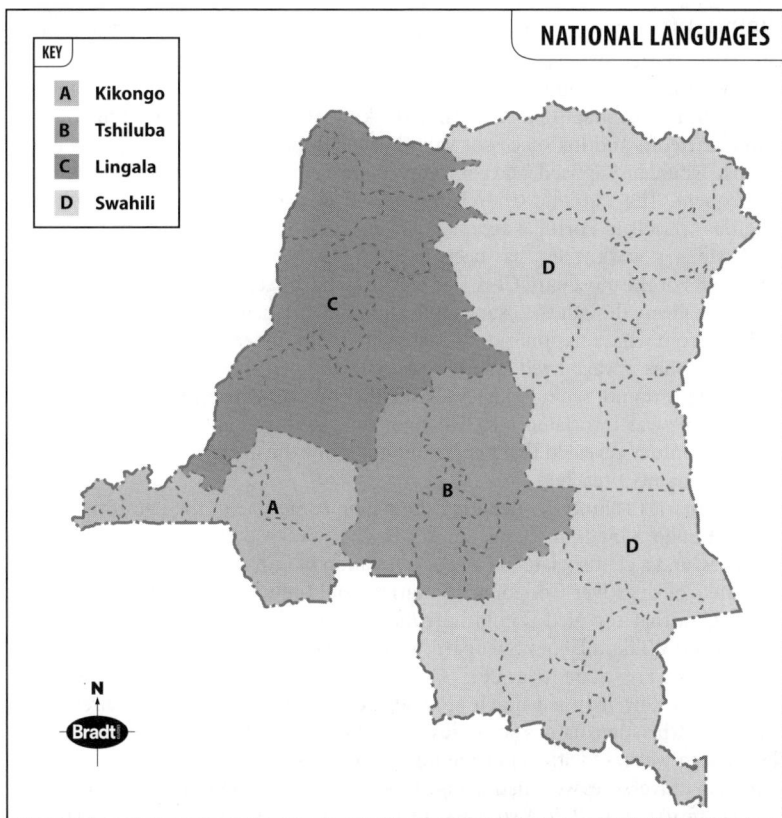

NATIONAL LANGUAGES

KEY

A	Kikongo
B	Tshiluba
C	Lingala
D	Swahili

N

Bradt

You don't have to speak it perfectly and, if you don't understand your interlocutor, simply ask them to speak more slowly (*parlez doucement, s'il vous plaît*). English is more widely spoken in Lubumbashi and other places in the provinces of Katanga, thanks to the mining industry and the proximity of Zambia, and in the tourist hotspots of Goma and Bukavu.

In addition to its official language, the DRC has four 'national languages': Lingala, Kituba/Kikongo, Swahili and Tshiluba. For many Congolese, their 'national language' is their second after their local language, of which there are hundreds in this vast country. **Lingala** is the lingua franca of Kinshasa and the northwest; it is also the usual language of *musique congolaise* (page 47) and has traditionally been the lingua franca of the armed forces. The **Swahili**-speaking area includes Katanga and the whole of eastern DRC, from Kisangani and Kindu to the Great Lakes. Congo-Swahili is effectively the same as the language spoken elsewhere in East and southern Africa. **Kituba**, or Kikongo, is the language of the southwest, including Matadi and Kikwit. **Tshiluba**, a language with its roots in the ancient Luba Kingdom that existed in the same region over a millennium ago, is used in Kasai.

Glossaries for these languages can be found in *Appendix 1* (page 227), along with some tips on speaking French for those who need them.

RELIGION

CHRISTIANITY The arrival of the Portuguese at the end of the 15th century saw missionaries preach the Gospel in the Kingdom of Kongo, and it would become immensely important to the first nations of the region, as well as play an important role in shaping their future. The king of the time embraced the religion wholeheartedly, and his successor would even adopt a Christian name – Alfonso. Alfonso would be baptised, and communications between Kongo and Europe would be frequent. The Catholic Church recognised Kongo as a Christian nation, and religious schools in Portugal accepted citizens from Kongo for religious training.

Missionary work, then, has been important to the make-up of the region for centuries. For the most part, Christian teachings have been followed enthusiastically by local tribes – though the exact application of Christianity may sometimes seem to differ from what missionaries brought with them. Indeed, Christian faith across the Congo has always lived side by side with the original animist practices, and many people do not seem to believe that either one is exclusive of the other.

The Bible was translated into Kikongo some centuries ago, though research in the 18th century revealed that people did not know the name of this singular 'God' that Christianity preached.

Missionaries voluntarily departed the region sometime in the late 18th century as the Kongo Kingdom dissolved. Yet in their wake they left numerous small churches, and a century later, as a new generation of European explorers arrived on the banks of the River Congo, missionaries would return. It would be missionary work again that revealed untold horrors perpetrated due to the rubber trade, in letters from William Henry Sheppard, as he worked his way deep into the territory of the Congo Free State (page 26).

Mobutu's Zaire banned much of what the Catholic Church had aspired to for centuries. Christian names were discarded for Congolese names, and dissent in the Church was met with expulsion for any bishops who opposed these measures. Christian universities were nationalised and Africanised. Mobutu's regime admitted it had gone too far in 1976, two years after he had banned celebrations of Christmas.

Pope John Paul II visited the DRC twice in his lifetime, in 1980 and 1985. Catholic bishops in the era of Mobutu were also outspoken opponents of his one-party regime, making their presence in the country unpopular with the authorities.

Protestantism is also prominent, and gained ground in the era of Zaire. While Catholicism opposed much of what Mobutu was aiming for in his religious reforms, the Protestant denominations sided with these policies as it gave the Protestant Church an equal status with Catholicism. The various Protestant groups that spanned across Zaire were merged into a singular unit, the Église du Christ au Zaire, or ECZ (now known as l'Église du Christ au Congo, ECC), and they gained political clout from this merger. In 1990, the ECZ, who had more or less acquiesced to Mobutu's requests, were in a position to lobby his government for democratic reforms.

Most Congolese still consider themselves to be Catholics. Every small town has at least one Catholic church, and there are impressive cathedrals in the larger cities such as Kinshasa and Lubumbashi. Roughly half of the population of the DRC is Roman Catholic, attesting to the lengthy history of the Catholic Church in the region.

Other Christian faiths are also present – around Lubumbashi there are small groups of Jehovah's Witnesses. With war and strife lingering in the eastern half of the country, evangelical groups have found an opportunity to capitalise on their problems by offering aid as well as preaching their own version of the Gospel.

ISLAM Zanzibari traders brought Islam with them as they delved deeper and deeper into central Africa seeking ivory and people to enslave. Thus, the majority of Muslims across the DRC can be found in the east. Descendants of Muslims who had been employed in various colonial armies have also migrated over the years into the east, bringing Muslim practices from Sudan, Uganda and Tanzania into the DRC's eastern provinces. The old slave routes possess the largest number of Muslims, even to this day: the province of Maniema, particularly the town of Kasongo which was once the capital of Tippu Tip's Sultanate of Utetera (page 21), still has the highest percentage of Muslims in the country. Islam subjugated animist practices, but did not eliminate them – much the same as what happened with Christianity. Many traditional practices of the east still continue, though under the name of Islam.

JUDAISM Jewish families immigrated to what is now the Democratic Republic of the Congo in the early 20th century, from eastern Europe, South Africa and the Greek island of Rhodes; by 1930, the community in Élisabethville was sizeable enough for a synagogue to be built. Jewish refugees from Europe came to the Belgian Congo fleeing Nazism and Fascism in the 1930s; the father of the Congolese politician Moïse Katumbi was one of those refugees. There was a smaller Jewish community in Kinshasa. The Association Sioniste du Congo Belge co-ordinated Zionist activities throughout the country. After independence in 1960, most of the Jewish community left, principally for Israel and South Africa. A few hundred Jewish people remain in the DRC, mostly in Lubumbashi, which has the country's only synagogue.

KIMBANGUISM This Christian religious movement was founded by Simon Kimbangu, a Baptist catechist, in 1921, when he first reported having visions calling for him to become a healer and apostle. He began his ministry, preaching faith healing, and soon a personality cult developed around him. Kimbangu successfully engineered a mass protest in 1921, and Belgian authorities, worried by Kimbangu's power over a large portion of the population, imprisoned him near Élisabethville (present-day Lubumbashi). He spent three decades there before perishing in jail in 1951. His followers, hunted by the authorities, fled to Brazzaville and may have been of assistance in founding the locally grown hybrid Christian sect, the Matsouanists.

Just prior to independence, in 1959, the Kimbanguist Church was recognised as an official religious organisation and allowed to practise openly. The Church did not have nearly as much clout as it did in the first half of the century, but today still has a large following in the DRC. Across Africa, Kimbanguism has an estimated 6 million adherents. It has its world headquarters in Kimbangu's birthplace in the province of Kongo-Central (page 110).

Kimbanguism is non-political and puritan. It rejects violence and teaches its followers to abandon many animist practices as well as avoid alcohol and tobacco, as well as dancing. Its worship follows Baptist lines. It holds large, well-organised services. Much myth and legend surrounds the life of Simon Kimbangu and his followers believe that he was the incarnation of the Holy Spirit. It was for this reason that the Kimbanguist Church was excluded from the World Council of Churches in 2021. It is estimated that roughly 10% of people in the DRC are Kimbanguists.

ANIMISM, SORCERY AND WITCHCRAFT Spiritual practices continued by the peoples that make up today's DRC have existed since time immemorial, and continue to exist: even with the organised religions of the world having a heavy footprint in every populated area, local people still believe strongly in the otherworld of spirits, superstitions and sorcery.

These beliefs have been used to great effect throughout the DRC's wars – rebels have indulged in cannibalism to gain strength and become invincible in battle; politicians may blame their opposing candidates of appealing to evil spirits to win, and gain favour from voters; children have been cast out of families for practising 'witchcraft' or 'sorcery'. These things are taken deadly seriously throughout central Africa, and understanding a bit about them can go a long way into understanding local behaviours.

The larger problem is that there are a wide-ranging number of practices relating to animist traditions, and simplification is not straightforward. Generally speaking, the dead are revered and so are their bodies; evil spirits are perceived to be real and haunt the living, and they need to be treated with some level of respect. Some people have offered potions to locals offering to ward off evil spirits – in December 2005, 64 people died after drinking one of these mixtures.

Children are believed to have close ties with the spiritual world, and in an unfortunate twist of fate, a family will cast a child out on to the street if they are suspected of practising sorcery. 'Sorcery' may, in fact, simply be bad luck – when there is a death in the family, or when someone loses their job. A family will cast out their most vulnerable member as atonement for this unfortunate turn of events – which, in recent times, has led to an increase in the numbers of street children – especially in big cities such as Kinshasa. Some Churches will offer to 'exorcise' the evil spirits from the child accused of sorcery, and put them through various forms of torture to cleanse their souls, before they are permitted to take refuge in their building. Many people pray to the Christian God to absolve their child of witchcraft or sorcery.

EDUCATION

The first educational system in what is now the DRC was established by Christian missionaries, who set up schools throughout the country to teach their Congolese flock enough literacy to read the Bible. In the early 20th century, the colonial administration of the Belgian Congo used this missionary structure to introduce a public education system. In the late 1920s, technical schools were set up in several large towns, where young women were taught housekeeping skills and young men were trained for various manual trades. In the 1930s, secondary and technical schools were decoupled from the Church; after World War II, education was free of charge and teachers were well paid. This continued after independence: school fees were covered by the state, there were bursaries for students who needed them, and new schools were built. In the 1970s, however, school fees were introduced, first for secondary and then for primary education.

From the early 1990s, instability and then war had a disastrous effect on children's education, as well as on so many other aspects of life. A host of reasons made it impossible for many children to attend school, and literacy and numeracy rates declined. Even after relative peace had been restored to large parts of the country, the difficult economic situation meant that many parents could not afford to educate their children. Since then, gradually, school attendance has improved. In 2021, 79% of girls and 86% of boys completed primary education (from ages 6 to 11); enrolment and completion at secondary level are much lower. The current government has increased the education budget and is rolling out a policy of free primary education throughout the country, apart from the cities of Kinshasa and Lubumbashi. But attending school is not enough; the quality of the education provided is often very low. UNESCO estimates that an astonishing 97% of children are unable to read an age-appropriate text by the age of 10. Parents whose means allow them the choice enrol their children in a Catholic school, where teacher–pupil ratios are better, or in private education, or send them abroad.

The DRC's public universities date back to the 1950s, when the University of Louvain founded what is now Kinshasa University (UNIKIN) and the University of Liège set up what is now the University of Lubumbashi (UNILU). They were followed in 1963 by the University of Kisangani. All three have a reasonably good reputation nowadays. These and other cities around the country also have private universities. As with primary and secondary education, parents who can afford it send their children to university abroad.

CULTURE

MUSIC The Democratic Republic of the Congo's greatest contribution to the cultural world at large is its music. Widely listened to across central Africa and beyond, *musique congolaise* regularly rings from bars and clubs as far away as Cameroon and Chad. Some Congolese musicians have also moved beyond the continent, building fan bases around the world, especially in Francophone nations. Paris is a hotbed for Congolese music and can in fact be a better place to sample it than Kinshasa, where live performances are hard to find.

The DRC's musical style originated in the 1940s with African jazz bands, evolving further in the 1950s as the Afro-Cuban musical style rumba really took off across the nation. Rumba became the basis for more experimentation as the DRC began to form a national musical style, with the *soukous* urban dance music style emerging in the 1960s. Congolese rumba is now part of humanity's 'intangible cultural heritage', inscribed as such by UNESCO in 2021. During the 1970s Kinshasa's suburbs became a hotbed for popular music, and during this period the most identifiable rhythms of Zairian music were established. The *sapeur* (page 236) Papa Wemba (1949–2016) was one of the most influential musicians of the 1970s and helped to introduce Congolese music to Paris in the 1980s. *Soukous* evolved in various directions, including *ndombolo*, which brought Congolese music to audiences in Africa, Europe and the Americas and influenced the development of French hip-hop. As well as Papa Wemba, his fellow *sapeur* Koffi Olomidé and the super-group Wenge Musica were prominent in this phase. Wenge Musica split in 1997, acrimoniously, and its stars J B Mpiana and Werrason set up rival 'Wenge' bands (see below). More recently, *musique congolaise* has diversified into electronic music known as Congotronics (see opposite).

VISUAL ARTS Traditional wooden masks and fetish sculptures from the DRC are highly coveted and incredibly popular – the exaggerated facial features and body parts of indigenous African art are said to have originated in the Congo, and these sculptures are often sold as souvenirs in neighbouring countries. This visual style is said to have originated with the original Kongo Kingdom, as well as the Kuba and Luba peoples.

Kinshasa is home to the famous Académie des Beaux-Arts, where traditionalist African styles of two-dimensionalism and symbolism are promoted and are taught to new students. The Académie also helps students to move beyond these styles and build a true contemporary visual art scene in the country. Artists such as Chéri Cherin and Chéri Samba have used the 'art naïf' style with political overtones, twisting the traditional symbols used in African painting to study the current socio-political issues confronting the DRC. The sculptor Bodys Isek Kingelez takes a different approach altogether, constructing highly detailed maquettes of

WERRASON

Werrason is hugely popular in his own country as well as abroad. He's toured across the Francophone world and performed in African music festivals in South Africa as well as closer to home. When I asked in Kinshasa who was the most popular of their contemporary musical acts, the answer was obvious. People always told me, '*C'est simple. Werrason.*'

He was born in 1965 in Kikwit and moved to the capital as a teenager. He was in the original line-up of Wenge Musica, which went on to become one of the best-known Congolese bands. They released their first album in 1988 and toured to Europe in 1991. After Wenge Musica split up, Werrason continued with his new band Wenge Musica Ma Mère, or WMMM. It was their 1999 release 'Solola Bien' which brought WMMM and Werrason to the attention of the French recording label Disque D'Or. They toured the record across the Western world and became the second African act (after Koffi Olomidé) to sell out the Palais Omnisports de Paris-Bercy, performing in front of 17,000 fans. Since then, Werrason has released eight more studio albums with WMMM and four solo studio albums, starting with 2001's *Kibuisa Mpimpa*, another great success and the beginning of his solo career. He has joined the ranks of other Francophone world music stars and continues to enjoy a large following in Europe, as well as Africa.

Werrason has also brought attention to the troubles of his country and to the plight of child soldiers. The Werrason Foundation is a non-profit organisation that helps orphans. He is a United Nations Peace Ambassador and has supported UNESCO campaigns to counter discrimination against people with AIDS.

KONONO N°1

Call it a modern-day appropriation of the 'noble savage' if you will, or perhaps a more idealistic approach at bringing to light the exciting and raucous music of Kinshasa to the world at large beyond central Africa – Konono N°1 is a widely heralded group who have played relentlessly together in Kinshasa since the 1960s. In the early 2000s, they were finally 'discovered' by French producer Vincent Kenis, who has made it his mission to bring the electrified grooves of the Congo to the world at large.

The group was founded by Mingiedi Mawangu, who adapted the *likembé*, a thumb piano, electrifying it with old magnets to great effect. Their music draws largely on Bazombo trance music. Konono N°1 numbers about 20 people, give or take, and they use a fascinating array of ad hoc musical instruments, many of which are made from scrap car parts, as well as featuring singers and dancers.

Using a wide variety of such homemade instruments, many of them jury-rigged with electronic wires to get distortion out of them, Konono N°1 has become something of a cult hit to Western audiences. Their first recording to be available outside the DRC was a 1987 compilation album, *Zaire: Musiques Urbaines à Kinshasa*, which first brought the group to Kenis's attention. He recorded their album *Congotronics,* released in 2004, and several other discs, most recently *Konono N°1 meets Batida* (2016). The band has performed at major electronic music festivals across the world since then. Mingiedi Mawangu died in 2015 and the group's lead *likembé* player is now his grandson Makonda.

Vincent Kenis's label Crammed Discs is devoted to not only promoting Congolese electro-traditional music, like Konono N°1 and Kasai Allstars, but world music from many other traditions. For more information or to buy physical or digital recordings, visit their website (w crammed.be).

futuristic cities that bear no relation to any urban area in the nation. European art communities have been especially supportive of contemporary artists from the DRC, and artists have gained a prominent standing in group exhibitions featuring African artists. There are contemporary art galleries in Kinshasa and Lubumbashi, where artworks can be purchased; see page 80.

Background Information CULTURE

1

2

Practical Information

WHEN TO VISIT

The Democratic Republic of the Congo has two seasons: wet (or rainy) and dry. The rains occur in different months in different parts of the country (this is why the rate of flow of the River Congo remains stable throughout the year, unlike – for example – the Amazon); see page 3 for details. It is very much easier to get around the country in the dry season, although it can be oppressively hot. With the start of the rains, many rural roads become impassable and even asphalted roads can become flooded. Visits into the rainforest are usually possible only in the dry season.

HIGHLIGHTS

Most people who visit the DRC do so for the wildlife. Until recently, the highlight for many was the chance to see **mountain gorillas** in Virunga National Park (w virunga.org), which has a third of the world's population of this endangered species. Unfortunately, at the time of writing, this park has been closed to visitors for several years due to the presence of armed militias in the area. Fortunately, though, it is still possible to visit Kahuzi-Biega National Park, the only natural habitat of the **eastern lowland gorilla**, where **chimpanzees** can also be seen. The dense forests on the left bank of the River Congo are home to the DRC's other unique primate, the **bonobo**; Lola Ya Bonobo (page 107), near Kinshasa, is a sanctuary for bonobos rescued from captivity. Mangroves National Park (page 120) has **manatees.** The national parks in Katanga (page 156), where the southern African **savannah** begins, have forest elephants, zebras and hippos.

The **River Congo** is a humbling and moving sight anywhere along its banks, and the history of central Africa's largest river is a great one (page 20). **Kinshasa**, the world's largest French-speaking city, is a fascinating cultural experience, particularly for those with an interest in Congolese music.

Hiking in the Rwenzori Mountains or ascending Mount Nyiragongo attracted many foreign visitors in the recent past. Unfortunately, like gorilla-trekking and for the same reason, Rwenzori is also out of bounds to visitors for the time being. There is nowhere else in the DRC which is oriented towards hikers.

SUGGESTED ITINERARIES

WEEKEND The only reasonable weekend itineraries in the DRC would require approaching the country from one of its neighbours. The difficulty and expense of obtaining visas mean that such a short trip is only worthwhile if you already have a visa (and a yellow-fever certificate) for the DRC and for whichever other country you are entering from; although see page 183 for information about 14-day visas.

From the **Republic of the Congo**, the two capitals of Brazzaville and Kinshasa face each other across the River Congo. The crossing by motorboat takes only 10 minutes, although the paperwork and payments to get on to the boat can take several hours. Kinshasa is one of Africa's great cities, with historic sites, world-famous nightlife and excellent places to buy craftworks and contemporary Congolese art; a weekend here would be an amazing introduction to the DRC.

From **Rwanda**, security permitting, a visit to Virunga National Park will be most people's top priority, to see mountain gorillas in their natural habitat. Hikers might prefer to ascend Mount Nyiragongo and camp overnight above its glowing crater. It would be difficult to combine both activities in a single weekend. Alternatively, cross the border to Bukavu, reputed to be the DRC's most picturesque town, and visit the eastern lowland gorillas in Kahuzi-Biega National Park.

From the Atlantic coast of **Angola**, Kongo-Central province is just across the border. In a weekend, you could visit Mangroves National Park and the historic town of Boma; a long weekend might give you time for Matadi and the Zongo Falls. If you find yourself in northeastern Angola, you could take the train to Dilolo, in Katanga, and visit the Lofoi Falls in Kundelungu National Park. From **Zambia**, it is easy to get to Haut-Katanga province, either to visit Kundelungu National Park or to spend the weekend in Lubumbashi, with its colonial architecture and vibrant nightlife.

From the **Central African Republic**, a Kinshasa-based tour operator can arrange an escorted tour from Bangui, downriver to visit Mobutu's palaces, including Gbadolite. The boat journey takes a full day in each direction.

ONE WEEK A week is not long in the DRC, but it would give you the option to explore a little more of the country than would be possible in even the longest weekend. At the time of writing, there are four international airports.

Flying into **Kinshasa** (or crossing from Brazzaville, as on page 57), spend at least one night in the capital – more if you are a fan of big cities or of Congolese music – then take a train or bus to Matadi, stopping at Lola Ya Bonobo and the Zongo Falls, and on to Mangroves National Park; or a plane to Mbandaka or Kisangani to see the great River Congo up close. Return to Kinshasa for at least a full day, preferably two.

Flying into **Goma**, security permitting, you could hike to the top of Mount Nyiragongo and trek into the forest in search of mountain gorillas, then take a speedboat (*canôt rapide*) down Lake Kivu to Bukavu, to visit the eastern lowland gorillas in Kahuzi-Biega National Park.

Flying into **Lubumbashi**, it becomes feasible to hire a car, with or without a driver. The main roads in Katanga are asphalted, which makes it possible to see a lot more sights in a shorter time than in most of the rest of the DRC. In a week, you could spend time in Upemba and Kundelungu national parks or visit the historic sites in and around Lubumbashi. The upgrading of Kolwezi Airport, under way at the time of writing, might make it possible to hire a car at one of Katanga's airports and return it at the other.

Crossing overland from **Uganda** becomes feasible with a week at your disposal. The only route that is at all safe is via Bujerere (see page 58 for security advice), which takes you to the Okapi Nature Reserve and onward to Kisangani.

TWO WEEKS A two-week itinerary, based on arrival into one of the international airports (as page 56), might include the following.

Flying into **Kinshasa**, spend at least one night in the capital, then take a train or bus to Matadi and on to Mangroves National Park; or take a boat upriver to track bonobos in Mai-Ndombe, then onward to Mbandaka for wildlife and a visit to an indigenous Pygmy community; or a plane to Kisangani, with the Stanley Falls and its traditional fishermen. Return to Kinshasa for at least two full days.

Flying into **Lubumbashi**, it becomes unexpectedly easy (for the DRC) to move around, either by public transport or by hiring a car. You could see a lot of Katanga in two weeks: historic sites and architecture, the linked national parks of Upemba and Kundelungu, the province's mining traditions, plus the Congolese music and international culture of Lubumbashi.

Options on arrival at **Goma** Airport will remain dependent on the security situation for the foreseeable future. See page 193 for suggested itineraries.

THREE WEEKS OR MORE It is so expensive to get to the DRC – not just the cost of flights, especially from Europe, but also the difficulty and expense of obtaining a visa – and so expensive to get around the country, that the longer you are able to stay, once you get there, the more cost-effective your trip will be. It is difficult to get to many of the country's magnificent national parks; having more time at your disposal will allow you to spend more time in them once you get there.

There are flights from **Kinshasa** to every city in the country (although see page 72 for airline safety advice). A three-week visit might start with a few days in and around Kinshasa, including a trip to Lola Ya Bonobo, the Zongo Falls, and Mangroves National Park; a flight from Kinshasa to Kisangani to see the Stanley Falls and the traditional fishermen; another flight from Kisangani to Goma (especially if Virunga National Park is open to visitors) and by ferry to Bukavu and Kahuzi-Biega National Park; and back to Kinshasa or out of the DRC from Goma international airport; *or* a few days in and around Kinshasa, as on page 51, then a flight to Kananga, to visit Upemba and Kundelungu national parks, and continue into Katanga for a few days, before flying from Lubumbashi to Kalemie on Lake Tanganyika, then leaving the DRC either by returning to Lubumbashi or Kinshasa, or via Goma.

TOUR OPERATORS

INTERNATIONAL

Global Bush Travel & Tourism Company Douala, Cameroon; +237 233 477 000; m +237 677 246 624; e info@globalbushtratour.com; w globalbushtratour.com. In the DRC, offers river trips by pirogue, overnight stays with Pygmy communities, & Kinshasa & Kongo-Central tours.

Laba Africa Expeditions Kampala, Uganda; +256 754 849 895; m +256 754 849 895 (WhatsApp); e info@labaafrica.com; w labaafrica.com. Tours of Kinshasa & Kongo-Central, including Mangroves National Park; can also arrange visits to Okapi Wildlife Reserve, 10-day river trip with on-shore camping, overnight stays with Pygmy communities, & gorilla-trekking in Kahuzi-Biega & (security permitting) Virunga national parks.

Soma Travel Tours Michigan, USA; +1 313 493 5320 (USA), +243 810 643 375 (Kinshasa); e info@soma-traveltours.com; w soma-traveltours.com. Offers excursions around Kinshasa & Kongo-Central, River Congo cruises & fishing trips for goliath tigerfish; also interpreting & translation services.

Undiscovered Destinations North Shields, UK; +44 191 296 2674 (UK), +1 1 800 614 2967 (US/Canada), +61 1 300 956 415 (Australia); e info@undiscovered-destinations.com; w undiscovered-destinations.com. In the DRC, offers expeditions on the River Congo, including the 1,000km voyage between Mbandaka & Kisangani.

Wild Frontiers London, UK; +44 20 3642 9136; e info@wildfrontiers.co.uk;

w wildfrontierstravel.com. Offers an itinerary from Kigali that includes gorilla-trekking in Kahuzi-Biega National Park (also, security permitting, Virunga National Park).

IN THE DRC The DRC's official tourist office, the **Office National du Tourisme** (ONT) can provide information on the various formalities in reaching any of the country's attractions. They can be a decent starting point for local brochures & suggestions on how to get there, but in the end it will come down to who you pay, & how much you pay. While they are friendly, they may not be able to offer much in the way of assistance – they will probably direct you to the ICCN office or a local travel agency.

Office National du Tourisme Av Lukusa 16, Gombe; m 089 323 4167; e contact@ officetourisme.cd; w officetourisme.cd. Website has information about the DRC's history & about each of its 26 provinces.
Congo Travel & Tours Kinshasa; \ +1 484 320 7442 (North American sales), +81 50 5809 3202 (Asia-Pacific sales); m Kinshasa: +243 971 542 597, with offices throughout the DRC; w congotravelandtours.com (contact form on website). Day trips in & around several cities; Kongo-Central tour including Mangroves National Park; expedition to track bonobos in the wild; 2-week River Congo trip; overnight stays with Pygmy communities; & a pioneering road trip from Kinshasa to Mbuji-Mayi.

Kivu Travel Goma; m +32 485 720 164 (WhatsApp); e info@kivutravel.com; w kivutravel.com. Year-round visits to Kahuzi-Biega National Park, including Lwiru primate sanctuary. Security permitting, Nyirogongo hikes & gorilla-trekking in Virunga National Park. Private tours to Garamba National Park can also be arranged.
Palma Okapi Tours Lubumbashi; m +243 99 878 91 87, +243 84 400 62 55; e palmaokapitours@gmail.com; w palmaokapitoursprl.blogspot.com. Specialises in visits around Katanga, including Kundelungu National Park & Bunkeya; city tours of Lubumbashi, Likasi & Kolwezi; & artistic & cultural experiences.
Ubuntu Voyages Goma; m +243 990 655 913; e info@ubuntuvoyages.com; w ubuntuvoyages. com. Gorilla-treks of varying lengths in Kahuzi-Biega National Park & (security permitting) in Virunga National Park; similar activities in neighbouring countries.
Virunga Amani Tours & Travel Goma; m +243 998 540 000, +243 814 023 590 (WhatsApp); e info@virungaamanitours.com; w virungaamanitours.com. Packages include a 20-day river trip from Kisangani to Kinshasa; a week in Ituri tracking okapi & foraging with a Pygmy community; & gorilla-trekking in Kahuzi-Biega & (security permitting) Virunga national parks.

RED TAPE

VISAS Visas are required by citizens of almost every nationality to enter the Democratic Republic of the Congo. These are not easy or cheap to obtain. Visa applications should be submitted to the DRC Embassy in or responsible for your home country an absolute minimum of three weeks before you are due to travel; your passport must have at least six months' remaining validity. A confirmed return air ticket, a confirmed hotel reservation and proof of your ability to cover the costs of your stay are required as part of your visa application, as well as various other documents including your yellow fever certificate. The cost of the visa varies according to the number of months you wish it to last and for citizens of different jurisdictions. British citizens are charged between £135 (one month multiple-entry) and £350 (six months); US citizens, between US$120 and US$450. You can apply online but will have to present yourself at the relevant DRC embassy, on a specified date, for the visa to be stamped into your passport.

It is occasionally possible to obtain a *'visa volant'* ('flying visa'), an e-visa which gets you on to the plane to the DRC and through the airport on arrival. On arrival at passport control, you are taken by an airport official to an office where

The Democratic Republic of the Congo has two time zones: the west of the country, including Kinshasa, is on GMT, throughout the year; the east, from Katanga and Kisangani, is on GMT+1, again throughout the year. Most of the country straddles the Equator and therefore has almost exactly 12 hours of daylight all year round; Katanga, further south, has slightly more of a difference between the December and June solstices.

you pay US$90 (at the time of writing) and your passport is stamped with a 'Visa AéroPortuaire'. This is valid for only seven days, during which time you must apply for a longer-term visa (if required). The process at Ndjili airport is reasonably well organised and fast. The e-visa also works for those arriving at a sea or lake port. Apply at w evisa.gouv.cd. The cost (at the time of writing) is US$300 (plus the US$90 payable on arrival). The advantage of a 'flying visa' is that the processing time for the application is very much shorter than for a full visa, in theory only 72 hours.

If you have booked a trip with a recognised tour operator, that operator will arrange your visa application for you. If you will only be visiting the national parks in eastern DRC (see page 65 for security advice), local tour operators can arrange a special visa for you, valid for 14 days; at the time of writing, the cost is US$105. It is possible to apply for a visa in one of the DRC's neighbouring countries, but given the length of time required for the application to be processed, this is unlikely to be a practical option for anyone who is not actually living in that neighbouring country, apart from overlanders with unlimited time at their disposal.

Once you have managed to obtain your visa and arrived in the DRC, this is unfortunately not the end of the red tape. Flying from one province to another (for example, from Kinshasa to Mbandaka, or from Lubumbashi to Goma) requires payment of an airport tax known as a 'Go-Pass'. These cost US$10 (for internal flights) and are purchased at the departure airport. There is also a passenger tax of US$5, again to be paid at the departure airport.

If you plan to self-drive while in the DRC, as opposed to hiring a car with a driver (page 95), you will need an International Driving Licence.

PERMITS A **park permit** is required to visit any of the country's national parks. These usually have to be obtained in advance, in the capital of the province where the national park is located. See the sections for each national park in later chapters for details. If you are travelling with an organised tour, your tour operator will arrange your park permit(s).

Photography permits are required in an astonishing number of circumstances in the DRC, for example in zoological or botanical gardens. Even with a photography permit, it is forbidden to photograph pretty much any institutional structure. Bans on photographing military buildings and personnel, or border areas, are common in many countries; equally, it is not unusual for it to be forbidden to photograph governmental buildings such as the presidential palace. In the DRC, however, taking a photograph of an institutional building as innocuous as a colonial-era railway station may well attract the enraged attention of a security guard. It should also be noted that the lower reaches of the River Congo mark the national border; so, in Kinshasa at least, any photographs of the river should be taken discreetly.

Within the national parks, the park permit includes permission to take amateur photographs; professional photography within the parks must be arranged separately and the charges are high.

INSURANCE Good travel insurance is essential. The medical cover should include evacuation – hospitals in the DRC are not equipped to deal with serious injury (page 65). Try to find an insurance policy that covers theft of cash, as well as cards and passport, and insure any electronic equipment against theft and damage. The updater of this edition had cash stolen from a locked safe in her hotel bedroom in the DRC. If you have had items or cash stolen, your insurance company is likely to require a police statement; in the DRC this is issued by the Renseignements Généraux (equivalent, very roughly, to the CID). Insurance companies usually expect any claim to be made as soon as possible after the event for which the claim is being made. It is especially important to contact your insurers immediately if hospital treatment or medical evacuation is required.

In the UK and other countries, no standard insurance company will cover travel in areas for which the respective government advises '**against all travel**' and, usually, 'against all but essential travel'. For the UK, at the time of writing, this includes all of Nord-Kivu and Sud-Kivu apart from the city of Bukavu; in other words, if you visit Kahuza-Biega National Park, you will not be insured if you meet with an accident. UK passport holders can check the areas currently excluded on the gov.uk website (**w** gov.uk/foreign-travel-advice/democratic-republic-of-the-congo). The only way to obtain cover for these areas is with war-risk insurance, which is naturally extremely expensive.

REGISTERING WITH YOUR EMBASSY In the DRC, things can change quickly and unexpectedly. Indeed, the spontaneity of events in the DRC is an integral part of what makes people want to visit it. Riots and military crack-downs can occur with little or no warning to travellers; a rebellion in a remote village can shut down that whole district or even region. Natural disasters can also strike with little or no warning – such as the 2021 eruption of Mount Nyiragongo and associated earthquakes that obliterated hundreds of buildings in northern Goma. Keeping in touch with your embassy is the best hedge you have against total disaster. One of an embassy's responsibilities is to assist its own citizens when they are in genuine need.

Anyone visiting the DRC for more than a few days should consider registering with their country's embassy in Kinshasa. Registering will ensure that, in an emergency, your embassy will know where you are and whether it is possible to evacuate you. Citizens of the European Union can approach any EU embassy. Otherwise, if your home country does not have an embassy in the DRC, find out which nearby embassy covers the DRC for your country, and try to register there. It should be noted, however, that British embassies worldwide no longer offer a system for citizens to register with them, even in countries as volatile as the DRC. It might be worth physically presenting yourself at the embassy in Kinshasa, with your British passport, and leaving a contact phone number with anyone who will speak to you there (the updater for this edition didn't bother).

EMBASSIES

To obtain a visa to visit the DRC, you will need to apply either in person or online. If your country is not listed on page 56, the best solution is to search online for the DRC embassy responsible for it. The website of the DRC's Ministry of Foreign Affairs is w diplomatie.gouv.cd, but it is of limited practical use.

DRC EMBASSIES ABROAD
Belgium Rue Marie de Bourgogne 30, 1000 Brussels; w ambardc.be. Also covers Luxembourg, the Netherlands & the EU.
Canada 18 Range Rd, Ottawa, ON, K1N 8J3; w ambassade-rdc-canada.com
France 32 Cours Albert 1er, 75008 Paris; w ambardcparis.com
South Africa 791 Francis Baard St, Arcadia, 0083 Pretoria; ☏ +27 12 343 24 55
United Kingdom 281 Gray's Inn Rd, London, WC1X 8QF (consular services); w ambardc.london, visa application at w forms.ambardc.london. Also covers Ireland, Finland & Norway.
United States 1100 Connecticut Av NW #725, Washington, DC 20036; w ambardcusa.org

EMBASSIES IN THE DRC
Belgium 133 Bd du 30 Juin (public access from Av des Jacarandas); consulate in Lubumbashi, Square Forrest; w rdcongo.diplomatie.belgium.be/fr
Canada 17 Av Pumbu; w international.gc.ca/country-pays/democratic_republic_congo-republique_democratique_congo/kinshasa.aspx
France Av du Colonel Mondjiba; w cd.ambafrance.org
South Africa 77 Av Ngongo Lutete; consulate in Lubumbashi, 2875 Av Lumumba; w dirco1.azurewebsites.net/kinshasa
United Kingdom 83 Av Roi Baudouin; w gov.uk/world/organisations/british-embassy-kinshasa; consular contact form w gov.uk/contact-consulate-kinshasa
United States 310 Av des Aviateurs; w cd.usembassy.gov

GETTING THERE AND AWAY

BY AIR There are three main international airports in the DRC: Kinshasa's Ndjili (FIH), Lubumbashi (FBM) and Goma (GOM). Kisangani (FKI) has occasional international flights with Ethiopian Airlines; when the upgrading of Kolwezi Airport is complete (expected in 2024), it, too, will meet standards for international flights.

As one might expect, **Ndjili** is used by more airlines than the others, with regular flights from Addis Ababa, Brussels, Doha, Istanbul, Johannesburg and Paris, as well as services to and from several other African countries and many internal flights. The airport has a reasonably good website, w aeroport-kinshasa.com, with some information about the airlines that use it, how to get there from Kinshasa and a particularly helpful section on DRC visa requirements. **Lubumbashi**'s Luano Airport has regular connections with Addis Ababa, Johannesburg, Nairobi and other African cities, as well as internal flights. **Goma** is mainly a hub for internal flights but is also connected with Addis Ababa, Kigali and Nairobi. See the relevant sections of the guide for practical information about these and the DRC's other airports.

Arriving on an international flight into any of the DRC's airports is initially fairly normal, but as soon as you are into the baggage reclaim area, you can expect to be surrounded by people offering to 'help' you. If you actually want some help with your luggage, ensure that you agree a price in advance. If not, politely decline their offers. If you have not made advance arrangements for your travel into Kinshasa from Ndjili Airport, use an official blue and yellow taxi outside the terminal, or download the Yango app to book a car. International departures at Ndjili are also more or less straightforward. You will have to pay an airport tax, which was US$50 at the time of writing; you do this at the RawBank office before heading for the check-in desks. Card payments may be possible, but you should keep back enough cash dollars, in case they are not.

BY BOAT The capital cities of the two Congos – the Republic and the Democratic Republic – face each other across the river that divides and unites them. Kinshasa and **Brazzaville** are connected by barge ferries, full to the gunwales with people and cargo, and by fast motorboats called *canôts rapides*. The latter leave Brazzaville from the port known as 'Le Beach' and land at 'Beach Ngobila' in Kinshasa; the crossing takes about 10 minutes. Unfortunately, as so often in the Congos, this short journey involves many different bits of paperwork and many different payments to the people processing said paperwork. You even have to pay the officers who search your luggage! There is also a port tax to pay on arrival in Kinshasa. The basic one-way fare on a *canôt rapide* is about US$35, but you should expect to shell out an absolute minimum of US$60 once the various payments are included. You could try to navigate the process yourself, but you risk never making it on to the boat at all. The usual way to deal with it all is to hire one of the informal fixers who tout for business at Le Beach ('*un démarcheur*'), who will make all the payments, in the right order, on your behalf, for a small fee. Alternatively, travel agencies in Brazzaville can arrange all the formalities a day (or more) in advance, although even with this assistance it can take a couple of hours before you can actually board. On Sundays, crossings end at noon. The luxury solution is a 'VIP service', on a private ferry, with all formalities expedited, and even access to a business lounge at Le Beach; Congo Travel and Tours (page 53), for example, charges US$850 per person for its VIP Express service. Whichever option you choose, you will, of course, need a visa for the DRC, unless you are a citizen of the Republic of the Congo, and a yellow-fever vaccination certificate.

From the **Central African Republic** (CAR), it is possible to cross the River Ubangi between Bangui and Zongo or Gbadolite. There are no scheduled passenger services, but Congo Travel and Tours can arrange escorted crossings. There are no scheduled passenger crossings across Lake Kivu, from Rwanda, or (at the time of writing) Lake Tanganyika, from Tanzania.

BY LAND If your main reason for visiting the DRC is to track gorillas, you will probably choose to enter the country from **Rwanda**. There are international flights from Kigali to Goma Airport (see opposite) and there are several land border crossings as well. Of course you will need a DRC visa and your yellow-fever vaccination certificate to be able to cross. See page 54 for advice on the two-week DRC visa valid only in Kivu-Nord and Kivu-Sud, the provinces within which Virunga and Kahuzi-Biega national parks are located. The **Goma**/Gisenyi border post is well used to foreign travellers and there is a public bus service from Kigali to Gisenyi (154km). When Virunga National Park is open to visitors, shuttle buses run from the Goma border to the park. For **Bukavu**, the border crossing from Rwanda at Cyangugu is convenient for Kahuzi-Biega National Park.

From **Burundi**, the only crossing is at Gatumba, between Bujumbura and Uvira. If you are in Bujumbura, this may prove to be your best option if the Rwanda/Burundi border is closed. However, at the time of writing, the road between Uvira and Bukavu is very dangerous, due to the activities of armed militias (and similarly south towards Kalemie). If the Ruhwa border crossing between Rwanda and Burundi is open, it will be preferable to use this route to Bukavu, via Cyangugu – a safer and better-surfaced road.

When Virunga National Park was open, many visitors approached it from **Uganda**, specifically the border crossing at Kisoro/Bunagana. Unfortunately, for the same reason that the park is closed to tourists, this crossing is inadvisable at the time of writing; Rutshuru, through which the road runs from Bunagana to Virunga or anywhere else, is one of the most lawless and dangerous districts of eastern DRC. It is possible, however, to cross from Uganda into the DRC at Bujerere; on the DRC side, this will give you access to the Okapi Wildlife Reserve (page 179) and onward to Kisangani. This road is not exactly safe, but it is policed to some extent in daylight hours. A professional security escort from the border to the Okapi Reserve is highly advisable.

From **Angola**, the principal crossing is Noqui/Matadi – it is a busy border with traffic in both directions. The road from Matadi to Kinshasa is reasonably good; there is also a rail service. An alternative border post in the Kongo-Central province is at Luvo. The border with Cabinda opens and closes intermittently.

The only international passenger train into the DRC is the Benguela Railway, built in colonial times to connect the central African Copperbelt with the Atlantic. The whole of the Angolan section of the line, over 1,300km, has been rehabilitated. Now known as **Lobito Atlantic Railway**, its main objective is to freight copper and cobalt from the mines in Katanga, a quicker and cheaper option than the existing routes. A passenger service also operates between Lobito to Dilolo, a few kilometres from the Angolan border in the DRC's Lualaba province. The 'express' leaves Lobito once a week and takes two days to get to Luau, the last station on the Angolan side. There is an onward passenger train between Dilolo and Kolwezi, 420km away; at the time of writing, this train runs only every two weeks, but the frequency of the service may improve. There is also a road border crossing at Luau/Dilolo.

For land access from **Zambia** to Katanga, see page 138.

When crossing land borders, it is likely that your luggage will be searched by hand and things can easily go missing. Keep anything of value in your immediate possession, and be vigilant at all times with whatever you are carrying.

HEALTH *with Dr Daniel Campion*

The Democratic Republic of the Congo is the most biologically diverse country in Africa and this includes a wide variety of infectious diseases. However, statistically you are far more likely to die in a traffic accident than from any of the hazards covered in the following pages. The DRC has one of the highest road traffic fatality rates in the world. Do what you can to reduce risks: always travel during daylight hours, always wear a seatbelt and refuse to be driven by anyone who has been drinking alcohol. Listen to local advice about areas you should avoid due to violent crime or militia activity.

PREPARATIONS Sensible preparation will go a long way to ensuring your trip goes smoothly. Particularly for first-time visitors to Africa, this includes a visit to a travel clinic (see opposite) to discuss matters such as vaccinations and malaria prevention. The following summary points are worth emphasising, however:

- Don't travel without comprehensive medical **travel insurance** that will fly you home in an emergency.
- Make sure all your **immunisations** are up to date. Proof of vaccination against yellow fever is mandatory for entry into the Democratic Republic of the Congo. If the vaccine is not suitable for you then you would be wise not to travel, as the fatality rate for yellow fever among unvaccinated visitors to endemic areas is close to 100%. It's also unwise to travel in the tropics without being up to date on tetanus, polio and diphtheria (which come in a three-in-one vaccine), hepatitis A and typhoid. Proof of vaccination against polio may be required on departure

from the DRC; there are fairly frequent outbreaks of polio in the country, so being up to date with your vaccination is a good idea even if your certificate is not checked. Immunisation against rabies, meningitis, hepatitis B, and in rare cases tuberculosis (TB) may also be recommended.

- There is a high risk of **malaria** in the DRC. Although two new malaria vaccines have been introduced as part of childhood immunisation programmes in Africa, they are not available for travellers. A variety of preventative drugs is available, including mefloquine, atovaquone/proguanil (Malarone) and the antibiotic doxycycline. Atovaquone/proguanil and doxycycline need only be started two days before entering the DRC, but mefloquine should be started two to three weeks before. Doxycycline and mefloquine need to be taken for four weeks after the trip and atovaquone/proguanil for seven days. It is as important to complete the course as it is to take it before and during the trip. The most suitable choice of drug varies depending on the individual and the country they are visiting, so visit your doctor or a specialist travel clinic for medical advice. If you will be spending a long time in Africa and visiting remote areas, consider taking an emergency treatment kit in addition to prophylaxis. It is also worth noting that no homeopathic prophylactic for malaria exists, nor can any traveller acquire effective resistance to malaria. Those who don't make use of preventative drugs risk their life in a manner that is both foolish and unnecessary.
- Though an advisable precaution for everyone visiting the DRC, a **pre-exposure course of rabies vaccination**, involving three doses taken over a minimum of 21 days, is particularly important if you intend to have contact with animals, or are likely to be 24 hours away from medical help. If you have not had this then you will almost certainly need to evacuate for medical treatment, as it is very unlikely that the DRC will have the necessary treatment.
- Anybody travelling away from major centres should carry a **personal first-aid kit**. Contents might include an antiseptic, Band-Aids, suncream, insect repellent, aspirin or paracetamol, antifungal cream (eg: clotrimazole), loperamide for diarrhoea (and possibly prescribed antibiotics for severe diarrhoea if you are at high medical risk), antibiotic eye drops, tweezers, condoms or femidoms, a digital thermometer and a needle-and-syringe kit with an accompanying letter from a health-care professional.
- Bring any **drugs or devices relating to known medical conditions** with you. That applies both to those who are on medication prior to departure, and those who are, for instance, allergic to bee stings, or are prone to attacks of asthma. Always check in advance to identify any restricted medications. Carry a copy of your prescription and a letter from your doctor explaining why you need the medication.
- Prolonged immobility on long-haul flights can result in deep vein thrombosis (DVT), which can be dangerous if the clot travels to the lungs to cause pulmonary embolus. The risk increases with age, and is higher in obese or pregnant travellers, heavy smokers, those taller than 180cm or 6ft, and anybody with a history of clots, recent major operation or varicose veins surgery, cancer, a stroke or heart disease. If any of these criteria apply, consult a doctor before you travel.

TRAVEL CLINICS AND HEALTH INFORMATION A full list of current travel clinic websites worldwide is available on w istm.org. For other journey preparation information, consult w travelhealthpro.org.uk (UK) or w wwwnc.cdc.gov/travel (USA). All advice found online should be used in conjunction with expert advice received prior to or during travel.

Practical Information HEALTH

2

COMMON MEDICAL PROBLEMS

Malaria This potentially fatal disease is widespread in low-lying tropical parts of Africa, a category that includes all of the DRC, and while the risk of transmission is highest in the rainy season, it is present throughout the year. Since no malaria prophylactic is 100% effective, it makes sense to take all reasonable precautions against being bitten by the nocturnal Anopheles mosquitoes that transmit the disease (see opposite). Malaria usually manifests within two weeks of transmission, but it can be as little as seven days and anything up to a year. Any fever occurring after seven days should be considered as malaria until proven otherwise. Symptoms typically include a rapid rise in temperature (over 38°C), and any combination of a headache, flu-like aches and pains, a general sense of disorientation, and possibly even nausea and diarrhoea. The earlier malaria is detected, the better it usually responds to treatment. So if you display possible symptoms, get to a doctor or clinic immediately (in the UK, go to accident and emergency and say that you have been to Africa). A simple test, available at even the most rural clinic in Africa, is usually adequate to determine whether you have malaria. You need three negative tests to be sure it is not the disease. And while experts differ on the question of self-diagnosis and self-treatment, the reality is that if you think you have malaria and are not within easy reach of a doctor, it would be wisest to start treatment.

Other insect-borne infections Although malaria is the insect-borne disease that attracts the most attention in Africa, and rightly so, there are others, most too uncommon to be a significant concern to short-stay travellers. These include dengue, Zika and other arboviruses (spread by day-biting mosquitoes), sleeping sickness (tsetse flies), and river blindness (blackflies). Bearing this in mind, it is clearly sensible, and makes for a more pleasant trip, to avoid insect bites as far as possible (see opposite). Anyone who is planning a pregnancy and is travelling to an area where there may be Zika virus should be aware of the guidance to wait before conceiving. Women travelling without their partners are advised to use barrier precautions for two months after leaving a Zika area; women travelling with their male partners should use barrier precautions during the trip and for three months after returning home.

Two other nasty (though ultimately relatively harmless) flesh-eating insects associated with tropical Africa are tumbu or putsi flies, which lay eggs, often on drying laundry, that hatch and bury themselves under the skin when they come into contact with humans, and jiggers, which latch on to bare feet and set up home, usually at the side of a toenail, where they cause a painful boil-like swelling. Drying laundry indoors and wearing shoes are the best way to deter this pair of flesh-eaters.

Tick bites Ticks may spread African tick bite fever and Crimean-Congo haemorrhagic fever along with a few other dangerous rarities. They should ideally be removed whole as soon as possible to reduce the chance of infection. The best way to do this is to grasp the tick with your finger nails as close to your body as possible, and pull it away steadily and firmly at right angles to your skin (do not jerk or twist it). If possible, douse the wound with alcohol (any spirit will do) or iodine. If you are travelling with small children, remember to check their heads, and particularly behind the ears, for ticks. Spreading redness around the bite and/or fever and/or aching joints after a tick bite imply that you have an infection that requires antibiotic treatment, so seek advice.

The Anopheles mosquitoes that spread malaria are active at dusk and after dark. Most bites can thus be avoided by covering up at night. This means donning a long-sleeved shirt, trousers and socks from around 30 minutes before dusk until you retire to bed, and applying a DEET-based insect repellent to any exposed flesh. It is best to sleep under a net, or in an air-conditioned room, though burning a mosquito coil and/or sleeping under a fan will also reduce (though not entirely eliminate) bites. Travel clinics usually sell a good range of nets and repellents, as well as Permethrin treatment kits, which will render even the tattiest net a lot more protective, and helps prevents mosquitoes from biting through a net when you roll against it. These measures will also do much to reduce exposure to other nocturnal biters. Bear in mind, too, that most flying insects are attracted to light: leaving a lamp standing near a tent opening or a light on in a poorly screened hotel room will greatly increase the insect presence in your sleeping quarters. It is also advisable to think about avoiding bites when walking in the countryside by day, especially in wetland habitats, which often teem with diurnal mosquitoes. Wear a long loose shirt and trousers, preferably 100% cotton, as well as proper walking or hiking shoes with heavy socks (the ankle is particularly vulnerable to bites), and apply a DEET-based insect repellent to any exposed skin.

Rabies This deadly disease can be carried by any mammal and is usually transmitted to humans via a bite or a scratch that breaks the skin. In particular, beware of village dogs and monkeys habituated to people, but assume that any mammal that bites or scratches you (or even licks an open wound) might be rabid even if it looks healthy. First, scrub the wound with soap under a running tap for a good 10–15 minutes, or while pouring water from a jug, then pour on a strong iodine or alcohol solution, which will guard against infections and might reduce the risk of the rabies virus entering the body. Whether or not you underwent pre-exposure vaccination, it is vital to obtain post-exposure prophylaxis as soon as possible after the incident. The full post-exposure treatment is unlikely to be available in the DRC if you have not had a pre-exposure course of the vaccine. Evacuate as soon as you can. Death from rabies is probably one of the worst ways to go, and once you show symptoms it is too late to do anything – the mortality rate is 100%.

Mpox The first reported case of human mpox (previously called monkeypox) was in 1970 in the DRC. Along with Nigeria, it is the country which reports the highest number of cases annually. In 2024, an mpox outbreak in the DRC was declared a public health emergency of international concern (PHEIC) by the World Health Organization (WHO) due to its spread to neighbouring countries. Symptoms usually begin with fever, joint pain and swollen lymph nodes, then a rash develops which goes through various stages until it forms scabs. An individual is contagious until all the scabs fall off and the skin underneath is intact. Mpox is usually mild; most people recover within a few weeks without treatment. In severe cases, antiviral drugs can be used. Most visitors are at low risk: a vaccine exists but is not normally available to travellers in many countries. Seek up-to-date advice from the online sources on page 59. To avoid contracting mpox, do not eat or prepare any type of bushmeat, wash or sanitise your hands often, and avoid close contact (including sexual contact) with anyone who has an unusual rash.

Bilharzia Also known as schistosomiasis, bilharzia is an unpleasant parasitic disease transmitted by freshwater snails most often associated with reedy shores where there is lots of water weed. It cannot be caught in hotel swimming pools or the ocean, but should be assumed to be present in any freshwater river pond, lake or similar habitat, even those advertised as 'bilharzia free'. The highest-risk areas will be within 200m of villages or other places where infected people use water, wash clothes, etc. Drying off vigorously with a towel after an accidental brief water exposure may help to prevent the *Schistosoma* parasite from penetrating the skin, but should not be relied upon. Bilharzia is often asymptomatic in its early stages, but some people experience an intense immune reaction, including fever, cough, abdominal pain and an itching rash, around four to six weeks after infection. Later symptoms vary but often include a general feeling of lethargy. If you may have been exposed, you can be tested or screened at specialist travel or tropical medicine clinics, ideally at least six weeks after exposure. Fortunately, bilharzia is easy to treat at present.

Meningitis This nasty disease can kill within hours of the appearance of initial symptoms, typically a combination of a blinding headache (light sensitivity), blotchy rash, and high fever. Outbreaks tend to be localised and are usually reported in local media. Fortunately, immunisation with the meningococcal ACWY vaccine protects against the most serious bacterial form of meningitis. Nevertheless, other less serious forms exist which are usually viral, but any severe headache and fever – possibly also symptomatic of typhoid or malaria – should be sufficient cause to visit a doctor immediately.

HIV Rates of HIV infection are high in most parts of Africa, and other sexually transmitted infections are common in the DRC. Condoms (or femidoms) greatly reduce the risk of transmission.

Ebola virus disease The spectre of the Ebola virus looms over the DRC but it is highly unlikely that any traveller would come into contact with it. At least three subtypes exist across the equatorial region of Africa, and most cases have occurred in or near the Congo region. The first outbreak was in Yambuku in 1976, and there have been at least 13 epidemics in the country since then. There was one in 2022, in Mbandaka; Equateur province has been a focal point for the disease, with three

COVID-19

The DRC's health-care systems have been greatly impacted by its own protracted conflict. This was exacerbated by the Covid-19 pandemic and by recurrent disease outbreaks such as cholera, measles, and Ebola. There are no reliable data on how many people died of Covid-19 in the DRC; probably most deaths occurred at home, far away from any health care. There has been significant vaccine hesitancy in the DRC, with limited demand, and there is evidence that Covid-19 has had a negative impact on the utilisation of health services since March 2020, with a decrease in hospital visits, a reduction in the number of antenatal care visits, reduced access to family planning and contraception, increased food insecurity and increased incidence of gender-based violence. Close to 23 million children missed out on routine vaccinations in 2020 due to the pandemic, the highest number in more than a decade, according to recent WHO/UNICEF data.

outbreaks in the space of three years. Fortunately, these frequent outbreaks mean that health workers in the DRC are now well prepared and familiar with outbreak control protocols.

The main route of transmission is from person-to-person contact through infected bodily fluids, and from treatment with contaminated needles. Other ways of contracting the virus include handling or eating contaminated meat from gorillas, chimpanzees, antelope and porcupines; airborne transmission between humans has not been proven. Many Africans have contracted Ebola during burial ceremonies from a dead relative, when handling the body in unsanitary conditions is common. It is almost always fatal within three weeks of transmission.

Initial symptoms of the disease are high fever, headache, exhaustion, dizziness and a sore throat. It could easily be confused with malaria or typhoid, which are far more common. Further progression of the disease includes bleeding from every opening in the body, low blood pressure and a weak pulse. Victims die of organ failure or excessive blood loss.

Avoiding Ebola is simple enough – keep up to date on regions that have had outbreaks, avoid handling dead animals, and avoid eating meat if you are travelling through the bush in these areas. Avoid contact with blood and other bodily fluids, and use appropriate measures such as gloves and a mask whenever confronted with people who are ill. Since this disease is so infamous, regions which have outbreaks are quickly sealed off from visitors.

Plague Plague is an infectious disease caused by bacteria (*Yersinia pestis*) that usually spreads to humans by bites from rodents' fleas. The most common form is bubonic plague – this is the variant that killed millions in Europe in the Middle Ages. Pneumonic plague is the most severe form and can be transmitted from person to person. There are reported cases of pneumonic plague in the DRC, in isolated mining camps and jungle towns. Symptoms include chills, diarrhoea, fever, headaches and swollen lymph nodes. Any of these can occur from two to seven days from the date of infection, and, without treatment, death can occur within a week. Anyone who is suspected of contracting plague should be isolated immediately, and all contact with them should be done with masks and gloves.

However, the likelihood of travellers coming into contact with plague is slim. In the DRC it tends to occur in isolated patches, far off the beaten track, and where there are horrendously bad sanitary conditions. Outbreaks are usually in illegal mining camps, deep in the rainforest, and death is common due to the lack of facilities for treatment. Plague requires the immediate administration of antibiotics, and supportive therapy to eliminate it from an infected person – and when this is done, most victims will survive. It is therefore critical that medical help is sought immediately if there is any indication that an individual is stricken with the disease.

Eye problems Bacterial conjunctivitis (pink eye) is a common infection in Africa, particularly for contact-lens wearers. Symptoms are sore, gritty eyelids that often stick closed in the morning. They will need treatment with antibiotic drops or ointment. Lesser eye irritation should settle with bathing in salt water and keeping the eyes shaded. If an insect flies into your eye, extract it with great care, ensuring you do not crush or damage it, otherwise you may get a nastily inflamed eye from secreted toxins.

Skin infections Any mosquito bite or small nick is an opportunity for a skin infection in warm humid climates, so clean and cover the slightest wound in a good drying antiseptic such as dilute iodine, potassium permanganate or crystal (or gentian) violet. Prickly heat is a fine pimply rash that can be alleviated by cool showers, dabbing (not rubbing) dry and talc, and sleeping naked under a fan or in an air-conditioned room. Fungal infections also get a hold easily in hot moist climates so wear 100%-cotton socks and underwear and shower frequently.

Altitude illness Along the eastern border of the DRC, in the Rwenzori Mountains, mountain peaks range from 3,000m to 5,000m above sea level. Above 1,500m, it is possible to suffer from some sort of altitude illness, and it is important to take a few precautions. The most common altitude-related illness is called acute mountain sickness (AMS), which has symptoms of headache, dizziness, fatigue and nausea. You should assume that any headache or dizziness at a high altitude is altitude sickness and treat it as such. The most important factor is the speed of ascent. If you ascend gradually, your body can usually adjust to the reduced oxygen levels. Avoid travelling from altitudes below 1,200m to 3,500m in a single day and, once above 3,000m avoid increasing your sleeping elevation by more than 500m a day. The key is to ascend slowly – and if you or anyone in your party shows symptoms, do not ascend further. If the symptoms worsen or are severe, start to descend. Never leave a person with altitude illness alone. Most people suffering from AMS will see it disappear as they descend. Acetezolamide (Diamox) can be used to prevent AMS by accelerating acclimatisation. However it can have side-effects and is not a substitute for gradual ascent. Like many medicines, it should not be used in the first trimester of pregnancy. If you think you might benefit from this medication, consult a doctor or mountaineering specialist before you travel.

Heat illness Heat exhaustion and heatstroke can be caused both by hot, dry weather and by hot, humid conditions; both extremes are found in the DRC, for example in the savannah of Katanga and in the open lowlands along the River Congo. Avoiding heatstroke is best achieved by observing how local people behave. Seek shade and stay out of direct sunlight, especially in the middle of the day; cover up with long, loose clothes; wear a hat or headscarf; and drink plenty of water. In hot conditions, you should be drinking at least 2–3 litres of water, or an equivalent liquid, a day. The glare and the dust can be hard on the eyes, so bring UV-protecting sunglasses.

Symptoms of heat exhaustion include dizziness, tiredness, nausea and headache. Use rehydration salts mixed with water to replenish fluids and salts and find somewhere cool and shady to recover. Some cases may progress to heatstroke, a more severe breakdown of temperature control. It can lead to reduced or absent sweating, flushed skin and disorientation leading to unconsciousness. Cool the body down quickly (cold showers are particularly effective), place the affected person under a fan and seek urgent medical treatment.

Snake bites and envenomation Snakes are very secretive and bites are a genuine rarity, but certain spiders and scorpions can also deliver nasty bites. In all cases, the risk is minimised by wearing closed shoes and trousers when walking in the bush, and watching where you put your hands and feet, especially in rocky areas or when gathering firewood. Only a small fraction of snakebites deliver enough venom to be life-threatening, but it is important to keep the victim calm, immobilise the affected body part, and seek urgent medical attention. In the DRC, Kinshasa is the only place where antivenom is available.

HEALTH CARE If you require immediate treatment, and if you are fit to fly, seek advice from your travel insurance provider about evacuation to South Africa or Europe. Hospitals in the DRC are poorly supplied and poorly sanitised, and you may be exposing yourself to even more risk by visiting one. If you have the right visa, you could also consider medical evacuation to Libreville in Gabon, Kampala in Uganda, or Lusaka in Zambia, all of which offer a higher standard of health care. The Centre Privé d'Urgence in Kinshasa and Centre Médical Diamant in Lubumbashi can stabilise your condition until you can fly. Unless it is immediately necessary to save your life, blood transfusion in the DRC should be avoided. Follow the advice of your travel insurance medical helpline.

If you need emergency care while in a small town or in the bush, ask at an aid agency clinic, if there is one, or seek help at the nearest church. For full wilderness trips, you should take a full medical kit, including a syringe and a tourniquet. Outside the cities, pharmacies may not have more than very basic medical items.

SAFETY

Much of the east of the DRC is very unsafe indeed, with many different armed militias operating throughout the region (page 40), violent conflicts between tribal communities and many villagers internally displaced by the fighting, now trying to survive in under-resourced camps in Kisangani, Goma or Bunia. It is for this reason that, at the time of writing, Virunga National Park and the Rwenzori Mountains are closed to tourists and the UK and other countries' governments advise against all travel to most of eastern DRC. If, despite this advice, you choose to try to travel through the region, you should seek local advice at every possible opportunity and hire security guards to travel with you. The huge freight trucks that ply these roads will often have gunmen on their roofs, to protect the cargo. A smaller vehicle without any sort of protection, and what's more occupied by foreigners, is a great opportunity for people to take their chances at relieving you of your vehicle and all your possessions.

Outside the areas of militia or intercommunal violence, the main safety concern for travellers is petty crime, especially in the big cities of Kinshasa and Lubumbashi. There is great poverty in the DRC and foreigners are seen as easy prey. Take care of your belongings, even within your hotel room, and be cautious about displaying your money or anything of value. Do not carry more cash than you immediately need while walking around town. Be especially careful at night. Never walk around at night in any major towns and avoid public transport; after dark, use a registered taxi (see pages 95 and 148 for suggested taxi firms in Kinshasa and Lubumbashi). As a foreigner, particularly if you are white, you are always being observed even if you do not realise it. In darkness, it would be far easier for a potential thief to take advantage of a momentary lapse of attention on your part.

There are two types of street children in the DRC. The Shégués are the ones you see everywhere. They may surround you and ask for money; they may try to pick your pocket or steal your handbag or watch; but they are not usually violent. The Kulunas, on the other hand, are urban gangs, much more dangerous, especially in times of tension such as pre-election periods. These youths are paid by unscrupulous adults to stir up trouble, for example by sabotaging opponents' campaign rallies or threatening other candidates. They are typically armed with knives or machetes and they require little provocation to use them. Kuluna gangs usually operate in the peripheral areas of cities, which means that, fortunately, most foreign travellers are unlikely to come across them.

CIVIL UNREST In cities across the DRC, as in other countries where political instability combines with widespread poverty, crowds can quickly accumulate from, apparently, nowhere, followed by security forces who are quite likely to seek to disperse those crowds by any means necessary. Peaceful protest is something that does not really exist in the DRC. The best advice is to stay well away from large public gatherings and to move discreetly away from any crowd you see forming. It is not necessarily obvious whether you are witnessing an organised rally or an unauthorised demonstration, and even the former can turn violent without much warning. If you find yourself embroiled in a demonstration, get yourself to a place of safety such as inside a hotel, restaurant or bank. Foreigners in plain view during chaotic moments can be far too inviting a target. It may be tempting to wait and see what happens, but you are risking your life in such situations.

CORRUPTION The largest problem most visitors will encounter is corruption – it is endemic across the DRC. As a foreigner, especially if you are a white foreigner, you will be viewed as an opportunity by many of the people you encounter, including government officials such as police. Being friendly can sometimes be misinterpreted as being a soft touch. However, remain polite at all times, even if you are directly asked for a bribe. Nobody, in any country, responds well to anger or threats and losing control will only make your situation worse. Just accept that randomly being pulled aside and constantly having your various documents pored over all come down to a quest for cash. If you keep this in mind and aim to minimise the amount you need to pay, your journey will be that much more enjoyable. Carrying a spare wallet with a few low-denomination US dollars can get you through tough situations. They will not count the money in front of you – they will be happy that you complied. It goes without saying that you should have your own paperwork in order at all times; if you don't want to carry your passport with you all the time while moving around within a city or town, take a photo of it on your phone to show at any police checkpoints.

When dealing with businesses, Western levels of punctuality, quality and trustworthiness can be elusive in the DRC. If you are visiting the country with the intention of doing business, you should seek (and follow) the advice of the commercial attaché at your country's embassy in Kinshasa. Several readers have had poor experiences with apparently reliable tour companies, who have either absconded with their money or offered less than stellar service. The key way to avoid this is to pay incrementally. Try to arrange a payment plan with the tour operator that includes a final tranche of payment at the end of your trip; pay guides and drivers on a day-by-day basis. Even with a reputable tour operator, it is not unknown for guides or translators to disappear with money they've been given to shepherd around tourists, even when the company has hired them in good faith.

ARTICLE 15

Understanding the 'Article 15' ideology of the DRC can go a long way to understanding why corruption is so rampant. It began in the 1960s with refugees fleeing revolts in central Congo, and demanding some supplies and shelter in their refugee camps. A prominent Luba leader, Albert Kalonji, told the dispersed population that the country was theirs, and it was up to them to fend for themselves – leave the government alone. It was widely popularised by Mobutu Sese Seko around 1990 as multi-party elections and government reform were anticipating the fall of Zaire. He admitted that it would be OK to 'steal a little'; this was widely printed in international newspapers, and taken to heart by the already corrupt bureaucracy around the country.

While 'Article 15' was the popular name for this behaviour, there is no such article in the DRC's Constitution or in any other legislation; it was Mobutu's comments, and the generally accepted behaviour that whatever is in the country is yours to have – not all of it, just a little. Take just a little. These words did a great deal to divert blame of the looming economic crash of the nation to other sources; no longer was the government obligated to pay its salaries on time to the vast public service, or even investigate petty theft. The dictator's popularity rose throughout these final years, at least until riots destroyed central Kinshasa. The writing was on the wall by this time, however, and people needed to continue the practice of 'Article 15' just to get some cash flowing in.

This mentality continues to this very day. It is a philosophy decades old, entrenched in the national psyche. Across the DRC, it is sometimes called the street economy – the economy that works, where one finds an angle any which way to bring more money in, while you wait for your month's overdue pay cheque from your 'real' job. In some ways it is intended to be a sideways and covert method for robbing people blind, and when the theory of relativity comes into play – that all foreign visitors make at least 100 times as much as a local – it can mean ridiculous amounts of money are demanded.

I've heard of customs officers seizing passports and demanding US$500 simply to give them back. A note in a ledger book can cost US$5–10, or US$100 if you are a business traveller. Get too uppity about it and they'll put you in jail for a while, until someone arrives with cash to bail you out. The arrival of UN peacekeepers saw prices shoot through the roof initially, as they were mandated to establish themselves in Kinshasa on huge expense accounts, and paid whatever was necessary.

Things can go missing from your bags and pockets (it's happened to me on several occasions) too easily. You may call the person a thief, but he or she may not even think twice about it. The notion of personal property is, therefore, a little blurred; perhaps they were 'taking just a little' to keep themselves going. And reporting these sorts of things to the police is just plain silly – you'll pay more to get it back than it's worth, if it's something minor. Prevention remains your best defence – ensure you don't have too much cash readily available, and always be ready to bargain in a friendly manner. Remember that aggression never works for foreigners in the Congo.

Spirits, magic and sorcery are all taken very seriously in the DRC, as in many other African countries. Any indication that a foreigner might be 'possessed', or assisted in his or her travels by elements from another world, could lead to your being physically attacked. Even worse, any Congolese person you might be travelling with, perhaps a driver or security guard, will have to answer to their community how it was they were dealing with someone who is obviously connected to demons and other unsavoury spirits of the other world.

I've run into a few travellers over the years who befriend the local population with some sleight of hand tricks, or similar minor 'magic' practices to break the ice. In other countries, this can be a great way to entertain the local population, especially children, but I implore travellers to refrain from these things while in the DRC. The risks are simply too great, and the beliefs in sorcery, animism and witchcraft too deeply entrenched in local culture, for it to be simply passed off as idle entertainment.

Even if it seems harmless at the time, suspicions can arise regarding anyone who comes into contact with you. Therefore, tell a joke, wear a stupid grin, be polite, but don't practise parlour tricks in the DRC. A large number of street children ended up on the streets because their families believed they were sorcerers.

WOMEN TRAVELLERS

Many women have travelled very enjoyably in the DRC, either alone or with other women. Naturally, for women as well as men, the further off the beaten track you go, the more challenging it becomes to travel alone. If you are mostly going to be in mid-range (or better) hotels in cities or large towns, you need no further advice than the 'Safety' section on page 65. You might get stared at in the street or attract some unwanted attention in nightclubs, but these are things you will probably be used to dealing with in your own country.

If you plan to travel in the interior of the DRC, you are probably a very experienced traveller and well aware of the difficulties you might face. Village accommodation with priests or nuns (page 75) is a safer option for women travellers than dossing down in the back room of a bar. You may wish to consider using a local tour operator to assist with activities like river trips or bonobo-trekking.

TRAVELLING WITH A DISABILITY

Depending on your disability, you may find it quite difficult to travel in the DRC. Only high-end hotels and supermarkets in Kinshasa and Lubumbashi are accessible to people in wheelchairs. Even Ndjili international airport is not fully accessible, although no doubt there are ramps somewhere around so that people in wheelchairs can negotiate the small flights of stairs. In Kinshasa, it may be possible for your hotel to locate a wheelchair-accessible taxi, but it is more likely you will have to be lifted in and out of the vehicle. If booking an organised tour, it will be helpful all round if you specify your requirements to the agency in advance.

Travellers with visual disabilities will find that city pavements are full of unexpected obstacles – shoe shiners, parked cars, fruit stalls, motorbikes and missing slabs. British Sign Language is unlikely to be useful as a means of communication; deaf people who can use French sign language or lip-read in French should have no difficulties beyond those faced by every traveller to the DRC. Nowhere in the DRC is well adapted to people with mental disabilities.

Albino Congolese are subject to great discrimination. Their families often believe them to be cursed and, in rural areas, albino people are effectively confined to their homes. If you are albino, you will similarly be treated with suspicion and fear by many people you encounter on your travels.

LGBTQIA+ TRAVELLERS

The Democratic Republic of the Congo is not an LGBTQIA+-friendly destination. Although Congolese law does not criminalise same-sex relationships, the penal code does criminalise 'public activities contrary to decency'. Attempts have been made by Members of Parliament to criminalise homosexuality, although their proposals were not passed. There are no openly gay public figures. Congolese LGBTQIA+ people generally suffer not only discrimination, but also verbal and physical attacks at home and in public places. Even organisations that support the LGBTQIA+ community have to 'disguise' themselves as generic human rights defenders. In 2023, tote bags in rainbow colours were distributed at a 'DRC Mining Week' event in Lubumbashi; the media regulatory body reacted by publishing a press release describing 'homosexuality, lesbianism and the like' as 'revolting and unconstitutional practices'. During voter registration the same year, dozens of transgender people were refused their right to a voter's card because their birth gender did not match their current appearance.

LGBTQIA+ travellers should therefore exercise considerable discretion in public. Hotels may refuse to provide a double room to a same-sex couple; there will not be much you can do about this, other than pushing twin beds together. Trans people who retain characteristics of their birth gender should be especially cautious in public places.

WHAT TO TAKE

Whatever you think you may need in the DRC, bring it. In small towns, it is difficult to find even mundane things, let alone speciality items. Basic things we take for granted in the West like bottle openers or pens can be difficult or even impossible to find outside major cities. Many Africans use naturally antibacterial twigs to clean their teeth, so it's not easy to find toothpaste or toothbrushes, except in the large supermarkets of Kinshasa and Lubumbashi. The DRC is not a country to pack light for – the variables are wide, the terrain difficult, and you need to be prepared for all eventualities. Some guidebooks advise taking half the stuff and twice the money when travelling; for the DRC, you should bring twice the stuff and at least three times the money.

If you are visiting the DRC on an organised trip or will mainly be staying in cities, you can get away with the minimum kit: a torch (flashlight) with extra batteries, insect repellent, a hat, a Swiss Army knife or similar (with bottle-opener, can-opener, scissors and tweezers), a power bank for your phone, and antimalarials if you are using them.

If you plan to travel around the country, you will need all this and more: sturdy, waterproof, hiking boots; a treated mosquito net (or permethrin spray for hotel nets); matches or a lighter; a torch that can also be used as a lamp (with lots of extra

One of the skills lost to the modern world – among others such as how to make fire without matches, find one's way without a compass or GPS, and build a home from sticks and mud – is perhaps that most pertinent to the visitor to the DRC: how to light an oil lamp.

If your torch batteries are dying and you're out of candles, you may suddenly become aware of the oil lamp lurking in the corner of a quickly darkening spartan room, somewhere between nowhere and a bus out sometime next week. In this case, conserving your battery power and using the local tools provided can be quite handy – saving your own materials for when there is really no other choice.

Faced with this portable lighting technology from the 18th century, the first thing to do is familiarise yourself with it. On one side is a lever that raises and lowers the glass casing that protects the wick (where the flame comes from). Below the wick is a knob, which one uses to increase or decrease the amount of fuel going to the wick – thereby creating a larger or smaller flame upon ignition. At the base is a lid, where the fuel goes in. Make sure you ask for the right fuel before refilling.

Lighting it, then, is simple enough – light a match, push down on the lever, and put the lit match to the wick. Adjust the knob to get the flame to the desired brightness. Carry around dark hallways at your discretion, or use it to light up your room. You may find it's not a bad way to get light after all.

batteries); and a map, if you can find one. See also page 59 for a suggested first-aid kit. If you have a GPS, you may want to bring it, but be warned that it will attract attention. Pack it in your hold baggage on internal flights, in as disguised a way as you can; in your hand baggage, it will definitely be found and might be confiscated. Use the GPS and even the map discreetly while in the field, to try to avoid local people thinking you are a spy. Pack all these things in a large backpack. Transport can be difficult or non-existent around the DRC and it is likely you will need to walk distances on footpaths between towns, or ride on the back of motorbikes on rough dirt roads. Picture yourself as going on a camping trip, even if you are planning to stay in hotels.

When in the jungle, do not be lean on what you bring – these are volatile areas and any problems you encounter will only be solved by what you have in your possession. These are not the kinds of places where one can simply head to the next village and find what you need. There are three things the author wishes he had taken on his first few visits to the Congo – a doorstop (for those cheap hotel doors that won't close, and for some added security when sleeping at night), hot sauce (for making those meals of canned tuna and canned corned beef almost palatable) and earplugs (to drown out the armada of screaming children on long bus rides).

ELECTRICITY The usual sockets in the DRC are the standard two-pin plugs used in continental Europe; the voltage is 220V. Travellers from the UK or outside Europe will need to bring adaptors for any electrical items, since they will be difficult if not impossible to find locally. Power cuts are frequent even in cities and large towns, although hotels usually have generators. A small power bank will be used more often than you can imagine. For torches, cameras or anything else battery-operated, bring more batteries than you think you can possibly need. Power surges are also common and can render rechargeable batteries useless.

MONEY AND BUDGETING

The national currency of the DRC is the Congolese franc (Franc congolais, Fc). US dollars, in denominations of US$5 and over, are accepted everywhere. They must be 'new'-format bills, with the big head of the US president (post-2009) and they must be in mint condition; even a small pen mark on a note is likely to cause problems. You should carefully check each note that you are given in change, whether in a hotel or on the street, and have no qualms about rejecting any note which is not in mint condition. US$1 and US$2 bills can only be used in the most upmarket hotels in Kinshasa; it is not really worth bringing them at all. Change of anything under US$10 is usually given in Fc. The most reliable way to exchange US dollars for Fc is on the street. Other major currencies, in addition to US dollars, can be exchanged at Western Union branches or at banks, although it is quite common to find they are unable to effect the transaction at the time you are there; they will come up with various excuses, but it usually means they don't have enough cash to spare for you.

ATMs are easy to find in cities and can even be found in smaller towns; they sometimes dispense US dollars as well as Congolese francs. Credit cards can be used in major hotels and supermarkets in Kinshasa, Lubumbashi and other cities; small shops and anywhere in small towns are cash only. International airline offices (eg: CAA) will accept credit cards for payment of flight tickets, but some smaller domestic airlines still require cash.

If you are not able to use your debit card in an ATM, or if your bank charges are unreasonably high, a reliable and fast method of receiving money is via Western Union. They have agencies in even the smallest towns in the DRC, some based within banks, others in the large hotels, and still others in small offices on the high street. Keep in mind, though, that it takes several hours for overseas transactions to be processed; it may require a day or more to receive a transfer from abroad.

BUDGETING FOR YOUR TRIP It would be difficult to see much of the Democratic Republic of the Congo on a very tight budget. Tourist visas are expensive, internal flights are expensive, park permits are expensive. Getting to some of the national parks requires chartering a plane! Those with no budget constraints whatsoever could easily spend thousands of dollars a day. The good news for everyone else is that there are ways to see at least some of the DRC's wonderful sights and wildlife without breaking the bank.

The biggest issue you will face is transport. Public buses are a cheap way to get around cities or, especially in Katanga (page 139), between towns, but to see anything off the beaten track – and a lot of the DRC *is* off the beaten track – will require either a 4x4 vehicle or a motorbike. Motorbikes are a form of public transport in the DRC and, for most trips, it should be relatively straightforward to hire a bike with its driver. It is also possible to rent 4x4 vehicles, with or without a driver; obviously this is a more expensive option. If you plan to spend a fair amount of time in the DRC, you might consider bringing a bicycle, although it would be hard going on the rough tracks in the bush.

Restaurants (page 78) are usually inexpensive, apart from those aimed at an elite, high-earning clientele, most of which are in Kinshasa and Lubumbashi. Street food, grilled in front of your eyes, is even cheaper. Mid-range hotels (page 75) are fairly affordable and, except in Kinshasa, there are always budget options too, as long as you have your own mosquito net.

The lowest realistic budget, not including high-cost items such as internal flights and park permits, would be around US$100 a day. This should get you a cheap bed anywhere outside of Kinshasa, two modest meals, bus travel on the days you move from place to place, and enough left over to buy mineral water and any other essentials in a grocery store. You could get by on even less, again outside Kinshasa, by shopping only at local markets, paying a few dollars a night for the cheapest bed in the back room of a bar, and cycling, walking or taking the cheapest public transport between towns; some travellers have managed this pattern with success.

For greater comfort and to see more of the country, a daily budget of US$150–200 should be enough to cover a mid-range hotel room, a snack and a restaurant meal a day, a couple of park permits every so often and perhaps one or two internal return flights, with other travel being done by bus or motorbike.

The high end in the DRC has no limits – the most expensive hotels, air tickets, park permits, 4x4 hire and payment for guides can run to several thousand dollars daily. If you are on this generous a budget, it makes sense to pay a local tour operator (page 53) to arrange your internal travel and park visits, rather than attempting to negotiate DRC officialdom on your own.

Some average prices at the time of writing include:

1.5 litre bottle water	Fc1,000
Large bottle of Primus or Simba beer	Fc6,500
Baguette	Fc800–1,000
Small bag of banana chips	Fc2,000
Litre of petrol	Fc3,000

GETTING AROUND

BY AIR To travel around most of the DRC, you will have no choice but to purchase a domestic flight. In most of the country, the roads are bad to impassable and in many areas they are insecure due to the presence of armed militias.

The internal air network is extensive, with numerous small operations running flights to most major towns. Their safety record ranges from appalling to poor; all DRC-registered airlines are banned from operating within the European Union. However, flying is the only way to get to some towns in the country and the only realistically feasible way to get between others. Compagnie Africaine d'Aviation (CAA; w caacongo.com) has one of the best (or least bad) accident records, with no fatalities since 2013. It is the updater's recommendation. CAA flies between Kinshasa and 14 other towns and cities. An alternative may be the government-owned Congo Airways (w congoairways.com), although at the time of writing its flights are suspended due to financial problems.

Even though flying is the only way for Congolese people to move easily around their vast country, airfares are expensive. CAA's fare from Kinshasa to Lubumbashi or Goma is around US$200 each way, to Kisangani only slightly less, and to relatively nearby Mbandaka, US$90. Each traveller must also pay a passenger tax known as a Go-Pass – US$10 per passenger at the time of writing – and an airport tax of US$5. In theory, the money raised from the Go-Pass is invested in bringing the DRC's airports up to international standards.

CAA flights can be booked on the company's website; for smaller airlines, the only reliable method of finding out which domestic flights are leaving on a given day may be to go to the airport and enquire there – most of these airlines are not registered on international booking systems.

BY RIVER The navigable stretch of the River Congo between Kinshasa and Kisangani is a classic river trip. Sadly, however, there are no regular ferry services nowadays. Occasionally a steamer runs the route, but most of the river traffic consists of old barges, tied together, carrying cargo and people sitting on top of it. The journey takes three to four weeks. These barges are often overcrowded and there have been instances of them capsizing. A less adventurous but undoubtedly more comfortable option is to book this trip with a tour operator, for example one of those listed on page 52.

Beyond the Stanley Falls, upriver from Kisangani, it may be possible to find a boat from Ubundu to Kindu, although the security situation in this region may deter local people from wanting to take you.

BY ROAD Except in Katanga, roads in the DRC vary from bad to virtually non-existent. It can be easier to travel between towns by crossing into a neighbouring country – for example, it is far less difficult to travel from Bukavu to Goma via the paved roads in Rwanda than attempting the rough road on the DRC side, not to mention less dangerous in terms of security. Of course crossing frontiers frequently brings its own sets of problems, not least the need for a multi-entry visa to the DRC and the appropriate visa for the neighbouring country.

In the dry season, road travel between certain cities is possible, and makes an interesting alternative to air travel. As you move from one province to another, and from one district to another within each province, a road toll is levied – the road equivalent of the Go-Pass for internal flights. For cars, including 4x4, the amounts are small; the roads authorities make their money from freight vehicles. Payment is always in cash, needless to say. Whatever the distance, you should leave at sunrise to ensure you arrive before dark even in the event of unexpected delays. For example, Kinshasa to Matadi, although the distance is only about 350km, can take up to 10 hours if the traffic jams in Kinshasa are especially bad. Kisangani to Goma would probably take two or three days, although at the time of writing the presence of armed militias throughout the region makes this route very dangerous. In the wet season, even these partially asphalted roads become much less passable.

Despite the terrible condition of the roads, freight is regularly moved over vast distances around the country, on massive trucks that you will want to steer clear of if you are travelling on the roads yourself. To get themselves from one town to another, or to send documents or other items, local people use motorbikes – the only vehicle capable of traversing the tracks through the rainforest. To travel serious distances overland in the DRC, you would need a very rugged 4x4 vehicle, lots of permits, lots of local advice and nerves of steel.

The exception to all this is Katanga, where the interests of the mining companies in the region have ensured that the main roads are in good condition. Asphalt runs from Sakania in the far south to Fungurume, about 100km short of Kolwezi. Katanga would be a very good option for anyone wanting to explore part of the DRC by car.

BY RAIL The rail network in the DRC, while by no means as extensive as it was in colonial times, is useful in some parts of the country. There are trains between

Matadi and Kinshasa (page 112) and between Kisangani and Ubundu. The most extensive network is in the south, radiating out from Lubumbashi. There are trains twice a month from Lubumbashi to Kalemie, with trains onward from there to Kindu; to Kananga, with trains onward from there to Ilebo (from where boats to Kinshasa can be found); and to Sakania in the Congo Pedicle. Some of these trains have a 'luxe' class; fares in all classes are very reasonable, considering the distances involved. See page 139 for further details.

OVERLANDING The glorious old days of overlanding through Zaire have long since passed, and even in those days crossing the country was something only the bravest would attempt. War in the east of the country and a ruined road network almost everywhere mean that even the bravest will think twice before attempting to cross the DRC overland. You would need the most rugged of 4x4 vehicles, a large amount of cash for permits and checkpoints, as much local advice as you can obtain and then a bit more, and plenty of time at your disposal. Even the route through Katanga, outlined below, could take up to a month, without any stops or detours. Attempting to cross to the east of the country would take longer, unless your trip was cut short by freelance militias murdering you on the way.

Enquire at major and minor towns along the way about checkpoints, insurgencies, permits and various other dangers as you continue. Regions can be sealed off by police and army forces for reasons that will likely always remain unclear to you. Anyone attempting to cross the DRC overland should employ a local guide/fixer from one town to the next. Do not rely on online maps or indeed paper maps; local guidance is your only friend in these circumstances.

The least unfeasible route across the DRC would start at Boma, if you are shipping your vehicle into the country, or wherever you cross the border from Angola or the Republic of the Congo (Congo-Brazzaville). From there to Kinshasa is relatively straightforward. Do not be lulled into believing it is all going to be like this! From Kinshasa to Kikwit is asphalted, but between Kikwit and Fungurume (page 73), beyond Kananga, will be rough road if you are lucky, rough track if you are not. You should hire an armed guard at least between Kikwit and Kananga. At Fungurume, at last, you will be back on asphalt and stay on it to any of the border crossings into Zambia (page 138). When (or if) the N1 highway is fully upgraded, this route will seem almost straightforward.

The security situation in the east means that, at the time of writing, all routes towards Uganda, Rwanda or Burundi are extremely dangerous. They should not be attempted without your own armed guard. DRC travel agencies, such as Congo Travel and Tours (page 53), can supply security escorts, or your local fixer may be able to provide one.

Preparing your vehicle Whatever you think may be needed on your trip, bring it. There are almost no places to repair a vehicle after you have left major urban centres. Bring at least an extra set of tyres (yes, that's four), enough fluids to replace everything in your vehicle twice, and a self-powered winch for any tight spots. Bring extra parts as well as the tools to fix them. If you're not a mechanic, take a basic course before setting out: if something breaks, there will be no-one around to fix it, and likely no parts to fix it with anywhere inside the country. This is by no means a comprehensive list.

Overlanding through the DRC requires a little more attention than for some other overlanding journeys in Africa. People will try and steal items from your vehicle while you are not looking, which means leaving nothing in full view if you're ever away from your vehicle, even for a few minutes to nip into a shop for some water. Have a few hidden compartments welded to the inside frame of your vehicle, where valuables can be stored. The chance of losing your vehicle outright is possible, but not likely; it is crucially important to have all of your papers in order, as corruption is still the main problem. Soldiers and police can conduct searches, and things will likely go missing.

Motorbikes can be bought in the DRC, but a decent touring bike will be expensive. These are the motorbikes that professional couriers use to transport passengers, documents or items for long distances through the jungle.

For more detailed advice, Bradt Travel Guides publishes a guide specifically for overlanding the continent called *Africa Overland: 4x4 · Motorbike · Bicycle · Truck*, which includes plenty of useful tips for getting ready.

ACCOMMODATION

From a hut in a roadside village in the deepest tropical jungle to the sparkling hotels in Kinshasa's elite neighbourhoods, your range of options is as vast as the country itself. Kinshasa has lots of high-end hotels and plenty of mid-range places, but almost nothing at the lower end where a budget traveller can crash.

In most cities, large and small, there is a choice of mid-range hotels. Typically, at least some rooms in these will have an en-suite bathroom and either a fan or air conditioning, and there will probably be a generator so the lights (and air conditioning) stay on, at least intermittently. At the budget end of the spectrum, you can expect cold water, or even no running water at all, shared bathrooms and insecure or non-existent locks to the rooms.

Away from the cities and large towns, unless you are with an organised tour, you will be looking at the accommodation options in villages. Sleeping under the stars is very much not recommended, for all sorts of security reasons. By far the best option will be the local Catholic priest, Protestant pastor or religious mission. Their houses usually have some space available for travellers, for which there will be a moderate charge; you will be safe, you will be well looked after, and you will have an invaluable opportunity to glean local information about your onward travel from people who move around their parish all the time. Most bars and music clubs have a few rooms at the back for a few dollars a night, if you can convince them to charge you the normal rate. These are usually intended for prostitution but will be rented to you if you can make a case for it. If you are on a long road trip, you will no doubt be shepherded to a place deemed 'safe' by your roadmates and made to feel welcome. Make sure you secure the door against intrusion. Shared toilets, or no toilets at all, are common across small villages. Washing from a bucket by candlelight is still something that occurs in the remote stretches of the Congo.

ACCOMMODATION PRICE CODES

Standard double room per night.

$$$$$	Exclusive	US$200+
$$$$	Expensive	US$150–199
$$$	Mid-range	US$100–149
$$	Thrifty	US$50–99
$	Budget	<US$50

EATING AND DRINKING

There is plenty of delicious fresh food in the DRC, although admittedly in small towns you may only be able to track it down in the local markets. Fruit and vegetables are highly seasonal; at different times of year you will find tomatoes, aubergines, pumpkin, okra, beans, corn and the ubiquitous manioc. Also on display is a baffling variety of green leaves – not just spinach, but also the leaves of sweet potatoes, a kind of hibiscus and a creeper called *fumbwa*. Market and street stalls are piled high with mangoes, pineapples, papayas, the small but delicious local bananas, oranges, coconuts and even apples from Ituri. Villagers sell fruit and vegetables at the roadsides, at the height of the relevant seasons, grown or harvested by themselves. Obviously the selection of fresh food is wider in the big cities than in small villages in the bush, but even in the latter it should be possible to find some fresh local produce.

The staple food in the DRC is manioc, prepared in many different ways. The classic is *chikwangue* or *kwanga*, a little cake of fermented manioc wrapped in leaves. You will see this being sold in markets and at roadsides everywhere in the DRC. *Fufu* is a paste made with manioc flour, while *pondu* consists of manioc leaves, chopped and cooked with onion, pepper and flakes of dried fish. These preparations are often served as accompaniments to meat or fish, but they are also very often eaten as they are. The other very common accompaniment is rice; fried plantain is also popular. Potatoes are served either sautéd or as Belgian-style *frites*.

Restaurants near the river and in Kinshasa serve the huge freshwater prawns called *cossa-cossa*. The Atlantic fish called *capitaine* is served as thick fillets, grilled or braised. Tilapia is usually grilled or fried. As for meat, smoked pork ribs, grilled goat, beef skewers and chicken in a sauce of peanuts, tomato and onion are some specialities worth trying. Unrefined palm oil, from a tree native to equatorial Africa (including the DRC), is the standard oil used in Congolese cooking.

The big cities have international restaurants, not only French cuisine but also Lebanese, Indian and, most recently, Chinese. The French restaurants are usually rather expensive, but the other international cuisines are quite affordable, not least because they are catering to their own communities who are not always on high incomes. Of course there are also restaurants offering high-quality local cuisine – fish, meat or vegetables prepared in interesting ways. Other than those within hotels, restaurants tend to close around 21.00, even in the big cities. Fresh milk is not always available, even in quite good hotels – powdered milk might be presented at breakfast along with Western cereals (the updater for this edition never grasped what she was supposed to do with the powdered milk, so she didn't eat the cereal).

Where there are Indian restaurants, vegetarians and vegans will find a choice of suitable dishes. Elsewhere in towns of any size, vegetarians should always be able to order an omelette with fresh bread or chips. Unless they are in accommodation where they can cook for themselves, vegans will have to make do with bread and tomatoes and fruit in their hotel rooms.

Once you are out in the jungle, although shops may have fridges, they probably don't have electricity often enough to keep food in them fresh. Because of the lack of refrigeration, non-perishable foods are most common outside the cities and major towns. Several types of tinned meat and fish can sit idle on shelves for months or even years before you pick them up. Check the sell-by date, if one is visible, make sure the can has not been opened, and bring your own can opener. Biscuits with artificial flavours are widely available; full of sugar, they will keep you going on long road trips. In the cities you can buy dried fruit and nuts, which are even better snacks.

THE DRC'S BELGIAN HERITAGE: BEER

The country now called the Democratic Republic of the Congo was ruthlessly exploited by its colonial power. However, one of the positive contributions of its Belgian rulers has to be its great beer. There are three main breweries in the DRC: Bralima and Bracongo in Kinshasa and Brasimba in Lubumbashi (the 'Bra' in each case is an abbreviation for 'Brasserie', 'brewery'). Most of the beers produced in the DRC are Belgian-style blondes – like Stella Artois or Jupiler – of around 5% APV, and most are available in a choice of 33cl and larger (65–75cl) bottles.

Bralima (w bralima.net), founded in 1923 as La Brasserie de Léopoldville, the colonial name for Kinshasa, produced its first bottles of Primus (5%), the DRC's best-known beer, in 1926. Primus is embedded in Congolese culture, with several now-famous musicians making their first breakthroughs with its advertising campaigns. Bralima's other beers include Mützig, a dark brown bock (5.5%), the amber Turbo King (6.5%) with its sexist advertising strapline 'a man's business' (*une affaire d'hommes*), a dark stout from high-roasted malt called Legend (7.5%) and, marketed only in Katanga, the blonde N'Tay (5%), the Swahili word for 'eagle'. Bralima is now owned by Heineken and is the importer into the DRC of bottled and canned Heineken.

The Belgian Congo's second brewery was Brasimba (w brasimba.com), set up in 1925 in what was then Élisabethville (now Lubumbashi) by Belgian mining expats longing for a taste of home. Brasimba is now owned by the Castel Group, which has been brewing beer in Africa since the 1960s. Its 5% Castel beer is pleasant enough and not as sweet as many African beers. More interestingly, it has its own range of signature beers, each with the Swahili name of an iconic Congolese animal: Chui (leopard) at 3.5%, with blonde and amber (Chui Black) versions; blonde Simba (lion) at 5%; and Tembo (elephant) at 5.9%, a darker beer with caramel undertones. Simba and Tembo are even exported to Belgium (w simbabel.be)! Some years, around Christmas and New Year, Brasimba brews a seasonal blanche called La Lushoise – 'the beer (or the girl) from Lubumbashi'. Peak 5.5 (5.5%), a sour blonde, and Peak 7.7 (7.7%), a dark bitter, are available only in the eastern DRC, from Brasimba's subsidiary brewery in Beni.

Bracongo (w bracongo.cd), also part of the Castel Group, is the youngest of the DRC's breweries, founded in Kinshasa in 1949. Its longest-running and best-known beer is 33Export (5.4%), marketed as a football fan's beer and first produced in 1975, when Zaire was in the top four footballing countries in Africa. Its newest is Nkoyi (5%), marketed mainly in Kinshasa and available in blonde and dark (Nkoyi Black) versions, both good beers although a little too sweet for British real-ale tastes. Its strongest beer is the dark Doppel Munich (6.5%). Beaufort (5%) has its origins in Cameroon, not Belgium, and is a light, refreshing lager; Bracongo's bottle-conditioned Castel is 5.2%. The Castel breweries in the DRC also brew Skol lager (5%) under licence; the DRC was the first country in Africa where Skol was launched, in 1965.

Beer aficionados will relish the challenge of working their way through the range on offer in the DRC. Those who are less devoted will no doubt find one or two beers they like and stick to those. Even those who don't like beer at all can take solace in the knowledge that not every colonial legacy is a bad legacy.

Along the roadside, you will see local people holding out animal carcasses or large fish as vehicles pass. Eating bushmeat is very risky; it is what caused Ebola and mpox (and possibly also Covid-19) to cross from wild animals into humans. There are a few restaurants, in Kinshasa and Lubumbashi, where you can try antelope and other game that has been handled and prepared safely. On no account should you encourage the sale of bushmeat from protected species such as bonobo or chimpanzee.

As for drinking, palm wine is the fermented sap of the same palm trees that produce palm oil. If you are spending time in small villages, you may see it being loaded and unloaded in large plastic jerry cans. It is rather sweet but not unpleasant. Foreigners drinking it in social settings will no doubt be quite a sight to local people, who are not used to seeing outsiders drink their 'national beverage'. The other national beverage in the DRC is beer – see page 77. Whisky, rum and vodka, often in unfamiliar knock-off brands, are available in liquor stores. The big supermarkets stock wine, mainly South African, at high prices, and internationally familiar brands of spirits, at even higher prices.

PUBLIC HOLIDAYS AND FESTIVALS

All administrative services and many restaurants and shops are closed on 25 December and 1 January. Some other public holidays are:

4 January: Martyrs' Day
16 January: Commemoration of assassination of Laurent-Désiré Kabila
17 January: Commemoration of assassination of Patrice Emery Lumumba
6 April: Kimbangu Day
1 May: Labour Day
17 May: Liberation Day
30 June: Independence Day

SHOPPING

Most artisans in the DRC have to combine their craft with other work that brings in a better income, usually all in the grey economy. This means, somewhat counterintuitively, that the best range of artisan goods can be found in Kinshasa, where craftspeople can send their items for sale from pretty much wherever they are in the country. The artisans' market in Kinshasa (le Marché des Valeurs) has a huge range of goods, although many visitors find it quite a challenging place to shop, with in-your-face salespeople and rather aggressive haggling. The big hotels in Kinshasa (page 102) have souvenir shops where it is easier to look calmly at the things you might like to take home.

Items to look out for are wooden masks and statuettes, jewellery made from wood, bone, stones or shells, and raffia carpets from Kasai. In Katanga, artisans use malachite, whose beautiful green colour comes from the copper ore within it, to craft jewellery, ornaments and other items inspired by traditional artefacts. The brightly patterned lengths of cloth known as *pagnes* make an attractive and easily portable souvenir, although none of it is produced in the DRC. You can buy a *pagne* and have it made up into a shirt or dress by a local tailor, sometimes within a few hours.

For details of contemporary art galleries in Kinshasa and Lubumbashi, see pages 80, 102 and 151. In theory, a permit is needed to export works of art or antiquities, though not required for handicrafts; check with the gallery before embarking on the (no doubt Kafkaesque) process at the Ministry of Culture (w culture.gouv. cd). For wildlife souvenirs, Lola Ya Bonobo (page 107) and Virunga National Park (page 208) sell T-shirts and other bonobo- or gorilla-themed memorabilia, on site and online.

CENTRAL AFRICAN ART MUSEUMS IN EUROPE

One of the tragedies of the Belgian Congo's colonial history is that it was not only its mineral wealth that was plundered. The colonisers also plundered much of the art produced in the kingdoms that they found. While contemporary art and culture thrive in the DRC, its museums are rather short of artefacts to illustrate the rich history of the indigenous people and those who later settled in the heart of Africa. The museums do their best to chronicle this history, using photographs and modern artisan items to supplement the few historic items at their disposal. For the best selection of artefacts, however, one must visit the museums in European capitals.

The best collection is, as one would expect, in Belgium: the **Africa Museum** in Brussels, formally called the Royal Museum for Central Africa and also known as the Tervuren Museum (w africamuseum.be). Created in 1898, it holds an unrivalled collection of objects from what is now the Democratic Republic of the Congo. It has biological and earth science collections, a huge photography and film archive, 8,000 musical instruments and 120,000 ethnographic objects, some of them acquired by coercion or outright theft. In a famous speech to the United Nations in 1973, President Mobutu demanded the return of 200 objects from Tervuren.

The museum collaborates with museums in Kinshasa and Lubumbashi, advising them on modern layout and presentation, and has returned some items from its collection to their homeland. Some of the items in its collection can be viewed on the museum's website.

Also in Brussels, the **Claes Gallery** (w didierclaes.com) specialises in West and central African art. As a child, the gallerist travelled around the villages of what was then Zaire with his father, who collected art for the Kinshasa museums. It's a good place to look at art from the DRC and, if you can, to buy it.

In Paris, the **Musée du Quai Branly – Jacques Chirac** (w quaibranly.fr) is France's national museum of the arts and civilisations of Africa and other parts of the world. At the foot of the Eiffel Tower, its collection includes many items from the former Belgian Congo, including ethnomusicology recordings, some from the 19th century.

Practical Information SHOPPING

2

ARTS AND ENTERTAINMENT

The DRC has a vibrant culture of visual arts; see page 48 for some background information. In Kinshasa, Symphonie des Arts (**f** Kinshasa Symphonie des Arts; page 102) is a long-established centre for displaying and selling work by Congolese artists. Also in Kinshasa, Kin ArtStudio (**w** congobiennale.art; page 103) occupies a large space in the former textile factory known as the Utex-Africa building, with artists' studios and workshops and a gallery for them to display their art. In Lubumbashi, the Waza gallery is run by a collective of local artists to promote their own work. The Dialogues gallery within the National Museum of Lubumbashi (page 152), set up with funding from the Lubumbashi businessman (and philanthropist) George Forrest, has a collection of contemporary Congolese art and erratic opening hours.

The French institutes and their Belgian equivalents (Wallonie-Bruxelles), in Kinshasa and Lubumbashi, often have exhibitions of work by Congolese artists and photographers. They also screen films (usually French-language) and are just about the only places in the DRC that you will find theatre or dance performances.

THE CONGO IN POPULAR FILM

The Congo has represented the great unknown that is the middle of Africa for much of its time in the Western consciousness. It was once the staging ground for numerous fictional adventures and in the middle of the 20th century, the word 'Congo' was synonymous with the Africa filled with wild animals and savage tribes that punctuated countless serialised adventures in popular cultures – especially in comic books, where the heroic white male characters of *Jungle Jim* and *Congo Bill* plied their trade rescuing damsels in distress and exploring the deepest jungles of the continent. These characters were hugely popular during the 1930s, 1940s and 1950s, and even spawned some movies – including *King of the Congo*, *Fury of the Congo* and *Congo Bill*.

The 'noble savage' was also a popular character theme for stories set in the Congo, with the comic-book character *Congorilla* making appearances in action comics throughout the 1940s and early 1950s. As the name suggests, he was a large gorilla who Congo Bill could assume the identity of to assist local people with their problems. Another recurring jungle character published by Fox during the 1940s was renamed *Jo-Jo, Congo King* – essentially a Tarzan lookalike, he battled large animals in the African jungle. And way back in 1930 the animated character Bosko wandered around the African jungle to the beat of jazz in one of the first fictional approaches to the region with *Congo Jazz*.

Hollywood cinema during its golden age warmed up well to the Congo. Audrey Hepburn starred in *The Nun's Story*, a 1959 film concerning a Belgian woman who spent some time in the Congo before various intrigues forced her to confront her faith. She would not be the only huge star to participate in a Congo-centric film – Orson Welles would narrate portions of the 1959 documentary *Masters of the Congo Jungle*, which explored the challenges faced by the men who lived in the Belgian Congo as well as the threats to wildlife there. The Congo would also be the setting for several camp films of the era, including *Panther Girl of the Congo*, a 1955 film depicting a short-skirted wildlife researcher who battles large mysterious beasts during her time in central Africa. *King of the Congo* from 1952 saw an air force pilot shot down in the Congo as he attempted to subvert Soviet influences

The only classical orchestra in the DRC is the Kimbanguist Symphony Orchestra (◼ Orchestre symphonique Kimbanguiste), founded in 1994, which occasionally performs in Kinshasa.

SPORTS AND ACTIVITIES

FOOTBALL The most popular sport in the DRC, by far, is football. The national team, known as the Leopards, was the first team from sub-Saharan Africa to qualify for a World Cup, in 1974 when the country was called Zaire. The Leopards have won the Africa Cup of Nations (AFCON) twice, in 1968 and 1974. More recently, they finished third in 2015 and fourth in 2023. They have also had success in the African Nations Championship (CHAN), winning the inaugural tournament in 2009 and lifting the trophy again in 2016. The DRC team just missed out on qualifying for the 2022 World Cup, losing its last qualifier against Morocco. Several Congolese footballers play in league teams abroad, including Yannick Bolasie and Dieudonné Mbokani, who both played for various English clubs before moving on elsewhere.

over African tribes. *Drums of the Congo* depicted a group of American adventurers searching for a mysterious meteor in the jungle.

After the independence of both the DRC and Republic of the Congo in 1960, interest in the Congo waned considerably. The continued revolutions there, as well as the fact that the great African colonial project had come to an end, saw the era of white adventurers and savage warriors become somewhat passé, if not yet entirely politically incorrect. Hollywood would approach the Congo again in the 1968 film *The Mercenaries*, an action-adventure yarn based on Mike Hoare and Bob Denard's exploits fighting the UN and everyone else during their time in the Congo. The year 1970 saw an English comedy called *Carry on up the Congo* reignite some stereotypes when their group of explorers was captured by jungle women. In 1977, Hong Kong's emerging film industry made a King Kong rip-off that came to be known as *Colossus of Congo* in some markets, though the country was never referred to specifically – nonetheless, this would be the last time that the Congo was used as a backdrop for stereotypical Africa until almost two decades later.

In 1995, the huge-budget Hollywood film *Congo*, based on the best-selling novel by Michael Crichton, brought modern stereotypes of the Congo to a wide audience – greedy multi-national companies intent on exploiting central Africa's mineral wealth at all costs. Diamonds buried in the jungle, missing researchers and evil businessmen all figure prominently in what is essentially a throwback to the earlier jungle movies that saw groups of white explorers delve deep into central Africa.

Big-budget non-fiction films surrounding the Congo's history have, comparably, been few and far between. Many were made during the time of the Belgian and French Congo, but after independence it is another story altogether. Two of the most recent (and easy to find) are *When We Were Kings* from 1996, a detailed account of 'The Rumble in the Jungle' – Muhammad Ali and George Foreman's Kinshasa fight in 1974. In 2000, a large-budget French film explored the life and death of Patrice Lumumba in *Lumumba*.

The national football league is called Linafoot, with three clubs usually tussling for the cup: the Kinshasa teams DC Motema Pembe and AS Vita Club, and the Lubumbashi club Tout Puissant (TP) Mazembe (w tpmazembe.com, in French). All three teams trace their history back to the 1930s. Known as the Ravens (les Corbeaux), TP Mazembe has won the African Cup of Champions Clubs (now the CAF Champions League) no fewer than five times, most recently in 2015. The Ravens played in the inaugural, and controversial, African Football League in 2023. People in Lubumbashi say that, when they are abroad and are asked where they are from, they don't bother mentioning their city's name, which nobody knows – instead, they reply that they are from the city of Mazembe, which gets instant recognition.

The DRC's women's national team has been playing internationally since 1998, when they achieved third place in the African Women's Championship. They got to the third round of the qualifiers for the 2020 Summer Olympics but were knocked out on aggregate. The current squad is drawn from the women's teams of national clubs, including TP Mazembe, and from clubs in Europe, Tanzania and Turkey.

OTHER SPORTS In 2023, Kinshasa hosted the ninth Jeux de la Francophonie, a sporting (and cultural) event for French-speaking countries, which included athletics and para-athletics, basketball, cycling, judo, table tennis, wrestling and, of course, football. Several teams in the US National **Basketball** Association have Congolese players, while the national women's **volleyball** team came fifth in the 2021 African Volleyball Championships. Foreign travellers looking for facilities to play **tennis** will find courts in some of the upmarket hotels or at tennis clubs in Kinshasa and Lubumbashi, for example Cercle de Kinshasa Tennis (f) and Cercle BELGE L/SHI (f). Kinshasa and Lubumbashi also have **golf** courses. **Jet-skiing** on Lake Tanganyika is offered by hotels in Kalemie.

FISHING Although the country is effectively defined by its huge river, sport fishing is not widely offered. Local people along the river fish for food, not for sport. However, a few agencies can organise fishing excursions (see page 52 for contact details). The coastal waters of the Atlantic off the DRC are rich in large game fish, including marlin, swordfish and the Atlantic tarpon (*Megalops atlanticus*), also known as the silver king. Tarpon are sought after by sports fishers because, in addition to being large, they are great acrobats, leaping and gyrating when they are hooked. Congo Travel and Tours can arrange tarpon fishing off Muanda (page 119), although you would need to bring your own fishing gear.

Unique to the Congo River Basin, including Lake Tanganyika, is the giant (or goliath) tigerfish (*Hydrocynus goliath*), a huge predatory beast. Its average length is 1.5m; its average weight is 50kg, although the largest recorded specimen weighed 70kg. It has gigantic teeth, up to 2.5cm long, that fit into grooves along its jaws. It feeds on other fish, even smaller members of its own species, and hunts by lurking in calm spots in river rapids and speeding out when it sees prey. Its sight and hearing are keen. Its only known predator, apart from humans, is the Nile crocodile. There have been (unverified) reports of giant tigerfish attacking humans. For the undaunted, Soma Travel Tours can organise expeditions to fish for giant tigerfish on the River Congo. Basic fishing gear can be provided, although keen sportspeople will probably prefer to bring their own.

A great book to learn about this fish, and the methods for catching it, is *The Largest Tigerfish in the World: The Goliath*, by Douglas Dann.

BIRDWATCHING The DRC has the largest recorded number of unique bird species in Africa. A total of 18 endemic species have been counted here – most importantly the Congo peafowl, Bedford's paradise flycatcher, Congo bay owl, Rockefeller's sunbird and three types of weavers. The best birding region, with one of the highest numbers worldwide of species unique to the area, is the Albertine Rift as it straddles the border of the DRC and Uganda. West of Lake Albert are the Itombwe Mountains, which have been a boon for researchers over the years. The mountains around Butembo and Lubero are especially remarkable, with 43 species unique to the area. Some migrate to the Ugandan side of the border, some don't. Highlights in this region include Albertine's francolin, Grauer's broadbill, Oberländer's groundthrush, Sassi's greenbull, Neumann's warblers, Grant's bluebill, Turner's eremomela and too many more to list here. Many others could exist, or migrate through the DRC; however, little real research has been done outside the eastern corridors. There are many other low-lying lakes and wetlands in the DRC where birding is an excellent option. Near Kinshasa is Lac Ma Vallée, once a popular birding site, which remains accessible. Mount Hoyo Reserve has numerous species unique to Ituri. The wetlands near Likasi and Upemba National Park are also especially abundant.

OPENING TIMES

Advertised opening hours in the DRC are more of a finger in the wind than a reliable indication. In general, banks are open from 09.00 to 15.00; Western Union agencies, other than those within banks, stay open for longer, sometimes until 18.00; the agencies within upmarket hotels often a little later. Small shops usually open very early in the morning and close quite early in the evening – don't rely on them being open after about 17.00. The international-style supermarkets in cities stay open the longest – 08.00–20.00 or even later. Nightclubs close before midnight; a little later at weekends. Museums are usually open Monday–Friday from around 08.00 until around 16.00, with an hour's break for lunch.

MEDIA AND COMMUNICATIONS

PHONE AND INTERNET The international dialling code for the DRC is +243, and the internet designation is .cd. Most businesses in the DRC, never mind individuals, have abandoned landlines and rely exclusively on mobile numbers. At the time of writing there are four licensed mobile networks. Coverage is generally good in cities and big towns. In rural areas – most of the country – it is non-existent or, at best, patchy. WhatsApp is very widely used throughout the country; it is the best way to communicate with people in rural areas, where they can pick up messages whenever they happen to have a signal. If you bring a phone into the country from abroad and put a DRC SIM into it, you will have to register your phone's IMEI; this can be done online and is not an arduous task. Practically all hotels in towns and cities have Wi-Fi, although it is not always very stable.

POST The beautiful colonial-era post offices in Kinshasa, Lubumbashi and other cities are better admired from without. If you need to send physical documents, international courier companies such as **DHL** are more reliable; there are DHL offices in the cities and most towns of the DRC.

RADIO AND TV Most Congolese get their news from social media, especially Instagram and TikTok. There are no terrestrial TV stations that cover the whole of this vast country. The state-owned RTNC (Radio Télévision Nationale Congolaise) has the widest network, with offices and transmission stations in every provincial capital, but even RTNC's TV transmitters only reach 50–100km beyond each capital. The big cities (Goma, Kinshasa, Lubumbashi) have their own local TV channels. Most private and 'community' media in the DRC is owned by political actors.

Radio Okapi, the United Nations' radio station in the DRC, manages a network of transmitters and is also available online (w radiookapi.net). This is the most objective source of news in the DRC, although admittedly the bar is set quite low. The BBC, Voice of America, RFI (Radio France) and DW (Deutsche Welle) broadcast on FM in the cities and are re-broadcast by many local and community radio stations.

CULTURAL ETIQUETTE

In business settings, suits and ties are not expected, although the other extreme of sleeveless T-shirts or shorts is not acceptable. While Congolese people may not always dress very formally, there are clear expectations about behaviour. Shake hands with your interlocutor(s) on arriving and leaving. Sit down if you are offered a seat (even if you have to sit there for 2 or 3 hours). Don't expect to be offered a coffee or even a drink of water while you wait. Women working with a male colleague should not be surprised if some (male) interlocutors address all their remarks to their male team-mate and make eye contact only with him.

See also page 54 for information on rules around photography.

TRAVELLING POSITIVELY

In the 21st century, the Congo colonial project has come full circle – what was originally seen as an escape from the continued quagmires of their African colonies became a point of blame for the European powers that carved up the continent in 1886. In those days, it may have been unclear as to what exactly the colonial future had in store for the Congo; yet, in many ways, their current existence is a direct by-product of the pretences from which they originated.

Nowhere else has there been such a perpetual and persistent meeting of international non-governmental organisations (NGOs) as in the DRC. This may be due to the fact that the 'nation', per se, was so badly managed by the Belgians, or to a sense of purpose by Western nations to correct the errors of the colonial agenda; both, perhaps.

This is the colonial legacy, and the Congolese must live it. Their duty is to make do, at least, with the institutions given to them while building new ones on their own. It is the obligation of Western governments, and aid organisations across the globe, to guide them along a path of order out of their current chaos.

The tourist should also make a contribution, one as critical to the nation's well-being as that of any other individual. The tourist can make known the great value that the DRC's cultural and natural institutions are to the world at large. Respect for their significance, in this case, flows from outward to inward. Only if the Congolese perceive their natural history and wildlife to be valuable will they ensure that they are protected while the rest of the nation develops. It is a parallel development that needs to take place – all the more critical, since once animal populations and wilderness are significantly damaged, they can never fully recover.

We all play a part in the preservation of a global heritage, and the promotion of a global culture where one can respect their origins, their landscape and their language. Amid the usual chaos and madness that can punctuate a visit to the DRC, try and envision this nation and these people for what they could become; and, if you see a way in which you can assist them to that goal, then the world at large will be a better place for your participation.

CHILDREN AND FAMILIES

Action Against Hunger
w actionagainsthunger.org. International organisation seeking to improve the health of families & eliminate hunger.
Congo Action w congoaction.co.uk. British charity working in Kivu Province that arranges child sponsorship, development of school facilities & livestock acquisition.
Oxfam w oxfam.org.uk. Operates both short- & long-term development projects in the DRC.
Save the Children w savethechildren.net. Focuses on protecting children & rebuilding their living environments as affected by war.
Watchlist on Children & Armed Conflict w watchlist.org. Advocacy group reporting violations against the rights of children in armed conflict.

GENERALIST AND OTHER GROUPS

ACTED w acted.org. French organisation (Agency for Technical Co-operation & Development) that assists with long-term economic development strategies. Active in both the DRC & the Republic of the Congo.
Amnesty International w amnesty.org. Advocacy group that monitors & reports human rights violations worldwide.
Care International w care.org. Large organisation aimed at fighting poverty worldwide.
Concern w concern.ie. Provides long-term development work for communities to experience an increased quality of life.
Global Witness Limited w globalwitness.org. Conducts field research & trains monitors to expose the link between the exploitation of resources & human rights violations.
Helen Keller International w hki.org. Provides training & assistance for vision & nutrition programmes.
Human Rights Watch w hrw.org. Conducts field research & reports on human rights violations. Active in both Congos.
Institute for War & Peace Reporting w iwpr. net. Trains local reporters to promote local journalistic efforts in covering conflicts.
International Crisis Group w crisisgroup. org. Conducts field research & political analysis to report on conflict regions & provide concrete advocacy plans to prevent, reduce or eliminate current or future conflicts.
SCDI (Staff de Chauffeurs Pour le Developpement Intégral) ✆ +243 816 08 1961/852 26 1938; e scdi@yahoo.fr. Local NGO based in Mbuji-Mayi dedicated to instructing & promoting an improvement in transport across the region as well as training new taxi drivers.
Telecoms Sans Frontières
w tsfi.org. Specialises in providing emergency telecommunications to regions in conflict.
Welthungerhilfe – German Agro Action
w welthungerhilfe.de. German group focusing on rebuilding agricultural lands, safe drinking water, crafts & small business training.
World Organisation Against Torture w omct. org. Coalition of organisations lobbying against detention & torture practices in the DRC. Provides assistance to victims & campaigns for the rights of women & children.

MEDICAL ASSISTANCE

Doctors Worldwide w doctorsworldwide.org. Provides aid & medical relief in regions where none exists & provides methods to prevent outbreaks of disease.
Medair w medair.org. Swiss-based medical organisation that provides emergency & long-term medical assistance in the DRC.
Médecins du Monde w medecinsdumonde. org. French-based group that provides medical assistance in the DRC.
Médecins Sans Frontières w msf.org. Provides emergency medical aid.

PARKS AND ENVIRONMENT

Africa Wildlife Foundation w awf.org. Partners with ICCN to create new wildlife refuges & promote sustainable land use.
Birdlife w birdlife.org. Provides assistance to ensure the conservation of bird species.
Dian Fossey Foundation w gorillafund. org. Dedicated to promoting the plight of the mountain gorilla.
Great Ape Survival Project w un-grasp.org. UN-sponsored organisation dedicated to protecting the traditional habitat of primates.

The Bushmeat Project w bushmeat.net.
Dedicated to raising awareness of bushmeat
hunting across central Africa.

Virunga National Park w virunga.org. English-
language webpage where individuals can purchase
supplies for the rangers of Virunga National Park
as well as donate to protect specific acreages in
the park.

Wildlife Conservation Society w wcs.org.
Partners with ICCN to create new wildlife refuges &
promote sustainable land use.

REFUGEES

International Medical Corps
w imcworldwide.org. Provides emergency
medical assistance to disaster- &
war-ravaged regions.

International Rescue Committee w rescue.
org. Provides short-term relief to refugees & assists
in long-term development projects.

Norwegian Refugee Council w nrc.no. Helps
protect internal refugees through food distribution,
legal assistance & shelter construction.

Première Urgence w premiere-urgence.
org. Multi-levelled aid organisation providing
emergency relief & post-disaster & post-war
development to affected regions.

Refugees International
w refugeesinternational.org. Provides assistance
to refugees, active in the DRC.

RELIGIOUS AFFILIATED GROUPS

Caritas w caritas.org. Catholic Church
organisation that provides long-term assistance to
developing regions.

**Catholic Agency for Overseas Development
(CAFOD)** w cafod.org.uk. Development wing of
the Catholic Church in England & Wales. Provides a
large variety of projects aimed at reducing poverty
& improving health.

Catholic Relief Services w crs.org. American
Catholic-based organisation that provides various
assistance to local communities.

Christian Aid w christian-aid.org.uk. Aid
agency of churches in the United Kingdom
& Ireland, working primarily through
local organisations.

Dan Church Aid w danchurchaid.org. Danish
organisation that provides long-term aid to reduce
poverty. Also active in landmine removal.

Development & Peace w devp.org. Caritas
Canada. Operates a wide variety of long-term
development projects.

Jesuit Refugee Service w jrs.net. Catholic-
based organisation that assists refugees.

Mennonite Central Committee w mcc.org.
Provides a multitude of assistance initiatives to
those affected by war in the DRC.

Norwegian Church Aid w nca.no. Promotes
human rights & development in co-operation with
local church organisations.

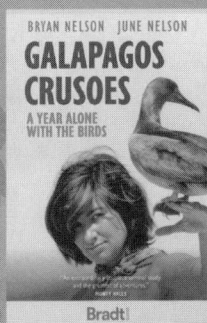

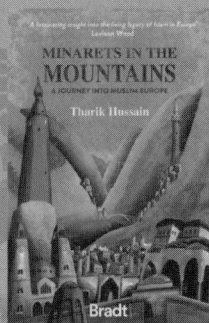

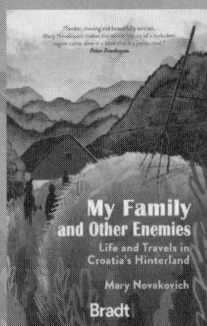

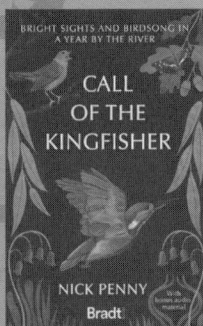

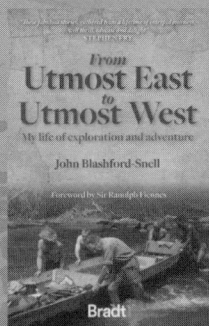

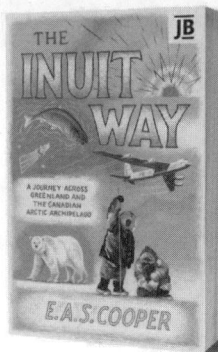

Part Two

THE GUIDE

3

Kinshasa

Rising out of the jungle, unlike any other sight in central Africa, are Kinshasa's towers, its lights, its chaos, its squalor. After spending weeks or months in the rainforests of the Congo, and arriving on to the streets of the capital, one can easily be overwhelmed – quiet evenings of darkness are overtaken by raucous clubs, cluttered evening markets, throngs of touts and beggars. Truly maddening traffic clogs the streets – from barely operating minibuses to convoys of tinted-window cars, thousands of people on the move in every direction, unknown faces of unknown people lurking in the corners of abandoned buildings, all living side by side in Kinshasa.

It is a cultural hub for the dreams and fortunes of all Congolese. With the DRC's high birth rate and an influx of refugees as war rages in the east, its numbers have swelled beyond any previous notions of size. Kinshasa is the world's most populous Francophone city: far surpassing Paris and Montreal combined. It is a city of deep divisions between rich and poor, of garish excess and poverty living as neighbours, with the privileged elites in their protected enclaves of a few international hotels, embassies and golf courses. It is more diverse and intimidating than any of Africa's largest cities. It is definitely not a place to miss – indeed, it is hard to visit anywhere in western or central DRC without passing through.

HISTORY

The place where Kinshasa now sits has always been a meeting point. Henry Morton Stanley opted to found the capital of the proposed Congo Free State on the eastern shores of what is now known as Malebo Pool, in between two well-known villages called Nshasa and Ntampo, in 1881. Stanley would name the new town Léopoldville, after his monarchic Belgian employer, yet the original inhabitants would continue to call the town Nshasa – and as the Lingala lingua franca began to dominate they referred to the town as Kinshasa, even though Belgian and European maps called it Léopoldville without exception. It became the stopping point for all expeditions further inland, as well as outward to the sea, with a railway completed to Matadi in 1898 to circumvent the Inga Falls that blocked the navigation of ships further upriver from the Atlantic. As the Congo rubber disaster unfolded (page 24), more of the disenfranchised were either forced to come to Léopoldville, or fled to its outskirts; the city would grow rapidly from local migrants, the European population brought in to administer the government infrastructure, and the missionaries and businessmen who needed a stopping point before heading upriver on their steamboats. Its upmarket establishments grew, with large mansions dotting the riverside, quiet tree-lined boulevards, and restaurants catering to the European diaspora.

Meanwhile Kinshasa's local neighbourhoods continued to balloon, and in those neighbourhoods the first glimmerings of independence appeared when

Joseph Kasa-Vubu and his ABAKO party were voted in as leaders of a suburb. His speeches incited riots, and those riots would pave the way for early independence from Belgium.

Joseph-Désiré Mobutu officially renamed Léopoldville as Kinshasa in 1966, and the nation as Zaire in 1971, and he began building a stronger infrastructure for the capital. With government-sponsored housing projects, unprecedented levels of public transport, and rapid expansion into the jungle, Kinshasa began to grow at an exponential rate throughout the 1970s. The tree-lined boulevards still survived, though, catering to the upper crust of Europeans doing business in Zaire, the new friends of Mobutu, and the emerging political elite of Africa. The high-class lifestyle was easy to find, yet out of reach for most of Kinshasa's population.

In the city's lower-class outskirts, though, its culture would make its mark in music; the first rumblings and beats of *musique Zaïroise* took over first the city, then central Africa, then the wider Francophone world. As gatherings were permitted, and public music systems became more available, so the dancers and singers of Zaire came to Kinshasa to find their fortunes. Nights became busy with music and dancing across the capital.

Local families prospered along with the economy in Kinshasa throughout Mobutu's reign, though the city was still highly dependent on jobs from the public service. Once it was announced that multi-party elections were to occur, the capital took a step back in history and descended again into rioting. Many were killed as the Forces Armées Zaïroises harshly put down the dissent. Corruption emerged as a serious threat to peace across the city. Soon Mobutu's government crumbled, and the rebel army from the east arrived, sending around another bout of looting, and open combat between soldiers loyal to the old Zaire and those loyal to Laurent Kabila. The last vestiges of Zaire evaporated quickly. Rattled by a half-decade of upheaval, the capital would remain modestly quiet until the outbreak of the Second Congo War.

As 1998 rolled around and Kabila's grip on power was in trouble, the capital was surrounded by his soldiers. Combat erupted on multiple fronts, with Rwandan and Ugandan troops marching from the east; Kinshasa was a genuinely dangerous place. Angolan, Namibian and Zimbabwean soldiers fought openly with the Rwandan and Ugandan armies; Chad also sent troops to reinforce the capital. Evacuations of Europeans from the city, as well as the few Congolese lucky enough to tag along, were common during this period of fighting. Without the intervention of outside forces, the capital would have been lost entirely to the whims of Rwanda's and Uganda's governments.

With the **Lusaka Peace Accord** in place, in theory at least, by 1999, armies slowly began withdrawing from around Kinshasa. Continued fighting had sent even more displaced people into the city searching for food and medicine; more than ever, it had become a refuge for the downtrodden, a place of sparkling towers on the river where those who had lost all they had to a conflict in the jungle might be able to begin a new life.

Yet turbulence continued. Laurent Kabila's assassination in 2001 sent more shockwaves throughout the city. Riots continued, although they were minor compared with the open chaos of the 1990s.

United Nations and aid agencies arrived in droves, transforming the city and injecting large amounts of cash into the capital. Other businesses arrived as well, as the transitional government signalled it would be fair to foreign investors. Supermarkets, nightclubs and restaurants all began to make new appearances in the districts across the capital.

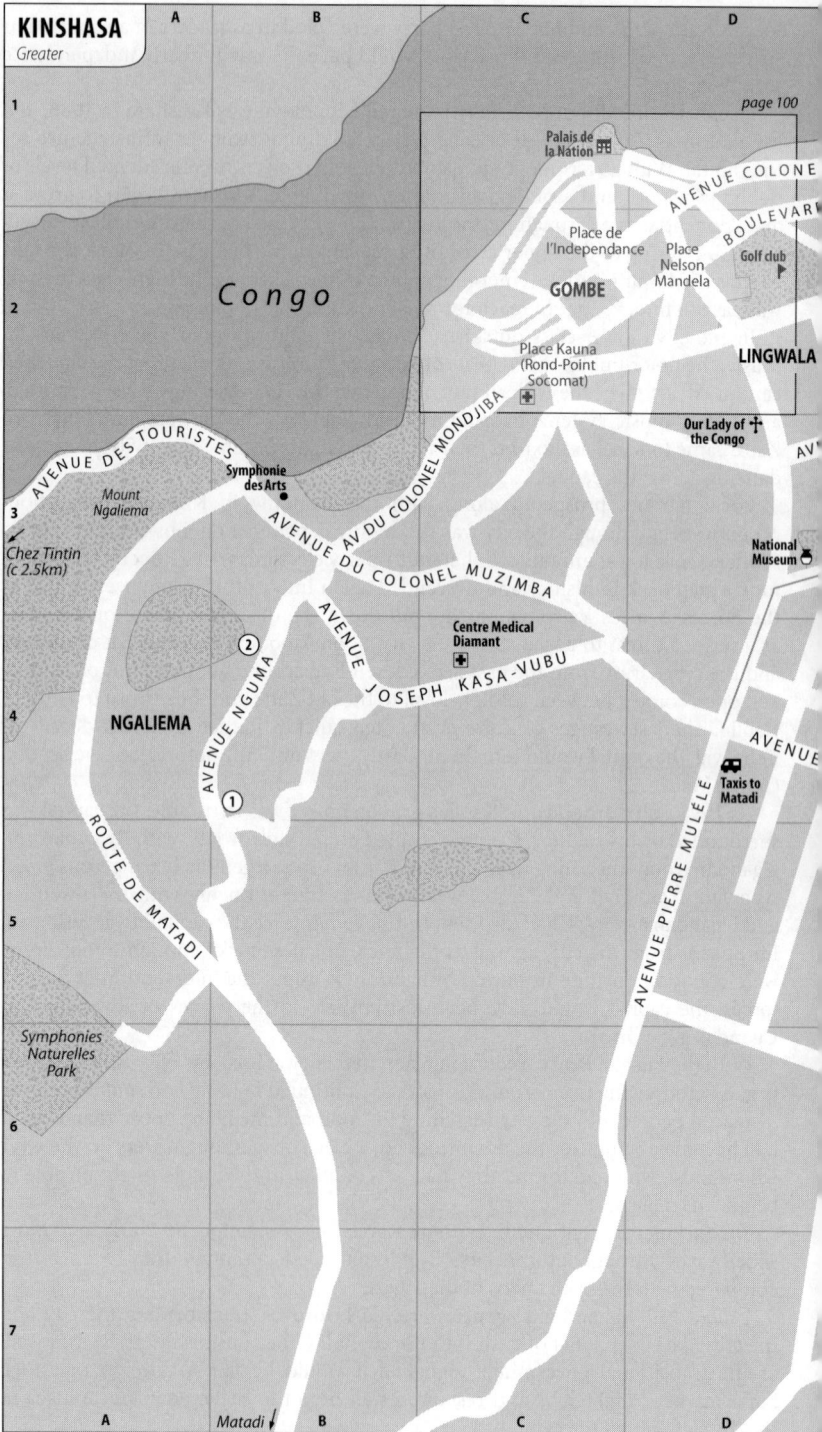

KINSHASA
Greater

Congo

AVENUE DES TOURISTES

Mount Ngaliema

Chez Tintin (c 2.5km)

Symphonie des Arts

AVENUE DU COLONEL MONDJIBA

AV DU COLONEL MUZIMBA

AVENUE DU COLONEL MUZIMBA

AVENUE NGUMA

AVENUE JOSEPH KASA-VUBU

Centre Medical Diamant

NGALIEMA

ROUTE DE MATADI

Symphonies Naturelles Park

Palais de la Nation

AVENUE COLONE

BOULEVAR

Place de l'Independance

Place Nelson Mandela

Golf club

GOMBE

LINGWALA

Place Kauna (Rond-Point Socomat)

Our Lady of the Congo

AV

National Museum

AVENUE

Taxis to Matadi

AVENUE PIERRE MULÉLÉ

Matadi

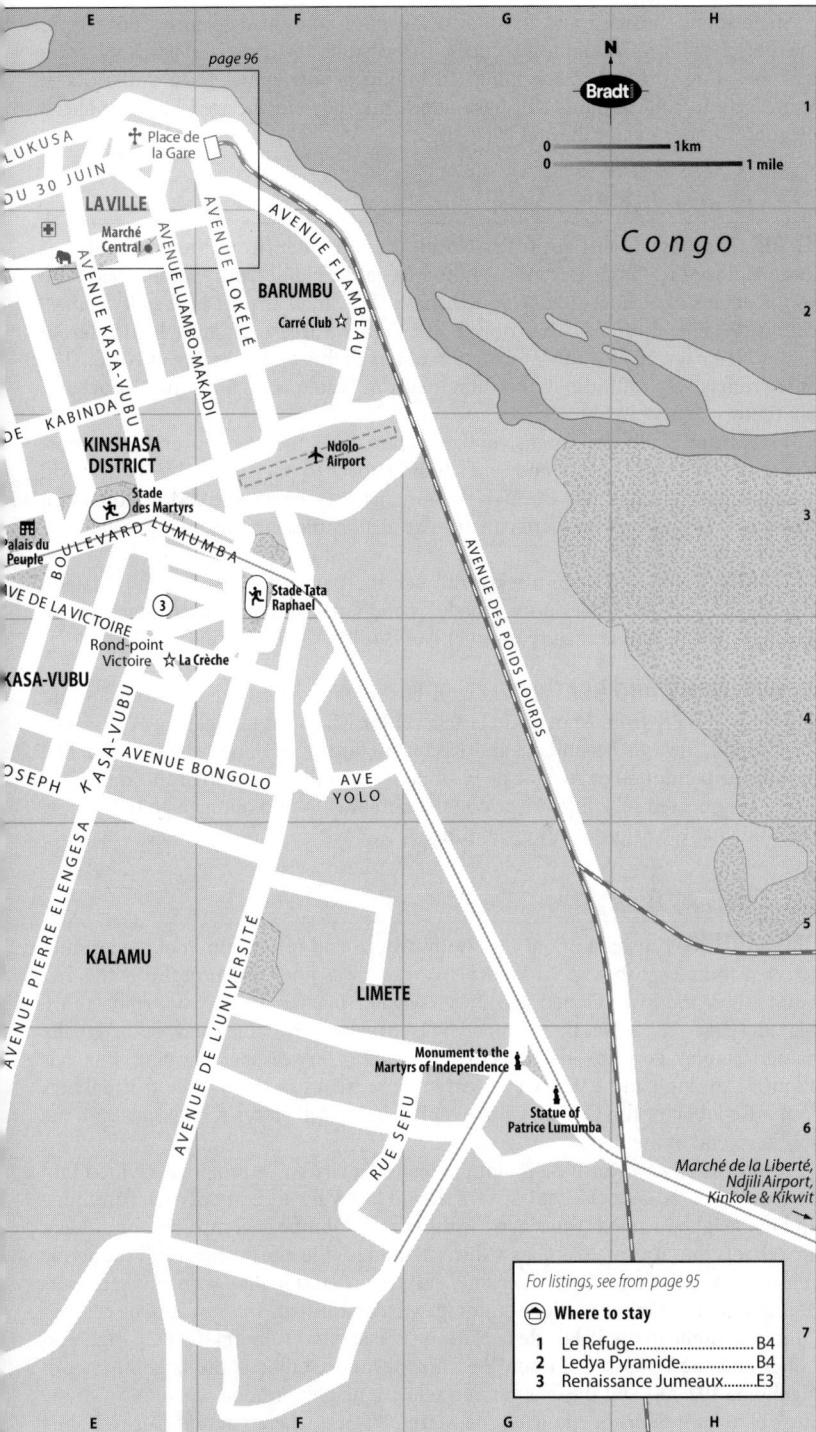

N

Bradt

1

page 96

LUKUSA

† Place de la Gare

DU 30 JUIN

LA VILLE

Marché Central

AVENUE FLAMBEAU

AVENUE LUAMBO-MAKADI

AVENUE LOKELE

Congo

2

AVENUE KASA-VUBU

BARUMBU

Carré Club ☆

DE KABINDA

KINSHASA DISTRICT

✈ Ndolo Airport

Stade des Martyrs

3

Palais du Peuple

BOULEVARD LUMUMBA

AVENUE DES POIDS LOURDS

VE DE LA VICTOIRE

③

Stade Tata Raphael

KASA-VUBU

Rond-point Victoire ☆ La Crèche

4

OSEPH

KASA-VUBU

AVENUE BONGOLO

AVE YOLO

AVENUE PIERRE ELENGESA

5

KALAMU

AVENUE DE L'UNIVERSITÉ

LIMETE

Monument to the Martyrs of Independence

RUE SEFU

Statue of Patrice Lumumba

6

Marché de la Liberté, Ndjili Airport, Kinkole & Kikwit

Kinshasa   HISTORY

3

For listings, see from page 95

⌂ **Where to stay**

1   Le Refuge..............................B4
2   Ledya Pyramide....................B4
3   Renaissance Jumeaux........E3

7

Since then, Kinshasa and its population have continued to grow. Poverty in the periphery has brought insecurity throughout the city – everything from pickpocketing, through kidnapping (including of foreigners) to violent riots. It is not safe to walk around Kinshasa after dark, beyond the well-lit and policed neighbourhoods of Gombe and Ngaliema.

GETTING THERE AND AWAY

BY AIR Kinshasa's main airport is Ndjili, located 30km from the city centre. If there is heavy traffic, it can take 2 hours to get to Ndjili from Gombe. See page 56 for details of airlines that serve Kinshasa. The small airport in the city centre, Ndolo [93 F3], these days has only a few flights a week, all short-haul internal routes. See page 56 also for information about flights and ticketing at Ndjili. The only reliable way to find out about flights from Ndolo is to go to the airport and ask there.

Taxis from Ndjili are expensive, like airport taxis the world over. The airport is a long way from the city and you should expect to pay about US$50. You will probably get a cheaper fare through the Yango app (see opposite). Most hotels of a reasonable (or higher) standard can arrange airport pick-ups for their guests.

BY TRAIN There is a once-weekly rail service between Kinshasa and Matadi; enquire at the railway station for schedules and fares, and buy tickets there too. In Kinshasa, the station is at the eastern end of Boulevard du 30 Juin [97 G3].

BY BUS, TRUCK AND BOAT Trucks and buses leave intermittently from around Kinshasa, usually from Marché de la Liberté for Kikwit or in Ngaliema commune for Matadi. Towards Mbandaka and Kisangani, at the section of the port reached by Avenue Bandundu or Avenue de la Douane, steamers occasionally head upriver. There are no fixed schedules or prices; the only way to find out is to go to the port and ask what is feasible at any given time.

GETTING AROUND

ORIENTATION Kinshasa lies at the southwestern end of Malebo Pool (sometimes referred to in English with its French word order as Pool Malebo); this is the first point where the River Congo becomes navigable upstream, after the rapids above Matadi (page 116). It was first mapped by Henry Morton Stanley and was originally named Stanley Pool. Its extent varies depending on seasonal flooding, but it is about 35km long and 23km wide, with a large island in the middle that belongs to the Republic of the Congo, whose capital Brazzaville faces Kinshasa across the southern end of the Pool.

Administratively, Kinshasa is simultaneously a city and a province, divided into 24 *communes*, or districts. Taxi drivers should know the location of each commune and the neighbourhoods (*quartiers*) within them. **Gombe** encompasses the affluent area that is the city's main embassy district and La Ville, the business and economic centre of the city – crowded by day and nearly deserted at night – with its skyscrapers dominating the skyline as older buildings are demolished. The residential sector of Gombe is home to the **Palais de la Nation** (Presidential Palace) [100 D2], high-end hotels and the Botanical Garden [96 D7]. Beyond Gombe is the large district of **Ngaliema** [92 A4] and the even more exclusive neighbourhood where most of the city's elite have their townhouses; the Marble Palace, where Laurent-Désiré Kabila was assassinated, is in the Ma Campagne neighbourhood of Ngaliema. Directly south of La Ville is Kasa-Vubu district and the **Rond-Point Victoire** [93 E4], sometimes called **La Cité**, a crowded roundabout that is the African centre of Kinshasa – the city's legendary music scene emanates from here. The national Parliament, the Palais du Peuple [93 E3], and the two big stadia, Stade des Martyrs [93 E3] and Stade Tata Raphaël [93 F3], are in Kalamu district. North is the district called 'Kinshasa' and the city's Central Market (Marché Central) [97 E7]. Continuing eastwards along the river, through the industrial district of Limete, one reaches **Ndjili Airport** and then the resorts on the Malebo Pool.

The city has two main thoroughfares. **Boulevard du 30 Juin**, an eight-lane highway through the city, runs parallel to the River Congo and is the largest street in the city. Some dare call it the Champs-Elysées of Africa. It extends from **'Beach Ngobila'** [97 H2], where boats and ferries pick up and drop off passengers to Brazzaville, and the railway station [97 G3], and continues through the upmarket Gombe district. Perpendicular to its middlepoint is **Avenue Joseph Kasa-Vubu**.

PUBLIC TRANSPORT Transco **buses** and shared taxis go up and down Avenue Joseph Kasa-Vubu to La Ville, as well as along Kinshasa's main suburban roads. Finding these vehicles in the daytime around Gombe or La Ville is relatively straightforward, but at night, especially if you are white, call a private **taxi**. A reliable firm with app-based booking is **Jeffery Taxi** (m 081 888 7777; w taxi.jefferytravels. com). There is also an Uber-type app called **Yango** (search for it on your phone or consult w yango.com), available only in Kinshasa. They offer rides in cars and on motorbikes; payment can be made only in cash to the driver. In case of difficulty, go into any reasonable-looking hotel and ask them to call a taxi for you.

Self-drive **car hire** is available in Kinshasa, although most car-hire companies rent their vehicles with their own drivers.

Avis Airport & Bd 30 de Juin; w avis.com
Congo Travel & Tours
w congotravelandtours.com

Kinshasa Car Rental
w kinshasa-car-rental.com

LOCAL TOUR OPERATORS

The DRC's official tourist office, the **Office National du Tourisme** (ONT) [96 B3], has its head office in Gombe; see page 53 for details. **Congo Travel and Tours** (w congotravelandtours.com) offers various Kinshasa city tours, day trips on the river and excursions to nearby attractions.

⌂ WHERE TO STAY

Kinshasa isn't the place to save money on accommodation. There isn't anything cheap in the city worth recommending, and even the lower-end places tend to be lacking in certain things – such as reliable electricity or running water – that the same money would get a traveller elsewhere in the country.

EXCLUSIVE There are several hotels that compete for the international elite in Kinshasa – they can all be booked online, either via their own websites or through the usual international booking portals. All hotels in this category accept credit card payment &, as standard, all guest rooms have 24hr electricity & water, en-suite bathrooms, AC, free Wi-Fi, complimentary mineral water & coffee/tea-making facilities, & TV with a range of international channels. They can provide transfers

KINSHASA
City centre

N

Bradt

| 0 | 250m |
| 0 | 250yds |

Congo

Station for boats upriver •

Congo Trade Centre

AVENUE DE LA DOUANE

☆ Chacha

Chez Ntemba ☆

AVENUE BANDUNDU

ℹ Office National du Tourisme

AVENUE DE LA GECAMINES Rond-Point AVENUE DE LA PAIX
Forescom

AVENUE DU COLONEL LUKUSA

AVENUE DU PORT

South Africa

AVENUE NGONGO LUTETE

AVENUE MONGALA

8

Centre Medical Diamant ✚

Avis 🚗

BOULEVARD DE 30 JUIN

AVENUE DU MARCHÉ

AVENUE DE L'EQUATEUR

AVENUE

RUE MPOLO

AVENUE WANGATA

AVENUE JOSEPH KASA-VUBU

Place du Marché

AVENUE DU HAUT CONGO

AVENUE DU COMMERCE

For listings, see from page 95

🛏 **Where to stay**

1	Belle Vie	F5
2	Memling	E4
3	Procure Sainte-Anne	F3

✖ **Where to eat and drink**

4	Al Dar	E4
5	Hunga Busta	E3, F4
6	La Patisserie Nouvelle	E3
7	Le Caf' Conc'.	E3
8	Le Chantilly	A4
9	NTV	F6

Kinshasa ✚ General Hospital

Botanical Garden

🐾 Zoo

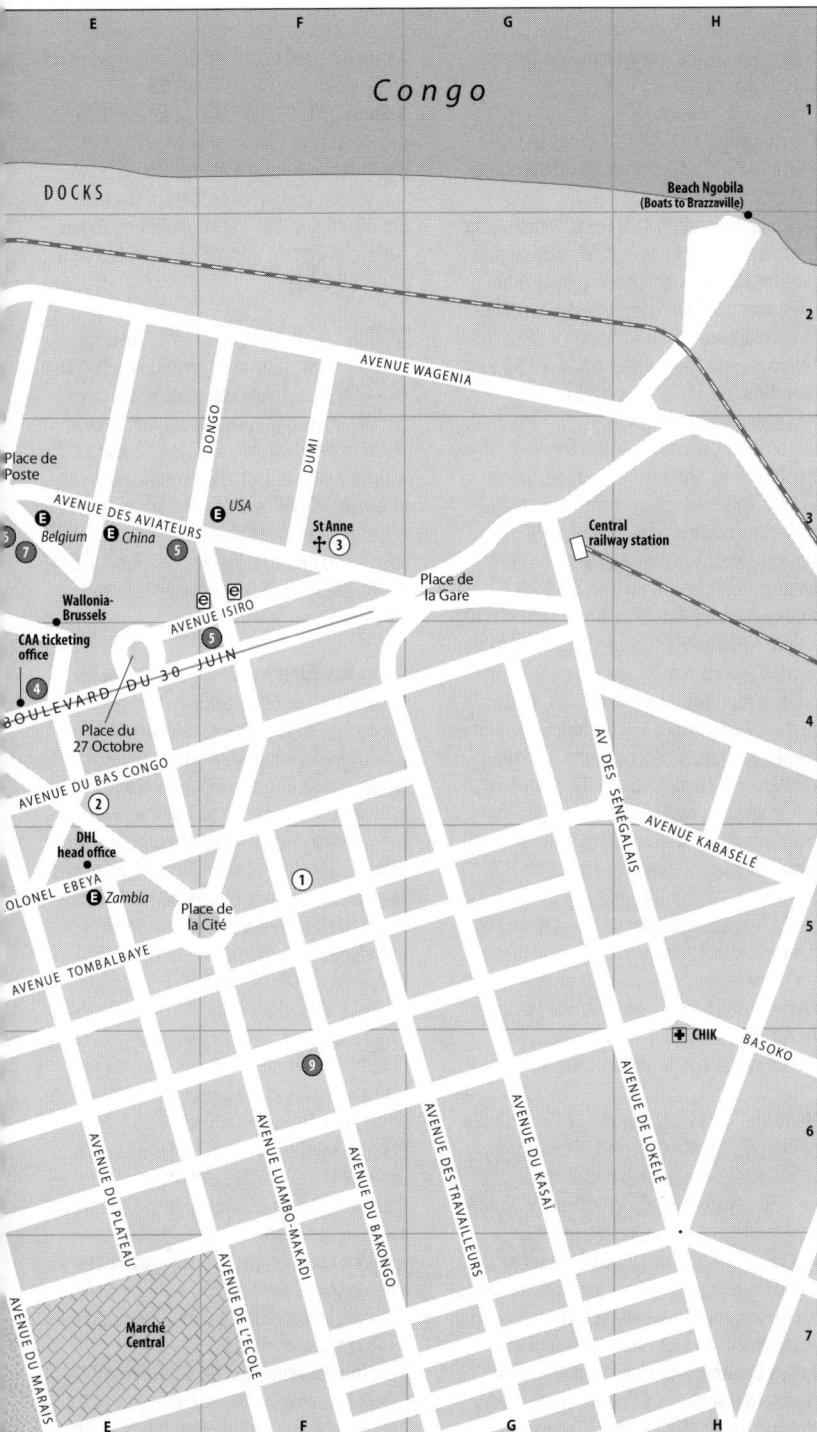

Congo

DOCKS

Beach Ngobila
(Boats to Brazzaville)

AVENUE WAGENIA

DONGO

DUMI

Place de
Poste

AVENUE DES AVIATEURS

E Belgium

E China

E USA

St Anne
✝ ③

Central
railway station

Place de
la Gare

**Wallonia-
Brussels**

e **e**

AVENUE ISIRO

**CAA ticketing
office**

BOULEVARD DU 30 JUIN

Place du
27 Octobre

AV DES SÉNÉGALAIS

AVENUE KABASÉLÉ

AVENUE DU BAS CONGO

②

**DHL
head office**

OLONEL EBEYA **E** Zambia

Place de
la Cité

①

AVENUE TOMBALBAYE

⑨

CHIK

BASOKO

AVENUE DU PLATEAU

AVENUE LUAMBO-MAKADI

AVENUE DU BAKONGO

AVENUE DES TRAVAILLEURS

AVENUE DU KASAI

AVENUE DE LOKÉLÉ

AVENUE DE L'ECOLE

AVENUE DU MARAIS

**Marché
Central**

to & from Ndjili Airport, book safe taxis to get around Kinshasa, & arrange transport for trips outside the city.

Fleuve Congo [100 A4] (207 rooms, 30 suites) Bd Col Tsatshi 119, Gombe; m 080 850 0600, 081 509 0153; w fleuvecongohotel.com. 22-storey skyscraper overlooking River Congo, with beautiful grounds sloping down to river. Full-sized outdoor pool, fitness centre, conference facilities, ATMs, 3 restaurants (including teppan-yaki), bars, lifts, tennis court, hot tub. All rooms with well-equipped bathroom, safe, desk, minibar & iron. **$$$$$**
Memling [97 E4] (180 rooms) 5 Av de la République du Tchad, Gombe; m 081 555 7700, 099 603 7000; e info@memling.net; w memling. net. Landmark high-rise in city centre, opened in 1937. Full-sized outdoor pool, fitness centre, conference facilities, 3 restaurants, bars, lifts, shopping area. All rooms with well-equipped bathroom, safe, desk & minibar. **$$$$$**
Pullman Grand Hôtel Kinshasa [100 B5] (190 rooms) 4 Av Batetela, Gombe; m 085 800 0111; e h9635@accor.com; w accor.com. Full-size outdoor pool, gym, spa, tennis courts, secure parking, 3 restaurants, bars, nightclub. Good Wi-Fi throughout; lifts, securely operated with key card. Extensive conference facilities; CAA ticket office; shopping mall including ATMs, pharmacy & mobile-provider agencies. Large, well-equipped rooms with safe, fridge & hairdryer. **$$$$$**

EXPENSIVE Hotels in this category are a bit more affordable than the elite hotels at the top of the range & their smaller size means they have a less impersonal feel to them. Standard facilities include AC throughout, credit card payments, swimming pools & on-site restaurants.

Belle Vie [97 F5] (72 rooms) 16 Av Tombalbaye, La Ville; m 097 605 0000, 081 544 3636; e hotelbelleviekinshasa@hotmail.com; w belleviehotel.com; f Hotel Belle Vie. Outdoor pool, garden, fitness centre, meeting room, restaurant with Indian, Chinese & European menus, bar, lift. All rooms en suite with free Wi-Fi, sat TV, safe, coffee/tea-making facilities. 2 smaller hotels also under same management. **$$$$**
Ledya Pyramide [92 B4] (21 rooms) 35 Av Nguma, Ngaliema; m 082 000 5454; f Ledya Pyramide Hotel. In the quiet Ma Campagne

neighbourhood; secure parking; pool, garden, terrace bar, good restaurant. Good-sized rooms, all en suite with fridge & sat TV. **$$$$**
Sultani [101 G3] (57 rooms, 8 suites) 30 Av de la Justice, Gombe; m 089 700 0113, 081 896 7000; w sultanihotel.com. Fitness centre, spa, terrace, conference facilities, restaurant, bar, lift. All rooms en suite with well-equipped bathroom, TV, safe, minibar & iron. Dbls **$$$$**, suites **$$$$$**

MID-RANGE AND THRIFTY There is nowhere really cheap to stay in Kinshasa. If you are on a tight budget, your best strategy is to move on somewhere else as soon as you can. Many of the more affordable guesthouses are popular with international staff based in Kinshasa, & can be persistently full as their rooms are rented into perpetuity. Call ahead of your arrival, or expect to spend some time hopping between places to find a room on short notice. Most hotels in this range require payment in cash.

Sunny Day Guest House [101 F3] (13 rooms) Av Comité Urbain 28/30 (ex-Colonel Vangu), Gombe; m 082 780 9686; e alaints@yahoo. it; w sunnyday-kinshasa.com. High-end studios geared towards long-term residents; discount for extended stay. English-speaking owner; online booking; 24hr electricity; Wi-Fi throughout. Peaceful tropical garden; short walk to riverbank. All studios have nice en-suite shower room, AC, sat TV, terrace, dining area & fully equipped kitchen. **$$$**
Le Refuge [92 B4] (10 rooms) Av Trèfle 4, Ma Campagne; m 081 010 0429; f Le Refuge. An affordable option by Kinshasa standards, with good-sized pool, garden, communal seated area with TV, shared covered terrace. Studio flats have en-suite bathroom, kitchenette, AC; suites also have separate sitting room. Studio flats **$$**, suites **$$$**
Procure Sainte-Anne [97 F3] (10 rooms) Av Dumi 1, La Ville; m 099 233 0739. The diocese of the historic St Anne's Church (built in 1903) has a few rooms available for visitors to the parish, including foreigners passing through. Peaceful haven in central Kinshasa. Small, simple rooms with basic en-suite facilities; small refectory where meals can be ordered. **$$**
Renaissance Jumeaux [93 E3] (10 rooms) Av Dibaya 2, Kalamu; m 081 492 8153, 089 637 7713; e jumeauxdistribution@yahoo.fr; f Hôtel

Restaurant Renaissance Jumeaux. Near Rond-Point Victoire; also has small restaurant. Rooms en suite with AC, TV, 24hr water; suite has kitchenette with fridge. **$**

✕ WHERE TO EAT AND DRINK

EXPENSIVE AND HIGH-END The upper crust is well taken care of in Kinshasa; in addition to the establishments listed below, all in Gombe district, the restaurants in the exclusive hotels (page 95) are usually excellent & in a similar price range.

Le Caf' Conc' [97 E3] 13 Av de la Nation; m 081 899 3090, 084 130 0116; w cafconc.com; ⏲ 07.00–19.30 Mon–Sat. French haute cuisine in city centre; fish, seafood, meat; renowned wine cellar, all French; sushi & oyster bar; private dining room. **$$$$**
Le Cercle Gourmand [101 H4] Av de Cercle 414; m 084 396 4402; e info@cercledekinshasa. com; w cercledekinshasa.com; ⏲ noon–14.00 & 19.00–21.30 Tue–Fri, 10.00–21.30 Sat. French haute cuisine within Kinshasa's golf club, catering to the city's elite. Interior decorated by the Symphonie des Arts. **$$$$**
Le Mandarin [101 H3] Bd du 30 Juin; m 081 884 1716; ⏲ noon–14.30 & 19.00–22.30 Tue–Sun. Chinese restaurant occupying the top floor of the INSS Bldg, with great views & secure parking, an extensive wine list & several set menus. All-you-can-eat lunch buffet on Wed & Sat; teppan-yaki grill; lengthy à la carte menu. **$$$**

MID-RANGE Every hotel of a decent size has some sort of restaurant, & they tend to offer food of similar quality to the rooms – they aren't a bad option if you are feeling less than adventurous & don't want to negotiate a taxi ride across town. Kinshasa's signature dish is *poulet mayo*, chicken in a spicy marinade, grilled & served with mayonnaise &, of course, *frites*.

Hunga Busta [97 E3 & F4] Av des Aviateurs & Bd du 30 Juin; m 081 514 1400; ⚑ Hunga Busta; ⏲ 08.00–22.00 Sun–Thu, 08.00–23.00 Fri–Sat. Outlets opposite the US Embassy & in Rosons Tower mall. Offers a slightly bewildering mixture of cuisines: grilled & fried chicken, meat & fish dishes, pasta & pizza, burgers & Lebanese snacks, including vegetarian options. Burger, shawarma, etc **$**, main meals **$$**

Quick Poulet Chez Beki [101 F6] Av des Forces Armées 25; m 081 885 3472, 099 824 8930; w quickpoulet.com; ⏲ noon–22.00 Mon–Thu, noon–23.00 Fri–Sun. Nicely decorated, great atmosphere, international without losing its Congolese roots. Offers sandwiches (**$**), grilled meat (inc goat) & chicken, fish & *cossa-cossa*, pizza. **$$**

BUDGET The best options for budget food in Kinshasa are in one of the city's many patisseries or the Indian & Lebanese restaurants. As ever, the Indian restaurants are a good option for vegetarians & vegans.

La Patisserie Nouvelle [97 E3 & 100 B7] Av de L'Equateur 343 & Av Col Mondjiba; m 081 998 9000, 081 422 6640; w patisserienouvelle. com; ⏲ daily, see website for hours. High-quality Belgian-style bakery; branches in Gombe & UTEX. Sells bakery goods, obviously, but also serves excellent b/fasts, soups, sandwiches, ice cream & main meals, including vegetarian options. **$$**
Al Dar [97 E4] Bd du 30 Juin; m 081 995 7888; ⏲ 07.30–22.00 daily. Popular Lebanese restaurant in the city centre, famous for its shawarma; also serves burgers, sandwiches & salads. Generous portions, fast service. **$**
Galito's [101 G6] Av de la Gombe 31; m 082 999 9998; ⚑ Galito's Kinshasa. South African chain, famous for its marinaded flame-grilled chicken. Fast service, safe, gets very busy at peak times. Various other outlets throughout Kinshasa, including Bandal, Sendwe & Bon Marché neighbourhoods. **$**
Le Chantilly [96 A4] 707 Av Colonel Lukusa, Gombe; m 081 710 8500, 081 710 8600; ⚑ Chantilly Kinshasa; ⏲ 07.00–18.00 Mon–Sat, 07.00–15.00 Sun. B/fasts, hot & cold filled baguettes, salads, main courses & ice cream; bakery goods, personalised cakes to order. Seating with AC, parking area. **$**
NTV [97 F6] Av Bakongo, Bon-Marché; m 082 700 0299; ⚑ Noor Taj Village. A local mini-chain, with restaurants in Boma, Muanda & Kinshasa. Indian, Congolese & international menu, including fish & tandoori; set meal offers vary throughout the week; Sunday b/fast specials. **$**

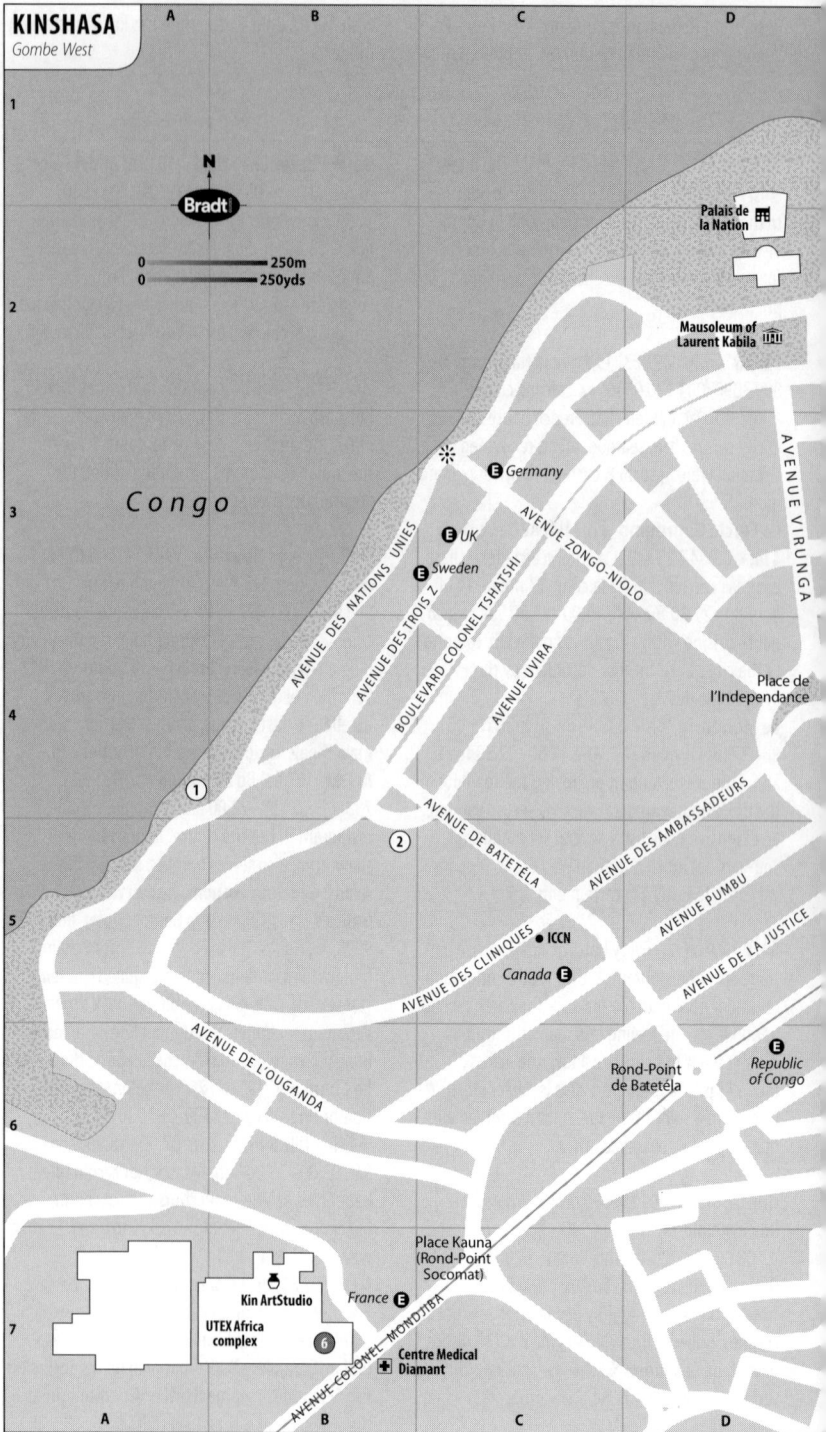

KINSHASA
Gombe West

N

Bradt

0   250m
0   250yds

Congo

Palais de
la Nation

Mausoleum of
Laurent Kabila

AVENUE VIRUNGA

Germany

AVENUE ZONGO-NIOLO

UK

AVENUE DES TROIS Z.

Sweden

BOULEVARD COLONEL TSHATSHI

AVENUE UVIRA

AVENUE DES NATIONS UNIES

Place de
l'Independance

①

AVENUE DE BATETÉLA

②

AVENUE DES AMBASSADEURS

AVENUE PUMBU

AVENUE DES CLINIQUES

● ICCN

Canada

AVENUE DE LA JUSTICE

AVENUE DE L'OUGANDA

Rond-Point
de Batetéla

Republic
of Congo

Place Kauna
(Rond-Point
Socomat)

Kin ArtStudio

France

UTEX Africa
complex

⑥

AVENUE COLONEL MONDJIBA

Centre Medical
Diamant

100

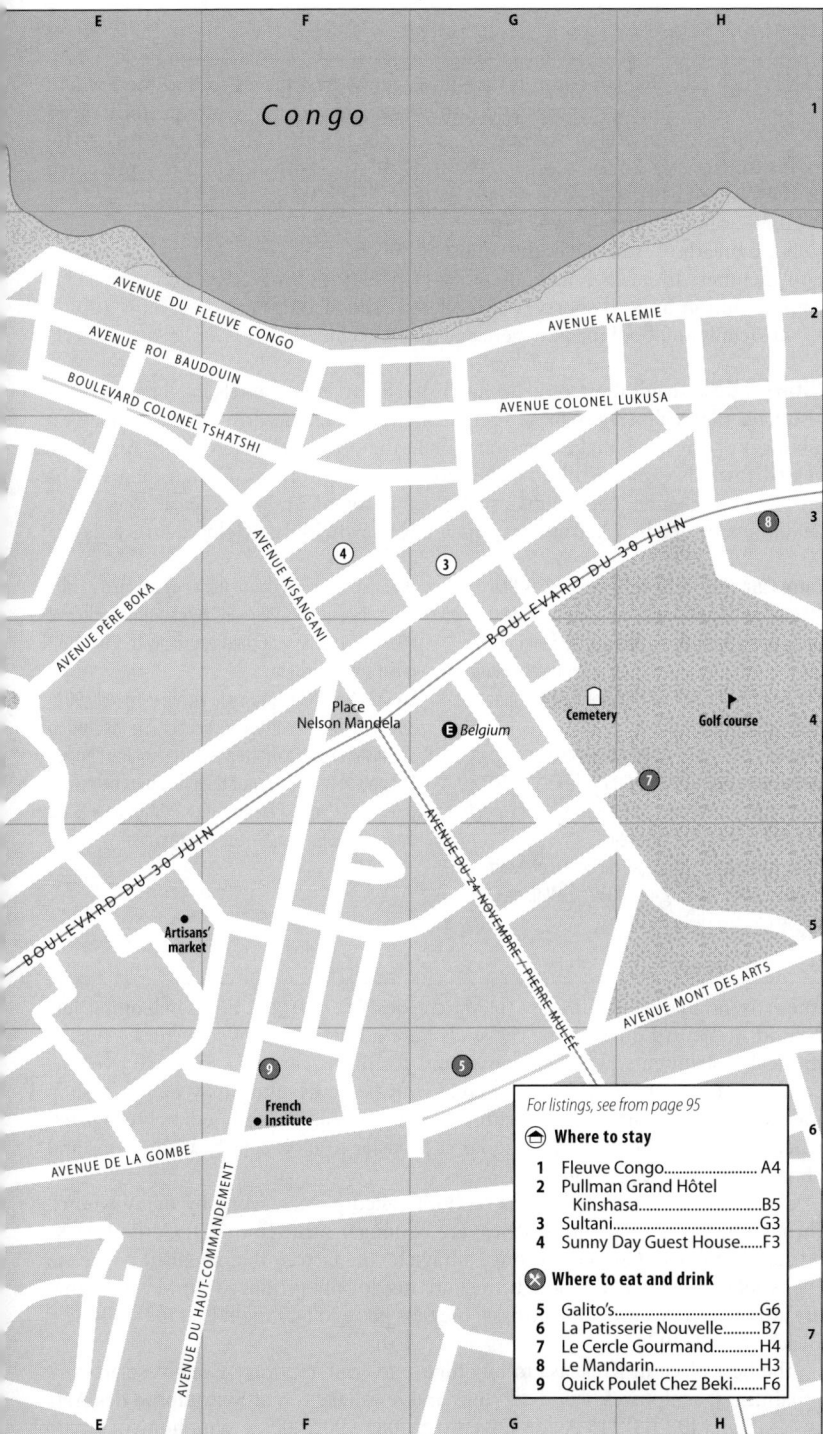

Congo

AVENUE DU FLEUVE CONGO

AVENUE ROI BAUDOUIN

BOULEVARD COLONEL TSHATSHI

AVENUE KALEMIE

AVENUE COLONEL LUKUSA

AVENUE KISANGANI

AVENUE PÈRE BOKA

BOULEVARD DU 30 JUIN

④

③

⑧

Place
Nelson Mandela

🅑 Belgium

☐ Cemetery

▶ Golf course

⑦

BOULEVARD DU 30 JUIN

AVENUE DU 24 NOVEMBRE–PIERRE MULELE

Artisans'
market

AVENUE MONT DES ARTS

⑨

French
• Institute

⑤

AVENUE DE LA GOMBE

AVENUE DU HAUT-COMMANDEMENT

For listings, see from page 95

🛏 **Where to stay**

1	Fleuve Congo	A4
2	Pullman Grand Hôtel Kinshasa	B5
3	Sultani	G3
4	Sunny Day Guest House	F3

❌ **Where to eat and drink**

5	Galito's	G6
6	La Patisserie Nouvelle	B7
7	Le Cercle Gourmand	H4
8	Le Mandarin	H3
9	Quick Poulet Chez Beki	F6

The French and Belgian cultural institutes are the best places to find literary and musical events, film screenings and, sometimes, dance and theatre performances. The French Institute is at Avenue de la Gombe 33 [101 F6] (m 085 107 4413; w institutfrancais-kinshasa.org; ⏰ 08.30–17.30 Tue–Sat); Belgium is represented by the Wallonia-Brussels delegation at Avenue de la Nation 206 [97 E3] (m 099 801 0800; w wallonie-bruxelles-rdc.org).

For a breath of fresh air in the centre of the city, the Cercle de Kinshasa admits non-members to its 18-hole golf course [101 H4], putting green and tennis clay courts. Tuition in both sports is also offered. The facilities are open daily, 07.00–17.00; details and booking at w cercledekinshasa.com.

NIGHTCLUBS In addition to the venues listed below, many hotels in all price ranges also have nightclubs. They make their money from selling drinks, so if you are on a budget of any kind, make sure you look at the prices before ordering. Anywhere geared towards expats is likely to be busy with sex workers; foreign men will be viewed as fair game. Nightclubs usually open around 21.00 (earlier at weekends), get quite crowded by 23.00 and stay open until dawn. Most are closed on Sundays.

Carré Club [93 F2] Av de Flambeau 230, Bon-Marché; m 081 990 3099; w carreclub.com. Large venue with disco, terraces, VIP rooms. Wide range of music genres including Congolese music, 3 DJ booths, light show; restaurant with Congolese, Indian & fast-food options.

Chacha [96 D3] Av du Port 4 (Forescom roundabout); m 097 386 0001; ⑤ Chacha Bar. Rooftop club & terrace. Well-known DJs at w/ends; free food buffet at some events.

Chez Ntemba [96 C3] Av du Port (Forescom roundabout); m 082 441 4042; ⑤ Village Chez Ntemba. Crowded dance floor any evening of the week, live music at w/ends & sometimes other evenings (admission charge, usually US$10–20), great sound system.

La Crèche [93 E4] Pl de la Victoire; m 099 993 3003; ⏰ from noon daily. A venerable institution of Kinshasa's on a rooftop terrace – many famous Congolese musicians got their first gigs here; live music at w/ends. Plastic chairs, Primus beer & an unpretentious, mostly Congolese crowd.

SHOPPING

The artisans' market in Kinshasa (le Marché des Valeurs) [101 E5] is in Gombe, just behind Boulevard du 30 Juin. The stalls have a huge range of souvenirs – masks, musical instruments, wooden statues and furniture, carpets – from all over the country. Those who feel uncomfortable with fierce haggling may prefer to shop for their souvenirs in the malls within the Pullman and Memling hotels (page 98) where, although the prices are higher, it is easier to look calmly at the items and choose what you really want.

The brightly patterned lengths of cloth called *pagnes*, worn by many women throughout West and central Africa, are no longer made in the DRC; the UTEX-Africa complex in Gombe was once a huge textile factory that supplied pagnes to the whole country. Even though they are not locally produced, however, pagnes are attractive souvenirs. In Kinshasa, the best place to buy them is at the stalls near Beach Ngobila [97 H2].

The best place in Kinshasa to buy high-end contemporary Congolese artwork – paintings, sculptures, wood carvings and jewellery – is at **Symphonie des Arts** in Ngaliema [92 B3] (15 Av de L'Avenir; m 081 990 1000; e symphoniedesarts@

gmail.com; **f** Kinshasa Symphonie des Arts; ⊕ 08.00–18.00 Mon–Sat). The goal of its founder, Christa Göpfert, is to support and promote Congolese artists; her gallery displays and sells their work. The gallery is set in a wonderful tropical garden that you can wander around, even if you cannot afford to buy any of the artworks on sale.

Those interested in contemporary African art may also like to visit **Kin ArtStudio** [100 B7] (Av Colonel Mondjiba 372, Ngaliema; **w** congobiennale. art; ◙ Kinartstudio). This non-profit organisation brings together emerging Congolese artists, building their capacity and promoting their work. Its space within the UTEX-Africa complex houses several studios and workshops, a library and a café-bistro.

There are many Western-style supermarkets in Kinshasa. They sell a range of imported foodstuffs, including dairy products, wines and spirits. Naturally they are more expensive than buying food in a market but, if you have been in the rainforest for a few weeks (or months), you will probably welcome the chance of a taste of home. They are also air conditioned!

OTHER PRACTICALITIES

There are **ATMs** everywhere in the city. Use an ATM inside a bank, where possible, and do not withdraw cash after dark. For money transfers, **Western Union** has the most agencies, but **Moneygram** and **BIAC** are two other options.

For postal services, use **DHL** [97 E5] (180 Av du Marché, Gombe; **m** 081 788 8810, 081 788 8811; ⊕ 08.00–17.30 Mon–Fri, 08.30–14.30 Sat).

HEALTH CARE Pharmacies are easy to find in the city centre. Both the Memling and Pullman hotels have pharmacies in their shopping areas. For minor injuries or ailments, there are a couple of health centres in Kinshasa that meet basic international standards. For anything more serious, however, medical evacuation to Europe or South Africa should be your first option.

Centre Medical Diamant w cmd.cd. Its main clinic in Kinshasa is in the Futur Tower building on Bd du 30 Juin, Gombe [100 B7] (**m** 090 777 7780; ⊕ 24hrs). Also 2 out-patients' clinics: in the Il Mercato building on Bd Mondjiba, Ngaliema [92 C4] (**m** 090 777 7781; ⊕ 24hrs); & in the Kinmarché building on Av Kasa-Vubu, Bandal [96 C4] (**m** 090 777 7782).

CHIK [97 H6] (Centre Hospitalier International de Kinshasa) Av Basoko 11, Gombe; **m** 082 740 1391, 090 000 1214 (ambulance); **w** chik.info; ⊕ 24hrs

WHAT TO SEE AND DO

Kinshasa is a city low on sights, but high on atmosphere. It may not have many historical monuments or cultural buildings, yet it is in many ways the real heart of central Africa, an immense social force in its own right. It is a city to be experienced; a city to hang out in; a city to speak to the locals; a city to have a drink; a city to get harassed by sex workers and pestered by street kids. Take a taxi or (better) a motorbike around, witness the vast night markets (but be very cautious and take nothing with you that you would be sorry to lose), hear blown speakers blasting Kinshasa's latest beats, and see where the DRC all begins and ends. It is an ever-shifting mass of people without an absolute focal point. It is the quintessential African city, created out of happenstance by Europeans and overrun by circumstances of conflict. It is a large disorderly mass; witnessing it,

3

Some 14 years after independence, and under the glowering presence of Mobutu Sese Seko, Zaire was seeking to revitalise its image – and tell the world that it was a new nation, filled with riches, a stable government, magnificent cities, and destined to be a prominent player on the international stage. As is always the case in the Congo, nothing is ever done in half measures, and Mobutu found an opportunity to promote his nation with some familiar and famous American sports celebrities: Don King, George Foreman and Muhammad Ali.

Don King himself was newly released from jail and itching to get Ali fighting Foreman. Storms of sports writers had been speculating on Foreman, the new boxing champion, and whether Ali could even last a few minutes in the ring with him. Yet to fight Foreman, Ali's camp wanted a significant sum of money – US$3 million. Don King agreed to get him the money, but warned that the fight would have to be held outside the USA in that case. Ali's handlers agreed – and Don King found his funding in Zaire's coffers.

Mobutu had agreed to pay US$10 million for the fight, split between Ali and Foreman. Their arrival in Kinshasa was a massive public relations coup for Zaire, and in the weeks of preparation leading up to the fight the nation was in the world's media spotlight.

The boxers would reside at the presidential village outside Kinshasa in N'sele, while journalists stayed in the city. The capital itself was under the microscope by Mobutu and the FAZ – one notorious evening, the president rounded up 1,000 of the city's highest crime leaders and brought them to the stadium. At random, he picked 100, and had his soldiers execute them on the spot – he warned the remainder that if so much as a pocket was picked while Ali and Foreman were in the country, everyone else would suffer the same fate.

and being a part of it, is what Kinshasa is all about. The central market (**Marché Central**) [97 E7] and the **Rond-Point Victoire** [93 E4] are excellent places to catch the feel of Kinshasa, during the daytime. Both areas are quite unsafe after dark.

Try not to be the outsider, the tourist, the observer: it can be your city as much as it has been that of anyone else. It is a city to construct your own experiences, to take away your own memories. It is never the same place twice, and while certain areas sort of keep up appearances in spite of it all, it was never meant to be anything more than a meeting point, a transit spot along Malebo Pool, rather than a permanent fixture. Kinshasa is more of a place to feel the rhythm of life than a place to tick off sights.

That said, however, there are several places that are worth taking the time to visit. Perhaps your first excursion should be a look at the River Congo. Start at the president's official residence, the **Palais de la Nation** [100 D2], an imposing building that was originally intended as the residence of the Belgian colonial governor. It witnessed several of the historic events around the nation's independence, including Patrice Lumumba's fiery speech at the independence celebrations (page 28). The building briefly housed the newly elected parliament, before Mobutu abolished it. Be careful taking photos here; the soldiers who guard the presidential buildings will be nervous that you are photographing them.

From the western end of the building, bearing right down Avenue des Nations Unies will lead you to a viewpoint of the great river [100 C3], near the German

Some say that while the Rumble in the Jungle was being staged, Kinshasa was the safest city on earth.

Muhammad Ali took advantage of this safety – he was seen continuously reaching out to the Zairians, talking to people on the street, gaining the favour of everyone in the nation. George Foreman, on the other hand, remained reclusive; by the time of the fight, Ali had all of Zaire rooting for him, and the trademark slogan 'Ali boma Ye', Lingala for 'Ali Kill Him', could be heard throughout Kinshasa.

The fight was originally scheduled for 25 September 1974, but Foreman was cut during a sparring match. Foreman's handlers asked that the fight be cancelled; Ali was furious. He begged Don King to fly in Joe Frazier, another prominent boxer, so the fight could go on in Kinshasa. Mobutu was not keen on having the fight cancelled either, and hinted to both of them that any attempt to leave Zaire before fighting was very unwelcome.

It was then delayed by five more weeks until 30 October. Foreman was seen as unbeatable, but over eight rounds Muhammad Ali wore him down in Kinshasa's intense humidity and won the fight. Both athletes went away with millions of dollars, in the largest purse ever to have been awarded to boxers up to that point.

Mobutu's Zaire came off better, having proven to the world that the African country, ridden by conflict for so long, could stage a major international sporting event. It remained the largest event of its kind ever held on the continent until South Africa hosted the football World Cup in 2010. It also changed the sport of boxing for ever – elevating the prizes and audiences to levels never known before.

To learn more about the Rumble in the Jungle read Norman Mailer's book *The Fight*, penned just after he left Kinshasa in 1974, and watch the 1996 documentary *When We Were Kings*, that centres entirely on this moment in sports history.

and UK embassies. Another place to look at the river is further west, at one of the bars overlooking the rapids in Ngaliema, beyond Symphonie des Arts; for example, **Chez Tintin** [92 A3].

Across the street from the Palais de la Nation is the **mausoleum of Laurent-Désiré Kabila** [100 D2], a curiously shaped structure supposed to represent a tent, symbolising the years that Kabila spent under canvas, in rebellion against Mobutu. A huge bronze statue of the late president stands before the entrance to the mausoleum. It is possible to visit the mausoleum and see Kabila's coffin; ask the guards for access, and be prepared to tip them after your visit.

The national **Parliament** meets in a monumental building, the Palais du Peuple [93 E3], constructed in the 1970s. When Parliament is in session, it may be possible to visit the building. Nearby, the **National Museum** [92 D3] (Musée National de la République Démocratique du Congo; 4422 Bd Triomphal; m 081 493 2524) is the perfect introduction to the history and culture of the country. There are said to be 12,000 objects on display, in three huge halls. They include masks, sculptures, musical instruments, archaeological finds and contemporary visual art. The museum also holds a collection of ethnographic recordings.

The stadium near the museum, **Stade des Martyrs** [93 E3] (the martyrs were the four government ministers hanged on Mobutu's orders in 1966), is the national football stadium. It has been upgraded to FIFA standards, although the renovations seem to be rather never-ending. The stadium is also used for concerts and other events. Kinshasa's other main stadium, **Stade Tata Raphaël** [93 F3] (Father Raphaël commissioned its construction in 1948), was the venue for the 'Rumble in the Jungle' boxing match in 1974 (page 104).

In the city centre, near the US Embassy, the **Church of St Anne** [97 F3] (Église Sainte-Anne; Av des Aviateurs) is a beautiful red-brick building, with columns and arcades. Built in 1913, it was Kinshasa's first permanent church. Various buildings were added later, in the 1970s, including the Procure Sainte-Anne (page 98). The city's cathedral, **Our Lady of the Congo** [92 D3] (Notre-Dame du Congo; Av du 24 Novembre), built in 1947, is another attractive building.

The **Zoo and Botanical Garden** [96 C7 & D7] (Av Kasa-Vubu; ⏱ 09.00–17.00; admission to garden Fc2,000, additional charge for photo permit) is one of the few green spaces in the city. Both were established, on the same site, in the 1930s. The zoo has not been maintained, although (as usual) there are plans to rehabilitate it. The garden, though, is a lovely place for a walk, with its trees (around 100 species) offering shade. Another nice green space, a little further out of town, is **Symphonies Naturelles** [92 A6], a park about 20 minutes' drive from Gombe. It has a bar and restaurant, as well as several walking trails among the forest.

MALEBO POOL
Kinkole [map, page 108] (✦ 04°19.35 S, 15°30.46 E) Kinkole is a fishing port on Malebo Pool (page 94) and is the site of Kinshasa's main fish market. At weekends, families go there from the city for a day of eating, drinking and posting on Instagram. There are riverside terrace bars and food-sellers by the roadside. The classic meal in Kinkole is *liboke*, chunks of fresh river fish, seasoned and wrapped in a palm leaf and smoked over charcoal. Excursions on the river, by pirogue or boat, can be arranged once you are there. Nowadays it is part of Kinshasa's urban sprawl; it is about 30km from the city centre, beyond Ndjili Airport, on a good road. The best place to look for a motorbike or shared taxi is the Marché de la Liberté.

Jardin d'Eden [map, page 108] (Av Delmo 144, N'sele; m 099 813 8197, 081 810 8502; e touristique_jardineden@yahoo.fr; w jardin-eden.populus.ch) A welcome breath of greenery and fresh air only 5 minutes' drive beyond Kinkole, the 'Garden of Eden' is a resort on the River N'sele, a tributary of the Congo. Most of its attractions are on a 16ha island in the river – a restaurant, picnic areas, rustic bars with music, and a small zoo. There is a beach from which you can swim, you can go fishing, or you can walk around the island. The resort has a speedboat (*canôt rapide*) and barges to transport guests over to the island (Fc7,500 & Fc3,500, respectively). On the mainland is a guesthouse (23 rooms; dbl **$$**, suite **$$$**) and campsite (US$35 for a 2-person tent). Jardin d'Eden would be a good option for your last night in the DRC, as it's within easy reach of Ndjili Airport but avoids the frustration and uncertainty of Kinshasa's traffic jams.

4

To Kongo-Central and the Atlantic

Head southwest from Kinshasa and you'll see some intriguing sights; it's not even necessary to have a 4x4 vehicle to reach most of them, although, as in most of the rest of the country, it will help. The urban sprawl of the capital is gradually enveloping more and more of the left bank of the River Congo, as people move to the big city in search of a better livelihood. With prosperity comes urbanisation, and families who have managed to save up a few hundred dollars buy small plots of land on the fringes of the city. They create modest-sized brick houses, do their best to grow small crops, and nurture them with the water from nearby rivers. What was once a wilderness is becoming suburbia. Attractions that, not so long ago, required a 4x4 can now be reached by public transport from Kinshasa.

Once you pass the periphery of Kinshasa, you reach the province of Kongo-Central (formerly called Bas-Congo). Kongo-Central has reasonably good infrastructure, because it has the country's only seaports, an extremely important bargaining chip with whoever happens to be in power in Kinshasa. It is sandwiched between the two territorial segments of Angola, helping further with imports and exports. It has minerals, beaches, bridges and the country's largest hydro-electric dam. After Katanga, Kongo-Central is the wealthiest region of the DRC. It also has many natural attractions, including Mangroves National Park, while its towns of Matadi, Boma and Muanda have some of the most historical monuments in the country. It's not only the gateway to the nation, but also a great option for travellers who don't want to battle with the difficulties of going too far inland.

SOUTH FROM KINSHASA

LOLA YA BONOBO (⊕ 04°29.07.78 S, 15°16.02.40 E; **e** info@bonobos.org; **w** bonobos. org; ⊙ 10.00–16.00 Tue–Sun; DRC residents US$5, non-residents US$10) 'Bonobo Paradise' (the translation of its Lingala name) is the world's only bonobo sanctuary, founded in 1994. Bonobos, with chimpanzees, are humans' closest relatives, sharing over 94% of the same DNA. They are unique to the DRC; their habitat is south of the River Congo, while chimpanzees live on the other side, which means the two species have never had to compete with each other for habitat. Bonobos have evolved to be more social and peaceable than the other great apes and their social structure is matriarchal; famously, they use sex as a means of social bonding.

Unfortunately, these beautiful creatures are targeted by poachers for bushmeat. Like chimpanzees, bonobos sleep in nests high up in trees. When the troupe goes up to its nests at night, the matriarch (the 'queen') makes a loud, very specific cry, which the poachers use to identify the troupe's location. They set traps at the foot of the trees while the bonobos are sleeping, so that they will be snared when they come down in the morning. The poachers are only interested in the meat of the adult animals;

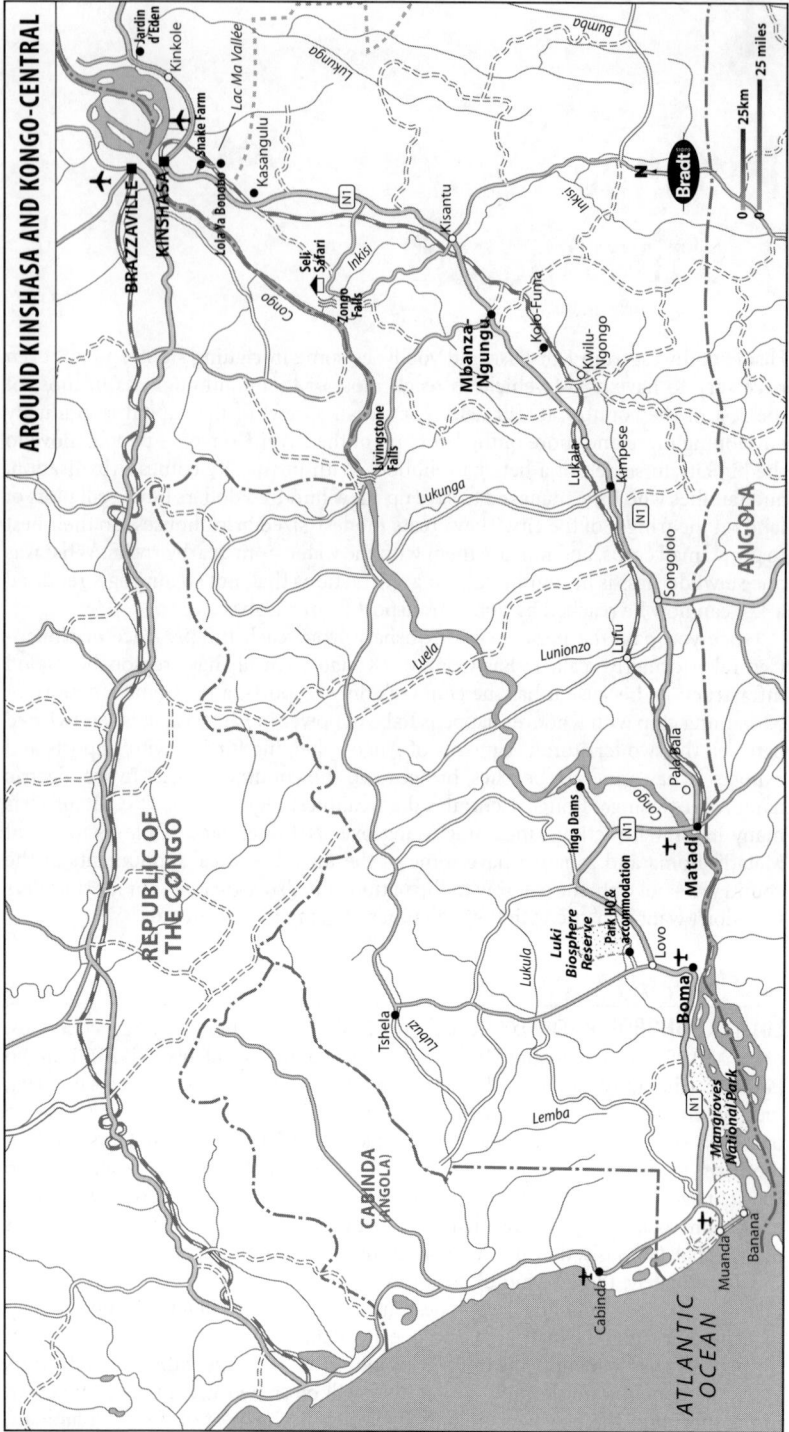

AROUND KINSHASA AND KONGO-CENTRAL

Jardin d'Eden
Kinkole
Lac Ma Vallée
Kasangulu
Snake Farm
Loka Bonobo
BRAZZAVILLE
KINSHASA
Congo
Seli Safari
Inkisi
Zongo Falls
Kisantu
N1
Mbanza-Ngungu
Kolo-Fuma
Kwilu-Ngongo
Livingstone Falls
Lukala
Kimpese
Lukunga
Songololo
N1
ANGOLA
Luela
Lunionzo
Lufu
REPUBLIC OF THE CONGO
Pala Bala
Congo
Inga Dams
N1
Matadi
Luki Biosphere Reserve
Park HQ & accommodation
Lovo
Lukula
Boma
Tshela
Lubuzi
CABINDA (ANGOLA)
Lemba
N1
Mangroves National Park
Cabinda
Muanda
Banana
ATLANTIC OCEAN

Congo
Lukunga
Lukunga
Inkisi

Bradt

0   25km
0   25 miles

108

they sell the babies to the pet trade but, without their mothers, the baby bonobos weaken and die. In 1994, the founder of Lola Ya Bonobo realised that the only way they could survive would be to give them a human 'mother' to care for and bond with them. The surrogate mothers are women from the villages near the sanctuary and they are the only humans who have any contact with the baby bonobos. Once the new arrivals have recovered mentally and physically from the separation from their bonobo mothers, they join one of the troupes in the semi-wild environment of the Lola forest. Visitors have no physical contact at all with the animals, which are very vulnerable to human diseases due to our physiological closeness.

However, there are many opportunities to observe the bonobos from a safe distance (safe for the bonobos). A footpath leads around the site, past two enclosures where the bonobo troupes spend their days. Their forest diet is supplemented with nutrient-enriched fruit, thrown to them from a distance; if you are there at the right time, you can observe the matriarch leading her troupe down from the forest to where she knows the food will arrive. The tour then passes the cabins where the new arrivals sleep. These are linked by a tunnel to their play area, where they spend most of their days with their surrogate mothers. Visitors can watch the little bonobos through large plate-glass windows as they play on their climbing frame and trampoline or cling to their 'mother'. The tour takes about 90 minutes. Scheduled tours leave the ticket office at 10.00, 11.30, 13.00 and 14.30. There is also the option of a private tour, including lunch, at a cost of US$50, which should be booked at least 48 hours in advance. There is a shop where visitors can buy bonobo T-shirts, wooden carvings and other souvenirs (also available on the website). There is even a guesthouse, where visitors can spend a night (or longer) within the sanctuary; see website for details.

Getting there and away Lola Ya Bonobo is just beyond the sprawling periphery of Kinshasa, off the N1 road to Matadi. Depending on traffic, it should take about an hour to get there from Gombe. A 4x4 is not essential. There is a public bus to within walking distance of the entrance to the sanctuary (Route Kimwenza). The sanctuary offers return transport to and from Kinshasa, at a cost of US$150 for up to three people. A taxi from Kinshasa will be somewhat cheaper but, of course, less convenient.

LAC MA VALLÉE (🅵 Africa Park Adventure; ⊕ Tue–Sun) Also off the Kimwenza road, the Ma Vallée reservoir is a little pocket of greenery and peace in the outskirts of the big city. It has been a place for people to enjoy themselves since the 1950s and is one of the closest remnants of rainforest to Kinshasa. You can walk through the forest all around the lake, only 6km, or hire a kayak or pedalo to explore it on the water, or even zip-line across it. Swimming, unfortunately, is not allowed. There is a restaurant on site, with snacks and various buffet options for food ($$–$$$) as well as, of course, a range of beers and soft drinks. You can order your meal before you set off on your walk or lake trip, so that it is ready for you when you return.

Lac Ma Vallée is leased by its owners, the Catholic Church in the DRC, to a private operator, Africa Park Adventure. Depending on traffic congestion in Kinshasa, it should take about an hour to reach the resort from Gombe. There is a small admission fee. Take insect repellent; it's a lake in the tropics, so naturally there are mosquitoes. With your own (or your own hired) transport, it would be very easy to combine a visit to Lola Ya Bonobo with a few hours here.

SNAKE FARM The DRC's only antivenom centre, part of the University of Kinshasa, is also an educational visitor experience. **Serpents du Congo** (Quartier Sebo,

Mont-Ngafula; m 081 991 8530, 099 991 8530; ⊕ 09.00–18.00 Tue–Sun, but call ahead to make an appointment; US$10) has a fascinating collection of snakes from around the DRC, including the deadly Gaboon viper and black mamba. The centre's experts show you the snakes and let you hold the non-venomous ones. The Snake Farm is off the road that leads to Lac Ma Vallée; follow the sign for 'Ferme Sogenak'.

KONGO-CENTRAL

The boundary between Kinshasa and the province of Kongo-Central is marked, as usual in the DRC, by a *péage* (road-toll) point. For private cars the toll is minimal; the roads authority makes its money from HGVs. The first town after the péage is Kasangulu, and about 80km beyond it are the first of Kongo-Central's unmissable sights: the Botanical Gardens in Kisantu. Further on lie the history-rich towns of Matadi, Boma and Muanda and the DRC's only marine national park.

KISANTU On the banks of the River Inkisi, the town of Kisantu started to develop at the end of the 19th century. Its cathedral, with its patterns of differently coloured bricks, dates from the 1920s and is the largest Catholic church in the DRC. The reason most travellers stop in Kisantu, though, is to visit its **Botanical Gardens** and take the detour to the **Zongo Falls**.

⌂ Where to stay

Mbuela Lodge (30 rooms, 10 chalets) On N1, just outside Kisantu; m 082 544 3322; w mbuelalodge.com. An 'agrotourism' resort of 100ha, with waymarked footpaths through the grounds; secure; bicycles, quad bikes & horses can be hired. Good-sized pool, gym, mini-golf, children's playground; restaurant & terrace-bar with music at w/ends. Rooms all en suite with AC, TV, safe, minibar, Wi-Fi; chalets have AC but share bathroom/shower facilities **$$$$–$$$$$**; tented accommodation also available.

Seli Safari Zongo, 60km from Kisantu; m 099 998 0280, 089 959 6646; ◻ SELI safari ZONGO. Resort on the banks of the River Inkisi, at access to Zongo Falls. Modern, comfortable accommodation in rooms, chalets, tents & deluxe villas. Swimming

pool, swimming area in river, forest walks. Tours to Zongo Falls & Inga Dams. Restaurant & barbecue grill. Transfers to/from Kinshasa can be arranged. Villas **$$$$$**, rooms/bungalows **$$$–$$$$**, tents **$$$**

Belle Vue (22 rooms, 5 chalets) On N1, Kisantu; m 089 723 0077. This historic hotel is showing its age & could do with some investment, but it is clean & its tree-shaded courtyard is a peaceful spot. Rooms en suite with fan; chalets have AC. **$$**

Centre Emmaüs Kisantu (50 rooms) m 099 121 2005. Run by Jesuit sisters; simple accommodation in utilitarian buildings; garden; kitchen & refectory; b/fast & other meals on request. **$**

What to see and do

Kisantu Botanical Garden (✦ 05° 07.55 S, 15° 06.07 E; m 081 147 7780; ⊕ 08.00–17.00 daily; US$7) Kisantu is a small town, but its botanical garden is a key site for conservation in central Africa, with more than 3,000 local and introduced species in its living collection. The herbarium is one of the oldest and richest in the Congo. There is an orchid house, a cactus greenhouse and a collection of aquatic plants. The Kisantu Botanical Garden was started in 1893 by a Jesuit, Justin Gillet, who planted European vegetables to improve the missionaries' diet. Gillet became interested in studying and collecting local plants, cataloguing almost 800 genera. After his death in 1943, botanical study at the garden continued and a horticultural school was set up. Unfortunately, during the uprising against Mobutu (page 32), rebels used the botanical garden as a military base. Most of the orchid collection was stolen and sold, along with many of the books and journals in the library. Since 2004, the garden has been rehabilitated, with the support of the European Union, WWF and Belgium's National Botanic Garden. A network of footpaths and vehicle tracks gives access to the 225ha site. Kisantu has become an environmental training centre and hosts several projects for biodiversity research and sustainable ecosystem management. Those with a particular interest in botany may like to look at the samples from the Kisantu catalogue on **w** plants.jstor.org.

Zongo Falls (⊕ 04°46.42.90 S, 14°54.27.96 E) The Zongo Falls are definitely worth the detour from the N1 between Matadi and Kinshasa. The waterfalls crash down almost 70m in spectacular fashion, creating a cauldron of steam and mist between two sheer cliffsides covered in foliage. The spectacle is at its most impressive at the end of the wet season, in January or February. The Inga hydro-electric dams (page 42) are on the River Congo, further downstream. Just south of Kisantu on the road towards Kizenga are several more small waterfalls: Luguya, M'fidi and Mosi. They're situated slightly away from the road, so it'll take a bit of asking around among the locals to locate them.

The best route to the Zongo Falls is via Kisantu, from where it is signposted. The falls are about 60km from Kisantu. The road is unpaved and it takes about 1½ hours. Motorbike taxis in Kisantu will probably do the run to Zongo. The **Seli Safari** resort at Zongo (see opposite) runs a bus service to/from Kinshasa at weekends, with packages including accommodation and visits to the falls and the Inga Dams.

MBANZA-NGUNGU (⊕ 05°15.06 S, 14°52.07 E) One thing that strikes visitors
to Mbanza-Ngungu is the pleasant climate: the acrid air of Kinshasa or the overbearing humidity of Matadi is non-existent here. It's high up in the hills and exudes a pleasant mountain-town quality, with crisp weather in the daytime and almost chilly temperatures at night. These are the hills that kept so many explorers from going further inland during their early visits to central Africa and over which Stanley's bearers hauled his boat *Lady Alice*. Its colonial name was Thysville; Albert Thys was the developer of the railway from Matadi to Léopoldville (page 73), which took eight years to complete before it opened in 1898.

Getting there and away Mbanza-Ngungu is about halfway between Matadi
and Kinshasa, although the duration of the journey to or from Kinshasa will be entirely dependent on how bad the traffic is. By public transport, the best way to continue your onward journey may be by train; the Matadi–Kinshasa railway stops at Mbanza-Ngungu. Buses between Matadi and Kinshasa don't always stop here; other than the train, a shared taxi or a motorbike to somewhere closer may be the only way to move on. As ever, you should agree the price before getting into or on to the vehicle.

There are two or three hotels in Mbanza-Ngungu, if you are stuck. If you plan an overnight stay between Kinshasa and Matadi, the Mbuela Lodge in Kisantu (see opposite) is a better option.

What to see and do The reason most travellers will stop in Mbanza-Ngungu
is to visit the **Thysville caves** in the nearby hills. There are several caves, linked and fed by tributaries of the River Congo and extending over an area of 750km². They are best known for a blind, albino fish that is unique to this cave complex: the Congo blind barb or *Caecobarbus geertsi*, first identified in 1921 and now listed as 'Vulnerable' by IUCN. In the 1950s, the total population was estimated at 7,000. Its

main threat is habitat loss; one of the seven caves where it was first discovered has now disappeared due to limestone quarrying. The cave complex has never been fully explored. The last expedition was by an American group in 1973, who spent three months mapping the caves but never reached the end of them. The theory is that the system emerges somewhere near Zongo Falls. Therefore, don't get lost.

To get to the caves, a 4x4 is absolutely necessary – though even with that you may find yourself walking part of the way as the road withers away into a grass trail after a few kilometres. You must get permission to visit from the local village chief at **Ntoto** (✛ 05°16.55.57 S, 14°52.06.26 E), who will generally ask US$20 per person for a guided tour. The village is only accessible by foot. He has lanterns available, but you should bring your own torch and an extra set of batteries. The caves are muddy even at the best of times, and slippery; wear waterproof boots and roll up your trousers.

MATADI Matadi is scenic and mountainous and historic and humid, the capital of Kongo-Central province. It is the terminus for the nation's very first railway and the furthest point upstream one can travel by boat before reaching the rapids that stymied many an explorer. At the time of writing, Matadi is the DRC's largest port, although it will be superseded when the new deepwater port at Banana is completed. In Matadi's early days, it was a small cluster of buildings right on the hill, buried among the mountains and cliffs of the shore, but in recent decades has enveloped the region entirely – with even Angola building its own port town right on the border. Business is booming, to an extent, with massive ships keeping the crane towers busy in the heavy, humid air. As is often the case with port cities, many products are available in Matadi that never reach the interior of the DRC, and it's a great place to stock up on supplies before going elsewhere.

History Diogo Cão first arrived on the shores of Matadi during his maiden voyage up the River Congo in 1485, eventually navigating the Mpozo River and leaving a mark at the furthest point he explored. The Portuguese founded the village of Noqui some kilometres from where Matadi would be established. Noqui would eventually be overrun and destroyed by the mid 19th century. Decades later, Henry Morton Stanley arrived on the former site of Noqui during his voyage downriver from the east. He founded the fort of Matadi, just past the rapids, in 1879 upon his first trip commissioned by King Léopold.

Matadi's existence was critical to opening up the Congo. The first railway of central Africa was completed in 1898, but during its construction a well-beaten trail of Congolese porters moved goods through the rough landscape northeast to Malebo Pool (then called Stanley Pool, page 90). Thousands died in these years, hauling tonnes of items through the hills.

In general Matadi escaped the worst of the wars that afflicted the rest of the DRC, with the exception of an invasion at the airport in 1998 by Rwandan troops, who staged a bold landing and marched to Kinshasa from the west. Otherwise, the province remained mostly unscathed.

Getting there and away Matadi is well served by buses and minibuses to and from Kinshasa. The buses leave Kinshasa from Rond-Point Victoire and take 6–8 hours; minibuses depart from Rond-Point Gabarre. The train service has been upgraded and is now perhaps the most comfortable way to make the journey, although it runs only once a week. The train takes about 8 hours and goes through spectacular scenery; a seat in second class costs about US$10. In the past Matadi

The seminal book *Heart of Darkness* grew from Joseph Conrad's own experiences in the Congo, and some published versions include his *Congo Diary*: a brief, yet illuminating account of his few months in the country.

What he experienced was based on his sojourn there as a labourer, working for an unscrupulous employer (referred to as Delcommune), and his long trek from the docks of Matadi northeast to the bustling capital of Léopoldville (which he refers to as 'Kinschassa') while the railway to Stanley Pool was still under construction. In Matadi he met Roger Casement, the activist, and Conrad was undoubtedly shaped by Casement's views on what was happening in the colony. He served on the ship *Roi des Belges*, experiencing further hardship along the way, and made one trip with the vessel upriver to Stanley Falls. He would return to Léopoldville three months later on 24 September 1890, and Matadi on 4 December. In all he spent less than five months in the Congo.

His time was not a pleasant one. The majority of Europeans he met, and the horrible conditions that Africans lived in, informed his best-known literary work. As a simple deckhand without any known ideologies, little would be hidden from him. Perhaps most intriguing is the lack of detail in his diaries regarding the worst excesses he may have seen in the Congo Free State; those were saved for his work of fiction.

The accounts of his time in the Congo are found in the *Congo Diary and other Uncollected Pieces*, published in 1978. Several editions of *Heart of Darkness* have at least partial excerpts from the *Congo Diary*.

also had flight connections with Kinshasa. The airport is on the north bank of the river. The only public transport to or from Boma is in cramped shared taxis, with a 2–2½ hour travel time.

Getting around One crosses the **Mpozo River** when arriving from Kinshasa, then winds along through the hills until finally arriving at the mouth of the River Congo and the primary ports of the nation. To reach points further west, one crosses the **Matadi Bridge** or Pont Maréchal, a feat of engineering that looms over the Matadi skyline. The city runs on a roughly north–south axis with most new businesses operating in the hills around Matadi while the old town centre becomes more and more cluttered. To the east of the city are high peaks from where the surrounding landscape can be surveyed. The city is split into districts (*communes*), the most notable of which for visitors is **Gombe**, the town centre – also referred to as Ville Basse. Head southwards and up in altitude and you arrive in **Haute-Ville**, a nicer neighbourhood and sometimes called **Ciné Palace** due to the large conference hall of the same name that dominates the district. On the road towards the Matadi Bridge and Boma is the **Commune de Kinkanda**.

📌 **Where to stay** *Map, page 114*

Flat-Hôtel Ledya (39 rooms, 11 apartments, 8 studios, 2 suites) Av Sita, Kikanda; m 082 451 0775; e flathotelledya@yahoo.fr; f Flat Hotel Ledya. Secure parking, Wi-Fi, fitness centre, pool, garden, 2 restaurants (Congolese & European). All rooms en suite with AC, TV, fridge, kitchenette. Dbl $$$–$$$$, suites $$$$$

Vivi Palace (22 rooms) Av Futi Muekono 10, Ville Haute; m 099 022 0410; f VIVI Palace Hotel Matadi. Restaurant with Congolese, European &

Chinese menus; bar with pool table, garden, secure parking, gym; all rooms en suite with AC, Wi-Fi, TV, safe, fridge, iron; 'superior apartments' have balcony; 2 wheelchair-accessible rooms. **$$$**, apartments **$$$$**

Fortune (21 rooms) Av Mpolo 11, Ville Basse; m 099 993 6548, 089 001 1545; w hotelfortunemtd. com. 2 restaurants, fitness centre, business centre; wheelchair accessible. All rooms en suite, good sized, with AC, satellite TV, Wi-Fi, safe, direct-dial telephone, tea/coffee-making facilities & minibar. **$$$**

La Fleur (16 rooms) Rte Kinkanda 30, Ville Haute; m 085 385 6018; e lafleurinfos2@ gmail.com; Hôtel La Fleur. Restaurant (**$$**) specialising in fish & game, pool in garden, lounge bar, parking. All rooms en suite with Wi-Fi, AC, TV, fridge. **$$–$$$**

Auberge de la Paix (11 rooms) Av Georges Puissan; m 081 033 9181. Simple accommodation set in peaceful garden with water feature; meals can be prepared. All rooms with simple en-suite bathroom, AC, b/fast inc. **$**

✕ Where to eat and drink *Map, above*

The hotel restaurants listed on page 113 and above are open to non-residents and are a good option for more formal dining.

Al-Amir Av de la Poste 14, Ville Basse (opposite police station); Resto Al Amir Matadi. Informal dining in city centre; fast food, fish, steaks; economical set lunches. **$**

Almadina Av de la Poste; m 084 500 0009;
f Restaurant Almadina; ⊕ 07.00–22.00
Mon–Sat, 08.00–22.00 Sun. Opposite the railway
station. African & international cuisine, from *cossa-
cossa* to pizza, all nicely presented; good service. $

Rehoboth Food Av La Plaine 12, Ville Basse;
m 082 390 4285, 089 741 4757; f Rehoboth
Food; ⊕ 08.00–22.00 daily. Congolese & European
cuisine, pizzas, pasta; patisserie; b/fast offers; all-
you-can-eat buffet at w/ends. $

Shopping The **Marché Gondola** just behind the cathedral is a small walkway
filled with craft kiosks, old postcards and other knick-knacks and good for a quick
gift stop. Near **Rond-Point 2415** are several decent small shops to stock up on food
and supplies before heading out of the city.

Other practicalities There are several **Western Union** agencies in Matadi,
mainly around the port, and **ATMs** at the banks in the town centre, such as BCDC
and Sofibanque.

If you're in Matadi waiting for a container to arrive, there are a few places to
check up on its delivery. At Rond-Point Ami-Congo, on the southwest side, is
a multi-storey building and on the top level is the **Agetraf office**. They are also
responsible for Delmas and Grimaldi containers that arrive in Matadi. For **Maersk**
(m 081 716 0443; ⊕ 08.00–16.30 Mon–Fri), head up Avenue de la Poste a little and
their office is on the second level. **Pacific Trading** (m 085 180 8807; ⊕ 09.00–16.30
Mon–Fri) is up the street on Rue de la Gare. A list of all shipping agents in Matadi
can be found at **w** portsdirectory.com/location/congo.

Matadi has an **Angolan consulate** in Haute-Ville (✆ 999 090; m 099 045 8051;
e josobar1952@hotmail.com, consuladogeral.matadi@mirex.gov.ao). Appointments
must be arranged in advance, by telephone or email.

As elsewhere in the DRC, if you are seriously ill or injured, seek medical
evacuation as soon as you are fit to travel. The **Memorial Center Hospital** can treat
minor injuries.

What to see and do A great place to begin one's visit to Matadi is the **Belvedere
viewpoint** to the east of the town centre – it's the highest spot in the city, with
wonderful views of the Matadi Bridge to the west and the mountains to the
northeast. It is quite a long, steep walk from the city centre; if you do not have
your own transport, take a motorbike taxi from the city centre. There is a bronze
map of the region which points out the peaks and the original roads and footpaths
used in the late 19th century. A fee of a few dollars must be paid for the map to be
revealed (and a bit more for a photo permit). From the Belvedere, **Peak Cambien**
(Pic Kinzau) can be seen, a rocky outcropping that is the highest peak along the
riverside and was used for initial surveying of the rail route northeast to Kinshasa.
Follow the Mpozo River northwards from Peak Cambien and you'll run into the
original **rail bridge** for the Matadi–Kinshasa railway, as well as the **Monument
to the Porters** who perished during the decades before the railway was built. The
monument is definitely off the beaten path, buried at the end of a grass trail near the
river – you'll have to cross the rail bridge and then wind around to ✪ 05°49.37.06 S,
13°29.44.39 E. From the road bridge it should take about half an hour.

The **Matadi Bridge**, often known in French as le Pont Maréchal – the 'Marshal'
being Mobuto Sese Seko who, as president, commissioned it in 1979 – is the only
bridge along the entire length of the River Congo (the bridges in the east of the
country cross its major tributary the Lualaba, not the Congo itself). It is also known
as the OEBK Bridge, after the abbreviation for l'Organisation pour l'Équipement
de Banana-Kinshasa. From its completion in 1983 until the opening of the bridge

across Maputo Bay in 2018, the Matadi Bridge was the longest suspension bridge in Africa. It's a toll bridge; if you are on foot, ask at the *péage* if you can walk across. You will probably be expected to make a small payment for this privilege, but it is worth it for the view from above the whirlpools that pose such a hazard to ships approaching the port of Matadi.

Matadi's **Hôtel Metropole** was built in the 1920s and opened in 1930. With its five floors, it was the first high-rise building in the Belgian Congo and offered its guests 'American-standard' comfort, with lifts, a spiral staircase and a casino. It closed its doors in early 2012, although the owners still hope to renovate and reopen it. It may be possible to see the interior of the hotel by asking at the entrance. Its central courtyard is designed in such a way that it always remains cool – a prime attraction in this always hot and humid region.

AROUND MATADI Hiring a motorboat is an excellent way to see two points of interest down the Mpozo River just east of the town. The **Rock of Diogo Cão** has several inscriptions by him, marking the furthest point reached by the Portuguese explorer during the maiden voyage of Europeans to the River Congo in 1485. Nearby are some **Fishermen's Caves** with excellent pastoral views of the river. At 12km east of Matadi is the village of **Pala Bala** (⊕ 05°49.49 S, 13°33.14 E), where the first Protestant church of the region was built. The village was also where one of Henry Morton Stanley's closest friends during his expeditions, Léon Johnen, perished in 1887 from disease. West from the city centre, on the riverbank, is the original Portuguese trading post in the area (⊕ 05°50.44 S, 13°26.05 E). Over the centuries it has seen the faces of many would-be explorers, including Sir Richard Francis Burton. It was also inhabited at the time of Henry Morton Stanley's arrival at the mouth of the river.

Follow Matadi's road north and you will arrive at several sets of rapids, first the **Yelala Rapids** roughly 15km outside the town. It requires a walk of several hours from the road, making it a full day's trip. Further north are the **Inga Dams** (page 42), built on a series of rapids called the Inga Falls, where the River Congo drops almost 100m. The road to Inga from Matadi is reasonable, if all you want is to see the rapids and the dams; local tour operators (eg: Congo Travel and Tours, page 53) can arrange visits to the turbine halls and control room.

Following the same road further north are the rapids of **Isangila**, which was also the point in the river which finally did for the expedition of James Kingston Tuckey almost two centuries ago – had he managed to continue, he would have discovered the navigable regions of the river, and history may have been distinctly different.

BOMA Boma's history is rich, and it was an indispensable cornerstone of administration for the Belgian Congo through many decades. Capital of the entire colony from its inception in 1886 until 1920, it remained the centrepoint of contact for Belgian officials until the administration moved completely to Léopoldville by 1929. Founded by the Portuguese centuries before the Belgians arrived, it was the primary stopping-off point for ships that wished to trade with the ancient African kingdoms. Later, James Kingston Tuckey and Sir Richard Francis Burton both stopped here for supplies, and established a base of communications for their expeditions upriver. It was the landing point of Henry Morton Stanley when he completed his momentous journey from the Indian Ocean to the Atlantic. It was also the site of a small formal ceremony in 1959 when Belgium officially handed over power of the colony to the new Congolese government.

Getting there and away Like almost everywhere else in the DRC, roads are rough and slow. You can catch a shared taxi from Rond-Point Boma on the north end of the city to Matadi, Muanda or Tshela. Traffic permitting, it takes 2–2½ hours to/from Matadi and 1½–2 hours to/from Muanda.

Where to stay *Map, below*

Candide (20 rooms, 2 suites) 1146 Fisher/Nzandi; m 097 852 2810, 082 006 5752 (WhatsApp); w hotel-candide.com. Great location right on the river; restaurant with river views & Congolese & international menu; good-sized pool overlooking river with poolside terrace & children's pool; boat trips can be arranged. All rooms en suite with AC, TV, b/fast, pool access & Wi-Fi inc. Dbl $$$, apartments $$$$–$$$$$

Mabuilu (21 rooms, 6 apartments) Av du Quai Congo 3; m 085 571 7270; e mabuiluhotel@gmail.com; ☐ Hôtel Mabuilu. Excellent restaurant specialising in fish & seafood ($$$); lounge bar, terrace bar; laundry service. All rooms en suite with good shower, AC, TV, Wi-Fi; some have river view. Dbl $$, VIP apartments $$$

Where to eat and drink *Map, below*

Boma's best restaurants are in the two hotels listed above; both are open to non-residents.

NTV Av 24 Novembre, Q/ Fisher; m 099 961 9838, 085 360 0002; ☐ NoorTajvillage Boma. A local mini-chain, with restaurants in Boma, Muanda & Kinshasa. Indian, Congolese & international menu, including fish & tandoori; set meal offers at w/ends. Vegetarian & vegan Indian options, of course. $

Auberge du Vieux Port Av du 24 Novembre; m 082 674 2444; ⏰ 11.00–22.00 daily. Also known as l'Auberge du Fisher. Wonderful location on the river, good place for a sundowner on the

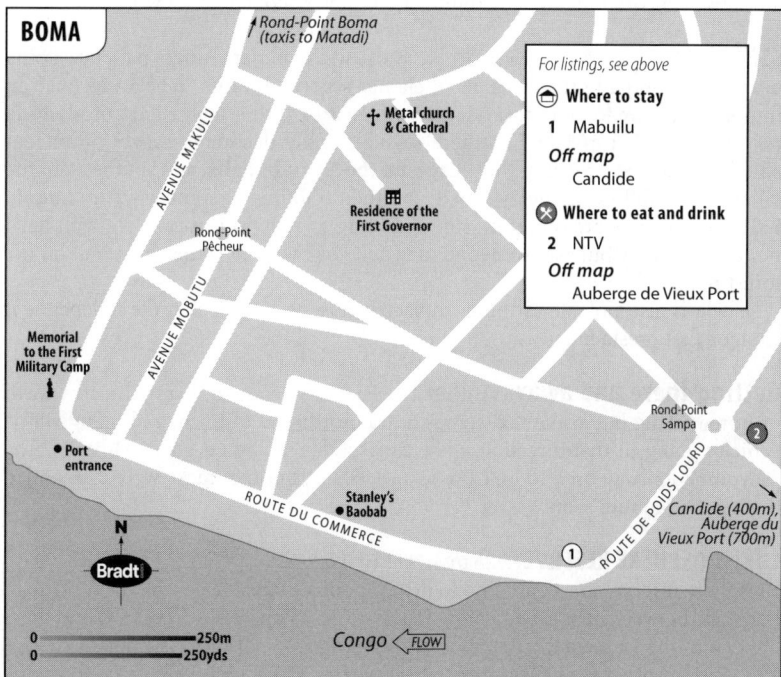

BOMA

Rond-Point Boma (taxis to Matadi)

AVENUE MAKULU

✝ Metal church & Cathedral

Rond-Point Pêcheur

🏛 Residence of the First Governor

AVENUE MOBUTU

Memorial to the First Military Camp

● Port entrance

ROUTE DU COMMERCE

Stanley's ● Baobab

Rond-Point Sampa

ROUTE DE POIDS LOURD

Candide (400m), Auberge du Vieux Port (700m)

N

Bradt

0 ──── 250m
0 ──── 250yds

Congo ← FLOW

For listings, see above

⊖ **Where to stay**
1 Mabuilu
Off map
  Candide

✖ **Where to eat and drink**
2 NTV
Off map
  Auberge de Vieux Port

wooden terrace, watching the cargo ships go by. Food may or may not be available, depending on management's frame of mind. Very basic accommodation (**$**) may, similarly, be available.

What to see and do Boma sits on a mountainside overlooking the mouth of the River Congo. There are many points of historic interest: a small **metal church** was the Congo Free State's first church and was erected here in 1890 – a kind of kit-church that was designed and built in Belgium, then disassembled and shipped to Boma. Beside it is the **cathedral**, built in 1920, with beautiful textile paintings within. Both churches are situated on a hilltop with good views of the town and river below. Further down the hill is the **Residence of the First Governor** of the Congo Free State, a three-storeyed mansion and a great example of Boma's 19th-century architecture. A 700-year-old **baobab tree** sits in town where, in 1877, Henry Morton Stanley was said to have spent his first night after his epic journey tracing the course of the River Congo – it's a large hollowed-out tree with enough room for a hammock, though you'd be hard pressed to have a snooze there these days. Behind it is a small museum with some paintings, and in front is a bar. They normally ask for a small admission fee.

The town still has many administrative buildings from its time as the colony's capital: the first barracks used by the Force Publique, several stopping points for traders and missionaries, as well as an ancient **cemetery** filled with graves of the first Europeans to set foot on these shores. Near the Auberge du Vieux Port are the **first cars** to have appeared in the Belgian Congo around 1905, but don't pay any money to see them – anything that could be removed from them, has been. They are little more than rusted hulks at this point: carcasses with tyres. Out in front of the port entrance is a small **Memorial to the First Military Camp** in the Congo, which was completed between 1886 and 1887. It's in the middle of a small market area and plenty of kids swarm around and pester visitors here.

TSHELA (✪ 05° 00.29 S, 12°57.34 E) For those with a fair amount of patience, going north from Boma to the town of Tshela has several rewards. Tshela was once an important centre for agricultural interests. Nearby is the small village of **Maduda** (✪ 04°55.21 S, 13°05.43 E), where several highly decorated graves of ancient chiefs are located. North of the village are the **Nyambi Falls**, and southeast of the village (after following the dirt road, and then walking for some way) are **Lukula Falls**. All of these areas require some walking to visit. This means you will need not only a guide, but also someone to watch your vehicle while you're out on the forest paths.

Tshela is also notable as the birthplace of Joseph Kasa-Vubu, the independent Congo's first president.

Getting there and away Visiting Tshela is easy enough, being directly north of Boma. Hang out at the taxi stands at the north end of town, and there will be vehicles going in that direction a few times a day. It should take 3–4 hours. The Mayombe Railway used to link Boma and Tshela, but the tracks were dismantled during the Mobutu years.

LUKI BIOSPHERE RESERVE *with thanks to Emilio Noorani*
Biosphere reserves are an attempt to bring about sustainable development through harmony between people and nature. They are co-ordinated by UNESCO and there are two in the Democratic Republic of the Congo: one of them is Yangambi (page 176) and the other is Luki Biosphere Reserve (✪ 5°37'25.5"S 13°05'57.7"E), in the

tropical rainforest to the north of Boma. The Luki area has been protected since the 1930s and it is the southernmost tip of the Atlantic Equatorial coastal forest, which stretches from Cameroon, through Guinea, to Cabinda and Kongo-Central. Luki has been included in UNESCO's Man and the Biosphere (MAB) programme since 1976. Camera traps have confirmed the presence of chimpanzees in the reserve: a very encouraging development, since human activities have driven them out of most of the rest of the region. The chimpanzees are completely wild and there are no plans to habituate them for tourism.

The Luki Biosphere Reserve is about 15 minutes' drive from Boma, turning left off the N1 at Lovo and then taking a track to the right after the village of Mangala. The reserve is managed by the DRC's Institute for Agricultural Studies and Research (INERA), which charges an entrance fee of US$10 (less for DRC citizens). Once inside the reserve, there are forest hikes (from a few hours to a few days), local communities to visit and learn from, river swimming, camping and other options. Guides are available for all these activities and more. Wear long sleeves and use good insect repellent, especially against sandflies.

Guest accommodation (**$**) is available, with mosquito nets, constant electricity from solar panels and batteries, and running water harvested from rainwater. Locally produced meals can be provided by arrangement (**$**). To reserve accommodation, contact **m** 081 862 8735 or **e** ernestinetipi@gmail.com or Entumba@wwfdrc.org.

MUANDA (✥ 05°55.00 S, 12°22.31 E) The Democratic Republic of the Congo's only true ocean town, Muanda (also spelled Moanda) has a distinctive colonial atmosphere with numerous old buildings built on the sandy shores of the southern Atlantic. It is a busy place these days, but feels a long way from Kinshasa and Matadi.

Muanda has an excellent stretch of beaches along the southern Atlantic Ocean, and in better days, when the roads were well maintained, it was a popular weekend spot for Kinshasa's expatriates. The best-known beach is **Tonde Plage**, at the foot of the cliffs edging the town. Boats can be rented for fishing here. Up the coast from Muanda is the small fishing village of **Nsiamfumu**, with its Plage Écologique and the other well-regarded beach in the area, **Kumbi Plage**. Apart from the attractions of the beaches, Muanda is the best base for visiting **Mangroves National Park**.

South of Muanda is the port of **Banana**, which was the first colonial outpost built in the Congo. It was occupied intermittently by Dutch and Portuguese interests, largely as part of the slave trade, before the arrival of the Belgians, and in 1873 it even had a regular passenger-ship service to Rotterdam. The redevelopment of Banana port is expected to be completed in 2025, when it will become the DRC's only deepwater port.

Getting there and away To or from **Angola**, the city of Cabinda is less than 50km from Muanda – you will probably spend more time waiting to cross the border than driving. If you are on foot or bicycle, it is feasible to hire a motorboat in Muanda and cross the river to the Angolan town of Soyo; make sure you have a visa for Angola before you try this.

Depending on traffic conditions, it should take 1½–2 hours to drive to or from **Boma** (104km). Shared taxis leave Boma from the RTNC roundabout. There is no longer a shared boat service. Motorboats can be hired privately; expect to pay several hundred dollars for the trip between Boma and Muanda. The drive to or from **Kinshasa** is just about possible within a day, although most people break the journey, for example in Matadi. Muanda has a small airport; ask locally if flights to Kinshasa are operating.

🏠 Where to stay

La Beviour (59 rooms) Rue de la Mission 1; m 081 777 7600, 099 997 7600; e info@labeviourhotel.com; w labeviourhotel. com; ☑ La Beviour. On the seafront; rooms in bungalows set in landscaped grounds studded with palm trees; private beach. Restaurant with sea views, pool, terrace bar overlooking beach, conference facilities. Kayaks, pedalos, jet skis for hire; boat trips & visits to Mangroves National Park can be arranged. Bungalows all en suite, with terrace, AC, TV, tea/coffee-making facilities; b/fast, Wi-Fi, access to beach & pool inc. $$$$–$$$$$

New Cliff (30 rooms) On N1 where it reaches sea; m 082 123 8479. On the main road towards Banana, overlooking the sea. Restaurant specialising in fish & seafood; rooms in chalets behind restaurant. All rooms en suite with AC, TV, Wi-Fi. $$$

Maison d'Accueil (30 rooms) Av de la Mission; m 081 506 8890, 081 003 6787. Run by the Catholic Sisters of Charity (Soeurs de la Charité). Simple accommodation blocks set around carefully tended garden; close to steps accessing beach (Plage Tonde); meals available by arrangement; reliable electricity & water. Rooms have simple en-suite bathroom, mosquito net, fridge & shared covered terrace. Rooms with fan $, with AC $$

✖ Where to eat and drink

NTV Bd du 30 Juin; m 097 894 6882, 089 011 111; ☑ NoorTajvillage Muanda. A local mini-chain, with restaurants in Boma, Muanda & Kinshasa. Indian, Congolese & international menu, including fish & tandoori; set meal offers at w/ends. Vegetarian & vegan Indian options. $

Plage Tonde Small kiosks on the beach serve portions of fish & *cossa-cossa*, with cold beers; very affordable. $

What to see and do

Mangroves National Park (Muanda Marine Reserve) (⊕ 05°45′S, 012° 45′E) Home to hippopotamuses, turtles and the elusive manatees, the mangrove forests of the Democratic Republic of the Congo's smallest protected area are the main reason many travellers visit Muanda. Mangroves National Park is a 'Ramsar' wetland of international importance. The central protected area covers a total of 768km², with a buffer zone stretching through the town of Muanda almost as far as the border with Angola's Cabinda exclave. It has three subdivisions: the mangrove islands, the coastal strip and the land along the river.

To visit Mangroves National Park, you will first need to buy a permit from ICCN's office, on Avenue de Commerce in Muanda (near the hospital). ICCN can give you information and provide you with a guide; alternatively, your hotel will probably be able to find a guide for you. In the **coastal** zone, the turtles nest from November to January – a wonderful sight, if you are fortunate enough to be there at the right time. In the inner section, along the **river**, you can see antelopes, crocodiles, buffaloes and, further upriver, hippos. The hippopotamus pod is quite far upriver; if you can afford it, a good option would be to pay a boatman to take you from Boma to Muanda, or vice versa, which would take you past the hippos (and mangroves) on the way. The **mangrove islands** are the most protected part of the national park, but they can be visited with the ICCN permit. There are several small villages on the islands, where you can learn how the villagers fish for prawns (*cossa-cossa*). One of the islands you can visit was a staging area for the slave trade; it was later used as a prison by the Belgian colonial authorities and by Mobutu (page 31).

Manatees are nocturnal animals, which means you are very unlikely to spot any on your trip, although it is nice to know they are there. Sadly, they are poached by nearby villagers for bushmeat. Apart from poaching, the main threat to their habitat is from charcoal-burning. The Congo mangroves are very large – up to 20m high, with aerial roots up to 10m long – which makes them a valuable resource for the charcoal trade. As the mangroves are felled, the manatees (and other river animals) have fewer places to shelter. This is a conundrum for conservation organisations; the villagers who live on the islands aren't allowed to clear land for agriculture, because they are in a protected area, but they have no other sources of income. Ecotourism – including the cossa-cossa lunches they offer to visitors – is their only sustainable alternative.

5

The Interior

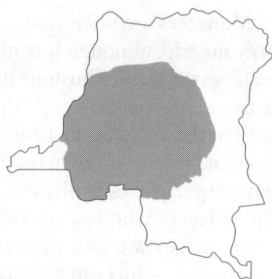

The central section of the Democratic Republic of the Congo has the least infrastructure, the fewest foreigners and the fewest amenities in the nation. It is difficult to get to, even by air; passenger boats no longer serve the river ports and only the largest towns have scheduled flights. Yet if you do visit, you will be seeing some of the most untouched wilderness left on the continent. Salonga National Park is the largest remaining undeveloped tract of rainforest in Africa, notoriously difficult to access. Salonga and other forest areas south of the river are home to our cousins, the bonobos; these are the only places in the world where they can be seen in the wild. The northwestern part of the region includes the linked wetland habitats from Lake Mai-Ndombe to the town of Mbandaka.

To the south of the region, the (relative) upgrading of the Route Nationale 1 (N1) has made it just about possible to drive to Kikwit, visit Gungu – site of the famous cultural festival – and continue to the Kasai provinces, where the deep equatorial rainforest slowly gives over to rolling savannah. These provinces have vast mineral wealth; the city of Mbuji-Mayi sits above one of the world's largest known diamond deposits. Kasai was home to the country's first secessionist movement in 1960; it is the only region where Tshiluba is widely spoken. For those with plenty of time, patience and commitment, this is an intriguing region to visit.

MAI-NDOMBE

Lake Mai-Ndombe is the southernmost lake in a huge wetland area that also includes the Ngiri Triangle and Lake Tumba (page 127). It is a vast expanse (twice the size of Belgium) of flooded tropical forest and it is designated as a Wetland of International Importance. Its ecological importance is due to all its vegetation, which makes the whole area a massive carbon sink. The trees also help to regulate flooding downriver, by absorbing water in the wet season and releasing it in the dry season. Lake Mai-Ndombe is very shallow, 10m at its deepest, and its water is acidic and swampy – its name means 'black water' in Kikongo.

Also in Mai-Ndombe province are **bonobos**! It was a surprise when, in 2001, a community organisation in the Bolobo district discovered that these wonderful primates were present in its territory – until then, conservationists had believed that this was not the right sort of habitat for bonobos. The local organisation, M'Bou Mon Tour (MMT), persuaded six villages to create 'community forests' and, with support from WWF-DRC, it trains and manages village tracker teams, who monitor and habituate the bonobos, collect data on their habitat and patrol the forest to deter poaching. The project is actively trying to develop ecotourism; visitors can go into the forest with village trackers to observe bonobos in the wild. MMT operates from a farm near the village of Nkala, where simple accommodation is available. WWF has five bungalows to rent, with toilets and showers, at its base

Bonobos are sometimes called the 'hippie apes'. They have evolved to avoid fighting, their social structure is matriarchal and, famously, they use social sexual contact to strengthen group cohesion and defuse potential conflicts. Unlike chimpanzees, to which they are closely related, bonobos have never had to share their habitat with other apes. They live only on the left bank of the River Congo (generally, south of the river), while chimpanzees and gorillas are found only on the right bank; none of the great apes can swim, so rivers are barriers for them. It is thought that chimpanzees have evolved to become aggressive because they had to be able to protect their territory from their rival apes.

The dominant bonobo in any group is always a female: the matriarch or 'queen'. Female bonobos have external genitalia, which swell in response to various situations, but – like female humans – they do not come into heat but are available for sex at all times. Females rub their genitals together to strengthen their relationships; if any bonobo in the group shows signs of being stressed or anxious, another member of the group will run over and use sexual contact to calm him or her; when the group is feeding, its members will have sex with each other to wish each other 'bon appétit'. They share food with each other and will even share it with strangers to the group.

Although bonobos and chimpanzees have very different approaches to conflict, they are closely related – to each other, and to us. Some 98.7% of the DNA in humans, bonobos and chimpanzees is identical. Until 1933, when they were recognised as a distinct species (*Pan paniscus*), it was believed that bonobos were merely a small type of chimpanzee (*Pan troglodytes*). Both species sleep in nests in the treetops, while gorillas sleep on the forest floor.

The main threat to bonobos comes from poachers, hunting the adults for bushmeat. When a group of bonobos retires for the night to their nests, the 'queen' makes a very distinctive loud cry ('Lights out!'). The poachers use this cry to locate the nests and lay traps below them while the bonobos are asleep. In the morning, they come down from the treetops and are caught in the traps. Juvenile bonobos are of no use to the poachers, because they do not have enough meat on them; they are usually sold as pets, but without the love and support of their mothers and the rest of their group, they pine and die. Nobody knows how many bonobos are left in the wild, but it could be as few as 5,000. Protecting the species requires not only safeguarding their habitat but also providing local human communities with alternative sources of income to selling bushmeat.

camp at Malebo. Further information can be found at **w** bonobosworld.org (search for M'bou Mon Tour) and **w** wwfdrc.org.

PRACTICALITIES It is not straightforward to get to Mai-Ndombe. The best option is probably a flight from Kinshasa to Nioki (weekly with **w** kinavia.com) and then arranging a boat or pirogue to the lake. To Nkala, the best option from Kinshasa is chartering a boat upriver. Alternatively, flying to Bandundu, a boat or pirogue to Mushie would at least get you to somewhere you might find a motorbike to take you the last stretch.

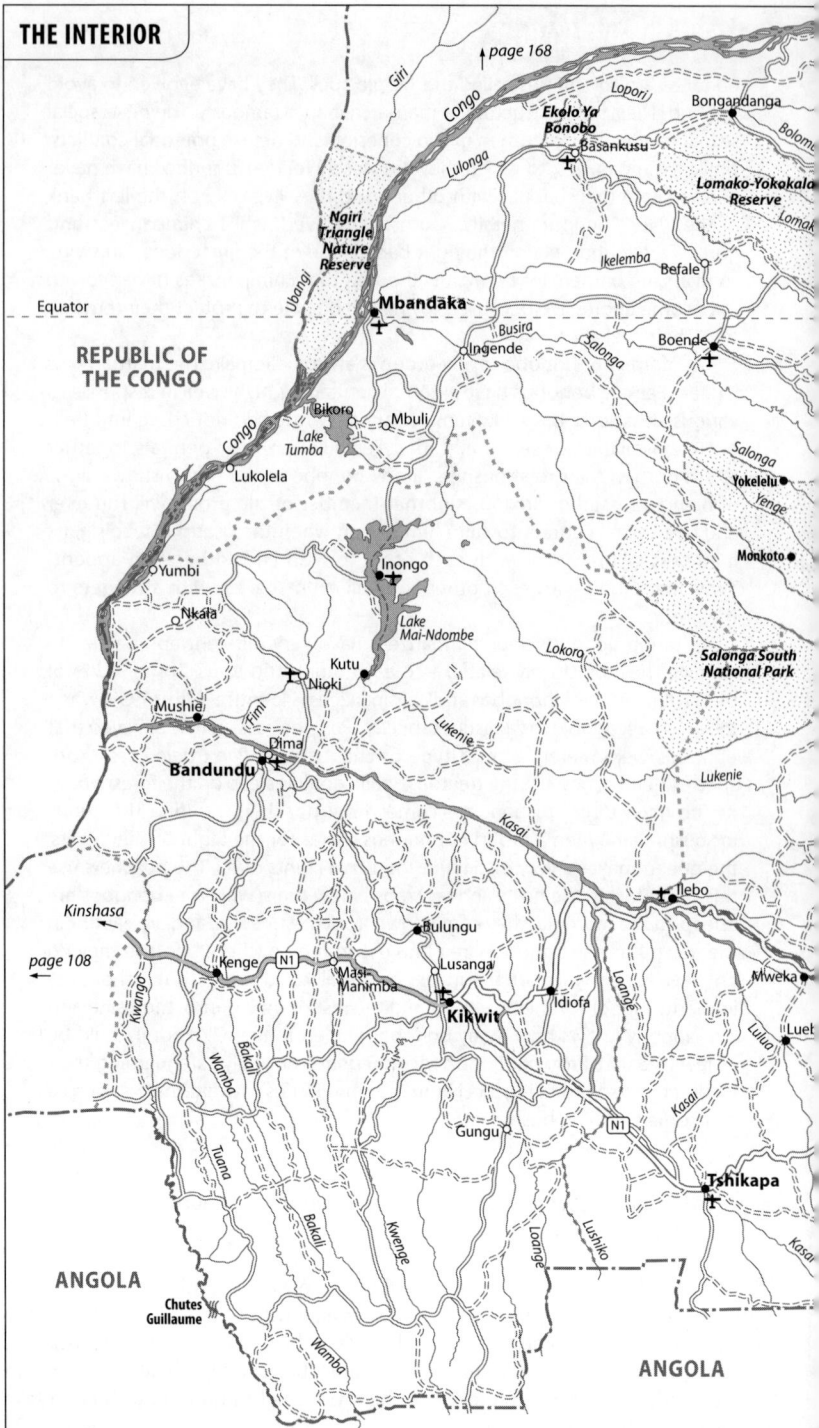

↑ page 168

← page 108

Giri
Congo
Lopori
Bongandanga
Bolom
Ekolo Ya Bonobo
Basankusu
Lulonga
Lomako-Yokokala Reserve
Lomak
Ngiri Triangle Nature Reserve
Ubangi
Ikelemba
Befale

Equator

REPUBLIC OF THE CONGO

Mbandaka
Busira
Ingende
Salonga
Boende

Bikoro
Mbuli
Lake Tumba
Lukolela
Salonga
Yokelelu
Yenge

Congo
Inongo
Lake Mai-Ndombe
Monkoto

Yumbi
Nkala
Lokoro
Salonga South National Park

Kutu
Nioki
Lukenie

Mushie
Fimi
Dima
Lukenie

Bandundu
Kasai

Ilebo

Kinshasa
Bulungu
Kwango
Mweka
Kenge
N1
Masi-Manimba
Lusanga
Loange
Luet
Wamba
Bokali
Kikwit
Idiofa
Luilua
Kasai

Tuana
Gungu
N1
Kasai

Bokali
Kwenge
Loange
Lushiko

ANGOLA
Chutes Guillaume
Wamba

ANGOLA

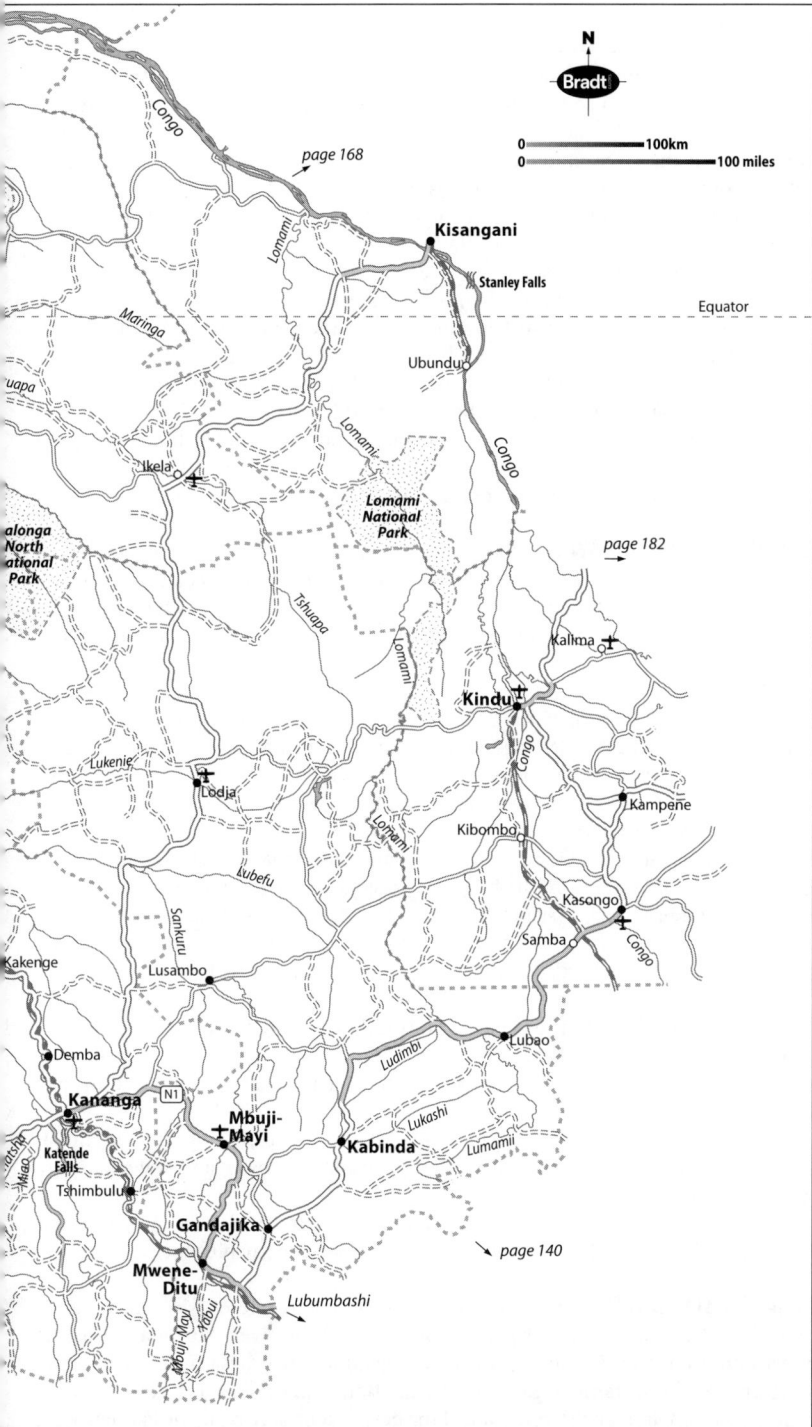

N

Bradt

0	100km
0	100 miles

page 168

Kisangani

Stanley Falls

Equator

Ubundu

Congo

Lomami

Maringa

Ikela

Lomami

Lomami National Park

page 182

alonga North ational Park

Tshuapa

Kalima

Kindu

Lomami

Congo

Lukenie

Lodja

Kampene

Kibombo

Lubefu

Sankuru

Kasongo

Congo

Samba

Kakenge

Lusambo

Demba

Lubao

Ludimbi

Kananga

N1

Mbuji-Mayi

Lukashi

Kabinda

Lumamii

Katende Falls

Tshimbulu

Lulua

Gandajika

page 140

Mwene-Ditu

Mbuji-Mayi

Lubilanji

Lubumbashi

Mbandaka (pronounced 'Ban-da-ka') is a humid city on the River Congo, where the river takes its turn south and starts to mark the border between the Republic and the Democratic Republic named after it. Henry Morton Stanley, on his original voyage down the river, stopped here briefly to mark the Equator. In fact, when Mbandaka was founded in 1883, it was originally called 'Equator'. Its name was later changed to Coquilhatville, after Lieutenant Coquilhat, who was with Stanley when they established the first river station here. 'Equateur' survives as the name of the province of which Mbandaka is the capital.

Mbandaka's claim to historical fame comes from the Coquilhatville Conference, held in 1961, which saw Moïse Tshombe come to the table to bargain with Joseph Kasa-Vubu about bringing Katanga back from secession (page 29). While the conference was unsuccessful, it was the catalyst that kept the new nation of Congo-Léopoldville together. Mobutu Sese Seko changed the name from Coquilhatville to Mbandaka during his 'Africanisation' campaign of the late 1960s, though the local inhabitants had used this name for decades before – as well as Wangata, which is still the name of one of the town's two administrative districts.

GETTING THERE AND AWAY Mbandaka Airport has direct flight connections, at the time of writing, with Kinshasa Ndjili a couple of times a week (w caacongo. com) and with Gbadolite once a week (w airkasai.cd). The river is the only other realistically feasible way to get to Mbandaka; see page 94 for advice on this option.

WHERE TO STAY

Benghazi (70 rooms) Av Bosomi 75; m 089 974 3319; ◾ Hotel Benghazi. 24hr water & electricity, Wi-Fi; secure; river views; restaurant, terrace. Apartment with AC, villa with AC & kitchen, both **$$$$$**, dbl rooms with fan **$$**
Emma (23 rooms, 2 suites) Ave Okito 6, Q/ Mambenga; m 082 199 8741, 099 811 4949; e auberge.emma@gmail.com; ◾ Auberge EMMA – Mbandaka Ville. 24hr electricity (solar panels); secure; free Wi-Fi; restaurant; transfers to/from

Mbandaka Airport by arrangement; responsive management. Rooms of various standards, all en suite, b/fast inc. Basic rooms have fan **$$**, others AC **$$–$$$**, 2 suites with 2 rooms, AC & sat TV **$$$$**
Notre Dame de SacréCoeur (5 rooms) Bd Lumumba; m 085 818 9998 (WhatsApp), 081 003 6735. Simple rooms beside the church, all en suite with running water, 24hr electricity & Wi-Fi; secure. B/fast & other meals available by arrangement. **$**

OTHER PRACTICALITIES The **General Hospital** in Mbandaka (Hôpital Général de Référence; m 085 811 9119) meets basic international standards. For serious illness or injury, if you are fit to travel, you should arrange medical evacuation to Europe or South Africa.

Wi-Fi is intermittent everywhere in Mbandaka, including in the hotels listed above. Make the most of it while it is available! Power and water cuts are also frequent.

Vehicles can be hired, with driver, from M Jacques (m 085 812 9915; US$100 per day plus fuel), or M Robert (m 099 810 4635; US$80 per day plus fuel).

WHAT TO SEE AND DO The River Congo, of course, is one of Mbandaka's great sights. In the past, when passenger steamers plied the river, Mbandaka was the most important transit point between Kisangani and Kinshasa. Just out of town, upriver, are the **botanical gardens**, Jardin Botanique d'Eala (w lejardindeala. wordpress.com, in French), once one of the best in central Africa. The gardens were created in 1900, with the goal of cataloguing the region's flora and assessing the commercial agricultural potential of the region. They occupy roughly 370ha and have over 3,000 species of trees and plants. Like everywhere else in the country, though, neglect and conflict have taken their toll; the gardens were occupied and looted by foreign fighters during the Second Congo War. ICCN, which manages the site, continues to seek international funding to restore the gardens to their former glory. It's still a good escape from town, however.

Across the river from Mbandaka, and covering nearly 3,000km^2 of swamp forest between the Congo and Ubangi rivers, is the **Ngiri Triangle Nature Reserve** (m 085 358 7167). Supported by WWF, it was the first project to be financed from the sale of carbon credits. The reserve has populations of African bush elephants, chimpanzees and hippopotamuses. A wildlife haven that is less difficult to access is **Lake Tumba**, about 100km south of Mbandaka, with many species of birdlife. The lake used to be famous for its tilapia and other fish, but the populations have been damaged by overfishing.

Mbandaka is one of the bases from which **Pygmy communities** can be visited; see page 180 for further information about the indigenous Pygmy peoples. Visits must be arranged through a tour operator. These communities are semi-nomadic and often move their settlements from one place to another – you can't just wander into the forest looking for them. See page 52 for national and international operators; alternatively, once in Mbandaka, ask at your hotel if they can contact a guide for you.

SALONGA NATIONAL PARK

In the heart of the DRC, Salonga National Park (w salonga.org) is the third largest forest protected area in the world, covering 3.6 million hectares – larger than Belgium! It covers such a huge area that not all of it has been explored. The national park exists to protect the equatorial forests and wetlands that occupy the middle of the DRC, criss-crossed with far more rivers than roads, and the wildlife that need them to survive. A 45km-wide corridor divides the two sectors of the park: Salonga North and Salonga South.

Salonga is home to several vulnerable endemic species, including the bonobo, found only south of the River Congo and thus only in the DRC. It also has slender-snouted crocodiles (*Mecistops leptorhynchus*), forest elephants (*Loxodonta cyclotis*), several species of pangolin, and hippos. Over 50 species of mammals are known to live in Salonga, including buffalo, leopards and nine kinds of antelope. Birdlife is vibrant – over 200 species! – including hornbills and the threatened Congo peafowl, the DRC's national bird.

It became a national park in November 1970 and a UNESCO World Heritage Site in 1984. In 1999, UNESCO added Salonga to its list of World Heritage Sites in Danger, because of the high level of poaching and illegal encroachments. ICCN and WWF, which co-manage the park, worked with UNESCO to address these problems, and in 2021 Salonga was removed from the Danger list. Poaching is still a problem, mainly for bushmeat but also for ivory, for which forest elephants are the target. There is also an international market for live animals, particularly bonobos, parrots and small primates. The park's excellent website has extensive information about the wildlife and human communities there.

GETTING THERE AND AWAY Visiting Salonga is one of the more difficult things to do in the DRC. The British TV presenter Simon Reeve went there as part of his

Wilderness series, first broadcast in 2024. Getting there required several days upriver in a pirogue, followed by two days on foot, hacking through the jungle, to reach an abandoned camp on the edge of the national park where he and his support team could shelter. Their water, food and medical supplies were brought by motorbike from the village where they spent the first night. The team then spent several days searching through the dense, swampy forest. They eventually came across a family of bonobos, and it must have been wonderful to see these beautiful creatures in the wild. However, Salongo is not for the under-equipped or under-resourced. Reeve (not a stranger to jungles) described it as the most difficult jungle he had ever been in. See pages 122 and opposite for fractionally easier ways to see bonobos in the wild.

The least difficult way to visit Salonga (unless you are a TV presenter) is to pay a tour operator to organise your trip. To attempt it individually – although it cannot be done without a guide – you first need to buy a park permit from the ICCN office in Kinshasa or Mbandaka. ICCN will be able to advise you on where to find a guide. To get to the park, you can either charter an aircraft to **Monkoto** (✛ 01°44.36 S, 20°41.09 E), where the park's administrative offices are located, or hire a boat or pirogue to take you there from Mbandaka – the estimated travel time is around seven days, one-way. To enter the park from the south, you could take a train or plane to Ilebo, then make your way (probably by a combination of pirogue and foot) to **Dekese** (✛ 03°29.09 S, 21°22.43 E) and hack your way through to Anga.

Within Salonga North, near the ranger station at **Yokelelu**, an ecotourism site is under construction at the time of writing. Once completed, it will include visitor accommodation, in solidly built bungalows, and a restaurant overlooking the river. Elsewhere in the park, there are ranger stations at Monkoto, Anga and Mundja in Salonga South and Mondjoku and Watsikengo in Salonga North. These stations do not provide accommodation, but the rangers may be able to assist you in a genuine emergency.

BASANKUSU (✛ 01°13.26 N, 19°47.54 E)

The small town of Basankusu, upriver from Mbandaka, is a base for visits to two bonobo habitats: Ekolo Ya Bonobo and Lomako-Yokokala. Friends of Bonobos, which co-manages Ekolo Ya Bonobo, and the African Wildlife Foundation, which co-manages Lomako-Yokokala, both have field offices in Basankusu. The town has an airstrip, but no regular flights; the most practical way to get there is by boat from Mbandaka. Simple accommodation is available.

LOMAKO-YOKOKALA RESERVE The Lomako-Yokokala faunal reserve, covering 3,625km^2 between the Lomako and Bolombo rivers, is designed to protect bonobos by supporting local people, tackling poaching and monitoring wildlife populations and habitat. It was created in 2006 and is managed by ICCN and the African Wildlife Foundation (w awf.org). AWF's support includes training for rangers, particularly in how to combat wildlife crime, and providing local communities with alternatives to selling bushmeat, including finance for micro-businesses. Antwerp Zoo's Centre for Research and Conservation (w antwerpzoofoundation.com) also supports the local communities and monitors the bonobo population.

In addition to bonobos, other animals make their home in the reserve's area, including the Congo peafowl, African golden cat, giant pangolin and forest elephants. While tourism is not the primary goal of the reserve, those involved recognise that small-scale tourism can bring benefits, with the income it generates and the encouragement it can give to the park rangers and local communities.

Groups who wish to track bonobos should be small – no more than four, and ideally only two at a time. A visit of three to four days should be sufficient to see them. If you're interested in the other animals in the reserve, other tours can also be arranged on request.

Practicalities Visiting this area takes time and the costs are high. From Basankusu, you take a boat down the Lomako River to **Iyema**, the field camp where the scientists researching bonobos and their habitat are based. They include a team of researchers from Antwerp Zoo, whose website (see opposite) has a simple map of the reserve as well as information about the team's activities. From Iyema, you can accompany one of the researchers as they track bonobos; this usually involves several hours' hiking through the forest. There is no tourist infrastructure at Iyema – visitors must bring their own tents and supplies. Alternatively, you could take the once-weekly flight (w airkasai.cd) from Kinshasa to **Lisala**, take a boat across the River Congo and continue by motorbike and on foot to Iyema.

EKOLO YA BONOBO Soon after the opening of Lola Ya Bonobo (page 107), its founder, Claudine André, started to look for a site where some of the orphaned bonobos could safely be returned to the wild. Like other great apes, bonobos can live into their forties, so it was unsustainable to keep them all in the sanctuary. In 2009, she led the first ever rewilding of bonobos, with the release of a group under its matriarch. A second group, of 14 bonobos, was released in 2022 (delayed by a combination of an Ebola outbreak, Covid-19 and legal and technical problems). Ekolo Ya Bonobo, which means 'Land of the Bonobos' in Lingala, now has 30 adult bonobos; healthy babies have been born in both groups. The reserve now covers 117,000 acres of rainforest, protected by a team of rangers.

In June 2023, Ekolo's installations were attacked by a group of young men, who also burned homes in nearby villages. Two bonobos were killed and the buildings at Ekolo's base camp were destroyed. The perpetrators were from one of the local communities, although their actions did not represent that community. In response, the management team has increased its engagement with local people and improved its channels of communication with them.

Ekolo Ya Bonobo is sandwiched between the Matoku and Lopori rivers, across the water from Basankusu. It is not open to visitors, at the time of writing, but you can sometimes see the resident bonobos on the riverbank from a pirogue.

KIKWIT

Kikwit is the first large city one arrives at east of Kinshasa – over 500km from the capital. Now that the N1 has been upgraded (to some extent), it is possible to drive there from Kinshasa within a day, as long as you leave early enough to beat the capital's traffic jams. Kikwit has an airport, but now that the road is better, there are far fewer flights than there used to be.

Kwilu, the province of which Kikwit is the principal city, was the centre of a rebellion between 1963 and 1965, at the same time as the better-known Simba rebellion in the northeast of the country. Its leader was Pierre Mulele, who had been minister of education in Patrice Lumumba's government and was inspired by Maoism. Kikwit next came to international attention in 1995 with an outbreak of Ebola. This was one of the first times that Ebola had been treated in a hospital setting. Provincial and national authorities did their best to control the spread of the infection, converting a ward in Kikwit general hospital into an isolation unit, staffed by volunteer health professionals. Despite these efforts, 245 people are known to have died in the outbreak. A happier reason to have heard of Kwilu is the festival of traditional culture at Gungu (see below).

With your own (or your own rented) 4x4 transport, there are waterfalls near the Angolan border that are worth a visit: **Chutes Guillaume** (also called **Chutes Tembo**), and slightly upriver **Chutes Kasongo-Lunda**. The roads to and from Kikwit have numerous bridges which pass over several picturesque waterfalls – on the way to Kinshasa and then between Tshikapa and Kananga.

WHERE TO STAY

Bikuna (31 rooms, 5 apartments) Av Lukengo; m 082 229 9066, 099 053 2949; f Flat hôtel bikuna kikwit. Has restaurant, garden, secure parking. All rooms en suite with AC or fan & TV. Standard rooms **$**, 7 larger rooms **$$**, bungalows with kitchen/diner **$$$**

Oasis Lorra (19 rooms) Av Lukoki 55; m 081 242 4241, 082 402 0782; e oasiskikwit@gmail.com; f Oasis Lorra Hotel. Simply furnished rooms, en suite with desk, AC, TV. **$$**

GUNGU

The people of Gungu belong to the Pende community and have retained many of their ancestral customs and traditions. They have celebrated these at the **Gungu Festival** since colonial times. The festival began in the 1920s as a commemoration of Belgium's National Day, 21 July. After independence in 1960, the festival fell into abeyance, although the Pende people of Gungu continued to celebrate their forefathers' traditions. These include initiation rites for boys entering adulthood, where the initiates learn to make the unique Pende raffia costumes and special masks and then dance on stilts. Different events – the installation of the chief of the community, funerals, etc – require different masks; the men also wear spectacular head-dresses and both men and women paint their faces and bodies with plant-derived dyes.

The Gungu Festival was revived in 1998, with the participation of communities from elsewhere in the DRC as well as the Pende. In theory it is held in alternate years in Gungu and in another part of the country; this being the DRC, the rotation is not altogether predictable. At the time of writing, the most recent festival in Gungu was in 2022.

Gungu's cultural heritage is also celebrated in its **museum**, which had assembled tens of thousands of traditional artefacts, mostly from the Pende culture, some from the late 18th century. In late 2021, the museum building caught fire and much of the collection was destroyed. The museum's founder and director managed to salvage about 10,000 artefacts and, until a new museum can be built, he stores and displays them in his home. The collection is open to the public and hosts visits from local schools.

Gungu is a short drive down a dirt track from the main N1 road, between Kikwit and Tshikapa. There is some simple accommodation in the village, although it is sure to be fully booked during the Gungu Festival.

ILEBO (⊕ *04°19.51 S, 20°35.02 E*)

Even before the arrival of the Belgian colonisers, Ilebo's strategic location made it an important settlement. It sits at the highest navigable point of the River Kasai, which flows into the Congo north of Kinshasa. For the Belgians, who called it Port-Francqui, it was a vital link in the export of minerals from Katanga and Kasai, which were brought by rail from Lubumbashi, then loaded on to riverboats. It is still used as a cargo port, although the mining companies now have other options – many truck the ore or concentrates to ports in southern Africa and the funders of the Lobito Atlantic Railway obviously hope that it will become a favoured route.

Trains run from Lubumbashi and Kananga to Ilebo several times a month. If you have made your way by rail to Ilebo, you are probably hoping to find a boat or pirogue to take you either upriver to Salonga National Park (page 127) or downriver to Bandundu for the sights in Mai-Ndombe (page 122). By road to Kinshasa, it would be a long, uncomfortable drive to join the N1, then several slightly less uncomfortable hours on the N1. If you arrive in Ilebo on the wrong day for a train, you will probably be able to find some kind of transport to Kananga.

WHAT TO SEE AND DO Going south from Ilebo on a bad road towards the village of Djokupunda are several notable natural sites, starting with the **Madimape Lakes** (also called the **Green Lakes**), once a popular spot for touring groups in the days of the Belgian Congo. Just south are some curious rock formations called **Baboon's Hole**, created by the irregular weather and drainage patterns in the region. The road exists, at least in theory, to the former colonial town of Charlesville, now **Djokupunda**, and just south of the town is a picturesque **waterfall** on the River Kasai. A road connects Djokupunda to Luebo which should allow you to get back on track.

KANANGA

Kananga's crumbling buildings and barren gravel streets have an aura about them of the USA's 'Wild West'. With a bit of imagination, one can still picture what this city was like in its colonial days: an administrative and transport hub for the whole Kasai region. It is still the second most important town in this Tshiluba-speaking region and, like its nearby neighbour Mbuji-Mayi, has an economy based on the mining industry. However, you'll see far less development in Kananga than Mbuji-Mayi.

Formerly known as Luluabourg, the town was the capital of the secessionist Federal State of South Kasai, or the Mining State of South Kasai, in 1960 and 1961. Luluabourg had been under consideration as the new nation's capital, but the rebellion put paid to that idea. The leader of the secession, Albert Kalonji, revived ancient Luba traditions and became *Mulopwe* (emperor) of the Baluba people and then king of the new state. However, retribution was swift and brutal – by the end of 1961 Kananga had been captured by soldiers from Léopoldville. Rebels persisted west of Luluabourg for several years in the Tshikapa region, until intervention by the UN in 1964 ended their rebellion for good.

GETTING THERE AND AWAY By **air**, CAA (w caacongo.com) has a couple of flights a week to Kananga from Kinshasa and from Lubumbashi. By **rail**, there are 'express' trains from Lubumbashi; 'regional' trains between Kananga and Ilebo; and connections with Dilolo, from where the Lobito Atlantic Railway runs across Angola to the Atlantic (page 139). All these connections from Kananga run every two weeks. Schedules can be checked and tickets purchased at any of these railway stations.

By **road**, the N1 between Kananga and Mbuji-Mayi has been upgraded (to some extent); it should take about 5 hours to cover the 180km between the two cities, rather than the entire day as in the past. Kananga from Mwene-Ditu, about 240km, should take around 6 hours via Tshimbulu. All other roads in the vicinity are atrocious.

GETTING AROUND The city sits on the railway line between Lubumbashi and Ilebo. On the far eastern end of the town is the **airport**, and close to the centre is the **railway station**. Cross the railway, pass the **CAA agency**, and head southwards along Boulevard Lumumba to reach the administrative centre, with the city hall and the governorate.

🏠 WHERE TO STAY *Map, opposite*

Ekaf (7 rooms) Cnr of Av Gécamines & Av Saio; m 081 032 7929, 081 998 1827. Beautiful courtyard, secure parking, good restaurant. Rooms in various categories, b/fast inc. With shower **$**, shower & TV **$$**, en-suite bathroom & TV **$$$**, apartments with living room, bathroom, TV, mini-bar **$$$$**

Kapi-Be Garden (24 rooms) 4 Av Mulamba Nyunyu, Q Plateau, Loc Oasis; m 099 359 3684, 081 869 1187; e mgardenkapyb@gmail.com; 🅵 Kapi-Be Garden MOTEL. Quiet location on outskirts of town, on airport road; secure parking, restaurant, terrace bar, pool; conference room; 4x4 hire available (US$120 per day); efficient management. All rooms en suite with AC & TV, some have balcony; b/fast inc. **$$$**, suite **$$$$**

Fine Fleur (4 rooms) Av Walikale 337, Q/Bianki; m 099 842 8469; 🅵 Fine Fleur Kananga. Small but comfortable guesthouse on the south edge of town. Has secure parking, terrace bar, restaurant. Rooms en suite with bathtub; AC, TV, fridge. B/fast inc. **$$**

Hôtel Med (24 rooms) Av Likasi 329; m 099 506 2049; e hotelmed@yahoo.fr. Large rooms with TV, fridge & AC, but power only runs for 4hrs a night. Secure parking available. B/fast inc, & they will make other meals upon request. **$$**

Grand (35 rooms) Bd Lumumba 700; m 085 328 0532, 097 321 2902, 081 223 0777; e grandhoteldekananga@gmail.com. Rooms in various categories, b/fast inc. Wi-Fi only on 1st floor. **$**; apartment **$$**

✗ WHERE TO EAT AND DRINK *Map, opposite*

Kananga's culinary scene is quite limited. The best dining in the centre is at the Ekaf and Kapi-Be Garden hotels (both **$$**). Apart from the hotels, **Mona Luxe** (**$$**), at the start of Boulevard Lumumba, is popular. For something truly cheap and Congolese, **Chez Maman Omos** (**$**) is a tiny, crowded little shop with a few plastic chairs; the dishes of the day are written on paper and taped to the window.

OTHER PRACTICALITIES Kananga suffers from frequent **power cuts** and water interruptions. Charge your phone and any other equipment whenever you can.

A **4x4 vehicle**, with driver, can be hired from New Dynamic Business (m 081 943 7994; e jmsquared007@gmail.com) and from Kapi-Be Garden hotel (see above).

For **souvenir shopping**, there are artists who will come by your hotel and offer you some finely crafted woodcarvings from across the Kasai provinces. These are well worth taking a look at – you'll see some amazing artefacts from the centre of the DRC for prices that one could only dream of in the major cities, let alone in Europe. Ask at the reception of your hotel for '*les artistes*' if you want to pick up some excellent Kasai souvenirs. It's worth noting that you should only buy a few pieces, certainly fewer than ten – any more and you could be accused of buying for commercial purposes, which requires an export permit. If you don't have one, you will either have to lose your souvenirs or bribe your way out of the problem on departure.

WHAT TO SEE AND DO Independence Square (Place de l'Indépendance), at the courthouse on Boulevard Lumumba, commemorates the **Luluabourg mutiny**. In February 1944, Congolese NCOs serving in the colonial army mutinied in Luluabourg. The mutineers failed to spread their insurrection to other garrisons and the leaders were executed.

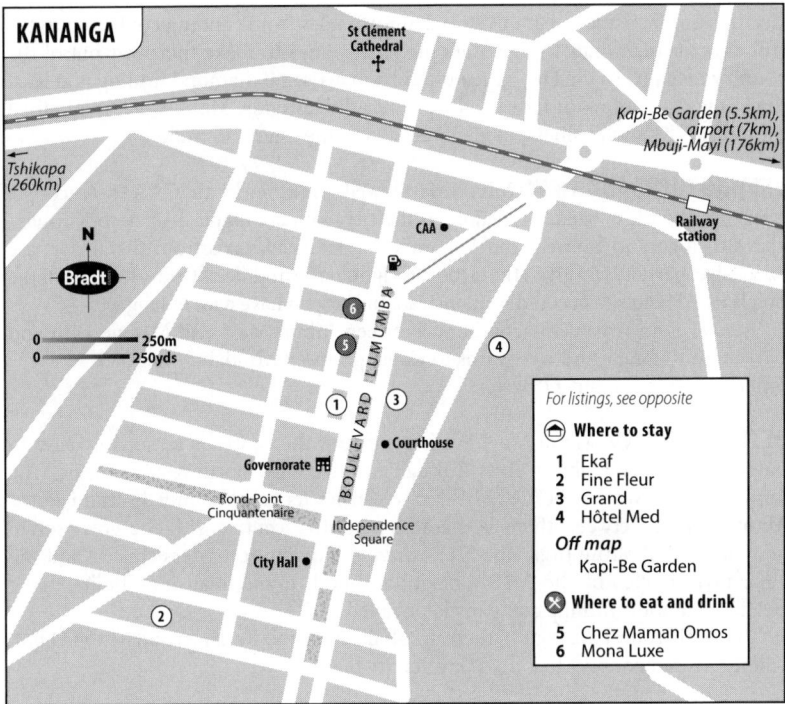

KANANGA

St Clément Cathedral ✝

Kapi-Be Garden (5.5km),
airport (7km),
Mbuji-Mayi (176km)

Tshikapa
(260km)

Railway
station

CAA ●

N

Bradt

⑥

⑤

④

0 ——— 250m
0 ——— 250yds

① ③

● Courthouse

Governorate ⊞

Rond-Point
Cinquantenaire

Independence
Square

City Hall ●

②

For listings, see opposite

🛏 **Where to stay**

1 Ekaf
2 Fine Fleur
3 Grand
4 Hôtel Med

Off map
   Kapi-Be Garden

✖ **Where to eat and drink**

5 Chez Maman Omos
6 Mona Luxe

Across the railway line is the city's **St Clément Cathedral**, an attractive example of colonial architecture, built in 1935. Kananga also has a decent waterfall just south of it, the **Katende Falls**, accessible via a road off the main highway to Tshikapa, west out of town. Downstream from the falls is an impressive **gorge** where the River Lulua passes through, though it takes a fair amount of walking from the nearest battered road – find someone to guide you to this.

On the road to Mbuji-Mayi is **Makumba Lake** (⊕ 05°46.27 S, 23°04.21 E), a spectacular scene right on the provincial border between Kasai-Central and Kasai-Oriental. There are some large governors' residences here for vacationing elites, as well as an airport if you feel the need to arrive by chartered aircraft. For the rest of us, once you reach the village of **Makumba** you can walk down a footpath to the lakeshore. There are no services at the village, so bring everything you need.

MBUJI-MAYI

Straddling the Bushimaie River, Mbuji-Mayi is the capital of Kasai-Oriental Province. It is the largest city in the Luba-majority, Tshiluba-speaking Kasais and, probably, the third-biggest city in the country (there are no reliable statistics for any of the DRC's cities). It is the largest urban centre where Tshiluba is spoken and it is the political heartland of the UDPS party, founded by Étienne Tshisekedi, father of the current president of the DRC.

The city sits above one of the largest diamond deposits in the world and the opportunities for employment have seen its population grow to several millions, as people have been drawn to Mbuji-Mayi from Kasai's villages and from elsewhere in the country. The DRC is a member of the multi-national Kimberley Process

Certification Scheme, meant to stop diamond sales from funding conflict, but it is still easy for diamonds from Kasai's informal mines to make their way out of the country illegally. In the DRC, the output from artisanal diamond mining is at least four times the output of industrially produced diamonds. Mbuji-Mayi is a hotbed for journalists and businesspeople interested in the diamond trade.

GETTING THERE AND AWAY Mbuji-Mayi is well connected by **air**. CAA (w caacongo. com) has the most reliable schedule to the city, with six flights a week to Kinshasa and also flights to Kolwezi and Lubumbashi. As usual, taxis from the airport are expensive, particularly given the airport is right in the middle of town. To some of the hotels listed below, you could walk instead, unless you have a lot of luggage.

The N1 is in reasonable condition between Mbuji-Mayi and Mwene Ditu and beyond to Katanga, and westwards to Kananga and beyond, but the roads in every other direction remain a disaster.

GETTING AROUND Mbuji-Mayi is a big city, but the centre is reasonably easy to navigate. The N1 highway runs through it diagonally, northwest/southeast. The airport is the western border of the city centre. Its eastern limit is **Rond-Point Mama Yemo**. Between them is the administrative centre, with the governorate and city hall; **Avenue Inga** (the N1), where the diamond traders cluster; and the concentric circles of the **MIBA** neighbourhood, grand mansions built by the Belgian diamond-mining company later called MIBA.

To travel around the region, there are **shared taxis** to Kananga and Mwene Ditu, where you can connect to a train or intercity bus.

🏠 **WHERE TO STAY** *Map, opposite*
There is a good range of accommodation in Mbuji-Mayi. Power cuts are frequent and even the more expensive hotels do not run their generators all day. Running water is subject to the whims of the city – get your shower in when you can.

Dilenga (17 rooms, 16 apartments) 1 Av de la Cathédrale, Dibindi; m 099 105 9129, 085 232 9900; ⬛ Flat Hôtel Dilenga. Apartments & some rooms in bungalows separated by landscaped open corridors; secure; restaurant with Congolese & international menus; terrace bar. Card payments possible; timetabled electricity, early morning & evening. Rooms en suite with TV, fridge, AC, Wi-Fi; b/fast inc. Dbl **$$$**, apartment **$$$$**
Gloria (50 rooms) Lusambo 71, Nkashi; m 085 621 0929, 082 274 7104; ⬛ HOTEL Gloria mbujimayi. Good security, 24hr electricity, good-sized pool, gym; restaurant with Congolese & international menu, terrace bar, nightclub. All rooms en suite with AC, TV, balcony, fridge; b/fast inc. **$$$**
Kadje (40 rooms) Av Salongo, Q/ Kalundu; m 081 578 7171, 085 431 6600; e kadjehotel@ yahoo.fr. Near the airport. Has small shopping mall; children's playground; pool, tennis court, secure parking, electricity. Restaurant, terrace

bar. Often block-booked for months or even years in advance. Rooms en suite with cable TV, AC, minibar. **$$–$$$**
Ka-be (48 rooms, 8 apartments) 66 Av Inga; m 085 616 3770, 099 731 2943 (WhatsApp); e hotelkabembujimayi@gmail.com. Very central, on main city strip; secure; 3 restaurants with Congolese & international menus, terrace bar, pool & conference room. Timetabled electricity, dusk to dawn; free airport transfers for guests. All rooms en suite with TV, AC. **$$**
Kebase et Fils (11 rooms) Av Lusambo 48, Q/ Mudiba; m 085 620 3971, 085 298 3303 (both WhatsApp); e hotelkebasefils0@gmail. com; ⬛ gerant hotel kebase et fils mbuji-mayi kinshasa. Small hotel in quiet neighbourhood; secure; timetabled electricity, early morning & evening. Free airport transfers for guests; restaurant. All rooms en suite with AC; superior rooms & apartments also with TV & fridge; b/fast inc. Standard **$**, dbl/apartment **$$**

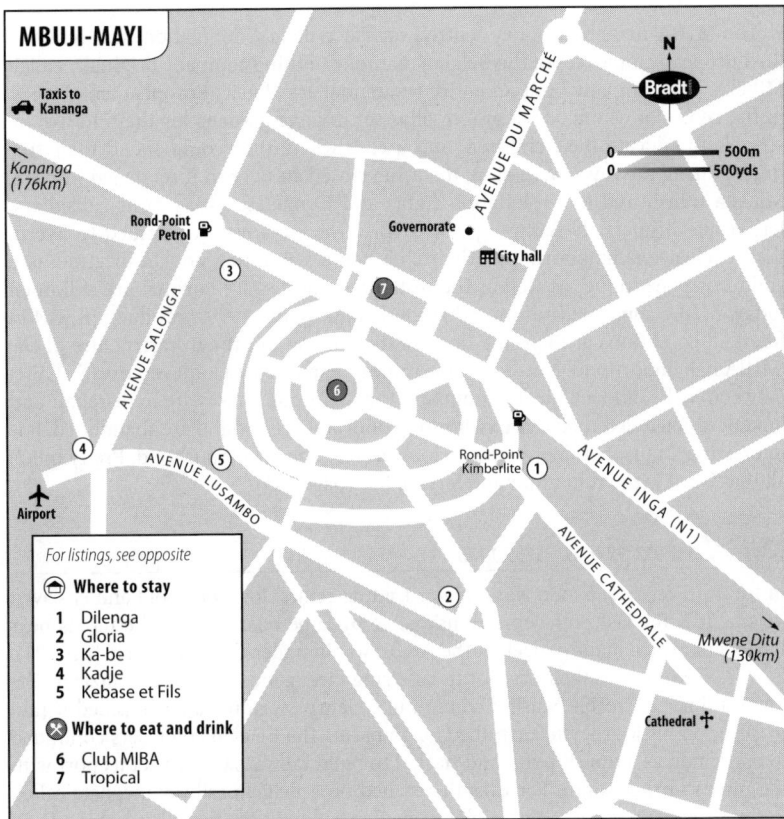

MBUJI-MAYI

Taxis to Kananga

Kananga (176km)

Rond-Point Petrol

AVENUE DU MARCHÉ

Bradt

N

0 ——— 500m
0 ——— 500yds

Governorate

City hall

③

⑦

AVENUE SALONGA

⑥

④

AVENUE LUSAMBO ⑤

Rond-Point Kimberlite ①

AVENUE INGA (N1)

Airport

AVENUE CATHÉDRALE

②

Mwene Ditu (130km)

For listings, see opposite

◉ **Where to stay**
1 Dilenga
2 Gloria
3 Ka-be
4 Kadje
5 Kebase et Fils

◉ **Where to eat and drink**
6 Club MIBA
7 Tropical

Cathedral ✝

✖ WHERE TO EAT AND DRINK *Map, above*

Club MIBA Pl de la Coopération 4; m 081 608 1406; ⏰ 07.30–22.00 daily. Once the preserve of the European employees of MIBA (page 136), nowadays open to the public; a breath of fresh air in the city. Congolese & European menu (fish, chicken, etc); the terrace becomes a nightclub in the evenings. $$

Tropical Av Inga 3; ⏹ Restaurant Tropical; ⏰ 08.00–23.00 daily. Congolese & Western dishes; secure parking; shady garden, interior with AC. $$

OTHER PRACTICALITIES The major banks around the city have **ATMs**, as do some of the larger hotels. Withdraw money from an ATM within a bank or hotel, if possible, and during daylight hours.

Vehicles (4x4, with driver) can be **hired** at the Kebase et Fils hotel (see opposite) for US$70 per day, US$100 if off-road; or from Mr Freddy Kabulu (m 085 612 7448; US$130 per day, US$200 off-road).

Mbuji-Mayi has two useful **petrol stations**: ML at the eastern end of the city centre, and another at Rond-Point Petrol. Both keep roughly the same hours, opening at 07.00 and closing at 22.00.

WHAT TO SEE AND DO Mbuji-Mayi's **cathedral** is an impressive colonial-era church, with a high bell tower and a beautiful vaulted interior with stained-glass windows. It may be possible to climb to the top of the bell tower, for good views of the city (and the bells).

The **MIBA** neighbourhood, centred on Place de la Coopération, was built for the European employees of the Belgian diamond-mining company originally called Mibeka. The company built an entire residential area for its European employees, in the centre of Mbuji-Mayi: grand villas set in large gardens for them to live in, schools to educate their children, and a club where they could spend their free time. During the Kasai Secession, the mine closed and, when it reopened in 1962, Mibeka transferred its exploitation rights and Congolese assets to its subsidiary, La Societé Minière de Bakwanga, or MIBA. The employees continued to live in their exclusive neighbourhood. Their club had a swimming pool, a theatre and a children's playground, as well as the restaurant and terrace bar that are still open today. MIBA continued to mine diamonds but, by the 1990s, production was in free-fall; conditions at the mine deteriorated and so did the infrastructure of the 'MIBA neighbourhood'. Nowadays, the mine is managed by a joint venture (SACIM) between MIBA and a Chinese company. The luxurious houses are in disrepair and linked by pot-holed roads. The swimming pool and playground are abandoned. It is interesting, but rather depressing, to look around the neighbourhood. Pretty much all that is left is the restaurant and terrace bar (page 135).

KINDU (⊕ 02°57.02 S, 25°55.11 E)

In the 19th century, Kindu was a major trading centre, for ivory, gold and enslaved people. It is the last point upriver navigable by large boats, before the rapids near Kisangani, which made it ideal for the Arab-Swahili traders, like Tippu Tip (page 21), for whom Kindu was their base for transferring these goods onward to Zanzibar. The town still has a sizeable Muslim community. Henry Morton Stanley reached Kindu in 1876, on his journey to map the Congo basin. The Belgian colonisers continued to use Kindu as a transit point and started to build railways to connect its port with the mines further south. For this, they called on a Belgian railway magnate called Édouard Empain. One of Empain's companies had built the first phase of the Paris Metro. In 1902, Empain founded a company to build railways in the east of the Congo Free State. The town of Kindu was renamed Port Empain in his honour.

In 1961, Kindu came to world attention after the massacre of 13 United Nations airmen. The victims were Italians, flying from Léopoldville to supply the UN garrison guarding Kindu's airfield. The Lumumbist troops who held the area believed they were Katangan planes, sent to bomb them; a crowd overpowered the airfield guards, killed the Italians and, it is alleged, ate their flesh.

GETTING THERE AND AWAY Trains run two or three times a month between Kindu and Lubumbashi, via Kalemie. The train is slow – the whole route takes the best part of a week – but gives you the chance to see parts of the country that aren't accessible by road, not only because most of the 'roads' are muddy (or dusty) tracks, but also because of the dangers from armed militias active between Kindu and Kalemie and around Lake Mweru.

There are no scheduled **river** services, but it may be possible to negotiate passage on one of the cargo boats that supply Kindu from Ubundu, or to hire a pirogue.

By **air**, CAA (w caacongo.com) has direct connections once a week with Kinshasa and once a week with Goma.

⌂ WHERE TO STAY

Karibu (17 rooms) Rte de l'Aéroport; m 082 306 7539, 081 249 2317; f Hôtel Résidence Karibu. Rooms set in blocks around landscaped gardens; hotel has restaurant, bar, gym, generator, Wi-Fi. All

rooms en suite (hot running water!), some with AC, others with fan. B/fast inc. **$$$**
Joli Rêve (13 rooms) Av des 3 Z 49; m 081 620 1505. Hotel has generator & restaurant/bar. Basic

rooms in small bungalows; more comfortable rooms, en suite. B/fast inc. **$**

WHAT TO SEE AND DO Most intriguing is the old **Slaves' Market** which tells a story of days gone by in Kindu's history – that of the Arab enslavers who traded here in the 19th century for human captives brought from the Congo's interior. A few decaying Arab- and colonial-era buildings survive in the town, including the cathedral. The small station will be of interest to railway fans; probably not to most others.

Lomami National Park grew out of scientific research over many decades by an American couple, John and Terese Hart, in the area between the Tshuapa, Lomami and Lualaba rivers (abbreviated as TL2). They confirmed the presence in these forests of bonobos, okapis, forest elephants and giant pangolins. Unfortunately, the forests also contained many poachers. The Harts worked for years to monitor the wildlife and reduce poaching. In 2012, a completely new species of monkey, *Cercopithecus lomamiensis*, was discovered on the left bank of the Lomami. An area of 9,000km² of TL2 was gazetted as the DRC's newest national park in 2016. It is co-managed by ICCN and the Frankfurt Zoological Society, whose website (w fzs. org) has more information about Lomami National Park.

Kindu is the nearest place to Lomami that can be reached by public transport. Onward travel to the national park is difficult – a combination of motorbike and foot. There are no supplies of food, clean water, or accommodation within the park. ICCN in Kindu may be able to arrange guides and porters; in any case, anyone hoping to visit Lomami, other than with an organised tour, will need to visit ICCN in order to buy a park permit.

6

Katanga

Katanga has always seen itself as different from the rest of the country. It was one of the original four large provinces created in 1914. Since local government reform in 2015, Katanga has been divided into four smaller provinces: Haut-Lomami, Haut-Katanga, Lualaba and Tanganyika. Geographically, the region marks the transition from the equatorial jungle around the River Congo to the dry savannah of southern Africa. The huge national parks of Kundelungu and Upemba are an example of this transition, with their marshy plains and forested savannah; Africa's highest unbroken waterfall is in Upemba National Park.

Katanga forms part of the central African Copperbelt and it is the country's most industrially developed region. Other minerals exploited in Katanga include uranium, cobalt and coltan. This industrial development means that Katanga also has the country's best infrastructure for visitors – good roads, several rail connections, international-standard hotels and restaurants, and so forth.

The last major kingdom in central Africa, the Yeke or Garanganze Kingdom, under its ruler Msiri, had its capital at Bunkeya, now in Lualaba province. Katanga was independent for almost two years in the 1960s before being pulled back into the fold through military force. Independence is not a forgotten dream – a separatist group called Bakata Katanga has claimed responsibility for sporadic attacks in the periphery of Lubumbashi and elsewhere in the region.

GETTING THERE AND AWAY

BY AIR Katanga's main international airport is at Lubumbashi (IATA code: FBM). Luano Airport, as it is known, has direct connections with Johannesburg, Addis Ababa, Nairobi and several other African cities, as well as Kinshasa. See page 72 for information about other internal flights. Like other airports in the DRC, Luano is challenging to navigate, particularly on departure. It is well worth paying an airport fixer to deal with airport taxes and check you and your luggage in. The local tour operators listed on page 148 can help with this. Alternatively, you can use one of the fixers at the airport; US$20 is a reasonable payment for their services. A rather sparse 'VIP lounge' offers respite from the chaos in the rest of the terminal; it is operated by Malabar Business Travel (page 148).

Kolwezi Airport (IATA code: KWZ) is undergoing major expansion at the time of writing and, in the lifetime of this edition, it may be that international flights start operating to and from Kolwezi.

BY LAND The main **border crossing** into the DRC from Zambia is at Kasumbalesa (page 153), said to be the busiest border post in Africa. It can take several hours to cross from one country to the other and lengthy traffic jams are frequent between

Kasumbalesa and Lubumbashi. The border posts at Sakania (page 153), across the border from the Zambian city of Ndola, and Mokambo, 20km from the Zambian town of Mufulira, are less busy alternatives. The road between Sakania and Kasumbalesa, through Mokambo, is excellent, although onward travel from either crossing to Lubumbashi will hit the same traffic that has come from Kasumbalesa. The border post on the eastern side of the Congo Pedicle, crossing the River Lualaba between Chembe and Mwenda, is essentially for freight.

Long-distance buses leave daily for **Johannesburg**; in Lubumbashi, they depart from behind the Park Hotel. The entire journey takes about a week and the one-way fare is US$150. The buses stop along the way in other major cities, including Lusaka and Harare, with part-route fares available.

The only passenger train to or from Katanga is on the Benguela Railway, built in colonial times to connect the central African Copperbelt with the Atlantic. Now known as **Lobito Atlantic Railway**, the line's entire Angolan section, over 1,300km, has been rehabilitated. Its main objective is to freight copper and cobalt from the mines in Katanga, a quicker and cheaper option than the existing routes. However, a passenger service operates between Lobito and Dilolo, a few kilometres from the Angolan border in the DRC's Lualaba province. The 'express' leaves Lobito once a week and takes two days to get to Luau, the last station on the Angolan side. There is an onward passenger train every two weeks between Dilolo and Kolwezi, 420km away.

GETTING AROUND

BY ROAD Katanga's main roads will come as a pleasant surprise to anyone who has driven elsewhere in the DRC. The **N1 highway** is asphalted from Sakania in the far south of the region to Fungurume in Lualaba province. Road upgrading is ongoing throughout the country and it may be that the remaining 100km to Kolwezi are asphalted during the lifetime of this edition. A toll is charged on each vehicle passing from one district to another; for an ordinary SUV or 4x4, the payment is negligible – a few hundred Congolese francs – while HGV drivers can be charged several hundred dollars along their route. Once you leave the N1, road conditions are a lot less predictable. Especially in the rainy season, many are impassable to vehicles other than expertly ridden motorbikes.

Buses connect the cities and towns of Katanga with each other. There are very frequent services between Kolwezi and Lubumbashi and between Lubumbashi and Kasumbalesa.

BY RAIL Lubumbashi is the headquarters of the national railway company, SNCC (w snccsa.com), and trains run from the station there to Kananga (page 131), Kalemie (page 163) and all the way to Kindu (page 136) on the River Congo. These are places that are otherwise practically impossible to reach other than by air, making the trains an appealing and affordable option for those with enough time at their disposal.

As well as the traditional *ordinaire* trains, there are 'express' services to Kalemie, Kananga and Mwene-Ditu, which have modern toilet and restaurant facilities. Between Lubumbashi and Kalemie, the express takes three to four days; in 2024, ticket prices on this route ranged from Fc416,200 in third class to Fc575,200 in 'luxe' first class. There are also regional trains from Lubumbashi to Sakania, Kolwezi to Dilolo and Kananga to Ilebo. Reservations for any train may be made either in person at a station or by phone on **m** 097 001 5616/7.

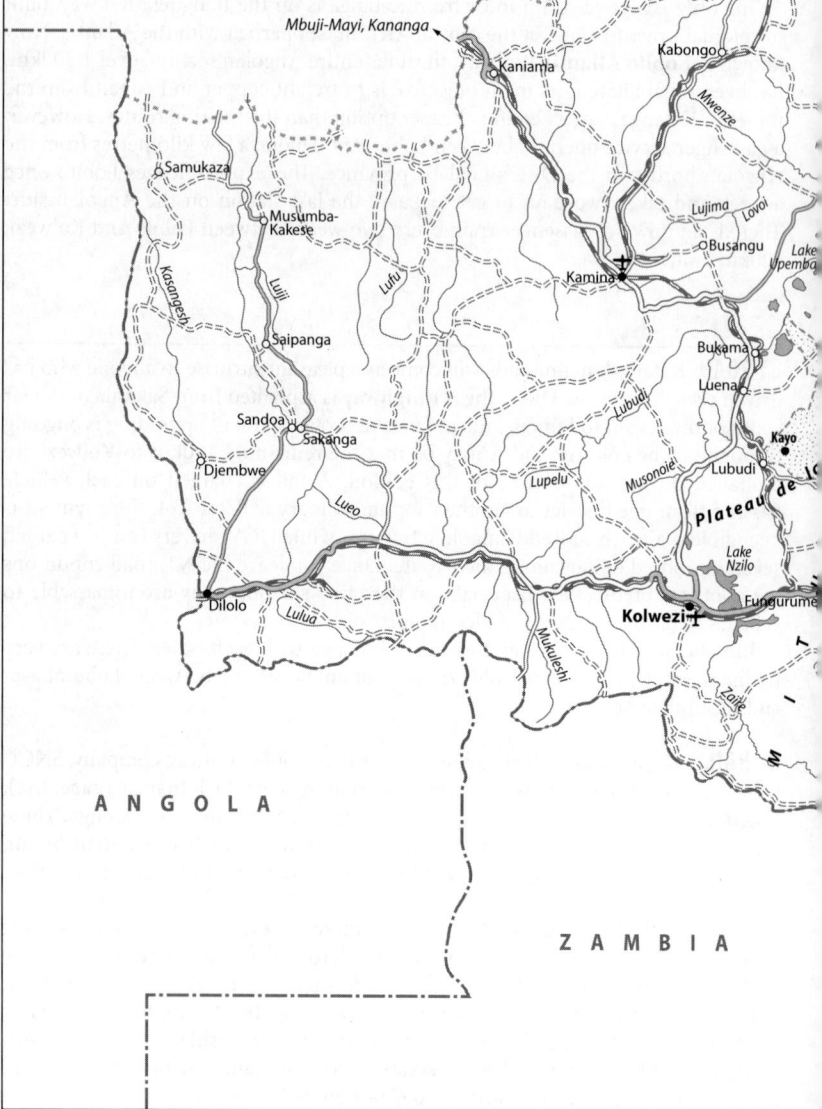

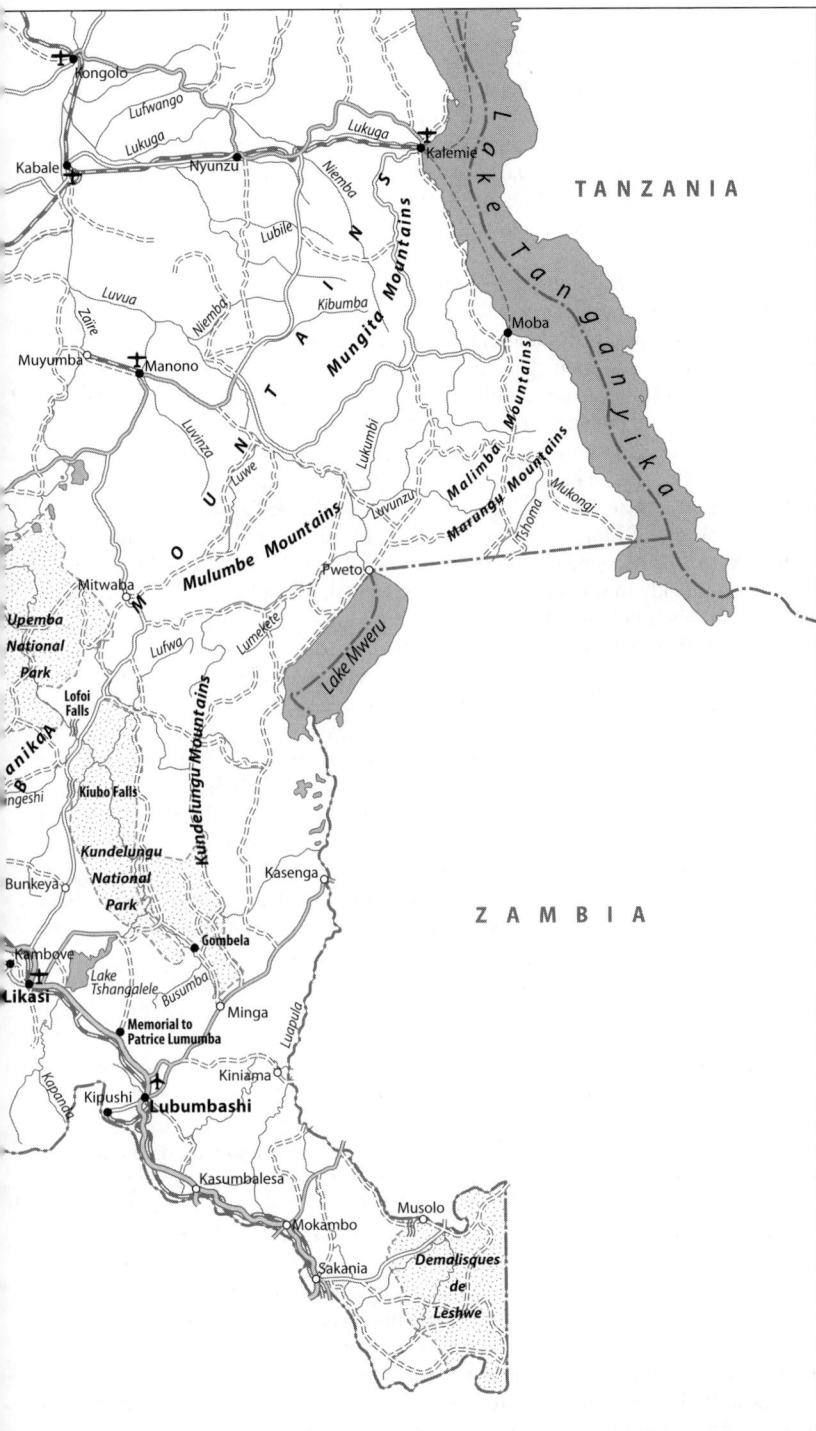

With its clean(ish), wide streets, its high-end restaurants and hotels, and its international-style supermarkets, Lubumbashi is probably the easiest city in the DRC in which to spend any length of time. Many foreigners are based here and many more pass through regularly, usually on mining business. The city has fine colonial-era buildings, including the magnificent Catholic cathedral, lively markets and even some green spaces.

HISTORY The city was founded by Union Minière du Haut Katanga (UMHK) in 1910, as a mining town. There had not been a settlement there before the arrival of the Belgians; it was a dry and empty scrubland. At the time, the Belgians were losing influence – and their Anglophone labour – in the region to British mining companies. A railway had been built all the way from South Africa into the southern Belgian Congo, and the majority of non-Africans in the area were not Belgian at all. UMHK and King Léopold sought to reassert their mandate over the Katanga region. The city was founded to keep these British companies in check, to expand Belgian influence, and ensure that the rumoured wish of the British to annexe Katanga would come to nothing. Its founders opted to build their new mining capital right next to a British smelter. With the railway already in place, supplies could be brought in quickly to transform an empty savannah into a bustling colonial town. In 1910, Élisabethville was born, with several hundred Belgian troops in tow, to demonstrate that they meant business in retaining control of Katanga.

The British would not disappear for long, though: as World War I raged in Europe, UMHK and Élisabethville found their Belgian funding inaccessible thanks to German interference. UMHK officials were eager to complete a railway line to Léopoldville, and invited further investment from British mining firms. The British maintained Katanga's infrastructure throughout the war and assisted in completing the rail line.

Yet the British presence was not welcomed by Belgian officials in Katanga, and they spent two years trying to reduce the number of Anglophone workers at mines across the province. Working conditions were deliberately made bad for migrant workers, and Africans were increasingly used for jobs that had normally gone to Europeans. In 1920, there was a strike and the British workers, eventually, received an increase in compensation; yet UMHK dismissed British workers once their contracts ran out and, between 1917 and 1922, the percentage of Belgian workers rose from 23% to 58%. Anglophone influence continued to wane and, by the early 1920s, Belgium solidly dominated the mining sector in Katanga.

Increased pressure on African and European labour created distress for Élisabethville's citizens during and after the great depression. Forced labour for local Congolese was still permitted, and UMHK officials were determined to get more productivity from their workers as profit margins were squeezed. The Belgian Congo had also created a secret police service, creating suspicion among locals as arrests without charge increased across the city. Life in Élisabethville was becoming less idyllic – Africans had their rations cut, and as World War II arrived, strife was rampant. A mass protest erupted in 1941, and was put down harshly by Belgian colonial forces – they killed 70 workers, and arrested numerous more Africans for conspiracy. Trade union reforms began during the war, but then lost ground after World War II ended and the colonial government sought to normalise the labour laws of their colony. Yet as African reform swept the continent in the late 1940s, Belgian attitudes were forced to progress in regards to their treatment of indigenous workers, and conditions did slowly improve as 1950 arrived.

If the notion of a European power assisting in the secession of a province in central Africa, then assisting its government in hiring mercenaries to engage in combat against the UN, sounds intriguing to you, the secession of Katanga (page 28) from 1960 to 1963 is indeed an intriguing story.

The entire engagement between foreign soldiers of fortune, usually referred to as mercenaries, against rebel forces loyal to Patrice Lumumba and UN 'Blue Helmets' is a curious footnote in the history of 20th-century Africa. Never mind the Belgian involvement, which was vast – their hopes of keeping the UMHK in a country friendly to Belgium, perhaps even allowing Katanga to exist as little more than a puppet state, speak volumes of European motivations for intervention across Africa to this very day.

The most troubling aspect of the secession, perhaps, is how forgotten it really is among world history. The DRC itself has seen a resurgence in its role across history texts with Mobutu Sese Seko's regime and the fallout from the Rwandan genocide that sparked the civil wars and internal strife that persist to contemporary times. Yet Katanga's brief years of independence are mostly buried, its history blurry and deep in the past, despite the modern-day parallels of the UN taking on greater roles to stabilise the very same country, and the increasing privatisation of conflicts in the Middle East and central Asia. These lessons have, at the very least, been pushed into a background largely ignored by pundits and analysts as the DRC struggles with all-too-familiar problems.

During the 1960s the Congo mercenaries were a big deal, celebrities of sorts, and many of them went on to write their memoirs of the Congo–Katanga affair. Robert Denard, the most famous, went on numerous other missions sponsored by the French government; however, he has never written his own personal accounts of his exploits.

Mike Hoare provides the largest base of first-person accounts available regarding Katanga. *The Road to Kalamata* is a short and simple read on the subject. Also by the same author is *Congo Mercenary*, which is a little hard to find, and *Congo Warriors*, which documents his time while working for the Léopoldville-based government and taking on rebels in the northeast. Jules Gerard-Libois's book *Katanga Secession* details the finer points of this moment in history from a political standpoint.

A compilation of articles on African guns for hire is available in *Mercenaries: An African Security Dilemma*. It discusses in detail the ramifications of the Congo's use of foreign mercenaries in the 1960s, which set a precedent for numerous other conflicts across the continent.

A solid analysis of UN involvement against Katanga's forces can be found in Trevor Findlay's book *The Blue Helmets' First War? Use of Force by the UN in the Congo, 1960–64*. Controversy remains over UN involvement and whether they did, in fact, overstep their boundaries when dealing with aggression from the secessionist province. Eric S Packham has a detailed account of the UN's involvement in the post-independence Belgian Congo with *Success or Failure: The UN Intervention in the Congo after Independence*.

Katanga LUBUMBASHI

6

With independence, the Europeans in Élisabethville saw a chance to stem the tide of African liberation and supported the secessionist government of Moïse Tshombe. Belgium also lent Tshombe's rebel government unofficial support, as

LUBUMBASHI
Greater

Karibu ↗

N

Bradt

0 _____ 500m
0 _____ 500yds

AV DE LA LIBERATION

Golf Club

Lubumbashi

⚑ Côte West

ROUTE DU GOLF

AV TSHINIAMA

ⓦ Côte West

④

⑥

⑨

⑫

⑬

AV RUWE

Kipushi ↙

Kasumbalesa ↘ D

For listings, see from page 148

🛏 Where to stay

1	Bethesda..................F2
2	La Source.................G2
3	Mota........................F5
4	Novotel....................C4
5	Planet Hollybum......G2
6	Pullman Grand Karavia..................B3

✕ Where to eat and drink

7	Casa degli Italiani...............G2
8	Cercle Héllenique...............G2
9	Complexe La Plage............B3
10	La Bonne Fourchette.......G1
11	Latte Lounge.....................F2
12	Lattélicious......................B4
13	Le Percheron....................B4
14	Nazem..............................G3
15	Saveurs et Viandes..........H1
16	Tony & Tony Mezepolis.....E3

Off map

Groupe Number One..........H7
Karibu...................................B1

Airport, Mulykap
bus terminal,
Muyambo Park,
Kolwezi

Centre Médical de
la Communauté ✚   1

N1

● Cercle
Belge

⑪   ②   2

⑤

BVD DU 30 JUIN

① AV DE LA REVOLUTION

Centre Médical
✚ Diamant

AV KILELA BALANDA

AV DU MUSÉE

⚑ National Museum
& art gallery

Provincial
Assembly

Lupopo
Stadium 🏃

⑧
⑦

Angolan
Consulate Ⓔ

SQUARE G A FORREST

Ⓔ Belgian
Consulate

⑭   3

⑯

AV SANDOA

BVD DU 30 JUIN

AV LUMUMABA

AV KIMBANGU

N1   4

AV RUWE

● Pétale d'Or
gift shop

● ICCN

AV KAMBOVE

③

AV N'DJAMENA

AV MUNONGO

✡

AV TABORA

Ruashi Market,
Kasenga

BD KAMANYOLA

✝

CHAUSSÉE LAURENT-DÉSIRÉ KABILA

✉

AV SENDWE

5

AV KASAVUBU

AV ADOULA

AV KAPENDA

AV MAMA YEMO

AV LOMAMI

6

Zoological &
Botanical Gardens 🐘

Restaurant
du Zoo ✗

AV MOÉRO

MANYOLA

AV DES USINES

AV LIKASI

N1

AV DU PARC

✝ Methodist
Church

page 147

E   F   G

TB Mazembe stadium,
Group Number One ↘ H

An infrastructure worthy of an independent nation was emerging in the secessionist state of Katanga as Moïse Tshombe began his year-long war against the government in Léopoldville. With the majority of extractable resources in Katanga as well as a sizeable and competent mercenary force behind him, Tshombe began accumulating planes with the aim of having an air force.

Avikat was, originally, simply a cargo outfit based in Lubumbashi. On independence, Tshombe purchased nine CM170 Magisters, small jet-engined fighters. Katanga therefore had an air force ready to fight in July 1961 – with European planes and European mercenary pilots to fly them. Avikat grew its numbers in October with the addition of Dornier aircraft from West Germany. Its main airbase was at Luano Airport outside Lubumbashi.

Avikat was initially a highly successful air force. They hit ONUC positions with their Magister aircraft and enjoyed several victories. There has been speculation that Dag Hammarskjöld's plane was shot down by Avikat in September 1961. ONUC eventually seized Avikat cargo planes in Lubumbashi and destroyed most of its fighter planes at Luano, while their own coalition air force of Ethiopian, Indian, Canadian and Swiss fighters attacked other airfields used by Avikat. By the end of 1961, Avikat was no more. The ground war continued for another year and more, before Moïse Tshombe officially ended the Katanga secession.

Very few books have been written on Avikat, though perhaps the most thorough is *Air Wars and Aircraft: A Detailed Record of Air Combat, 1945 to the Present*, by Victor Flintham (out of print, but available secondhand).

Katanga continued its mission to retain autonomy from Congo-Léopoldville. The Belgians secretly funded the mercenary army that gave the United Nations a run for their money; the possibility of losing control of UMHK and the numerous lucrative mines scattered across the province was unattractive to European interests in Katanga. African opinion of the Katanga secession was sharply divided and, when UN forces invaded in 1961, the province saw more upheaval.

Mobutu's Africanisation programme saw the city's name change to Lubumbashi and the vast majority of European workers evicted from their positions across Katanga, which was renamed Shaba Province. The workforce was largely African, and UMHK was nationalised and renamed Gécamines. The city ballooned in size, with people moving from elsewhere, particularly Kasai, to seek work in Lubumbashi.

The year 1990 would be another critical time in Lubumbashi and for all of Zaire – Mobutu's troops used lethal force to suppress a student protest at the university, killing 11. Kinshasa was scheduled to host a Francophone summit soon after, but international pressure against Mobutu's response to the protests meant that the summit location was switched at the last minute. This put further pressure on the dictator for change; during this time Shaba was renamed back to Katanga.

The city did not suffer much fighting as Laurent Kabila and the AFDL moved westward from their bases near Rwanda; it fell to the rebel forces in April 1997. Several weeks after the invasion of Lubumbashi, Kabila declared himself the new president of the Democratic Republic of the Congo; Mobutu fled Kinshasa soon after, and Kabila's march to the capital continued.

As fighting ensued between militias backed by Rwanda and Uganda, refugees started to arrive from the northern interior of Katanga. The mining industry under Gécamines continued amid the chaos. Lubumbashi largely escaped the open conflict of the Second Congo War, allowing it to retain the same economic importance to the country that it had enjoyed since its foundation.

GETTING AROUND Lubumbashi is bisected by the rail line, which runs roughly north–south through the city. If you follow the street west from the train station, you'll pass through an area where the roundabout near the **Park Hotel** [147 D2] marks the historic town centre. The **River Lubumbashi** marks the western edge of the city centre and on its other side are residential neighbourhoods, including **Quartier Golf**, where the golf course [144 B2] is located on the shores of a small artificial lake, beside the Pullman Grand Karavia hotel. To the southwest, another landmark is the massive black slag-heap next to the copper smelter.

Around Katanga, the most reliable **bus** company is Mulykap [145 H1] (m 097 345 1177; f Mulykap SARL), which has its own modern terminal on the outskirts of the city. Mulykap operates shuttle buses to its terminal from Avenue Adoula. Other buses to Likasi, Kolwezi and other points in Katanga leave from Avenue Kapenda at Avenue Des Usines.

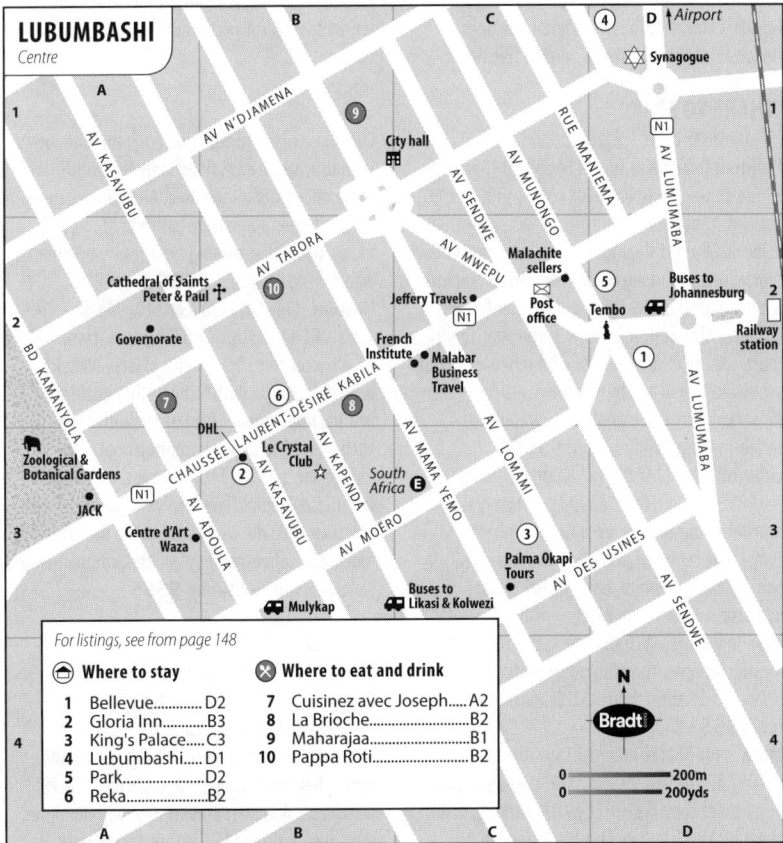

LUBUMBASHI
Centre

Airport
Synagogue
AV N'DJAMENA
City hall
RUE MANIEMA
N1
AV LUMUMABA
AV KASAVUBU
AV SENDWE
AV MUNONGO
AV TABORA
AV MWEPU
Malachite sellers
Cathedral of Saints Peter & Paul
Jeffery Travels
Post office
Buses to Johannesburg
Tembo
Governorate
French Institute
Malabar Business Travel
Railway station
BD KAMANYOLA
CHAUSSÉE LAURENT-DÉSIRÉ KABILA
AV KAPENDA
AV MAMA YEMO
AV LOMAMI
AV LUMUMABA
DHL
Le Crystal Club
Zoological & Botanical Gardens
N1
South Africa
AV ADOULA
AV KASAVUBU
AV MOÉRO
JACK
Centre d'Art Waza
Palma Okapi Tours
AV DES USINES
AV SENDWE
Mulykap
Buses to Likasi & Kolwezi
N

For listings, see from page 148

⊖ **Where to stay**
1 Bellevue D2
2 Gloria Inn B3
3 King's Palace C3
4 Lubumbashi D1
5 Park D2
6 Reka B2

⊗ **Where to eat and drink**
7 Cuisinez avec Joseph A2
8 La Brioche B2
9 Maharajaa B1
10 Pappa Roti B2

Bradt

0 ——— 200m
0 ——— 200yds

Lubumbashi's Art Deco **railway** station [147 D2] is open for business and the schedules are posted in the information hall, next to the station building. Tickets can also be bought here. Destinations include Sakania, Kolwezi and Kalemie. See page 139 for further details of the routes served.

For safety, use **taxis** arranged by your hotel rather than hailing one in the street. Everybody in Lubumbashi uses motorbike taxis, which can get round the traffic jams more easily than a car.

Vehicles can be **hired**, with driver, at a cost of between US$150 and US$200 a day within the city limits, US$300 a day outside Lubumbashi. The local tour operators listed below can assist with this. Some additional phone numbers are:

Agrizex m 099 702 6749, 081 505 0728
Bethanie m 099 702 5894

CFAO m 089 930 9900
Yan m 089 002 0441

LOCAL TOUR OPERATORS

Congo Star Safaris m 097 577 0629; f. Operates Kiubo Falls Lodge (page 157) & Kafubu River Lodge. Offers hotel bookings, ticket bookings, airport assistance & transfers.

Jeffery Travels [147 C2] 62 Av Mzee Kabila, LAC Bldg; m 081 999 1101, 099 027 9535; f Jeffery Travels – Lubumbashi. Offers hotel bookings, vehicle hire, ticket bookings, airport transfers.

Malabar Business Travel [147 C2] The Piazza; m 081 662 0479, 081 599 5588; f. Operates the 'VIP lounge' at Lubumbashi Airport & can help with other travel requirements.

Palma Okapi Tours [147 C3] 42 Av Mama Yemo; m 097 579 0444; f. Offers tours to various tourist spots & cultural events.

WHERE TO STAY

Exclusive and expensive

Pullman Grand Karavia [144 B3] (197 rooms) 55 Rte du Golf, Q/ Golf; m 081 152 5519, 099 997 8006; e haot4-sb@accor.com; w accor.com. Set in lovely grounds sloping down to lake, next to golf course; secure parking. Wide choice of restaurants & bars; nightclub; Wi-Fi throughout, conference facilities, ATM, souvenir shops. Large pool, tennis court, spa. All rooms en suite with toiletries; b/fast inc, reputed to be the best in town; AC, flat-screen TV, safe, minibar, complimentary water, tea/coffee-making facilities, desk. $$$$$

Lubumbashi [147 D1] (32 rooms) Av 30 Juin; m 081 977 7111, 083 222 2233; e reservation@hotellubumbashi.com; w hotellubumbashi.com. Large central courtyard with good-sized pool & café; restaurant, bar, spa, hairdresser, gym; conference room, Wi-Fi. Stylish rooms all en suite with AC, TV, fridge, desk, tea/coffee-making facilities, complimentary water & b/fast inc. Smallest rooms $$$, most $$$$, suites $$$$$

Mota [144 F5] (103 rooms) 1597 Av Kasavubu; m 097 378 0330, 099 589 7339; e reception@hotel-mota.com; f HOTEL MOTA. Parking; good restaurant with Indian, Chinese, European &

Congolese menu ($$); good Wi-Fi throughout; seating areas on each floor; large function/conference room on top floor. All rooms en suite with toiletries, some have bathtub; AC, TV, safe, fridge, tea/coffee-making facilities, complimentary water, desk, b/fast inc. $$$$

Novotel [144 C4] (120 rooms) Av Mpala 1; m 084 442 2215; e HB714@accor.com; w all.accor.com. Great views of lake; wheelchair accessible; rooms with facilities for people with hearing impairments. Restaurant with open kitchen, café, lounge bar; rooftop pool with terrace bar, gym; Wi-Fi throughout, conference facilities. All rooms have lake view; all en suite with toiletries, AC, safe, work-table, large flat-screen TV, fridge, tea/coffee-making facilities, complimentary water; some have balcony. $$$$

Mid-range

Gloria Inn [147 B3] (62 rooms) 555 Av Kasavubu; m 081 887 6546, 097 775 1415, 084 729 0868; e gloria.inn.ishi@gmail.com; w gloria-inn.com. Secure parking; restaurant, terrace bar; good-sized pool, small gym; Wi-Fi, laundry service. All rooms en suite with toiletries, some have balcony; AC, TV, safe, fridge, desk, tea/coffee-making facilities, complimentary water, b/fast inc. **$$$–$$$$**

King's Palace [147 C3] (32 rooms) 15 Av Lomami; **m** 099 678 8888, 082 411 1111; **e** reservation@hotelkingspalace.com; **w** hotelkingspalace.com. Restaurant, bar, garden, conference facilities, hairdresser; parking; airport transfers available. All rooms en suite with nice shower; AC, flat-screen TV, safe, fridge, complimentary water, tea & coffee-making facilities; b/fast inc. **$$$**, suites **$$$$**

La Source [145 G2] (65 rooms) 72 Av Kilela Balanda; **m** 099 020 7462; **e** contact@hotellasource.org; **w** hotellasource.org. Restaurant with Congolese & international menu, good-sized pool, terrace bar with tables screened from each other. Wi-Fi throughout; credit cards accepted. 12 3-bedroom furnished apartments (**$$$$$**). All rooms en suite with AC, TV, fridge; b/fast inc. **$$$**

Planet Hollybum [145 G2] (16 rooms) 975 Kilela Balanda; **m** 099 703 0256; **w** planet-hollybum. com. Rooms in bungalows set around a garden with swimming pool; friendly, professional service; secure parking; credit cards accepted. Wheelchair accessible. Popular restaurant/pizzeria; disco at w/ends. All rooms en suite with AC, TV, fridge, complimentary water. **$$$**

Park Hotel [147 D2] (80 rooms) 50 Av Kasai; **m** 099 703 2330; **e** info@parkhotelcongo.com; **w** parkhotelcongo.com. Beautiful Art Deco building from 1930s. Central courtyard with bar & outdoor restaurant seating; excellent restaurant (the Safari Grill); shops, conference room, gym open 24hrs; Wi-Fi, room service. All rooms en suite, most with bathtub as well as shower; nicely decorated, with AC, TV, safe, minibar. **$$–$$$**, suites **$$$$**

Thrifty

Bellevue [147 D2] (26 rooms) Av Mwepu, coin Kasai; **m** 097 010 1555; **e** eximint2@ hotmail.com, hotelbellevuelubum@gmail.com; **w** bellevuelubum.com. On 'Tembo Square', beautiful colonial building with glazed balconies. Small but clean rooms, all en suite with fan or AC; b/fast inc. **$$**

Bethesda [145 F2] (18 rooms) 1034 Av Idiofa; **m** 081 273 6008; ◻ Hotel Bethesda. On small street between Av de la Révolution & Rue Kilia Balanda. Secure parking; rooms set around central courtyard. All rooms en suite, with TV, fan, Wi-Fi; b/fast inc. Mostly sgls; dbls have AC. Sgls **$**, dbls **$$**

Reka [147 B2] (37 rooms) 696 Av Kapenda; **m** 099 704 5132, 085 447 5503; **e** hotelrekardc@ gmail.com. Restaurant, courtyard terrace, laundry service, Wi-Fi. Friendly reception staff. All rooms en suite with AC, TV, mosquito net; 'superior' rooms have bathtub as well as shower. Sgls **$**, dbls & suite **$$**

WHERE TO EAT AND DRINK Lubumbashi has a vibrant restaurant scene, with plenty of options for those seeking some culinary variety. All of the larger hotels have restaurants open to the public. Planet Hollybum's wood-fired pizzas are justifiably popular, as is the Park Hotel's Safari Grill. **Complexe La Plage** [144 B3] has restaurants focused on meat and fish (called Le Boucher and Le Catch, both **$$$$**) and a patisserie as well as Legends Bar. There are a few Indian and Chinese restaurants around town; some of the hotel restaurants also have Indian and Chinese menus.

Expensive

Groupe Number One Restaurant [145 H7] 33 Av Kapwassa, Rte Munama; **m** 082 200 9839, 099 054 2042, 099 072 3055; **e** groupenumberonercd. restaurant@gno-rdc.com; **w** gno-rdc.com; ⏲ only on Sun & pub hols, noon–16.00; Sun brunch 1st Sun of the month, 10.00–13.00. Formerly called Le Bush Camp; set in the Katangan countryside north of Lubumbashi. High-quality meat from the company's farms, slaughtered in on-site abattoir; grills & salads; European & South African wine list. Butcher's & charcuterie shop on site. **$$$$**

La Bonne Fourchette [145 G1] 88 Av de la Révolution; **m** 082 322 259. Contemporary cuisine with an African touch. Formal indoor restaurant; informal poolside terrace. Grilled meat, fish, vegetarian options; Sunday buffet. **$$$$**

High-end

Saveurs et Viandes [145 H1] 2003 Bd Msiri; **m** 083 012 2295, 099 054 2042; **w** gno-rdc.com; ⏲ noon–15.00 & 18.30–22.00 Mon–Sat. Owned by Groupe Number One. The only menu of its kind in Lubumbashi, with imported luxuries such as lobster Thermidor, Wagyu beef, caviar & 1.5kg

Katanga LUBUMBASHI

6

tomahawk steak. Also meat, fish & chicken baked in charcoal oven. French & South African wine list. $$$–$$$$

Casa degli Italiani [145 G2] Av Lumumba 2900; m 099 702 5756, 081 333 1157; ⏰ from 19.00 daily. Excellent European dining in a long-standing Italian restaurant. Secure parking. $$$

Cercle Héllenique [145 G2] 3000 Av Lumumba; m 081 607 0539. Not just a restaurant but a social & sporting centre for Lubumbashi's large Greek community; serves authentic Greek dishes including pitta sandwiches ($) & Greek coffee. $$$

Karibu Restaurant [144 B1] 9 Chemin Public, Q/ Golf; m 099 826 8470. Part of Kalubwe Lodge hotel ($$), in lovely setting with small gardens. African & European-inspired menu. $$$

Le Percheron [144 B4] 4 Av Shiwala; m 081 400 0057; ⏰ 11.00–22.00 Mon–Sat. French bistro with Congolese accent; grilled chicken & *cossa-cossa*, steaks. $$$

Tony & Tony Mezepolis [145 E3] 13 Av Mama Mobutu; m 081 078 3600; e tony.tony. mezepolis@gmail.com; f Tony & Tony Mezepolis; ⏰ 10.30–14.30 & 18.30–22.30 Mon–Sat. Genuine Greek food, with special menus for Orthodox Easter ($$$$). $$$

Mid-range

Maharajaa [147 B1] 1073 Av Lomami, behind the Mairie; m 081 021 2020. Quiet dining space offering good-quality Indian menu, including vegetarian & vegan dishes. Food that's both tasty & affordable. Decent portions. $$

Pappa Roti [147 B2] Hypnose Mall; m 090 688 1104. Indoor & outdoor seating. Indian-run; menu mainly standard international fast food but includes a few daily specials for the manager's family & friends. Fish, chicken & vegetarian options usually available. $$

Cuisinez avec Joseph [147 A2] 117 Rue Adoula, coin Zambezi; m 081 888 4861. Informal local restaurant with creative chef (Joseph); tilapia or chicken baked with vegetables & smoked pork ribs, as well as more simple grilled dishes. Highly recommended. Set lunch $, à la carte $–$$

Budget and fast food
The best options for budget food, apart from snacks from street stalls, are the fast-food chains, which have branches in all the main shopping malls. They include the South African chains **Pizza Inn**, **Chicken Inn** (both self-explanatory) & **Galito's** (also grilled chicken).

Nazem [145 G3] Av Kimbangu. Does a brisk trade in Lebanese flatbreads, with *za'atar* or cheese topping, made while you wait. Has a few sit-in places but is essentially a take-away. $

Patisseries

Lattélicious [144 B4] 8485 Av Panda; f Lattelicious Panda; ⏰ noon–22.00 daily. A South African chain, serving b/fasts, smoothies, bar meals, coffee & alcohol. $$

Latte Lounge [145 F2] Av Kilele Balanda 1446; f Lattelounge Lubumbashi. Part of the South African Lattelicious brand. Coffee, cocktails, ice-cream sundaes, bar meals. Family-friendly, children's play area. Live sports on big screen. $$

La Brioche [147 B2] 75 Chaussée Laurent-Désiré Kabila & in Complexe la Plage; ⏰ 07.30–22.00 Mon–Fri, 07.30–18.30 Sat, 07.30–20.00 Sun. B/fasts, sandwiches, crepes, waffles; also patisserie & good coffee. $–$$

ENTERTAINMENT AND NIGHTLIFE Côte West [144 C3] (m 099 584 8358), on Route de Golf, is a big expanse of green space on the lakeside, with tables and chairs scattered around it and a covered terrace bar. The tilapia are home-reared; grilled chicken and brochettes are also served. More than for the food, though, it is a place to relax and get some fresh air. There's a pool table and fishing on the lake.

The **French Institute** [147 C2] (63 Chaussée Laurent-Désiré Kabila; m 081 999 1314; w institutfrançais-lubumbashi.com) holds exhibitions of art by Katangan artists, screens films and lays on musical, theatre and dance events. There is also a café, with seating outside in the peaceful courtyard.

Le Crystal Club [147 B3], on Avenue Kasavubu, has a resident DJ, playing mostly Congolese music, every night until about midnight.

For sport, the best option is the **Cercle Belge** on Avenue Kilela Balanda [145 G1] (m 099 521 6020; ⏰ 10.30–22.00 Tue–Sun). It has six clay tennis courts, a football pitch, a volley-ball court and a pétanque rink, as well as table tennis, bowling, darts, pool and children's games. For the less energetic, the club also broadcasts major sporting events on its big screen. **Complexe La Plage** [144 B3] has a swimming pool, a beach volleyball court, and paddleboats for hire. The **golf course** [144 B2] is open to non-members, who can rent clubs.

SHOPPING Across the street from the Park Hotel [147 D2] are stalls selling souvenirs made with **malachite**. For a wider range of local handicrafts, the artisans' stalls at the **Ruashi** (or Kamalondo) **Market** [145 H5] have sculptures, masks and many items in copper and malachite. Several of the larger hotels have souvenir shops, for example, the Pullman Grand Karavia, Planet Hollybum, and the Lubumbashi and Park hotels.

Petale d'Or [145 G4] (128 Av Munongo; m 099 702 8833) is a cosmetics and lingerie shop which also stocks Congolese textile items (although the fabrics themselves are not made in the DRC). They can also make jewellery to order. For contemporary Congolese art, **Centre d'Art Waza** [147 A3], on Avenue Adoula, is run by an artists' collective and showcases their work.

For general groceries, there are numerous supermarkets around town. Many supermarkets offer a range of hot and cold take-away meals, western and Congolese: a good option if you don't want to eat in restaurants every night.

OTHER PRACTICALITIES There are **ATMs** at most bank branches and within the larger hotels; they issue Congolese francs and, in some cases, US dollars. Use an ATM within the bank (or in a hotel), where possible, and always in daylight hours. **Western Union** agencies can be found everywhere around the city. Those linked to banks close mid-afternoon. Some of the agencies in the city centre, and those within the larger hotels, have later opening hours.

Several countries have **consular representation** (sometimes an honorary consul) in Lubumbashi. They include Belgium [145 F3] (Sq Forrest; m 099 552 6800), Angola [145 E3] (Sq Forrest; m 081 181 9394) and South Africa [147 C3] (Av Mama Yemo; m 097 101 3063).

Lubumbashi's **post office** [147 C2] is in the aptly named Place de la Poste. Items will reach their destination more quickly and reliably with **DHL** [147 B3] (Av Kasavubu; ⊕ 08.00–17.00 Mon–Fri, 08.00–noon Sat).

There are many pharmacies throughout the city. As elsewhere in the DRC, if you are seriously ill or injured, seek medical evacuation as soon as you are fit to travel. **Hospitals** in Lubumbashi that meet international standards are:

Centre Médical Diamant [145 F2] 1034 Av Kilele Balanda; \090 777 783; w cmd.cd; ⊕ 24hrs)

Centre Médical de la Communauté [145 H1] Av de Nyanza; m 084 189 0997, 099 152 8400, (emergency) 084 189 0999; w cmclubumbashi.com

WHAT TO SEE AND DO The historic centre of the city is symbolised by the 1930s statue of an elephant in the middle of the roundabout – the Swahili word for elephant is *tembo* and so this roundabout is known as Rond-Point Tembo [147 D2]. It is surrounded by fine colonial-era buildings, notably the Bellevue hotel, and with fruit and vegetable sellers; it is always busy with people. The Park Hotel and the railway station are a short distance away, both good examples of colonial architecture.

Chaussée Laurent-Désiré Kabila leads from the Park Hotel to the modern administrative centre, with the provincial Governorate [147 A2]. Across Avenue Kasavubu from the Governorate is the Catholic **Cathedral of Saints Peter and**

Paul [147 B2], one of the most impressive buildings in the city and the largest cathedral in the country. Its beautiful ochre brickwork, colonnaded entrance and square bell tower form a harmonious whole. The original chapel became a cathedral in 1922 and today's building was completed in 1935. Lubumbashi also has the DRC's only **synagogue** [147 D1]. It was completed in 1930 when European settlement was booming in then Élisabethville, and much of the Belgian Congo's Jewish population lived there. The structure has withstood the numerous incursions through the city's turbulent history. These days there are very few Jewish people left in Lubumbashi; services are held irregularly, and the building is usually locked up.

The **National Museum of Lubumbashi** [145 F3] (Musée Nationale de Lubumbashi; Av Kasai; ⊕ 07.30–noon & 13.00–16.00 Mon–Fri; US$10 for foreign citizens) tells the story of the city, the province and the region, from its geology, through the little archaeological research that has been done, to its wildlife and the beliefs and customs of its people. There is a replica of the Ishango Bone (page 15), and there are masks and items that demonstrate a chief's power. Very informative panels (in French) explain each stage of this story. The upper halls display the ethnographic collection, with textiles, shells, wooden statues and basketry. Finally, the entomology section has a collection of dried insects, arachnids and a small crocodile. Also in the museum's complex is Dialogues, a gallery of contemporary art; unfortunately, despite its opening hours (⊕ 09.00–15.00 Mon–Fri, 09.00–13.00 Sat) being displayed at the entrance, it never seems to be open.

The **zoological and botanical gardens** [145 E6] are a welcome area of green space in the city centre. The trees are labelled with their scientific, French and local names. Paths lead round the cages and enclosures, with helpful signage in places. There is a glass-fronted cage of snakes, including the beautiful but deadly Gaboon viper. There are lots of primates – many species of monkeys and baboons, and a chimpanzee. The cages are large, with plenty of trees for the animals to exercise and play in. There are also tigers, lions, zebras and waterbuck, all in (separate) huge wooded enclosures, which means they are not often visible, as well as a couple of eagles and various species of crocodile. There is even a café, and toilets (Fc100). You could quite easily spend most of the day in the zoo, especially if you wanted to wait and watch for some of the more elusive animals. Admission is US$15 for foreign adults; a photo permit costs an additional Fc3,000. The gardens are open from 09.00 to 18.00, with last admission at 17.00. Just outside the entrance, at the side of the car park (Fc4,000), is the Restaurant du Zoo (m 099 217 3365; ⊕ 10.30–21.30 Tue–Sun; $$), serving Congolese dishes and pizzas.

In the territory of the zoo, but separated from it, is **JACK** [147 A3] (entrance on Bd Kamanyola; w jackchimpscongo.org, in French; w jacksanctuary.org, in English), a sanctuary for chimpanzees and other primates that have been trafficked or poached. They welcome visitors, but it is best to contact them first via their website.

In the outskirts of the city, on the road towards Likasi, **Muyambo Park** [145 H1] (m 099 990 4101; ⊕ 09.00–15.00 daily) is a small safari park, with giraffes, ostriches, antelopes and hyenas. Buggies and bicycles can be rented to get around the park. There is an artificial lake there, with boats and pedalos to hire.

If you have a vehicle, a good day trip heads 100km east to the town of **Kiniama** (✪ 11°28.05 S, 28°18′50 E). After some walking you can see where the **Kafubu and Luapula rivers** merge. This creates some fancy whirlpools and the trip there has some decent scenery. There is accommodation in the vicinity, at the Kafubu River Lodge; contact Congo Star Safaris (page 148) for information or to book.

Traditional musicians perform at special community occasions and also, sometimes, at festivals
above (X/A)

Wooden masks are a central element in traditional culture and, nowadays, are also highly sought after by museums and collectors PAGE 48
below left (PM/S)

In eastern DRC, traders use handmade scooters (*chikudu*) to transport their cargo
below right (TRP/S)

Rural communities use face and body decoration to mark significant events such as coming-of-age celebrations
bottom right (SS)

above
(SS)
Kindu, deep in the DRC's interior, is the birthplace of politician Matata Ponyo, whose statue stands in the town PAGE 136

below left
(BRB/S)
The only bridge across the River Congo is in Matadi, in Kongo-Central PAGE 115

below right
(GG)
The plane in which Patrice Lumumba was flown to his execution is displayed at the memorial site to him, in Haut-Katanga PAGE 156

bottom right
(JdN)
The beautiful 1940s library is the pride of Lwiro's Centre de Recherche en Sciences Naturelles PAGE 204

Bukavu is perhaps the most picturesque town in the DRC PAGE 194

above
(OE/S)

Many colonial-era railway stations have Art Deco features;
Lubumbashi's is a good example PAGE 148

below
(IB/A)

above (WC/S)
The rolling hills around Bukavu contrast with the tropical rainforest elsewhere in the country PAGE 194

left (OE/S)
The people who live near Lake Kivu use the lake to get around and to fish for food PAGE 205

below (EM/S)
The Zongo Falls, between Matadi and Kinshasa, are especially spectacular in the wet season PAGE 111

Garamba National Park has been a protected area since 1938; villagers who live in the park help to protect its rich wildlife PAGE 178

above
(MW/AP)

Mount Nyiragongo is an active volcano but, when it is safe, visitors can hike to the crater and camp nearby overnight PAGE 211

right
(DK/S)

Green Lake, near Goma, has formed inside a volcanic crater PAGE 193

below
(TM/S)

above (MV/S) — Forest elephants are smaller than their bush cousins; their hard tusks make them a target for ivory poachers PAGE 6

below left (JH/D) — The elusive okapi is unique to the DRC and is related to the giraffe PAGE 6

below right (DH/S) — Chimpanzees live in deep rainforest and sleep in nests high up in trees PAGE 8

bottom right (DK/S) — Mountain gorillas have long black fur to protect them in their high-altitude environment PAGE 8

The Kordofan giraffe is smaller than other giraffe subspecies and, in the DRC, it is found only in Garamba National Park PAGE 178

above left
(RW/AP)

White rhinos, poached to extinction in Garamba National Park, have recently been reintroduced there PAGE 6

above right
(RW/AP)

Africa's emblematic big cats, lions can be spotted in national parks in eastern DRC PAGE 7

right
(KW/AP)

Buffaloes move in herds that number in the hundreds or even thousands PAGE 5

below
(MvR/AP)

left
(SS)
African grey parrots are targeted by poachers who sell them as pets PAGE 11

above
(SS)
The DRC has many species of snake; the egg-eaters are non-venomous PAGE 13

below left
(OP/S)
The large, beautiful swallowtail butterfly will delight anyone who spots it PAGE 13

bottom left
(SS)
Liberian banana frogs are tree frogs, living in forests; the DRC has many species of frog, more often heard than seen PAGE 12

bottom right
(SS)
The Congo peafowl, the DRC's national bird, is threatened by habitat loss in its rainforest home PAGE 11

Further along this road towards the Zambian border, about 210km and 6–8 hours' drive from Lubumbashi, is the town of **Kasenga** (⊕ 10°23.29 S, 28°36.55 E) where the **Lualuba Rapids**, also called **Johnston Falls**, create some incredible sights. They're the largest rapids in the DRC, bordering Zambia, and absolutely in the middle of nowhere. There is no public transport and a robust 4x4 vehicle will be needed.

KASUMBALESA

If you're arriving by bus from Zambia, Kasumbalesa will be your first stop just across the border in the DRC. It's a crowded, chaotic place where any number of trucks and people and cargo containers get stuck for days, weeks or even months. Many sit in limbo waiting while their goods are inspected and reinspected, or while they weave through the byzantine bureaucratic procedures to discover who exactly needs to be paid off for their journey to continue. If you are bringing your own vehicle, check and recheck that all of your documentation is in order: these officials see a huge number of foreign vehicles and know their game inside and out.

Cheap accommodation and cheap food are easy to find in Kasumbalesa. However, if you are travelling light, your stay here should be reasonably short, as Lubumbashi is only about 2 hours' drive away on a well-paved highway. Minibuses ply this route frequently.

PRACTICALITIES Kasumbalesa has a modern border-crossing post with nice paid washrooms and theoretically smooth entry and exit procedures.

The **bus station** is right in the middle of the market, and there are a few cheap hotels buried along this crowded stretch of road. Further up the street away from the border is **Boulangerie Victoire** (⏲ 06.00–20.00; $), a decent place to stock up on bread and pastries.

The best hotel in town is **Hôtel de la Paix**, on a small unasphalted street parallel to the main road, about 2km from the town centre (23 rooms; m 080 895 0148; **$$$**). It has secure parking; the Tijo Restaurant is connected to the back of the hotel and meals can be ordered there. Rooms have simple en-suite bathroom (with shower and WC), double bed, hot water, fan and TV. If you're crossing, cross as early in the morning as you can: large trucks moving copper and other minerals tend to arrive in the afternoon, creating chaos at the frontier and huge traffic jams, often lasting for hours, on the highway towards Lubumbashi.

SAKANIA

Sakania is the southernmost town in the 'Congo Pedicle', which divides neighbouring Zambia into its familiar 'butterfly' shape. The Pedicle is a hangover from the colonial Scramble for Africa: Belgian and British negotiators deciding the borders between their respective colonies, in 1884–85. In Katanga, Belgium wanted as much as it could get of the game-rich Bangweulu Wetlands, while Britain wanted as much territory as it could get in general. The king of Italy was called in to arbitrate, and the line he drew created the Congo Pedicle. The two 'arms' of Zambia are separated by 75km of the DRC.

Sakania is a busy town thanks to the two border crossings nearby, particularly the one with Ndola, only a few kilometres away. The other place of interest in its territory is the nature reserve called Demalisques de Lechwe, the extension of those Bangweulu Wetlands awarded to the Belgian Congo back in the 1880s. Lechwe

(*Kobus leche*) are beautiful, big antelopes; the males have large spiralling horns. They live in marshy areas and use flooded meadows as protection from predators. The black lechwe (*K. leche smithemani*) is found only here and across the border in the Bangweulu Wetlands national park. The organisations involved in administering the Zambian park hope one day to create a wildlife corridor with the reserve on the DRC side.

Near the eastern border of the Congo Pedicle with Zambia, close to the village of Musolo on the River Luapula, are rapids and a waterfall usually known by their Zambian name of Mumbotuta. They extend over several hundred metres along the river, though they don't fall a great height. In colonial times, they were named after a Belgian officer, Giraud, who discovered them while traversing the river in 1883. On this expedition he would be captured only a few dozen kilometres downstream by local villagers, and die in their custody.

GETTING THERE AND AWAY Sakania is about 4 hours' drive from Lubumbashi, if there are no traffic jams (a big 'if'). The road between Kasumbalesa and Sakania is excellent. There are also trains from Lubumbashi, although they are infrequent. To visit the Demalisques de Lechwe and the Mumbotuta/Giraud falls, a very robust 4x4 is essential.

🏠 WHERE TO STAY

Angel's Inn (41 rooms) Av Maman Aimée, Q/ Douane; m 082 089 5091, 097 808 4775; e angelsinnguesthouse@gmail.com. In a quiet neighbourhood a few mins' drive from town centre. Secure parking, restaurant (**$**), terrace bar; bakery & butcher's within complex, under same management. Reception building & most rooms set round a central courtyard; some rooms further away along poorly lit footpath. Wi-Fi only in reception building. All rooms en suite with AC or fan, mosquito net, TV, fridge; 'de luxe' rooms (**$$$$**) have huge bathrooms, AC, tea/coffee-making facilities, iron, desk, armchairs & table. **$$–$$$**

LIKASI

Likasi is at the heart of Katanga's Copperbelt, more or less halfway between Lubumbashi and Kolwezi. Copper was being used in this area as far back as the 16th century, worked by skilled artisans. It is the reason the town exists – it was founded in 1917 when the Likasi mine was opened. By 1931, the settlement had grown into a town and was named after a Belgian engineer called Jean Jadot. Opulent mansions and public buildings, set on wide avenues, gave Jadotville an urban coherence lacking in less carefully planned towns in Katanga or beyond. Nowadays, Likasi is still an important mining centre, for copper and cobalt; the industrial mines are operated by Chinese companies, and many people work as artisanal miners – a higher number than the employees of the industrial mines.

The old colonial neighbourhoods are an interesting sight: the carefully planned suburbs for mine workers, in their grid pattern, and the quiet tree-lined boulevards of the town centre, with the Art Deco town hall (built in 1928) and railway station particularly worth a look.

GETTING THERE AND AWAY Likasi is roughly a 2-hour drive north of Lubumbashi, on a decent paved road. There is little traffic, and roadworks do occur from time to time. It is, however, a 'Péage' route, meaning that a small fee is collected in each direction. The toll for a normal-sized 4x4 vehicle is less than US$2. Regular buses stop in Likasi from Lubumbashi en route to Kolwezi.

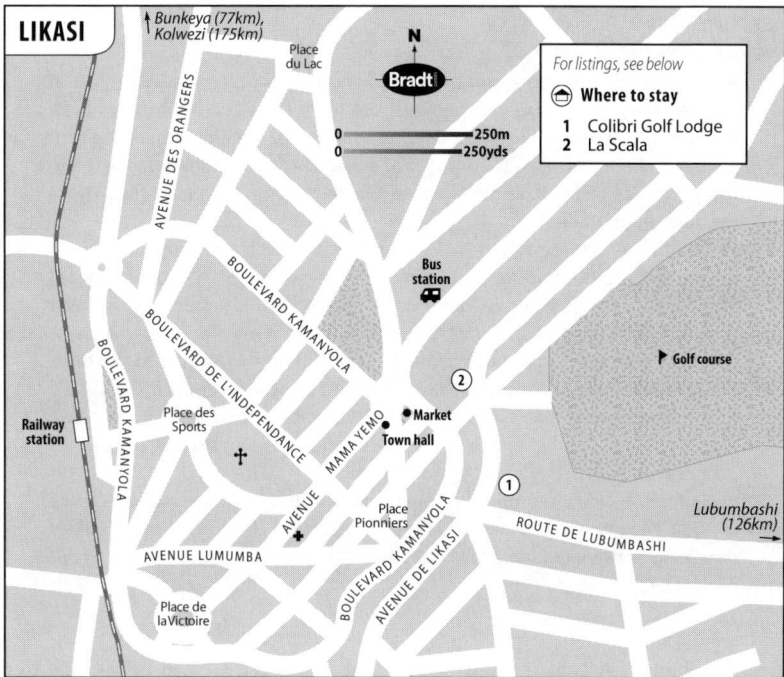

LIKASI

↑ Bunkeya (77km),
Kolwezi (175km)

Place
du Lac

N

Bradt

0 ———— 250m
0 ———— 250yds

For listings, see below

⊖ **Where to stay**
1 Colibri Golf Lodge
2 La Scala

AVENUE DES ORANGERS

BOULEVARD KAMANYOLA

BOULEVARD DE L'INDEPENDANCE

BOULEVARD KAMANYOLA

Bus
station

Golf course

Railway
station

Place des
Sports

②

AVENUE MAMA YEMO

● Market
Town hall

①

Lubumbashi
(126km)

Place
Pionniers

BOULEVARD KAMANYOLA

AVENUE DE LIKASI

ROUTE DE LUBUMBASHI

AVENUE

AVENUE LUMUMBA

Place de
la Victoire

WHERE TO STAY *Map, above*

Colibri Golf Lodge (20 rooms) 1212 Av du Football; m 097 701 1406; e colibrigolflodge@gmail.com; w colibrigolflodge.com; ⧉ Colibri Golf Lodge. Has restaurant, pool, rooftop lounge-bar, gym. Good-sized, nicely decorated rooms, all en suite, with AC, TV, fridge & tea/coffee-making facilities. **$$$**

La Scala (12 rooms) 1287 Av de la Mine; m 081 409 2020; ⊙ lasc.ala. Has restaurant/pizzeria ($$); Chinese restaurant; covered terrace bar; secure parking; pool tables. Rooms in bungalows set around courtyard; all en suite with AC, TV, fridge; b/fast inc. **$$**

AROUND LIKASI There are plenty of great excursions in the Likasi area, aside from the national parks. Nearby is **Lake Tshangalele**, a very popular site for migrating birds. The turn-off is 90km before arriving in Likasi; turn right, and follow the road to the north shore. Also in this area are the **Lufira Falls** near **Mwadingusha** (⊕ 10°44.55 S, 27°14.41 E), sending water from the Kundelungu Plateau rushing into the lake. This was where the DRC's first hydro-electric plant was built, one of the country's most important before the creation of the Inga Dams near Matadi.

Southwest of Likasi are the **Kashinge Caves**, between two rivers, near the Moaishi and Kashinge streams. These caves were used as hiding spots during periods of inter-tribal war, and can be considered something of an archaeological site. They're not easy to find, so a guide is more necessary than usual.

Anyone interested in the political history of the country will want to visit the **Memorial to Patrice Lumumba**, just off the N1 highway about 70km from Likasi and 50km from Lubumbashi. The memorial is at the place where Lumumba and his allies Maurice Mpolo and Joseph Okito were executed in January 1961 (page 29). The tree against which they were shot is still there and still shows the damage

An unmistakeably large presence near Likasi is the colonial-era mine of Shinkolobwe. Even from the road into the town from Lubumbashi, you will notice the massive 'tailings' of the copper and cobalt mines, where the run-off has spilled into semi-solid pools of soil and cast-off minerals. These are the remnants of Shinkolobwe, whose place in history is guaranteed by its production of uranium.

The mine was first opened in 1921, and the ore was transported to Belgium for processing into radium and uranium. Some of the Shinkolobwe ore fell into German hands when Belgium was occupied in 1940. During World War II, the United States became interested in Shinkolobwe's uranium, which was thought to amount to about half of the world's known reserves at the time. Some Shinkolobwe ore had been warehoused on Staten Island; this was sold to the Manhattan Project and an agreement was reached that Shinkolobwe would continue to ship ore to the USA. This uranium was used in the bombs dropped on Hiroshima and Nagasaki in 1945.

Shinkolobwe continued to supply the USA until Congolese independence in 1960. The mine was sealed and officially declared closed in 2004. It is likely that some artisanal mining continues, with the uranium being smuggled out of the DRC overland.

from the bullets. A golden statue of Lumumba has been erected next to the tree and a mausoleum has been built over the spot where the three men were originally buried, before they were disinterred, chopped up and dissolved in acid. The plane they were flown in to Katanga has been moved here. There are paths through the trees around the site, leading to statues of Mpolo and Okito, and of Laurent-Désiré Kabila. The whole site is very peaceful and moving.

The guard at the entrance gate will attempt to charge for admission; if there are foreigners in the car, the amount will be extortionate. Do not pay! There is no entry charge to the site. The people who maintain it will show you around (in French) and should be rewarded for their time; US$10 or Fc20,000 is a reasonable amount.

KUNDELUNGU AND UPEMBA NATIONAL PARKS

with thanks to ICCN Haut-Katanga

Although now managed as separate parks, Kundelungu and Upemba have the same types of landscape and habitat and, until 2016, were administered together. Together they cover over 2 million hectares, about the size of the Netherlands. The River Lufira bisects Kundelungu from south to north and continues through Upemba before, eventually, joining the River Lualaba. Along the river are lakes and wetlands; as the terrain rises, the habitats change from rainforest and miombo forest to savannah grasslands. The highest point is in Kundelungu, 1,700m above sea level. Part of the river valley is a Ramsar Wetland of International Importance. The river has several beautiful waterfalls and cataracts. **Lofoi Falls**, in Kundelungu, is the highest unbroken waterfall in the whole of Africa – a fall of 300m. Another waterfall, only slightly less spectacular, is at Masansa. Upemba has the **Kiubo Falls**, also set in forest and tumbling about 60m over sandstone.

The parks are home to iconic **animals**. There are many hippos in the wetlands and, higher up, several species of antelope, including kudu and sable antelope. Upemba also has forest elephants, around 300 of them, and the DRC's only wild zebras, also a thriving population. Kundelungu once had white rhinos, but they had become locally extinct by 1994. Cheetahs, which were thought to be present at one time, are also locally extinct. Lake Upemba is particularly rich in **birdlife**.

Upemba and Kundelungu national parks, in common with other protected areas in the DRC, are threatened with poaching, illegal settlements and mining, and by the presence within them of armed militias, in this case Mai-Mai groups (page 41). In 2012, the Chief Warden of Upemba National Park was ambushed and murdered by Mai-Mai.

These national parks are co-managed, under a public–private partnership, by ICCN and the Forgotten Parks Foundation (w forgottenparks.org), with support from IUCN (w iucn.nl). New, young rangers were recruited and given full training; the villagers who live around the lakes in the parks were helped to reduce overfishing; and the park management became more focused on conservation science than before.

PRACTICALITIES The first step in visiting the Upemba–Kundelungu park complex is to buy a **park permit** from ICCN in Lubumbashi (see map, page 144). The price for foreign citizens is US$50.

The entrance to **Kundelungu National Park** is at Gombela; the park administration office is at Katwe, where there is a guesthouse (US$25 per night pp) with room for four couples. There are cooking facilities, but nowhere to buy food; you have to bring everything with you, including drinking water (or the means to purify unsafe water – see page 64). At Masansa and Lutshipuka there are camps with tents set up; you will need your own sleeping bag and, of course, food and water. Armed guides can be hired at all three places. The main entrance to **Upemba National Park** is at Lusinga; see below for accommodation at Kiubo, 30km away. There is also an entrance near Kayo. Armed guides can be hired at both entrances.

The easiest way to get to these national parks is in a **4x4 vehicle**, but getting around within the parks can only be done on foot. From Lubumbashi, it is 180km to Katwe, asphalted as far as Minga (about halfway). To Upemba, the road is asphalted as far as Kiubo, 400km from Lubumbashi. The park entrance, at Lusinga, is a further 30km on the Mumbolo road. It is also possible to approach Lusinga from Mitwaba, 45km away (unasphalted), but see page 163 for security concerns in the Mitwaba area. The upmarket **Kiubo Falls Lodge** (m 097 930 9955; f Congo Star Safaris; **$$$$**), 30km from the Lusinga entrance, has ten chalets, with Wi-Fi and air conditioning; there is ample parking, as well as a restaurant, pool and children's playground.

The best way to reach the Kayo entrance of Upemba National Park is by **train**. The *rapide* train from Lubumbashi to Kananga stops at Lubudi. From there, a taxi or motorbike can take you the 15km to Kayo and possibly the further 10km to the park entrance. There is a small hotel in Lubudi, and accommodation available at the convent there.

BUNKEYA

In many ways, Bunkeya (⊕ 10°23.51 S, 26°58.10 E) is the spiritual heartland of Katanga. Before the arrival of the Belgians, the political authority in the region was the Kingdom of Msiri, at its height from 1856 to 1891, which stretched through most of central Katanga. Its king, Ngengelenwa Msiri, has been documented as either a crazed despot or an astute politician who sought to mitigate the incursions from the Europeans as they began their colonisation of the continent during the final decades of the 19th century. Katangans and Congolese in general speak highly of him, while European records consider him a twisted old man who brutalised his servants. These days he is highly regarded among Bunkeya's population as one of the few chiefs across central Africa who did not wish to bend to European colonialism.

HISTORY Msiri had established the capital of his kingdom in Bunkeya sometime around 1850 by consolidating tribes and driving away the Lubas, who commonly raided the region. The kingdom stretched from the west bank of the River Lualaba to the west of present-day Kolwezi, a vast area larger than Great Britain. The rich mineral deposits made his kingdom a trading centre, shipping ivory and gold west to Portuguese ports and slaves east to Arab holdings. He struck a deal with Tippu Tip, who was running his own state east of the River Lualaba, for protection from his attacks in exchange for a steady supply of slaves. Ngengelenwa Msiri was no fool, and managed to form an army of 3,000 to protect his kingdom; unlike other African leaders before colonial times, his astute trading practices had amassed a huge cache of rifles and ammunition. His army was as well armed as any European outfit in the region.

He was ardent at keeping out intruders, refusing permission from any explorers who may have arrived in the Garaganze, the original name for Katanga. It was not until 1886 that Msiri invited Protestant missionaries to establish themselves at Bunkeya. He also hired Arab advisors related to Tippu Tip, and sought advice on how to limit European expansion into his territory, surrounding himself with people from other cultures, to learn from them and better understand what their motives might be.

Msiri was eventually approached by explorers from both Britain and Belgium, who were seeking to expand their territorial mandates in the region. The British South Africa Company arrived in Bunkeya in 1890 and presented the king with a treaty, which he demanded to be translated before agreeing to it. He deemed the treaty unfavourable to his kingdom and rejected it outright, sending the company on their way. By this time the Berlin Conference had adjourned and his kingdom was within the Congo Free State, though he was not made aware of this fact.

His downfall would come in 1891 when William Grant Stairs, a Canadian military commander who had travelled with Henry Morton Stanley arrived in the region. Military campaigns across the east were driving out African leaders to secure the region ahead of the Arabs, and at Bunkeya they were equally relentless. Stairs was charged with ensuring the region was soundly under control of forces loyal to the Congo Free State, and he sent a Belgian officer, Captain Omer Bodson, to arrest Msiri; on 20 December 1891, after an altercation, Bodson shot Msiri dead; Bodson was then killed by a nephew of Msiri.

Msiri's death did not precipitate the end of the kingdom, however, and the people appointed a new chief, Mukanda Bantu. He agreed to have the kingdom incorporated into the Congo Free State, something Ngengelenwa Msiri was set against. Subsequent attacks occurred on members of Stairs' expedition by those who thought the entire deal was bad, yet the transition was relatively peaceful.

Moïse Tshombe was descended directly from the Msiri kings, or so it is said, and this bolstered his leadership during the years of Katanga secession in the 1960s.

PRACTICALITIES Bunkeya is 75km north of Likasi on a brutal dirt road and should take the better part of a day by private transport. There are some minibuses that ply this route as well, at Likasi's market. There should be one or two basic **hotels** in town, and if not, try one of the various Christian missions to get a room. None should cost above US$10.

WHAT TO SEE AND DO The town itself is a modest affair with several Catholic and Protestant missions. The best thing worth seeing is the **Tomb of Msiri**, and every 20 December his death is commemorated in an elaborate ceremony. The town has held fast to its ancient traditions and you can see plenty of unique costumes, robes and furniture around. Whenever a new king is appointed there are elaborate celebrations; the last was held in 1997. The nearby **Mount Mkulu** is an ancient burial site.

KOLWEZI

Kolwezi was an important mining centre in colonial times, and there are still examples of colonial architecture around the city – the mansions of the white bosses and the Catholic cathedral, for example. After years of decline, Kolwezi has seen a resurgence in the last decade, as foreign (mostly Chinese) mining companies have returned to exploit the huge copper and cobalt deposits in the area, constructing entire new neighbourhoods to house their employees. The presence of so many foreigners in the city has also led to an improvement in the quality and range of hotel accommodation and restaurants.

GETTING THERE AND AWAY Frequent **buses** connect Kolwezi with Lubumbashi; the N1 road is asphalted as far as Fungurume and the journey takes about 5 hours, depending on traffic. Road upgrading continues throughout the country and the asphalt may reach Kolwezi during the lifetime of this edition. The bus station in Kolwezi is quite far from the city centre – there are taxis and motorbikes to ferry passengers around.

CAA (w caacongo.com) has direct **flights** from Lubumbashi and Mbuji-Mayi, three times a week; they connect with flights to and from Kinshasa.

WHERE TO STAY Map, page 160

Expensive

Moon Palace (50 rooms) 4351 Route Likasi; m 082 303 3333; ￼ Hotel Moon Palace Kolwezi. Secure parking, airport transfers available; Wi-Fi; restaurant, bar, good-sized pool, gym. All rooms en suite with AC, TV, tea/coffee-making facilities; some have balcony. **$$$$**

Town Lodge Executive (30 rooms) Av Araucarias 114, coin Av Kasa-Vubu; m 089 989 8888; e Kolwezi@TownExecutiveLodge.com; w townexecutivelodge.com; ￼ Town Lodge Executive. Part of the small Colibri regional chain. Airport transfers & parking inc. Outdoor pool, garden, gym, 2 restaurants, free Wi-Fi throughout. All rooms en suite with toiletries; AC, TV, minibar, coffee machine. Standard rooms **$$$**, deluxe **$$$$**, suite **$$$$$**

Mid-range

Colibri Inn Hotel (32 rooms) 27 Av Prof Joseph Yav; 27 Rue Colibri; m 082 399 9828; e kolwezi@lodgecolibri.com; w lodgecolibri. com; ￼ ColibriHotelKolwezi. Airport transfers (4mins from airport) & parking inc. Outdoor pool, gym, games room, garden, restaurant with African & international cuisine, terrace bar. All rooms en suite with toiletries, AC, TV, tea/coffee-making facilities; some have balcony; b/fast inc. Dbl **$$$**, suite **$$$$**

Kampi Ya Boma (52 rooms, 4 suites) Av Imini Lufupa, Q/ Joli Site; m 081 380 0099, 099 266 3579; e resv@kampiyaboma.com; w kampiyaboma.com. Very convenient for Kolwezi Airport, 3km from city centre. Wheelchair accessible. Secure parking, 24hr electricity,

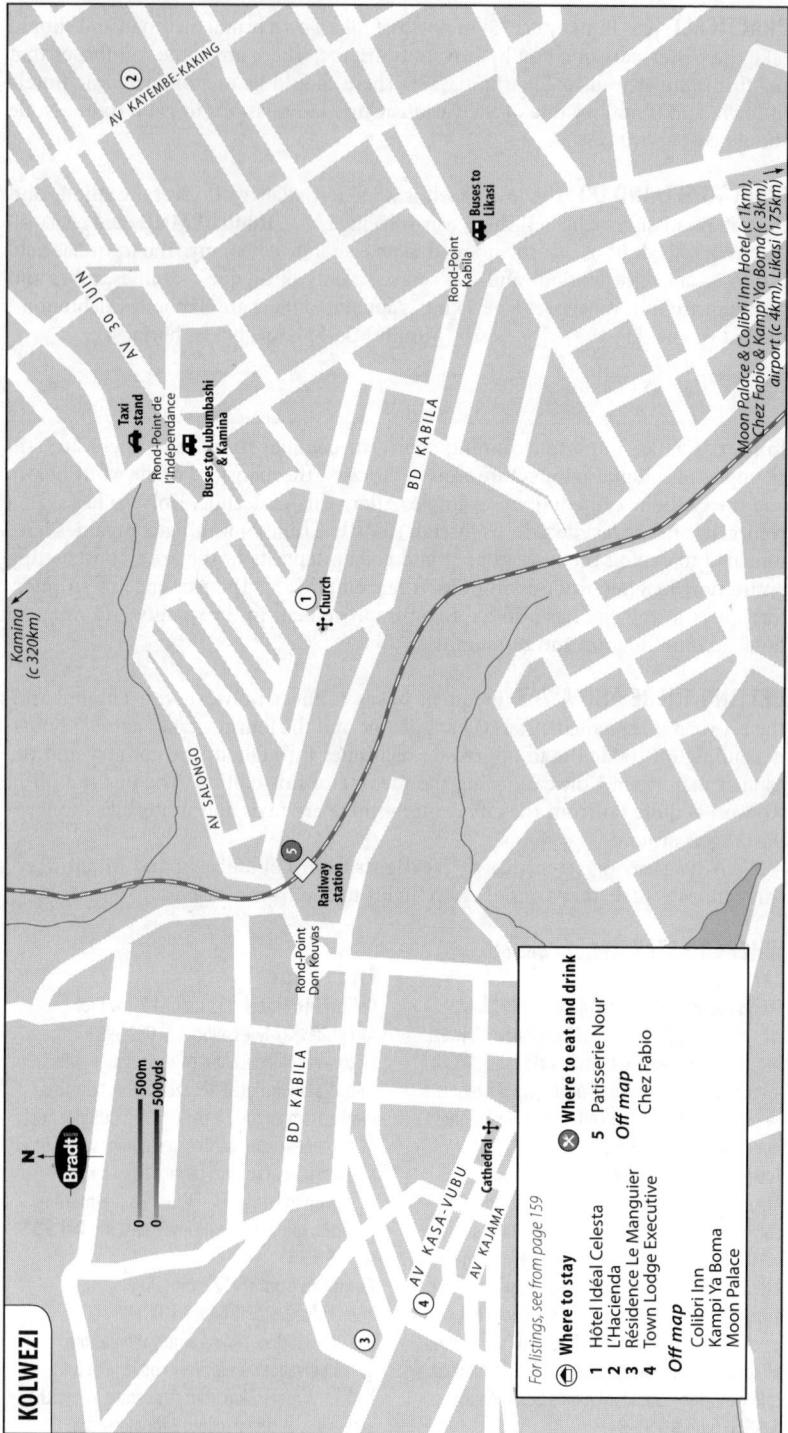

KOLWEZI

N

Bradt

0   500m
0   500yds

Kamina ↖ (c 320km)

AV KAYEMBE-KAKING   ②

AV 30 JUIN

Taxi stand
Rond-Point de
l'Indépendance
Buses to Lubumbashi
& Kamina

✝ Church   ①

BD KABILA

Rond-Point
Kabila
Buses to
Likasi

Moon Palace & Colibri Inn Hotel (c 1km),
Chez Fabio & Kampi Ya Boma (c 3km),
airport (c 4km), Likasi (175km) ↓

AV SALONGO

Rond-Point
Don Kouvas

Railway
station
⑤

BD KABILA

AV KASA-VUBU

④

AV KAJAMA

Cathedral ✝

③

For listings, see from page 159

⬤ Where to stay

1   Hôtel Idéal Celesta
2   L'Hacienda
3   Résidence Le Manguier
4   Town Lodge Executive

Off map
  Colibri Inn
  Kampi Ya Boma
  Moon Palace

✖ Where to eat and drink

5   Patisserie Nour

Off map
  Chez Fabio

large outdoor pool, gym, choice of restaurants with Congolese, European & Indian menus, laundry service, bar with pool tables & TV screens, conference room. Standalone chalets set in spacious grounds, all en suite with AC, sat TV, Wi-Fi, mosquito net, seating area; suites also have kitchenette, living room & guest toilet. $$$–$$$$

Residence Le Manguier (27 rooms) 63 Av Kasavubu; m 099 362 0063; e info@lemanguierhotel.com; w lemanguierhotel.com; f Le Manguier Hotel Kolwezi. Secure parking, bar, restaurant; Wi-Fi throughout. Good-sized pool, sauna, gym. Airport transfers available. All rooms en suite (some with tub as well as shower), with TV, AC, coffee/tea-making facilities, fridge; superior rooms have balcony. $$$, suites $$$$

L'Hacienda (26 rooms, 1 apartment) 420 Av Kayembe Kaking, Q/ Mutoshi; m 099 774 5960, 081 404 3789; e haciendakolwezi@gmail.com; f L'hacienda Hôtel-Kolwezi. Secure parking; outdoor pool, landscaped grounds, restaurant with European & Congolese menu, bar with pool table. All rooms en suite, nicely decorated in Latin American style with AC, TV, Wi-Fi & coffee/tea-making facilities. $$$

Thrifty

Hôtel Idéal Celesta (20 rooms) 1675 Av Kamina; m 099 137 2129; e ipomrdc@gmail.com. Secure parking, restaurant/bar, helpful reception staff. All rooms en suite, some with shower, some with bathtub; AC, TV, fridge, Wi-Fi; b/fast inc. Superior rooms have garden view, others look on to street. $$

✗ WHERE TO EAT AND DRINK *Map, opposite*

The restaurants of the hotels listed on page 159 and above are open to non-residents. An alternative is **Chez Fabio** (m 081 191 5666), run by the chef of La Bonne Fourchette restaurant in Lubumbashi (page 149), just off the road out to the airport, on the way to Kampi ya Boma. It serves high-quality French dishes with daily specials ($$) and à la carte ($$$). For a lighter meal, **Patisserie Nour**, in the city centre, offers fresh bread, sandwiches and snacks ($).

OTHER PRACTICALITIES Kolwezi has several supermarkets that stock imported goods; Kinmarché, on the main road into town, just past the airport, is easy to find. Banks in the city centre have ATMs. Western Union and DHL both have agencies on the main road, near the general hospital.

WHAT TO SEE AND DO The open-cast **Mutoshi Mine** was the first to be exploited in Katanga. No longer in use, the open-cast pit is now filled with water, given its turquoise colour from the traces of malachite within it. You can't swim here, but it is nice to look at.

Lake Nzilo curves around the city to its east and northeast. On its southern shore, the **Katebi Lodge** resort (w gpmkatebi-lodge.com; $$$$) has two swimming pools with views of the lake and a beach volleyball court; boat trips on the lake are available. At the other end of the lake is a series of rapids called the **Nzilo Falls**, which drop over 30m through an impressive gorge. This is the source for one of the hydro-electric plants that power the mines.

South of Kolwezi are the **Lufunfu Caves** near the village of **Lufunfu** (⊕ 11°11.60 S, 25°37.00 E) at the source of the river of the same name.

KAMINA

Kamina's importance stems from its location as a major rail junction in colonial times. This is where the colonial railway divided (page 58) between the mines in the south and the river transport to the north and west. Nowadays, the timetables are more limited, but there are still **trains** from Kamina to Mwene Ditu, Kananga and

THE OCCUPATION OF KOLWEZI

Catching the eye of the world in 1978 was yet another rebellion in Zaire; most rebellions in the country were local insurrections, put down harshly by Mobutu's FAZ and barely a whimper was made of such things to the outside world. Yet like most events in the Congo, once Europeans become embroiled, the country rose to global consciousness.

The prime example of this is the tragedy of Kolwezi. Katangese rebels, 4,000 strong, had received funding from Angola to begin their insurrection against Mobutu's rule as well as European domination of the resources there – they lived and worked in the Gécamines properties, enjoying comfortable lives in upper-class company-manufactured homes. Early on the morning of 13 May 1978, the rebels marched straight into Kolwezi and sealed the town off, fighting briefly with FAZ soldiers. This was definitely a good way to get the world to notice, as there were 3,000 Europeans in town during the invasion. The Katangese forces declared on 14 May that the second war of Shaba had begun, and announced their international assistants – Angola, Zambia and Cuba.

The rebels were ruthless inside Kolwezi – they killed with impunity and set fire to buildings without much thought for who or what may be inside them. Mobutu's FAZ tried an unsuccessful counter-attack, and the dictator later begged for military assistance from the USA, France and Belgium to end the brutal uprising. Whole families were being executed by the rebels: a systematic extermination of the town's population was occurring. This included Europeans, and because of that, European soldiers would arrive shortly.

In the early hours of 18 May, French paratroopers arrived in Kolwezi in what was called Opération Bonite. They dropped by parachute and quickly took the airport. Katangese guerrillas retreated mostly into the forest where they staged counter-attacks on the evenings of 19–20 May. Europeans began evacuating from Kolwezi. Belgian soldiers arrived, primarily with an interest in organising the evacuation. European forces were fast and organised, overwhelming the Katangese rebels quickly.

In total, some 250 rebels were killed before they fled on 21 May 1978. But the civilian toll was massive – as many as 700 Congolese and 170 Europeans lost their lives.

A memorial to the soldiers who lost their lives in the Shaba wars, built by Mobutu in the 1970s, sits beside the main road as you enter Kolwezi from the south.

the terminus in Ilebo (page 130), from where there are still cargo boats up the River Kasai and onwards to Kinshasa; to Kabale, Kongolo and on to Kindu (page 136), from where some river traffic still runs up to the start of the rapids at Ubundu; and a spur line to Kalemie (see opposite), on Lake Tanganyika – in colonial times a major port.

Kamina was the seat of the last king of the Luba empire (page 16). More recently, after World War II, a large air base was built by the Belgian military. During the 1960s, it supported foreign troops coming in to put down the Katanga secession (page 28). It was then used as a forward base for aircraft during Operation Dragon Rouge as they arrived in the Congo from Ascension Island en route to Stanleyville (page 170). It is now a Congolese Air Force base. The civilian airstrip, near the town centre, is no longer in use.

WHAT TO SEE AND DO Kamina is a good starting point for some natural wonders in the region, especially **Pitanshi Caves** (✛ 07°55.60.00 S, 25°19.60.00 E), which follow the River Kilubi. These caves were created by river erosion underground and are lit by sunlight through naturally created shafts. Generally they're only accessible during the dry season. A road heads to them northeast from **Kipukwe** (✛ 08°06.11 S, 25°10.07 E) and then doubles back on to the main road to Kabongo at **Samba** (✛ 07°55.14 S, 25°13.13 E). Continue on this road to **Kabongo** (✛ 07°20.29 S, 25°34.57 E) where **Lake Boya** is right beside it. The lake is popular with birdlife and surrounded by high reeds. Follow the road northwest along the railway for a few hundred kilometres and arrive at **Kaniama** (✛ 07°30.43 S, 24°10.26 E), which has a worse road going northeast towards the modestly impressive **Kaye Falls**.

There is a brutal road north to here which eventually reaches the village of **Mani** (✛ 06°28.01 S, 25°20.58 E), right on the border between Lomami and Haut-Lomami provinces. Mani has a few natural sights, not least the **Kabale Lakes** which can be good for birdwatching. The geography also begins to shift from Katanga's arid brush to moist forest foliage. The River Lomami is west of Mani, and if followed upstream for about 10km it will bring you to the **Lubangule Falls** in a shallow valley. The Lomami merges here with the River Lubangule. Keep going along the road from Mani to **Kabinda** (✛ 06°08.10 S, 24°28.50 E) and the road should link up with Mbuji-Mayi after grinding away for several days.

Northeast from Kabongo, the railway arrives in Kabale, where the line divides again: north to Kindu or east to Kalemie. If for some reason you are here in a (very robust) 4x4 vehicle, driving north to **Kongolo** might be worth a try: the **Hinde Rapids** are an impressive sight at the point where the River Lualaba squeezes between two valleys and ends the navigable portion of the river. The rail bridge here that crosses the Lualaba is also impressive, spanning over 500m. There is no direct road link between Kabale and Kongolo. There is a dirt track northward to **Kasongo** (✛ 04°25.34 S, 26°40.06 E) in Maniema province. Hire an armed escort and stock up on petrol.

THE TRIANGLE OF DEATH

Since it became a battle zone during the Second Congo War, the area that lies, roughly, between the southern end of Lake Tanganyika, the River Lualaba and Lake Mweru has become known as the 'Triangle of Death'. Many Mai-Mai groups are active in the area; some are villagers who have armed themselves to defend their communities, while others are much more sinister (page 41). It doesn't make much difference to foreign travellers. Manono, Mitwaba and Pweto are not only dangerous places, but they are almost impossible to get to except on foot or motorbike. The motorbike couriers who transport documents or valuables on government business are often from the indigenous Pygmy peoples, partly because they are known to be hard-working and reliable, but mainly because of their deep knowledge of the forest and any intruders who are roaming around in it. Any traveller who decides to explore this dangerous region is strongly advised to hire a guide/driver from the indigenous Pygmy community.

KALEMIE

This city of a quarter of a million has a lengthy colonial history – dating back to Arab traders who established a port on the western shore of Lake Tanganyika, as a transit post for their trade in enslaved people and ivory. Belgian missionaries began to found Catholic missions around the lake in the late 1880s, but came under attack by Tippu Tip and others. In 1891, an expedition arrived to relieve the missionaries' defenders. The motivation for the expedition was primarily from anti-slavery groups, led by a cardinal of the Catholic Church, who lobbied the government to send troops. On 30 December 1891, the expedition's leader founded the military post of Albertville, around 15km from the site of the modern town of Kalemie. After the Arabs had left, the name of Albertville was transferred to the site of their old port at M'Toa. The railway and the port made it once more a busy centre for imports and exports, via Tanzania and the Indian Ocean. Albertville was an important base during World War II – a fleet of seaplanes launched from here destroyed the German fleet in Lake Tanganyika.

Mobutu's *authenticité* policy saw the city's name changed to Kalemie and reinforced its status as the southeastern transportation hub for Zaire. Yet during the 1990s, Kalemie's remoteness compounded its problems, as revolution spread across the DRC and the city became a transit point for soldiers and supplies coming from Tanzania. In the countryside surrounding Kalemie, Mai-Mai groups have become increasingly active since the turn of the 21st century, and this has brought a large number of refugees into the area, as well as UN peacekeepers to try and resolve the conflict. Matters were not helped when the town was struck by a 6.8 (Richter scale) earthquake in December 2005, collapsing houses and buildings across the region. See page 40 for information on the security situation at the time of this update.

GETTING THERE AND AWAY CAA (w caacongo.com) has **flights** to Kalemie from Goma and Lubumbashi. The schedules change rather frequently. As ever in the DRC, the best way to check what flights there are, and when, is to go to the airport and ask there.

There are two **trains** a week between Lubumbashi and Kalemie (1,320km), via Likasi, Kamina and other stations. The 'express' takes between three and four days in each direction; fares (as of 2024) range from Fc575,200 in 'Luxe' first class (AC, modern toilets, meals and drinks served to your seat) to Fc416,200 in third class. The *ordinaire* (a 'stopping train') takes longer and costs less: Fc194,300 in first class, Fc175,900 in second class, and Fc155,200 in third class. There are also trains from Kalemie to Kindu (page 136).

A privately owned cargo and passenger **ferry**, the *MV Amani*, operates between Kalemie and Uvira, at the northern end of Lake Tanganyika. It leaves Uvira (Kalundu) on Sundays and returns there from Kalemie on Thursdays. In the past, the same ship has taken passengers across the lake to the Tanzanian port of Kigoma; there has also been talk of a connection to Bujumbura (Burundi). In the meantime, the international crossings are made by boats of unreliable safety; the most recent fatalities were in April 2024, when ten passengers died.

It is highly inadvisable to travel by **road** much beyond the town. Not only are the roads in terrible condition, but Mai-Mai groups are active throughout the region.

GETTING AROUND Kalemie sits on the west coast of Lake Tanganyika, with the River Lukuga creating its northern boundary. **Avenue Lumumba** runs north–south along the lake, the main boulevard in the original layout of the Belgian town. The city centre's infrastructure dates almost entirely from the time of the Belgian Congo, giving the town a unique look – this also means it looks a bit more ragged than some other cities. The airport is near the north end of town.

WHERE TO STAY AND EAT

Tcham (38 rooms) Bd Lumumba 6493–5; m 081 801 2900; w hoteltcham.com. On lakefront, secure. 2 good restaurants (**$$**), 24hr room service; terrace bar & restaurant with lake views. Wi-Fi throughout, laundry service, airport transfers & day trips offered. Pool, gym, tennis court; jet-ski & quad-bike rental. All rooms with good en-suite bathroom, AC, flat-screen TV, safe, minibar, iron with board, phone; some have balcony with lake view; b/fast, gym, pool, tennis all inc. **$$$**

Rio Beach ('Chez Rio') Bd Lumumba. Great setting on lakeside (take mosquito repellent). Grilled chicken, brochette or steak with frites; wide choice of beers; shorter wine list. Relaxed, friendly atmosphere. **$**

WHAT TO SEE AND DO The main sight in Kalemie is **Lake Tanganyika**: the largest in the Albertine Rift, and second largest in Africa, after Lake Victoria. It is extremely deep and has a wide variety of unique aquatic life amid clear blue water – both scientific and commercial divers work in the lake. Most of the town's economy is based on fishing. The fishers head out at dusk to fish by lantern and, in the evening, the waters of the lake near the town are dotted with the light from their lamps. The

CHE GUEVARA AND LAURENT KABILA

Che Guevara's time in eastern Congo was punctuated by a notable lack of grass-roots leadership from the rebel force's highest commander, Laurent-Désiré Kabila. Che had, in fact, sent numerous letters to Kabila and kept in regular contact for a period of years both before and during his arrival in eastern Congo. The two historical figures, though, would only meet twice.

The first time was in Dar es Salaam, in 1964 – Laurent Kabila was travelling across Africa petitioning governments friendly to his cause for support, key among them President Julius Kambarage Nyerere's in Tanzania. They met in Dar es Salaam, along with Laurent Kabila's Simbas, their commanders, and a Cuban delegation led by Che Guevara. Che spoke fondly of Kabila, and while his words were harsh for the other rebel leaders of Africa who were only seeking to feather their own nests and lead a revolution from the posh hotel rooms of capital cities, he was impressed by Kabila's presentation, presence and eloquence. Guevara agreed to provide support for the Simbas as soon as possible, and departed for Cuba.

The second meeting was nearly a year later. Guevara had been in the Simba training camps for several months in the mountainous regions northwest of Kalemie. After another cordial but urgent request for Kabila to make his presence known in the Simba rebel enclave, Kabila repeated his mantra of 'arriving soon'. Finally, three months after Guevara's arrival in the Congo, Kabila arrived in the Simba stronghold. Guevara remarked in his journals of how Laurent Kabila could impress the local population with his energy and natural charm, telling people what they wanted to hear while still maintaining an air of authority. Guevara continuously requested that Kabila assist him in organising a force to carry out attacks as soon as possible; Kabila, though, was evasive on this subject and always changed the topic of conversation when it started to revolve around his involvement in military action.

They spent five days together touring the rebel enclave, and very little progress was made for a definitive plan of action for the Simbas. On 11 July 1965, Laurent Kabila told Guevara he needed to cross Lake Tanganyika to Kigoma for a meeting with some rebel leaders and would return in two days. Kabila never returned, and the two of them never met again.

terrace bars on the lakefront (Boulevard Lumumba), including Rio Beach (page 165), are ideal spots from which to observe this, with a cold drink close to hand (and mosquito repellent on your hands and any other exposed skin).

The disintegrating houses of the Belgian colonial neighbourhood can be explored on a hilltop that overlooks the town and the lake. There are views of the surrounding countryside towards eastern Katanga (full of Mai-Mai, better viewed from this distance) as well as across the lake to Tanzania. You can also see pieces of **artillery** from World War II scattered about the hilltops, which were aimed at the Germans in Tanganyika.

If you follow a rough road 25km southwest from Kalemie on the road to Muhila (security permitting), you will reach **Koki Falls**, flowing out of the Muhila Mountains east of the lake. The water in the falls is hot, flowing from an underground spring. The road south has some excellent scenery, passing through lush bamboo forests along a winding road that follows the plateau.

Along the coast south of Kalemie is the smaller lakeside town of **Moba** (✪ 07°02.53 S, 09°46.36 E), similarly established by Belgian missionaries in 1893. In town there is a small chapel, and a monument to its founders. It is not accessible by road, but it may be possible to hire a boat or pirogue from Kalemie.

7

Kisangani and the North

The wild north of the Democratic Republic of the Congo is a place of sparse population, terrible roads and amazing wildlife. In a general sense, one could say the north of the country is the area on the right bank of the River Congo between its two big turns, then eastwards to Lake Albert. Its only large city is Kisangani – a historic outpost, located at the river's last point navigable by large boats.

The north has parks and reserves with the country's most emblematic animals: great apes, okapis and forest elephants. Its northeast corner has the crumbling remains of the spectacular palaces that Mobutu had built in his home province, in Gbadolite and Lisala.

As well as Garamba National Park and Okapi Wildlife Reserve, this chapter also covers Maiko National Park; the province of Ituri, with its capital Bunia, is covered in *Chapter 8* (page 224).

KISANGANI

A mid-sized city of old concrete buildings and towers looms against a vast network of jungle and rivers where mud huts are the norm – it is a true contrast of the region and a curiosity to see all of this infrastructure, dilapidated though it may be, so far away from anything similar. Kisangani has always been the centrepoint for the northeastern end of the Democratic Republic of the Congo; its founding pre-dated the entire existence of the country. Motorbikes zip along deteriorating roads, the sun seems to burn even through thick cloud, and crowds of people wash their clothes along the shores of the River Congo. Without the river, there would be no Kisangani, as it is the furthest point one can travel from Kinshasa without encountering rapids and, throughout its history, it has been the major transit point for the region. Kisangani has seen many transformations, as its history narrates.

HISTORY The history of Stanleyville/Kisangani is sprawling, complicated and bloody – it has changed hands several times, and has seen combat in its streets. Its chronology can be a source of confusion; perhaps it was doomed to this fate as the geographical centre of Africa, as well as being the oldest and most remote outpost of the wild and undeveloped Congo Free State.

European and Arab arrival Henry Morton Stanley arrived on the spot where Kisangani would be founded in 1875; Swahili Arab traders, among them Tippu Tip, were already active in the area and helped Stanley create a trading centre that would suit not only the needs of the Arab ivory and slave trades, but also the colonial interest in an outpost at the terminus of the navigable waters of the River Congo. The area was already an important trading centre for local tribes who traded fish and handicrafts

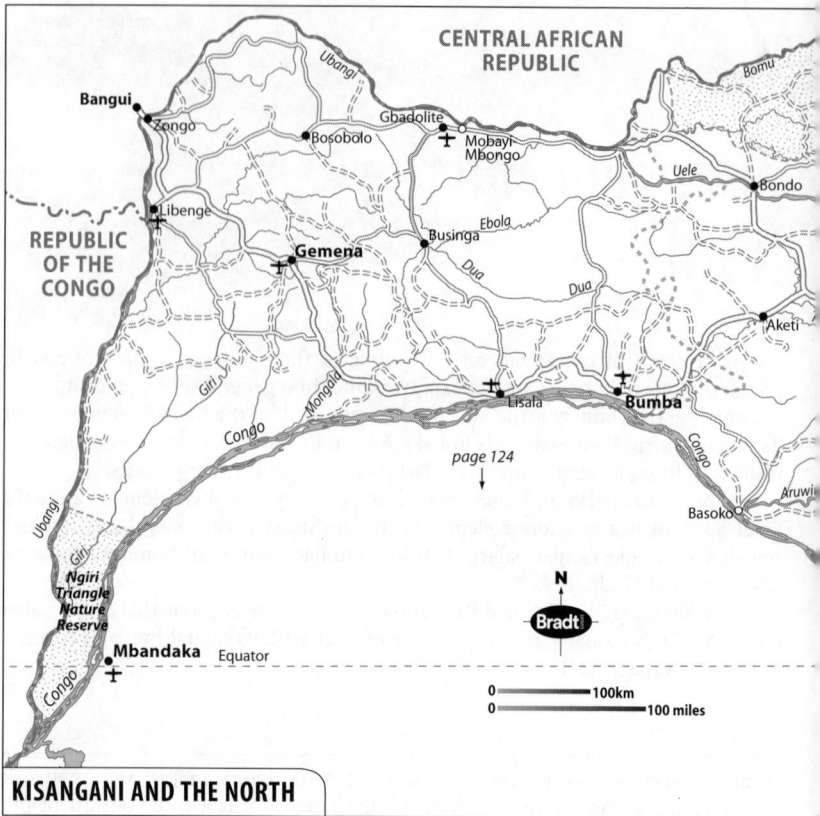

KISANGANI AND THE NORTH

on the river's shores. It was where the Congo started to flow westwards, fed by the Lualaba to the south, the Tshopo to the east and the Lindi rivers to the north.

Tippu Tip, his sons, and other Swahili Arabs loyal to the Zanzibari sultans ruled Stanleyville from its founding in 1875 until 1893. King Léopold sent the first Belgian officials there in 1883, though Arab traders protested strongly – finally, in 1886, setting fire to the fledgling outpost, and burning it down. This act prompted the Belgians to negotiate with the Arabs. Tippu Tip and his men retained control of the outpost, but local trade began to shift towards Belgian interests after this.

In the 1890s, there was intense dispute over the increasing tendency to ship ivory westwards, to Belgian interests, rather than to the Arab ports in the east. At the same time, anti-slaving groups were clashing with Arab slave traders in the region. Major clashes erupted in 1892, pitting Arab traders against Belgian soldiers. The Arabs were defeated, and were driven out of Stanleyville entirely. Tippu Tip's State, ruled from Stanleyville, had dissolved into Léopold's territory.

The Belgian system was a step backward from the Arab system of trade that had worked, more or less, with the local people for some decades – the forced labour, kidnapping, and total lack of interest in any kind of exchange with the population ruined the fledgling commercial economy, broke emerging ties between the colonisers and the colonised, and almost entirely erased the status of Stanleyville as a trading hub; it became merely a shipping port, a relationship of exploitation that saw goods flow only one way. The town existed solely as an administrative centre, ultimately being designated as regional capital for the whole of the eastern half of the Congo Free State in 1897.

With the arrival of the railway in 1912, the city gained ground – Congolese people were paid to work on it, bringing cash to the local population and reintroducing fledgling trade to the region. Agriculture followed after World War I, and weekly markets began to form; the river and rail connections brought more commercial businesses to the city, along with thousands of Europeans to run them.

While much of the local population was still relegated to work camps, requiring permits to travel far afield, the town grew into a city as World War II arrived and passed. It experienced population booms during this time, as more economic activity arrived, driven by European and American interest in war materials. Congolese people began to start their own businesses in the 1950s, and the more affluent owned their own houses. The Belgians completed the Tshopo Dam in 1956, giving the city its own reliable source of electricity. Stanleyville was flourishing. Yet, when independence arrived and the country itself began to disintegrate, all that changed. The city would be a central flashpoint in the 1960s, when the structure of the entire nation was in question.

The 1960s – invasions and rebellions With independence came the fracturing of the Congo state, and when Patrice Lumumba was arrested, a rival government loyal to him fled to Stanleyville. Led by Cyrille Adoula and Antoine Gizenga,

page 182

they represented the Lumumbists among the Congolese. Subsequent conferences brought them back into the fold of Léopoldville.

The death of Patrice Lumumba had created the ideal conditions for a leftist rebel movement to emerge in the east of the Congo and, in 1964, a fighting force emerging from the rural areas near Albertville (now Kalemie) began to capture villages without much resistance. Albertville fell first, then Port Empain (Kindu); and there, they coalesced behind a name, the Simbas, and also behind a man – Nicolas Olenga.

The Simbas of the time were a ragtag force. They used spiritual charms to protect themselves in battle – rituals that each soldier believed would protect him from bullets. Their ferocity scared the national army (ANC), which often fled in disarray rather than fight them. Soon after they captured Port Empain, they moved north to Stanleyville and, as they stood at the outskirts of the city, the European population was evacuated.

Throughout the following months, as ANC soldiers fought with the Simbas, thousands of white Europeans were caught in the crossfire. This prompted various European governments to act, but only slowly. In the meantime a new rebel government had been assembled and was operating out of Kisangani. Nicolas Olenga, while retaining the real power of the regime, would appoint Gaston Émile Soumialot to the position of prime minister.

The town's African population was supportive, as they had begun to deify the deceased Patrice Lumumba. Soumialot appointed a president, Christophe Gbenye, and declared the Simba territory the People's Republic of the Congo (not to be confused with the one in Brazzaville). Gbenye's presidency was short-lived, though, and he was sacked by Soumialot and the Simba military leaders later once the tide began to turn against them.

Indeed it did, and rather quickly. Moïse Tshombe, now prime minister, called upon his old mercenary friend Mike Hoare for some assistance. The decision to use mercenaries was unpopular with both the Léopoldville government and their main international supporters, namely the USA and Belgium, yet they allowed it anyway, rather than see the Congo partitioned and embroiled in a rebellion that they perceived as communist in nature.

Port Empain was finally liberated on 5 November 1965, by a mercenary army with some assistance from anti-Castro Cubans; only much later would the latter realise that their communist compatriots were also involved in this conflict, supporting the Simbas. Hoare's mercenaries moved slowly across rugged roads, anticipating ambushes at every corner as their poorly equipped trucks became stuck in muddy tracks. Yet they were ruthless to the Simbas, and even though heavily outnumbered, suffered few casualties.

A few weeks later Operation Dragon Rouge was initiated – US aircraft dropping Belgian paratroopers over Stanleyville, to rescue the Europeans still trapped and held hostage in the city (several missionaries, including the American Paul Carlson, had been shot by the Simbas). Simultaneously, ANC columns broke through the Simbas' defences and reached Stanleyville. Operation Dragon Noir, a similar operation in Isiro, followed. Some Europeans were saved, but others were not.

The main rebel forces had been dispersed, but large areas of the east were still under Simba control. It was late 1965 before the rebellion was finally defeated, mainly because the Simbas' foreign supporters, including Cuba, had abandoned them.

The Simba occupation destroyed Stanleyville's economy entirely – almost all Europeans had fled, and the vast majority of African men of working age had either been murdered or were hiding in the jungle. Yet their problems would not be over as the ANC's authority was minimal, and the city was mostly controlled by mercenaries.

The mercenary rebellions Some of Mike Hoare's mercenaries, veterans of the Katangan conflict, used their position as occupiers of Stanleyville to their advantage – they seized the radio station and airport, then demanded safe passage back to Katanga, where negotiations on its independence were to occur. Other mercenaries, led by Robert Denard, remained in Stanleyville as well and played a waiting game with the Léopoldville government. As Mobutu, already in control of the military, gained power, he paid Denard in July 1967 to run the Katangese mercenaries out of Stanleyville. With Mobutu's rise, Moïse Tshombe had recently fled the Congo, but his interest in its politics was still far from over – and Stanleyville would remain its focal point for a while longer.

Yet Denard, after having run the first Katangese rebels out of Stanleyville after being paid by Mobutu, quickly received word from Tshombe that he wished to engineer a coup to overthrow the future dictator. He put Bob Denard and another old mercenary hand – Jean Schramme, who had backed him in Katanga – in charge of this operation. Schramme controlled a huge swathe of territory in eastern Congo, from Kindu to Bukavu, and Denard, still in control of mercenaries in Stanleyville, had been in contact with Tshombe. Tshombe himself was in Spain, and agitating for a coup against Mobutu and seeking to create an environment where he could return to the Congo; but he was captured, his plane hijacked by Mobutu's operatives near Algerian airspace. Schramme and Denard did not know this until later; Schramme's forces attacked Kisangani, expecting assistance from Denard's men stationed there, but Denard had failed to organise his men for the attack. The ANC responded, summarily executing some of Denard's men and fighting off both groups of mercenaries.

Mobutu begged the USA for help, but they were reluctant to aid the country once again – they eventually supported the ANC with four cargo aircraft. So, mostly on their own, the ANC pursued the mercenaries southeast to Bukavu, where they became surrounded. Mobutu arranged safe passage for most of them, airlifting them out of the country on Red Cross aircraft, on the promise that they would never return to Africa.

The rout of the mercenaries solidified the authority of the ANC across the whole country; from then on, the nation would be a dictatorship under Mobutu. As he began his Africanisation of the country's names, he renamed Stanleyville as Kisangani.

From Mobutu to chaos, again Under Mobutu's rule, businesses began to arrive back in the city, creating a new generation of factories, breweries, and industries surrounding textiles and paint. An international-standard airport was completed in 1977, although less than a year later Kinshasa halted all international flights due to a scandal over ivory smuggling.

In 1986, the discovery of diamonds in the region around Kisangani proved to be a major setback for the city – the infamous corruption of Zaire's officials and the slow disintegration of Mobutu's government led to numerous internal conflicts between officials, departments and foreign traders, legal and illegal, all fighting for a share of the diamond trade. It is no coincidence that as Kabila's army moved west in 1997, Kisangani was occupied quickly by both Ugandan and Rwandan troops under the banner of the RCD; yet once again, driven by greed, they fought each other. In June 2000, over a thousand civilians were killed in what became known as the 'Six-Day War', at the end of which the Ugandan troops had been pushed out of the city. The RCD fractured into two groups: RCD-ML, based in Kisangani and led by well-known philosopher and political theorist Ernest Wamba Dia Wamba,

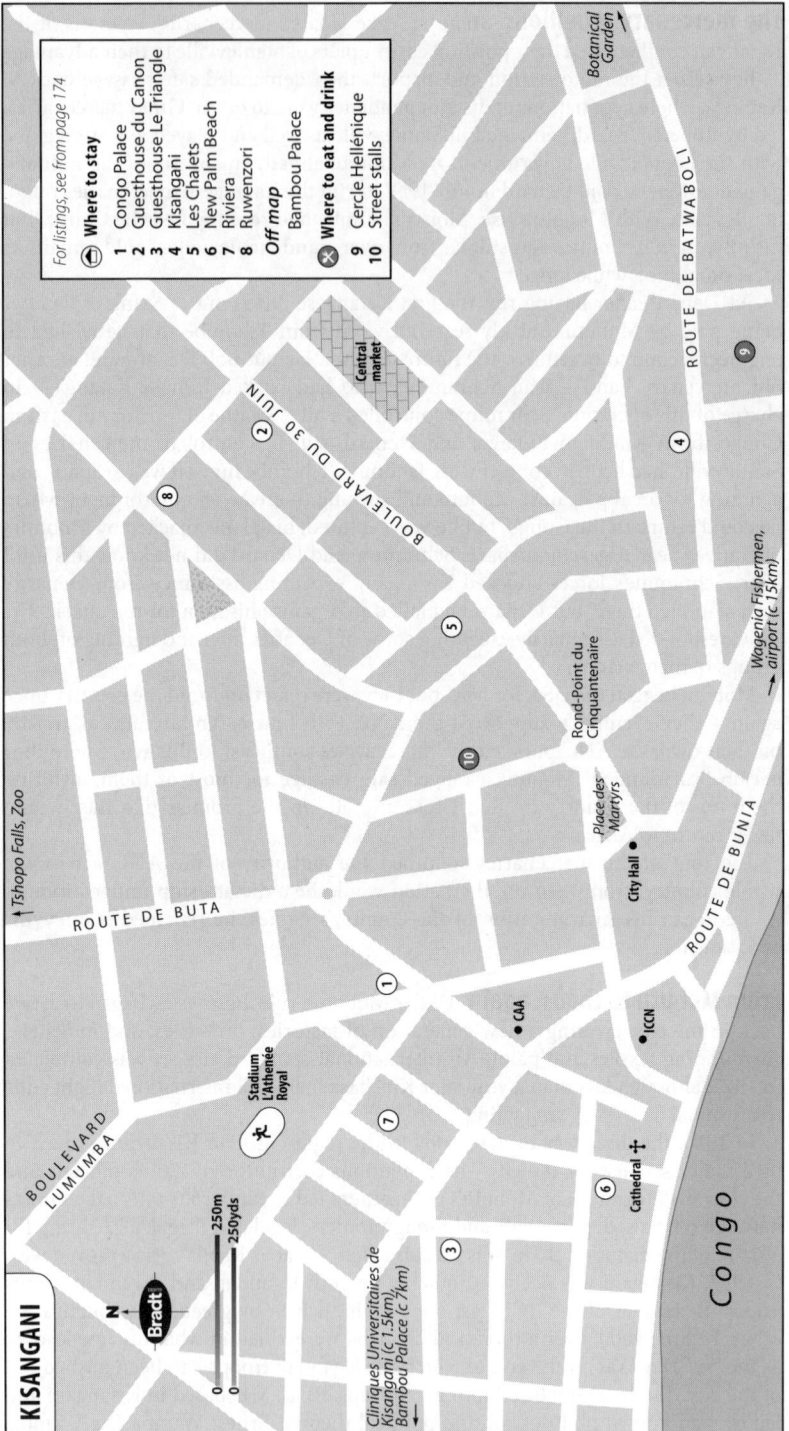

KISANGANI

For listings, see from page 174

Where to stay
1 Congo Palace
2 Guesthouse du Canon
3 Guesthouse Le Triangle
4 Kisangani
5 Les Chalets
6 New Palm Beach
7 Riviera
8 Ruwenzori

Off map
Bambou Palace

Where to eat and drink
9 Cercle Hellénique
10 Street stalls

Tshopo Falls, Zoo

BOULEVARD LUMUMBA

ROUTE DE BUTA

Stadium
L'Athenée
Royal

Cliniques Universitaires de
Kisangani (c 1.5km),
Bambou Palace (c 7km)

CAA

ICCN

Cathedral

City Hall

Place des
Martyrs

Rond-Point du
Cinquantenaire

BOULEVARD DU 30 JUIN

Central
market

ROUTE DE BATWABOLI

Botanical
Garden

ROUTE DE BUNIA

Wagenia Fishermen,
airport (c 15km)

Congo

250m
250yds

N

Bradt

and RCD-Goma, unsurprisingly based in Goma. As RCD-ML were driven out of Kisangani, their retreat into the forests of Ituri anticipated the future conflict there.

In May 2002, an attempted mutiny of RCD soldiers in Kisangani escalated, with military prisoners being released and the radio station captured. Within a few hours, the RCD had sent two plane-loads of reinforcements from Goma and recaptured the city from the mutineers. Unfortunately the troops loyal to the RDC then embarked on a harsh crackdown. Leaders of the mutiny were summarily executed on the Tshopo Bridge and their bodies thrown into the river. Dozens of policemen were also executed. Looting was widespread. The subsequent UN investigation by UNHCR concluded that 183 people had been killed by RCD forces, 103 of them civilians. The people of Kisangani expected United Nations forces (MONUC) to intervene to protect them, but they had no mandate to do so at the time. A month after the massacre, a UN Security Council resolution at last provided the basis for the MONUC mission to be authorised to protect civilians under imminent threat.

After Africa's world war, Kisangani was devastated – all of the major local businesses were either shut down or operating at a minuscule capacity, the river port had been all but destroyed, terminating river transport, and no public transport existed. Wave upon wave of soldiers looted the city as it subsequently changed hands again and again. People made their way around on foot, or on bicycles. All progress that had been made between the rebellions of the early 1960s and the latest chaos of the late 1990s had evaporated. Kisangani entered the new millennium in the worst condition of all the DRC's cities.

Since then, progress has been intermittent. The river once again brings cargo from Kinshasa, but prices in the city are high. The roads that connect Kisangani with the rest of its province are poor and, in the wet season, often impassable even to freight trucks. The airport is functional, but flights are few and far between; at the time of writing, it has no international connections. There is some industry and people are getting by, but the city is not exactly thriving.

GETTING THERE AND AWAY Kisangani's Bangoka **Airport** (FKI) is much larger than the number of flights it now receives would justify. It was upgraded to international standards in the 1970s and, in the past, Ethiopian Airlines operated direct flights there from Addis Ababa. At the time of writing, however, CAA (w caacongo.com) operates only a couple of flights a week to or from Kinshasa and another couple to or from Goma. Check-in procedures are difficult and stressful; unless you are on the tightest of budgets, it is well worth paying US$20 or so for an airport fixer to handle all of them for you. The airport is situated 17km east of the city; ask your hotel to arrange a car for you a day or two in advance, in case there are fuel shortages (page 175). If you have little or no luggage, a motorbike will be easier to find than a car.

The roads around the province are in bad condition. In the 2023–24 wet season, even the huge trucks that bring fuel from Uganda were unable to get through. Throughout the region, the roads are dangerous due to inter-ethnic violence and armed militias (the freight companies pay for a FARDC escort where required).

Ask around at the central truck station for vehicles heading to Buta or Isiro. The road from Bunia to Kisangani has been repaired and sees regular minibuses travelling in each direction.

GETTING AROUND The city lies at the confluence of the Lualaba and Congo rivers, and slightly upstream of where the River Tshopo flows into the Congo. The civilian airport, Bangoka, is to the east of the city; there is also a small airfield near the city centre, used for UN and humanitarian flights. The administrative centre, with the city hall, is near the port, around Martyrs' Square (Place des Martyrs). Boulevard du 30 Juin leads roughly northeast past the main market. North from Place des Martyrs leads to the Tshopo Bridge, the zoo and the city's northern suburb.

WHERE TO STAY *Map, page 172*

Congo Palace (60 rooms, 30 studios, 10 apartments) 19 Av de l'Église; m 082 985 3346, 099 171 3935; w hotelcongopalace.com. Emblematic building in city centre, built in 1954 (as Zaire Palace). Large pool, sauna & massage, well-equipped gym; conference facilities; secure parking, laundry service. Fast Wi-Fi throughout; bars, restaurant; b/fast inc, 24hr room service. All rooms have modern en-suite bathroom with good shower & toiletries, AC, widescreen sat TV, minibar, work table. **$$$$**, suites **$$$$$**

Bambou Palace (12 rooms) 48 Av Munyororo, Simi-Simi; m 089 821 9999 (WhatsApp), 082 822 2265; e reservations@bamboupalace-congo.com; w bamboupalace-congo.com. Beautiful setting on riverbank, a few km out of town beyond UN airport; gardens & 'hanging gardens' with river views; pool; boat trips offered; airport pick-up available; secure parking, 24hr electricity, Wi-Fi. Bar, restaurant (**$$–$$$**) with menu including fresh fish (grilled or *liboke*). Twin & dbl rooms, also 3 large suites & 1 apartment; all with modern en-suite bathroom with good shower; AC, TV. **$$$**, apartments **$$$$–$$$$$**

New Palm Beach (40 rooms) 6 Av Colonel Tshatshi, Makiso; m 089 700 4096, 081 222 2734; e newpalmbeach03@gmail.com. Has 24hr electricity, secure parking, bar, pool, well-equipped gym, nightclub, good restaurant; b/fast inc. Rooms all en suite with AC, TV, Wi-Fi. **$$$**, apartment **$$$$–$$$$$**

Guesthouse Le Triangle (38 rooms) Rond-Point Msgr Grison, Av Munyororo 1; m 084 311 9757; e ghletrianglekis@gmail.com. Has 24hr electricity, secure parking, garden with trees, restaurant (**$$**).

All rooms en suite & well equipped, with AC or fan, Wi-Fi. **$$**, apartments **$$$**

Les Chalets (26 rooms) 4 Rue de L'Industrie, Makiso; m 099 850 8407, 085 171 4295, 099 822 4316; e safimonique@hotmail.com. Has 24hr electricity, secure parking, good restaurant (**$$**), bar, pool; laundry service, b/fast inc. Well-maintained rooms, all en suite, with Wi-Fi, sat TV, hot running water, fan; apartments have AC. **$$**; apartments **$$$**

Riviera (23 rooms) 5 Av Bondekwe; m 085 400 2075. Restaurant at rear with pool table; terrace bar in front, under shady trees; Wi-Fi; b/fast inc. Some rooms share bathroom, others en suite, with AC or fan, TV, running water. **$$**, 2-room apartment **$$$**

Guesthouse du Canon (36 rooms) 37 Bd du 30 Juin, Makiso; m 081 305 6055, 099 747 3281; e ducanonguesthouse@yahoo.fr. Has 24hr electricity, secure parking, restaurant; b/fast inc. All rooms en suite, with AC, TV, running water, Wi-Fi. **$$**

Ruwenzori (28 rooms) 44 Av Lumumba, Makiso; m 081 532 9000; e carkisangani@yahoo.fr. Has 24hr electricity & water, secure parking, restaurant; terrace bar in gardens; b/fast inc. Rooms all en suite, with AC, sat TV, Wi-Fi. **$$**

Kisangani (15 rooms) Av Lumumba, Makiso; m 097 894 7242. Colonial Art Deco building, could do with some renovation; rooms set around tree-shaded courtyard; hotel also has apartments in bungalows opposite. Large restaurant with colonial-era furniture & pool tables. Some rooms share bathroom, others en suite with running water, all with AC. **$**

WHERE TO EAT AND DRINK *Map, page 172*

Kisangani restaurants have something of a supply problem, given the issues with barge and road transport to the city, which means prices are quite high. The cheapest option is to buy bananas and peanuts from roadside vendors, or head to the **Central Market** to pick up some fresh local vegetables. During the evenings there are **street stalls** which make up decent chicken and grilled goat (**$**) as well as fried plantains and whatever else happens to be circulating in the area that day.

For a sit-down meal, the restaurants in the hotels listed above are open to non-residents and often good value. The **Cercle Hellénique** (Bd Mobutu, Makiso;

m 084 715 5509, 084 451 0004), next to the Orthodox church, offers Congolese dishes, including fish, regular buffet lunches, occasional barbecues, and – when they can get the ingredients – Greek specialities. It has a pretty garden and a basketball court.

OTHER PRACTICALITIES Kisangani's poor road connections mean that prices are generally high and, especially in the wet season, there are shortages of fuel. There are **ATMs** at the major banks, but it is not inconceivable for them to run out of cash. Withdraw cash in daylight hours and, where possible, use an ATM inside the bank. It is always wise to keep a reserve of cash dollars. There are several Western Union agencies in the city.

For **emergency health care**, Cliniques Universitaires de Kisangani (CUKIS; m 097 424 8538) meets basic international standards. If you are fit to travel, you should arrange medical evacuation to Europe or South Africa.

A **4x4 vehicle**, with driver, can be hired from 'Maison the Light' (m 099 704 1396, 081 042 4158) for US$130 per day.

WHAT TO SEE AND DO The **Wagenia fishermen** are top of many people's list for things to see in Kisangani. The Wagenia villagers use a unique fishing technique, first documented by Henry Morton Stanley, across the rapids – the Boyoma Falls, once known as the Stanley Falls – that block navigation further upriver. The fishermen build complex wooden structures across the rapids, to which they attach baskets; the baskets are lowered into the river, the fish swim into them and are caught.

The Boyoma Falls are about 5km from the centre of Kisangani. There are seven cataracts, extending for over 100km between Ubundu and Kisangani, with a total drop of over 60m. The fishermen's structures are over the last of the cataracts, the one closest to Kisangani – it is often called the Wagenia Falls. Unfortunately, visitors are often mobbed by young men demanding payment for the right to look at the fishing structures; to avoid this harassment, it is better to go with a Congolese friend, or with an organised tour. The fishing community lives on the small island in the middle of the river, and you can take a pirogue across and meet the chief (for a fee, obviously). Artisans sell souvenirs, mostly fish-related, around the site.

In the city centre, the **cathedral** is an imposing white building, with a great view of the river from its parvis. It was built in 1899, although it has been restored several times; it was shelled during the street fighting in June 2000 (page 171). The **botanical garden** is attached to the Science Faculty of the University of Kisangani; it was originally planted in 1975 and is now a little patch (a hectare) of tropical forest in the middle of the city. There are even some monkeys that have set up home in it. Next to the garden is the Centre for Biodiversity Monitoring (w centresurveillancebiodiversite.org), a multidisciplinary collaboration between the university and Belgian institutions to improve the study of the DRC's extraordinary biodiversity. The centre has a small zoological museum, open to the public.

On the road north out of town is the **Tshopo Bridge**, which crosses the river of the same name and provides a good view of the hydro-electric dam that keeps Kisangani's power running (sometimes) while it tends to cut out in neighbouring cities. Follow this road a bit further and you'll find the turn-off to the **zoo**, an almost-abandoned place with about five animals. Most of the others were killed in one insurgency or another. Just below the zoo is the pleasant **Linoko Beach** where you can sit and have a beer, with a decent view of **Tshopo Falls**. The place can get a bit raucous on Saturday nights and Sundays, but is quiet enough in the daytime.

The people of Kisangani are proud of the time that Hollywood came to town, even though it was over 70 years ago. The blockbuster film *The African Queen* starred Humphrey Bogart and Katharine Hepburn as a Canadian boat captain and English missionary out to attack a German ship during World War I, on Lake Tanganyika. Despite not being set in the Congo at all, most of it was filmed near Ubundu (then called Ponthierville), upriver from Kisangani.

Filming in central Africa was a unique challenge in itself and the stars were not immune to the elements. Hepburn notoriously fell ill with dysentery from drinking too much local water. Bogart and director John Huston claimed they avoided illness by living on Scotch whisky. Bogart later wrote 'Whenever a fly bit Huston or me, it dropped dead.' Hepburn recounts her time in the Congo in her memoirs *The Making of The African Queen: Or, How I went to Africa with Bogart, Bacall and Huston and almost lost my mind*, published almost 40 years after the movie's release.

The movie itself is a good chance to see the River Congo and some of its local wildlife during the era of the Belgian Congo. It earned Bogart his only Academy Award, for best leading actor. The film was nominated for four other awards, including Huston for best director (and, jointly, for best screenplay) and Hepburn for best leading actress.

For production, an entire village was constructed for their set, west of Ponthierville, at Biondo, along the Ruiki River. Bogart, Hepburn and the production staff lived rough in the middle of the Congolese jungle for several months shooting the movie, learning Swahili, washing with buckets and trying to avoid mosquitoes – Hepburn described her conditions as 'luxury primitive'. Scenes in the water were shot back in England, as concerns over the actors performing in Congolese rivers had come to light.

Unfortunately the movie credits do not honour the country, with the final credits indicating only that it was 'Filmed in Africa'.

And finally, most obviously, the **River Congo** is a sight in itself. You can hire a canoe to visit surrounding villages, and on certain mornings the floating river markets begin from here – there are entire villages that exist solely as rafts on the river, drifting between shores, and they trade their goods along the way.

YANGAMBI BIOSPHERE RESERVE

In colonial times, Yangambi was an important research centre for tropical agriculture and forestry research. It had the richest herbarium in central Africa, with 125,000 specimens; trial plantations of rubber trees, oil palms and coffee plants; laboratories; and a well-stocked library. It employed over a hundred researchers in different fields. After independence, however, the research centre fell into disuse, until 1977, when it was designated as one of the DRC's two Biosphere Reserves (the other is Luki; page 118). Its importance for biodiversity is mainly because of the huge diversity of its trees – an incredible 32,000-odd different species, according to UNESCO. Its most threatened animals are forest elephants, which may already have disappeared from the area; more positively, the presence of chimpanzees was confirmed in 2018. Human communities live within the reserve too, growing crops, hunting, fishing and also doing some artisan gold-mining. Some of their members have now been trained as instructors in agricultural techniques. The Meise Botanic garden (**w** plantentuinmeise. be) in Belgium, which also supports the botanical garden in Kisangani, is digitising Yangambi's herbarium, which has over 150,000 dried specimens.

The Yangambi Biosphere Reserve (**w** yangambi.org) lies on the right bank of the River Congo, downriver from Kisangani. The only way to get there is by boat or pirogue from Kisangani. To arrange a visit, use the contact form on the website or, once in Kisangani, you could enquire at the botanical garden there (page 175).

MAIKO NATIONAL PARK

Maiko National Park was created in 1970 and occupies roughly 10,000km² between the Lubero and Maiko rivers. It is not possible to visit most of this park at the time of writing, due to the presence of armed militias. They are exploiting the mineral resources, in particular the component minerals of coltan, and poaching the wildlife within the park. They call themselves the Simba Mai-Mai, although they have little connection, beyond the name, with the Simbas of the 1960s.

In recent years, villages on the western edge of the park have created three community forests. Patrol teams from these communities have joined park staff from the southern sector of Maiko in monthly monitoring patrols. In 2022, the teams found over 300 traces of okapi. They are also recording the presence of eastern lowland gorilla groups, chimpanzees and other threatened species. When they come across poachers' snares, they remove them.

PRACTICALITIES If security in Maiko National Park were to improve during the lifetime of this edition, it would still not be an easy place to visit. It has no airstrips, no accommodation and no infrastructure – even 4x4 trails don't exist, aside from a southeasterly road from Bafwasende down to village populations living in the park. It would be wise to hire a guide or two; the largest settlement where people familiar with Maiko hang out is **Lubutu** (⊕ 00°44.53.10 S, 26°34.54.46 E). There are two options for visiting the park – one involves heading northwest from Bukavu (also extremely dangerous at the time of this update) or southeast from Kisangani to the town of **Mahulu** (⊕ 01°01.42.94 S, 27°16.15.78 E) and slowly working your way in from there on foot. The other option is through **Bafwasende** (⊕ 01°00.00.03 N, 27°09.21.91 E), where a road winds southeast to **Angumu** (⊕ 00°06.58.75 S, 27°42.06.73 E) and then to **Matshitshi** (⊕ 00°13.29.57 S, 27°45.57.40 E), where you can begin excursions into the northern part of the park. In theory, this road trail winds along to Kanyabayonga near Virunga National Park – if you manage it, ask someone to give you an award.

Also remember that a park permit would be required. It should be bought at **ICCN** in Kisangani; they will also be able to advise on security within the park and help you to find a guide.

ISIRO

Isiro (⊕ 02°46.15 N, 27°37.12 E) is the largest town in the northeast of the DRC and is the closest major town to Garamba National Park. If you are trying to get to Garamba overland, Isiro is where you will end up on the way to the park.

In colonial days the town was named Paulis, after Colonel Paulis, a prominent local businessman involved with the Congo railway system of the era. It was the hub for transportation, mining and farming in the province during the first half of the 20th century. The town was also the home of the first beatified Congolese woman, Marie-Clémentine Anuarite Nengapeta, who was killed by Simba rebels in 1964. Pope John Paul II travelled to Kinshasa in 1985 to complete the beatification ceremony. Her body is buried in the Catholic church in Isiro.

GETTING THERE AND AWAY Isiro has an airfield, but there are currently no scheduled flights. The road from Kisangani is used by freight trucks and is relatively secure. It should be possible to hitch a lift with a trucker; otherwise, 4x4 is essential. The routes from Bunia are only passable in the dry season and pass through territory controlled by armed militias.

GARAMBA NATIONAL PARK

Garamba has a long history, some of it bad and some of it, more recently, quite good. The park was founded in 1938, the second national park created in Africa, after Virunga. UNESCO declared it a World Heritage Site in 1980. It has one of the largest populations of forest elephants and the last remaining Kordofan giraffes in the DRC; it also used to have white rhinos. Over the decades that followed the UNESCO declaration, Garamba's wildlife populations declined due to armed conflict and wholesale ivory poaching. The Lord's Resistance Army, who had moved into Garamba's forests in 2004 or 2005, smuggled Garamba's resources across the borders to South Sudan and Uganda, in a highly professional operation involving pack animals to transport the ivory, and used the proceeds to buy more and more powerful weapons.

In 2016, African Parks (w africanparks.org), which co-manages Garamba National Park with ICCN, reviewed its strategy and introduced systems to enforce conservation law and bring stability to the park and its surroundings. Since then, wildlife numbers in the park have begun to increase and local communities have seen investment in sustainable development. Solar grids now provide electricity to over a thousand households and small businesses around the park; schools and a hospital have been built and equipped. The elephant population (a unique hybrid of forest and savannah elephants) has stabilised, the recorded number of Kordofan giraffes now totals over 80 and, perhaps most excitingly of all, 16 white rhinos were relocated from South Africa to Garamba in 2023. The park also has lions and chimpanzees.

ELEPHANT TRAINING

In its original days, Garamba was off-limits to tourism entirely, an animal reserve where elephants were captured for domestication. Throughout the late 19th century the African elephant proved to be an impossible animal to work with, and was never used as a beast of burden; however, Garamba proved the rest of the colonialists wrong, and a successful domestication programme was established around 1927. Elephant domestication in the region dates back to the time of the Congo Free State in 1902, and involved selecting a young elephant from a herd, capturing it, and then forcing it to undergo rigorous training. With captive breeding programmes well developed before independence, the domesticated elephants were rented out as labour for several decades, but the breeding programme halted throughout the park when the Congo began reinventing itself as Zaire. The programme was restarted during the 1970s and 1980s, but fell into disarray again as the country disintegrated in the 1990s. The last remaining domesticated elephant, Kiko, died in 2008 at the age of 56.

PRACTICALITIES The only practical way to get to Garamba National Park is by **air**, to the airstrip at **Nagero** (⊕ 03°44.58.30 N, 29°31.05.50 E), Garamba's main population centre. There are no scheduled flights and a small plane must be chartered. Most visitors fly in from Bunia (page 225), with Kisangani as an alternative; it may also be possible to charter a plane in Arua, on the Ugandan side of the border.

From Kisangani, about 900km away, the journey by **road** would take several days; Bunia is closer (about 400km), but the roads are only passable in the dry season and, even then, militia presence means they are unsafe.

Park permits can be purchased on arrival in the park. In Nagero, accommodation is available in the chalets of **Garamba Lodge** (e garamba.lodge@africanparks.org; **$$$$** FB). The lodge has a restaurant and a well-stocked bar. They offer a variety of safaris from Nagero, including aerial safaris in their small plane. The village of **Gangala Na Bodio** (⊕ 29°31.05.50 N, 29°08.17.10 E) also has an airstrip. Simple accommodation may be available there. This village was where the Garamba elephants were trained (see opposite).

OKAPI WILDLIFE RESERVE

Occupying 13,700km² of the Ituri Forest, the Okapi Wildlife Reserve was established in 1992 to protect the habitat of the creatures after which it is named – the enigmatic *Okapia johnstoni*, unknown to science until 1901. The okapi is the only surviving relative of the giraffe, with the same kind of extra-long tongue. It is instantly recognisable from its striped hindquarters, which act as camouflage in forest clearings. It is found only in the forests of northeastern DRC and has been protected, at least on paper, since 1933. Its habitat is being fragmented by illegal mining and logging, the animals themselves are hunted for bushmeat, and most of the area where they live has been occupied by armed militias for decades. The Ituri Forest is also the heartland of the BaMbuti and Efe communities, indigenous Pygmy peoples who live by harvesting the resources of the forest; they have also suffered from the illegal activities in their ancestral lands.

The reserve's operational base – the Conservation and Research Centre – is at Epulu. It had been set up in 1928 as a capture station for okapis which were then sent to zoos in North America and Europe. Later, the captured okapis were kept at the Epulu Station, to give visitors the chance to see the animals and to educate local schoolchildren and others about their importance. In 2012, militia armed with AK47s attacked the centre, probably in retaliation for a crackdown on ivory poaching, and killed seven people, including two park rangers, and all the captive okapis. The Epulu Station was rebuilt, but it was decided not to restock it with captive okapis, but to focus on protecting the wild animals in the reserve.

The okapi programmes in the reserve are operated by the Okapi Conservation Project (w okapiconservation.org), whose website has a wealth of information about the animals and indigenous people there. The reserve itself is co-managed by ICCN and the Wildlife Conservation Society (w drcongo.wcs.org).

PRACTICALITIES Epulu is best visited from Kisangani – a day's journey by private vehicle, otherwise a complicated set of negotiations for motorbikes over a day or two. If the security situation improves, it is also possible to get to Epulu from Beni, again about a day's journey. From the east, the road between the border and Mambasa passes through territory controlled by armed militias and is unsafe. There is no infrastructure within the park for visitors. The rainy season here runs roughly between August and November, when all roads are likely to be impassable.

The indigenous Pygmy peoples were the first inhabitants of the Congo rainforests. They are genetically very different from all other human populations, suggesting that their ancestors diverged from Africa's other early humans around 60,000 years ago. In the DRC, there are between 1 and 3 million indigenous people, from many different tribal communities. They are specialised hunter-gatherers, moving around the forest to locate resources that they can extract from it: honey, bushmeat, caterpillars (a valuable source of protein, widely consumed in parts of the Congo) and medicinal herbs. They consume some of these resources themselves and trade the surplus with sedentary (Bantu) farmers, in exchange for food they need, basically starch (eg: cassava).

Indigenous Pygmy communities have consistently been discriminated against, marginalised and driven from their historic habitats. An estimated 6,000 BaTwa people were expelled from their territory, without compensation, when Kahuzi-Biega National Park was extended in 1975. During the Second Congo War, indigenous Pygmy communities found themselves caught between rebel militias and government troops. In Ituri, a genocidal campaign known as 'wiping the slate' ('*effacer le tableau*') led to the deaths of an estimated 60,000 BaMbuti people; the UN investigated reports that MLC and RCD-N fighters were killing BaMbuti people and eating their flesh, in the belief that it had magical powers.

After years of campaigning by indigenous Pygmy groups in the DRC, a new law was passed in 2022 that formally protects the traditional customs and institutions of the country's indigenous Pygmy peoples (*peuples autochtones pygmées*) and establishes a number of provisions of positive discrimination, including free access to health care, justice and education. Discrimination against indigenous people is punishable by fines or imprisonment. The passage of the 2022 law was a great achievement by campaigners, who have now transferred their efforts to ensuring that its provisions are upheld. Meanwhile, the forests of eastern DRC are still full of armed militias and they still come into conflict with indigenous Pygmy communities. The 2022 law is unlikely to be of much help to these groups.

BUTA

Buta (✛ 02°48.35 N, 24°44.21 E) was once a stopping point on the important rail link between Bumba on the River Congo and Isiro in the northwest of the DRC. Those days, of course, are gone, and Buta is an incredibly isolated place on a stretch of bad road, 300km north of Kisangani or roughly three days' drive by 4x4. It is the only town of any size in this remote region and a staging ground for the sights along the border with the Central African Republic. There are huge hunting reserves here – **Bomu** and **Bili-Uere** together occupy over 36,000km² along the border, quite likely the largest hunting domains on the planet. Just south of Buta is the hunting reserve of **Rubi-Tele**, and you will pass through this area by road from Kisangani.

Head northwest from Buta and you will arrive in the town of **Bondo** (✛ 03°48.49 N, 23°41.00 E), which was once a strategic mining town and still sports the remnants of a rail line. Arab influences can also be seen – the region was ruled by Sultan Djabir in the late 19th century and when Belgian interests arrived, they clashed with the Arab business of gathering enslaved people and ivory. You can continue on a rough dirt road north to the village of **Gangu-Bili** (⊕ 04°14.11.45 N, 23°36.40.22 E) and hire a canoe to visit **Gangu Falls** a few hours' upstream. Northwest of Bondo, on the 'road' to the Central African Republic town of Bangassou, is **Monga** (⊕ 04°12.02.09 N, 22°48.44.25 E), situated on the north bank of the Bili River. On the road here from Bondo there is a waterfall.

MOBUTU'S PALACES

Way up in the tropical jungle, on the border of the DRC with the Central African Republic, is **Gbadolite** – the first town built in the DRC after independence. Mobutu turned his home village into a town whose inhabitants enjoyed 24-hour electricity (from its own hydro-electric plant), well-paid jobs and, when the president came visiting, his handouts of cash. Gbadolite's airport had its runway refitted to handle jumbo jets and even Concorde, which Mobutu chartered to visit his properties in Switzerland and Belgium. It was incredibly isolated, about 1½ hours northeast of the capital by jet. Mobutu built a mansion in Gbadolite and two residences nearby. Dignitaries from around the world were invited to dine at the lavish mansion, far from the daily bustle of Kinshasa. The stories were unbelievable – massive doors over 3m tall, huge statues, a gigantic pool and huge arching hallways. Mobutu's entourage were accommodated in its numerous guesthouses. He imported wedding cakes made the same day in Paris for his children, and even dairy cows – all of it delivered by Concorde or huge cargo planes.

The money that went into the 'Versailles of the Jungle', and then evaporated, was enormous. After Laurent-Désiré Kabila's victory, the building was gutted by looters. Gbadolite is now a ghost town; tropical vegetation is taking over its wide boulevards and magnificent houses. It is a fine reminder that power does not last forever.

Mobutu also built a riverside palace in **Lisala**, a complex of three marble buildings. Long abandoned and looted, some of the ruined rooms are now used as makeshift schoolrooms.

On the road from Gemena to Zongo and into the Central African Republic at Bangui are two different waterfalls, though local guiding and your own transportation are essential: **Mole Falls** are east of the main road towards Zongo on the Mole River, and **Kotobongo Falls** on the Lua River, near the village of Bokada.

PRACTICALITIES Despite its appearance as a small place of dirt roads and shacks buried in the jungle, **Gemena** (⊕ 03°15.16 N, 19°46.38 E) is the largest town in this far northwestern corner of the DRC. The **Catholic Mission** can rent out rooms for a few dollars. At the time of writing, CAA (**w** caacongo.com) has two flights a week between Kinshasa and Gemena. Gbadolite is about 200km away on a poor road that requires a good 4x4 or motorbike. Lisala is about the same distance on a fractionally less bad road.

Gemena is a usual stopping point for those travelling to or from the Central African Republic. Expect a three-day journey to the border from here, or at least two weeks to Kisangani via road, when there is transport through Buta and the river ports of **Lisala** (⊕ 02°09.11 N, 21°30.51 E) and **Bumba** (⊕ 02°11.10 N, 22°28.04 E). There are riverboats from Kisangani to both of these towns, and you can catch a truck onward from there. Alternatively, you can also wait at the river and find some barges heading towards Kinshasa.

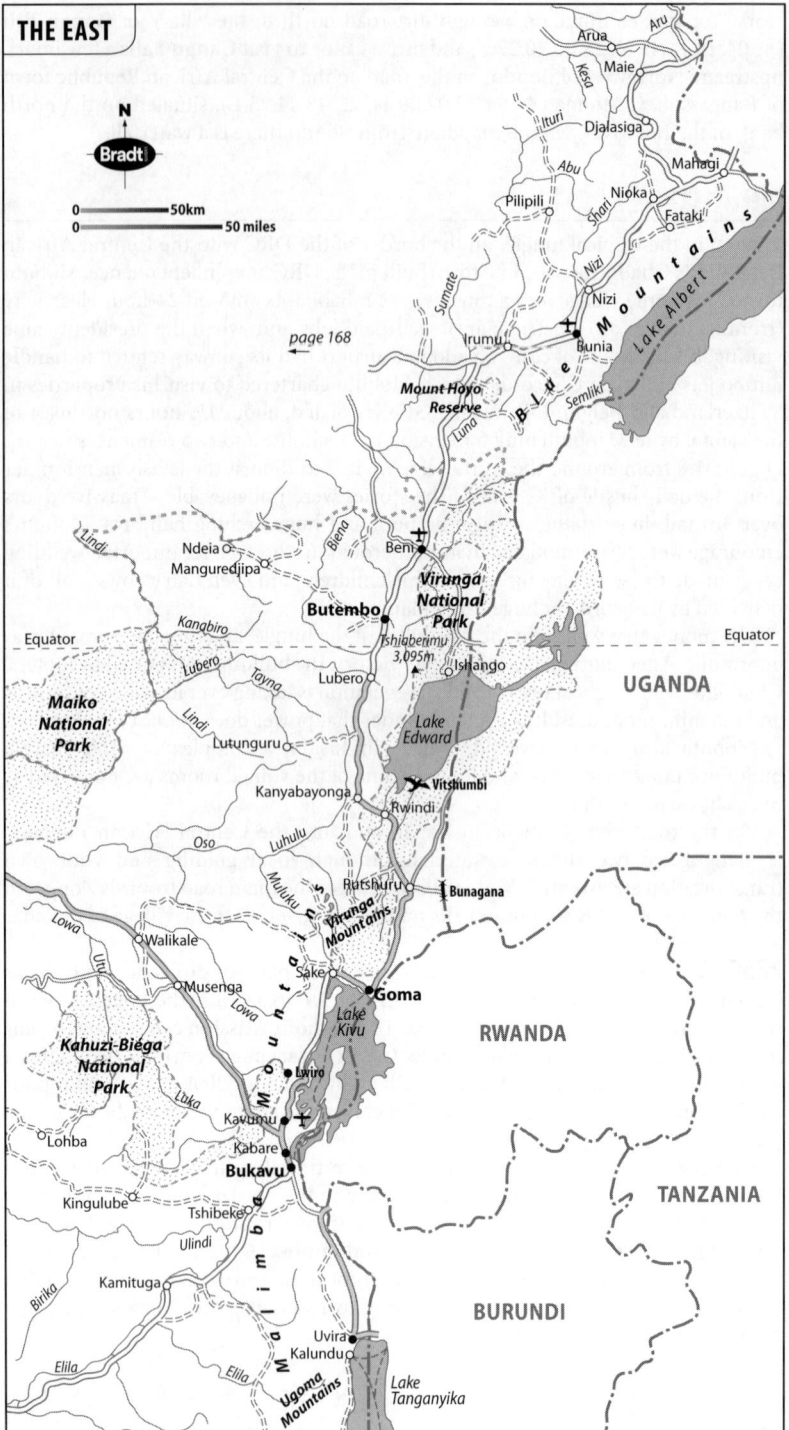

THE EAST

N

Bradt

0   50km
0   50 miles

← page 168

Arua
Aru
Kesa
Maie
Ituri
Djalasiga
Abu
Mahagi
Shari
Nioka
Pilipili
Nizi
Fataki
Sumate
Nizi
Irumu
Bunia
Mount Hoyo
Reserve
Luna
Semliki
Lake Albert

Blue Mountains

Lindi
Ndeia
Manguredjipa
Bena
Beni
Kangbiro
Butembo
Virunga
National
Park
Lubero
Tayna
Lubero
Ishiabenmu
3,095m
Ishango
Equator
Equator

UGANDA

Maiko
National
Park
Lindi
Lutunguru
Lake
Edward
Kanyabayonga
Vitshumbi
Oso
Luhulu
Rwindi
Rutshuru
Bunagana
Lowa
Muluku
Virunga
Mountains
Walikale
Sake
Musenga
Lowa
Goma
Lake
Kivu
Kahuzi-Biega
National
Park
Luka
Lwiro
RWANDA
Lohba
Kavumu
Kabare
Bukavu
Kingulube
Tshibeke
Ulindi
TANZANIA
Birika
Kamituga
BURUNDI
Elila
Elila
Uvira
Kalundu
Lake
Tanganyika
Ugoma
Mountains

Malimba Mountains

8

The East

The eastern frontier of the Democratic Republic of the Congo is a unique landscape, with towering mountains, active volcanoes, rare gorilla species and other wildlife. The area is a geographical wonder of Africa, and it is no surprise that it sits along the border as many of these landmarks make natural frontiers – Mount Stanley, third-highest peak on the continent; the volcano ranges that sit between the DRC, Rwanda and Uganda; and the Great Lakes of Africa's Rift Valley.

Unfortunately, the people of the DRC's eastern provinces – Sud-Kivu, Nord-Kivu and Ituri – have borne the brunt of civil conflict for over 30 years. Dozens of different armed groups are still active in the region, an alphabet soup ranging from the ADF through CODECO, FDLR and M23 to the Zaire/FPAC. See page 40 for some background to this. United Nations peacekeepers, known in their current iteration as MONUSCO, have been present in the region for many years but began their phased withdrawal in 2023. At the time of writing, MONUSCO had withdrawn from Sud-Kivu and most of the rest of the DRC; the UN intends to withdraw from the last two provinces, Nord-Kivu and Ituri, by the end of 2024.

Nord-Kivu and Ituri have been under a 'state of siege' (*état de siège*) since 2021. This means that civilian authorities, such as local councils, are suspended and have been replaced with a military authority with enhanced powers to maintain law and order and, if necessary, restrict fundamental freedoms, such as freedom of assembly or of movement. Foreigners are often kidnapped for ransom and sometimes killed. In February 2021, the Italian ambassador to the DRC and his convoy were murdered, in an apparent kidnapping attempt, on the N2 close to Virunga National Park, on their way to visit a World Food Programme project. The Facebook page ⓕ North Kivu Life has updates from international organisations, reporting on security and humanitarian concerns in the province, as well as less trustworthy posts from more partisan sources.

Most government travel advisories explicitly warn against visiting eastern DRC. At the time of writing, for instance, the British government advises 'against all travel' to both Kivus and Ituri (among numerous other provinces). The only exception to this is the city of Bukavu. Even if you choose to disregard this advice, be aware that a government warning of this sort will invalidate most travel insurance policies.

See page 53 for entry requirements to the DRC. If you have prebooked a package in Virunga and/or Kahuzi-Biega national parks, and are not heading deeper into the country, it is straightforward to arrange a 14-day single-entry visa in advance through any affiliated tour operator or Virunga National Park's website (ⓦ visitvirunga.org/visa). The 14-day visa currently costs US$105 and requires two weeks to process; it will be delivered by email. Note that visas arranged by Virunga National Park are accepted only at the border crossing between Gisenyi and Goma, and those arranged by Kahuzi-Biega only at the crossing between Cyangugu and Bukavu; exiting at a different border is fine, provided you do so within the 14-day limit. See page 53 for information about obtaining standard visas that allow you to travel beyond the Kivus.

GOMA

Thanks to Sean Connolly, contributor to Bradt's guide to Rwanda, for his research in Goma, on which this section draws heavily.

Capital of the volatile province of Nord-Kivu, Goma lies on the north shore of Lake Kivu, practically contiguous with the Rwandan lake port of Gisenyi. It has traditionally been the main gateway for travellers heading to the southern sector of Virunga National Park, home to the DRC's population of mountain gorillas. The lake lies at an altitude of 1,500m above sea level, which gives Goma a very pleasant climate with temperatures ranging between 20°C and 30°C all year round.

Goma's northern skyline is dominated by the spectacular volcano Nyiragongo. It is an active volcano and erupts quite frequently, most recently in 2021. The 2002 eruption obliterated the city centre. A 1km-wide river of lava flowed through the city, destroying more than 4,500 buildings, killing at least 250 people and displacing most of the human population until the eruption ended and reconstruction could begin; the city is now 2m higher above sea level than it was before the eruption. An earlier eruption, in 1977, had also wiped out the town and killed 2,000 people.

Black volcanic rock permeates Goma's landscape, lending it a unique look in the DRC. It is everywhere – used to build walls, roads, crushed and reconstituted into bricks. The city is a mixture of diffused black and grey colours, surrounded by lush green hills which create some of the best farmland in Africa. Huge lava fields northwest of Goma attest to the city's precarious position.

HISTORY Belgians arrived in the area now known as Goma at the turn of the 20th century, encountering small settlements of Bantu and indigenous BaTwa peoples. They created a permanent settlement in 1906 as a counterbalance to a German outpost built around the same time in Gisenyi. This proximity to the German colony gave Goma strategic importance during World War I. It was made the administrative centre for Nord-Kivu in 1948, and saw a major increase in population after this.

Goma became an important post for NGO staff during the Rwandan genocide, as thousands fled the civil war in that country. It then became a centre of conflict as Rwandan troops chased Interahamwe militias into Congolese territory, and armed Laurent-Désiré Kabila, marching west with him all of the way to Kinshasa. Unfortunately for Goma, the conflicts there continued throughout the Second Congo War (page 33). In October 2008, clashes between the Congolese army and the rebel Congrès National pour la Défense du Peuple (CNDP), the latter led by the Tutsi general Laurent Nkunda, resulted in thousands of casualties and forced a quarter of a million civilians to flee their homes. Despite several calls for ceasefires, the fighting continued intermittently until January 2009, when Nkunda was arrested after crossing into Rwanda, where he remains under house arrest to this day.

In April 2012, the rebel Mouvement du 23 Mars (M23), led by Bosco Ntaganda, was formed by mutinous former CNDP soldiers who had been integrated into the Congolese army after the 23 March 2009 peace accords (from which M23 took its name, claiming that the Kinshasa government had not fully implemented them). The rest of the year saw sporadic M23 attacks throughout Nord-Kivu, culminating in the seizure of Goma on 20 November 2012. M23 was driven out within two weeks, however, and intense military and political pressure saw Ntaganda turn himself in to the US embassy in Kigali in 2013. Following a four-year trial by the International Criminal Court, Ntaganda was convicted on 18 counts, including rape, murder and sexual slavery, and sentenced to 30 years in prison.

With M23 in hibernation, Goma enjoyed a period of relative peace between 2013 and 2018. The city had an agreeable and vibrant atmosphere over this period, and the lively nightlife curtailed by the civil war resumed with vigour. Although solidified flows of craggy black lava from 2002 still lay beside some of the roads, most of the town had been cleared and rebuilt by this time (though one striking informal monument to the eruption, a group of planes trapped where they stood when the lava flowed through, can still be seen at the airport on the left side of the road towards Nyiragongo and the national park).

Sadly, the situation in Goma has deteriorated greatly since 2018. Natural disasters have played a part in this. An Ebola outbreak in 2019 was followed by the Covid-19 pandemic in 2020, then by another violent Nyiragongo eruption in May 2021 – resulting in at least 32 deaths, the evacuation of 400,000 people, the destruction of 1,000 properties and a lava blockage on the N2 road north to Beni.

However, the main problem has been increasing violence by M23 and other armed militias. At the time of writing, M23 occupies several major towns in the province, controls much of the N2 and other major roads leading to Goma, and occupies large tracts of Virunga National Park. Thousands of people have fled the fighting and live in packed refugee camps around Goma. Fighting between M23 and the Congolese army frequently reaches the outskirts of Goma. In May 2024, two camps for internally displaced people (IDPs) from conflicts elsewhere in the region were bombed, allegedly by M23. At least 12 IDPs were killed and hundreds were injured. Tension in Goma is likely to continue for the foreseeable future, with a strong military presence around town. At the time of writing there is a 22.00 curfew throughout the city.

GETTING THERE AND AWAY

By road Assuming you have a visa and a yellow fever vaccination certificate (page 58), getting to Goma from **Rwanda** could scarcely be more straightforward. The place to cross is the Grande Barrière [189 D7] at the west end of Gisenyi's main lakeshore road, which now has a shiny new integrated border post. The Grande Barrière currently operates from 06.00 to 15.00 only. Travellers with the special 14-day 'park visa' would be better to cross during business hours, just in case the DRC border police need to confirm anything with the ICCN office (which now, conveniently, stands alongside the new Grande Barrière border post).

Coming from elsewhere in Rwanda, there are plentiful minibus taxis to Gisenyi (Rubavu), and a motorbike taxi from the bus station to the border costs around Rfr400. Once you've crossed to Goma, several hotels lie within easy walking distance of the border post, or you can get a motorbike to the town centre (around Fc1,000).

At the time of writing, the roads north to Lake Edward and south to Lake Tanganyika are occupied by dozens of different armed groups. Rutshuru is one of the most dangerous districts in the entire country. For overlanders, the westward road via Walikale may be a relatively safe route to Kisangani; enquire locally. It is highly advisable to hire an armed escort.

By air Goma Airport (GOM) [187 G1] is one of the best served in the DRC. At the time of writing, Ethiopian Airlines (w ethiopianairlines.com) flies several times a week to/from Addis Ababa and operates connecting flights to major cities in Africa,

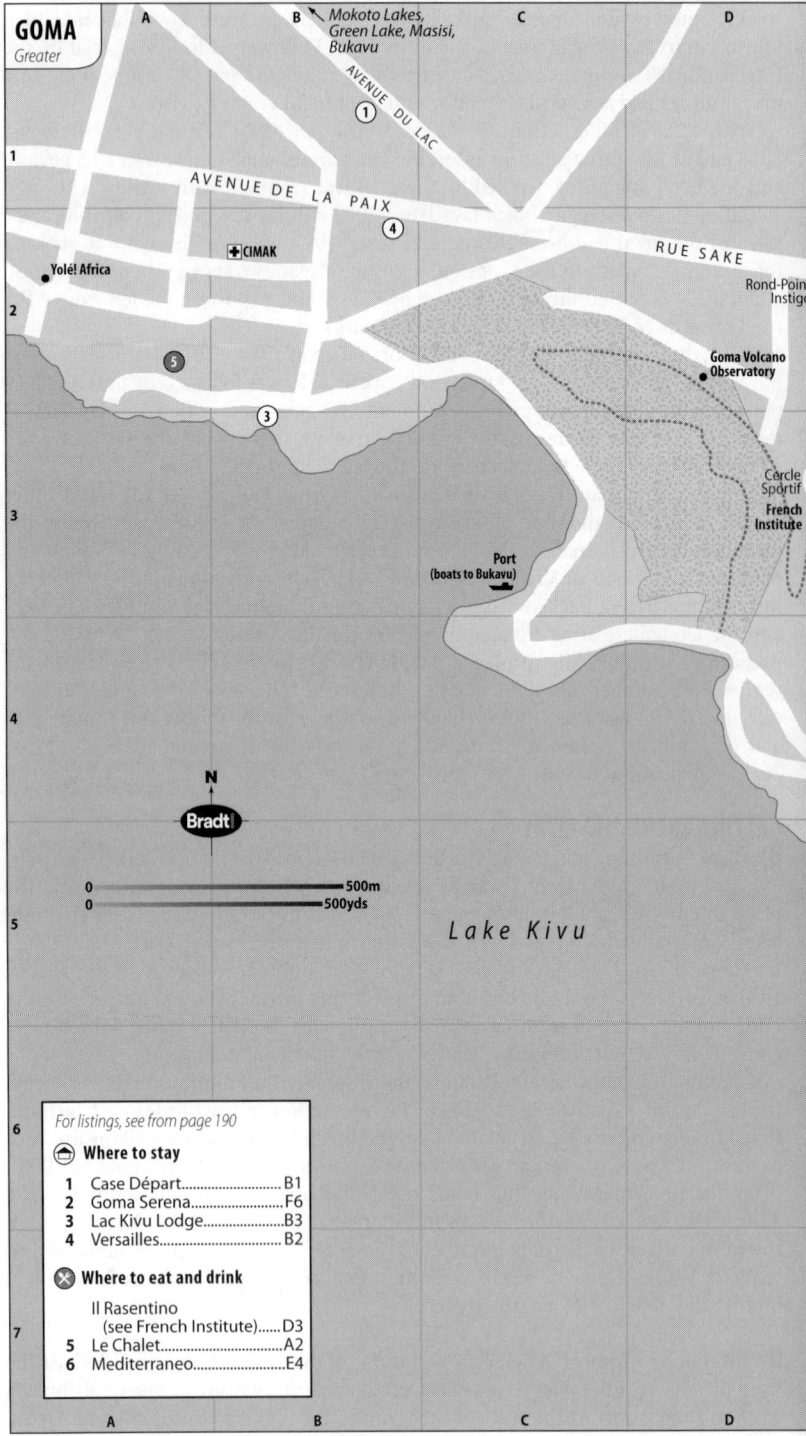

GOMA
Greater

Mokoto Lakes,
Green Lake, Masisi,
Bukavu

AVENUE DU LAC

AVENUE DE LA PAIX

RUE SAKE

CIMAK

Yolé! Africa

Rond-Point
Instige

Goma Volcano
Observatory

Cercle
Sportif

French
Institute

Port
(boats to Bukavu)

N

Bradt

| 0 | | | 500m |
| 0 | | | 500yds |

Lake Kivu

For listings, see from page 190

🛏 **Where to stay**

1	Case Départ	B1
2	Goma Serena	F6
3	Lac Kivu Lodge	B3
4	Versailles	B2

✖ **Where to eat and drink**

	Il Rasentino	
	(see French Institute)	D3
5	Le Chalet	A2
6	Mediterraneo	E4

Destroyed cathedral (200m), ↑
Marché Virunga

↑ Lava Field,
Nyiragongo, Kiwanja

✈
Airport

1

🚐 Minibus station for
Rutshuru & points north

RUE SAKE

● Foyer Culturel
de Goma

Rond-Point
Segners

2

● Goma
University

● Jambo Safaris
office

SITE OF
LAVA FLOW

Rond-Point
Rutshuru

Rond-Point
Bralima

3

Librairie Lave
Littéraire ●

SITE OF
LAVA FLOW

RUTSHURU ROAD

4

6

LYN LUSI

⊠

page 189

Rond-Point
BDGL

5

SITE OF
LAVA FLOW

BOULEVARD KANYA-MUHANGA

6

②

Rwanda

𝑖

Lake Kivu

7

Asia, Europe and North America. For visitors to Rwanda and Goma, it would be worth looking into the possibility of an open-jaw itinerary with Ethiopian Airlines, eliminating the need to backtrack to Kigali for a return flight. Jambo Jet (w jambojet. com), the low-cost arm of Kenya Airways, operates several flights a week between Nairobi and Goma. See page 56 for details of international flight taxes.

Within the DRC, CAA (w caacongo.com) has six direct flights a week between Goma and Kinshasa and direct flights to Kalemie, Kisangani and Kindu. At the time of writing, flights from Goma to Butembo and Beni are operated by Busy Bee Congo (m 099 068 8210; w busybeecongo.com), based in Goma; as ever in the DRC, the most reliable way to check on current flight schedules is to go to the airport and ask. For internal flights, each passenger has to pay taxes, probably only in cash; see page 54.

By boat There are no international passenger services across Lake Kivu. Between Goma and **Bukavu**, the safest and quickest way to travel is by boat. The fastest and most reliable option is the Ihusi Express (m 094 464 5680/099 481 3235; e ihusiexpress@gmail.com), *canôts rapides* (speedboats) with two daily departures in each direction daily. It takes about 2½ hours, with a stop on Idjwi Island (page 205). The best place to check for up-to-date information about these boats and to buy the US$50 tickets is the Ihusi Hotel (page 190). The public boats (*vedettes*) are operated by the national rail company, SNCC (w snccsa.com). There is a 'Vedette VIP' with a one-way fare of US$50, and *vedettes ordinaires* for US$35. The public boats call at various places on Idjwi Island; part-route fares are cheaper.

Note that there is an immigration check when you are getting on the boat – the special 14-day 'park visa' (page 183) is fine to go to Bukavu and Sud-Kivu (assuming it's in date), though the people checking your passport may try to convince you otherwise; have the park office number on hand. Also know where you're planning to stay in Bukavu and relevant details of your itinerary, as you may be asked for them.

GETTING AROUND Goma sprawls westward along the lakeshore and northeast between the Rwandan border and the airport. In the middle is the **port** [186 C3] and Mount Goma, a hill overlooking the city. The city centre is a large roundabout, officially called Rond-Point de l'Indépéndance but usually referred to as **Rond-Point BDGL** [189 B2] (pronounced *Bay-Day-Zhay-Ell*), after one of the buildings that surround it. **Boulevard Kanya Muhanga**, once called Avenue Mobutu, is the main thoroughfare through town, and after the Rond-Point BDGL it gets a little rough – the northern half was flooded by lava. If you follow the main road west out of town, then bear left after the hospital, you'll get to the pleasant lakeside road that winds through numerous old Belgian holiday residences and some of the city's nicest hotels. The main road becomes the N2 that continues around Lake Kivu to Bukavu and beyond (but note security advice on page 185).

LOCAL TOUR OPERATORS
Tourist information The booking office for Virunga National Park [189 D7] (w visitvirunga.org; ☉ 08.30–17.00 Mon–Fri, 08.00–noon Sat), on the DRC side of the Grande Barrière border post, is the place for independent travellers to arrange or collect prebooked gorilla-tracking and other park permits. When the security situation allows, the efficient staff here can also arrange transport to the park's various attractions at fixed rates, advise on accommodation, and offer assistance with most other queries relating to tourism in and around Goma.

GOMA
Centre

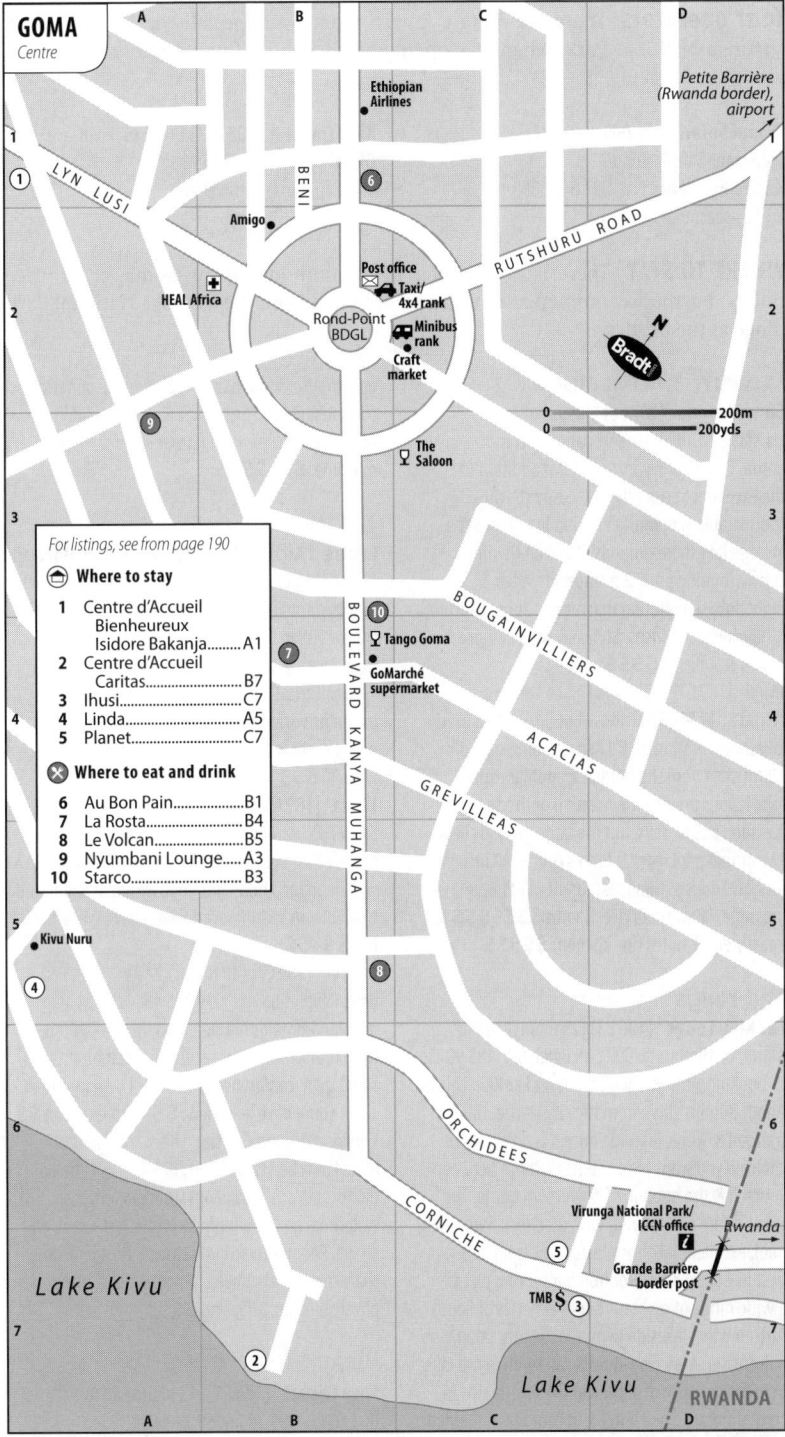

For listings, see from page 190

🛏 **Where to stay**

1 Centre d'Accueil
   Bienheureux
   Isidore Bakanja.........A1
2 Centre d'Accueil
   Caritas...........................B7
3 Ihusi...............................C7
4 Linda...............................A5
5 Planet.............................C7

✖ **Where to eat and drink**

6 Au Bon Pain....................B1
7 La Rosta..........................B4
8 Le Volcan........................B5
9 Nyumbani Lounge......A3
10 Starco.............................B3

Ethiopian
Airlines

LYN LUSI

BENI

Amigo

HEAL Africa

Post office
Taxi/
4x4 rank
Rond-Point
BDGL
Minibus
rank
Craft
market

The
Saloon

*Petite Barrière
(Rwanda border),
airport*

RUTSHURU ROAD

N

Bradt

0 ————— 200m
0 ————— 200yds

BOUGAINVILLIERS

🍷 Tango Goma
GoMarché
supermarket

ACACIAS

BOULEVARD KANYA MUHANGA

GREVILLEAS

Kivu Nuru

ORCHIDEES

CORNICHE

Lake Kivu

Virunga National Park/
ICCN office
Rwanda

Grande Barrière
border post

TMB $

Lake Kivu

RWANDA

Tour operators There are quite a few in Goma, all specialising in tourism to Virunga National Park, when it is open, and to Kahuzi-Biega National Park. See also page 52.

Amani Safaris m 099 066 1474;
f Amani-Safaris-Congo
Kasitu Eco-Tours m 097 646 5888;
f kasituecotours

Kivu Travel m 081 313 5608; w kivutravel.com
Okapi Tours m 082 556 6810;
w okapitoursandtravel.org

WHERE TO STAY There is no shortage of accommodation in Goma, at all price points. Further recommendations can be obtained from the Virunga National Park office at the border.

Exclusive and expensive

Goma Serena [187 F6] (109 rooms)
m 081 370 1000; w serenahotels.com/
goma. This award-winning 5-star addition to the excellent Serena chain is easily the most comfortable & upmarket option in Goma. Set in large lakeshore grounds, it has an Olympic-size swimming pool, 2 restaurants, a bar & nightclub; spa offering massages, sauna, nailcare & hairdresser services. Stylish & well-equipped rooms & suites. **$$$$$**
Ihusi [189 C7] (75 rooms) 16 La Corniche;
m 081 312 9560; w ihusi-hotel.com. In a pretty lakeshore location on Bd Kanya Muhanga, only 100m or so from the border; a popular expat rendezvous prior to the opening of the Serena. It has seen better days, but the large grounds have swimming pool, gym & tennis courts, all included for hotel guests. Good restaurant, Wi-Fi; sauna & massage, laundry service. Rooms **$$$–$$$$**, apartment & suites (inc kitchen) **$$$$$**

Mid-range

Lac Kivu Lodge [186 B3] (28 rooms) 162 Av Alindi, Q/ Himbi; m 097 589 6483, 097 183 9028;
e booking@congo-lodge.com; f Lac Kivu Lodge. About 30mins' drive from the city centre, this tranquil & scenic lakeside retreat is an excellent choice if you want to put some distance between yourself & the hubbub of downtown Goma. The grounds are overflowing with greenery. Swimming pool, excellent lakefront restaurant (said to be best in Goma) & bar; rooftop bar serving pizzas, a wide range of cocktails & 140 varieties of South African wine; lakeside gym, spa, beauty salon, hairdresser, ATM. Non-guests can swim in the lake here for the price of a drink at the bar. Rooms in contemporary-style hotel & in Congolese-themed

guesthouse; some have private terrace or balcony overlooking lake. Sgl rooms & suite available. All rooms en suite with flatscreen TV & espresso machine. **$$–$$$$**

Thrifty

Centre d'Accueil Bienheureux Isidore Bakanja [189 A1] (35 rooms) Av Lyn Lusi; m 097 046 9994. Run by Catholic Church (Isidore Bakanja [d1909] was beatified in 1994), centrally located near Heal-Africa hospital. Bar-restaurant set in green & geometrically hedged garden, serves good & inexpensive Congolese meals. Clean tiled rooms with TV, hot water, fan & fitted nets. **$$**, rooms with AC **$$$**
Linda [189 A5] (65 rooms) La Corniche; m 099 548 7783; w lindahotelgoma.com. Very close to Grande Barrière, on lakeside; secure. This reliable & well-managed hotel has pool, excellent restaurant, garden with seating overlooking lake; Wi-Fi; b/fast inc. **$$–$$$**
Planet [189 C7] (40 rooms) 27 Av de la Révolution; m 099 346 4644; w planethotelgoma.net. Modern hotel 100m from Grande Barrière; secure. Bar-restaurant (**$$**), small gym, conference rooms, Wi-Fi. All rooms en suite, some have lake view. **$$**, with jacuzzi **$$$**
Centre d'Accueil Caritas [189 B7] (37 rooms) 68 La Corniche; m 089 190 7871. Run by Catholic diocese; attractive buildings set in carefully manicured waterfront grounds; business centre; restaurant; Wi-Fi; secure. Rooms simple but well kept; cheaper rooms share communal showers, others en suite, many with private terraces. B/fast inc. **$$**

Budget

Case Départ [186 B1] (12 rooms) 28 Av du Lac; m 099 340 4059, 084 089 3354;

e casedeparthotel@gmail.com. Rather out of the way & (despite its address) not on lakeside, but a pleasant option for budget travellers. Restaurant serving delicious grilled chicken; terrace between the 2 wings of the hotel; Wi-Fi; b/fast inc. Rooms in the newer wing are bigger & better equipped. Old wing **$**, new wing **$$**

Versailles [196Aa B2] (6 rooms) Av de la Paix; m 085 924 9901. An adequate budget hotel with running water, fair restaurant; Wi-Fi in public areas; b/fast inc. All rooms en suite & clean, with mosquito net; some have AC, some have TV. **$**

WHERE TO EAT AND DRINK
All the hotels listed opposite have restaurants open to the public and serve good or very good food (**$$–$$$**), but there are also plenty of standalone restaurants. A selection follows.

Nyumbani Lounge [189 A3] 29 Rond-Point BDGL; m 082 900 7748; ⏀ daily. Great atmosphere, has big screens showing football matches, small intimate rooms, shisha & cigars. Creative menu includes well-prepared international dishes; open for b/fast with home-baked bread, croissants, etc; free Wi-Fi. There's a long menu of cocktails & shisha pipes to keep you entertained in the evenings. It's probably the slickest address in town, & is reliably packed with locals & expats, seeing & being seen. **$$$–$$$$**

Le Volcan [189 B5] 28 Bd Kanya Muhanga; m 089 627 5009; ⓕ levolcanrestau243; ⏀ daily. This popular pub-style restaurant & bar serves great burgers, Indian & African dishes. DJ nights & live music; check Facebook page for details. **$$$**

Mediterraneo [187 E4] Rue Lyn Lusi; m 097 766 0386; ⓕ Restaurant-Mediterraneo-Goma; ⏀ daily. Italian restaurant, with beautiful garden. Specialises in pasta, antipasti, risotto, wood-fired pizza; Italian coffee(!); also barbecued T-bone steaks & lamb. **$$$**

Le Chalet [186 A2] Av du Lac; m 099 998 8014; ⓕ lechaletgoma; ⏀ daily. Set in pretty lakeshore gardens about 5km west of the town centre, this popular upmarket eatery is known for its Sun lunchtime buffets & excellent pizzas; menu of international & Congolese meat & fish dishes. Gets very busy, especially at w/ends. Also rents kayaks, should you fancy getting out on the water before or after your meal. An attached café, Le Petit Chalet, serves a healthy variety of salads & fresh juices. **$$–$$$**

Il Rasentino [186 D3] 171 Av des Ronds-Points; m 097 146 6525. Within the French Institute (page 192), popular lunch spot with the NGO community. There's a daily buffet at 12.30; also serves good Italian cuisine, including pizzas. Tue is cinema night. **$$**

La Rosta [189 B4] Av Accasias; m 082 122 2212; ⏀ 11.00–late Tue–Sun. Formerly Lapa Goma, this breezy & stylish resto-bar is known for its signature cocktails list, regular themed nights & tasty pizzas, grills, pasta & *plats du jour*. There's indoor seating & a wide wooden terrace. **$$**

Starco [189 B3] Bd Kanya Muhanga; m 099 000 9000; ⏀ 08.00–21.00 daily. Offering great Lebanese cuisine, popular with expats & NGO workers for Fri drinks & dinner. **$$**

Au Bon Pain [189 B1] Bd Kanya Muhanga; m 081 286 0011; ⏀ 07.00–19.00 Mon–Sat, 10.00–15.00 Sun. Home-baked bread, sandwiches & patisserie; small dining area. Popular with expats & Goma bourgeoisie. **$–$$**

ENTERTAINMENT AND NIGHTLIFE
Cultural centres
No matter what calamity befalls Goma, its indefatigable cultural scene seems to be among the first things to bounce back. Today there are several admirable cultural centres and festivals in the city and, given the difficulties Goma has suffered and continues to suffer, the cultural calendar puts a number of cities around the continent (and indeed the world) to shame.

Foyer Culturel de Goma [187 F2] 2 Av du Collège; m 099 503 9505; w foyerculureldegoma.org. Offers classes in music, art & theatre, in addition to regular concerts & poetry events. They also organised the first Amani Festival (w amanifestival.com) in 2014, which featured African superstars like Tiken Jah Fakoly, as well as Congolese acts including the Goma-based Will'Stone and Bill Clinton Kalonji; the most recent events took place in Feb 2022 and 2023 (the latter was hosted in Bukavu for security reasons).

French Institute [186 D3] 171 Av des Ronds-Points/Rue Lyn Lusi; m 084 119 3479; w institutfrancaisgoma.org; ⊕ 08.30–17.30 Tue–Sat. Hosts an active calendar of cultural events & courses; also home to Il Rasentino restaurant (page 191). The old Alliance Française

– building, archives, library – was destroyed in the 2002 Nyiragongo eruption.

Yolé! Africa [186 A2] Av Pelican 8; m 099 712 3055; w yoleafrica.org. Puts on weekly film screenings on Sat afternoons at 16.00, along with dance competitions on the last Sat of the month & a variety of other cultural programming in between – check their website for the latest. They're also involved with presenting the week-long Salaam Kivu International Film Festival every Jul.

Nightlife Goma is known for its lively nightlife and has many bars and nightclubs worth exploring; note that, at the time of writing, a 22.00 curfew is in force throughout the city.

Tango Goma [189 B4] Av Kanya Muhanga; m 097 015 4203; f. Popular & central lounge bar serving international cuisine ($$) & cocktails. Wed is happy pizza night (2 for the price of 1).

The Saloon [189 C3] Av Kanya Muhanga; m 097 452 5148; f thesaloongoma. This nightspot is famous for its Thu after-work drinks & live DJ. Also serves food ($$).

SHOPPING For those climbing Nyiragongo or visiting other attractions in Virunga National Park on a self-catering basis, the GoMarché [189 B4] (m 099 170 5350; ⊕ 08.30–21.30 Mon–Fri, 10.00–21.30 Sat, 09.00–21.30 Sun) is the biggest and best-stocked supermarket in Goma. Also worth a try is Amigo [189 B2] (m 097 979 7971), which has a good selection of packaged goods, along with meats, cheeses and alcoholic drinks. **Local products** to look out for are Goma cheese, Kivu coffee and Virunga chocolates.

The city's main **market**, Marché Virunga [187 F1], is just over 2km north of the Rond-Point BDGL, near the rebuilt Cathedral Saint-Joseph. The market is by far the biggest in town: expect non-stop, multi-sensory stimuli, and thousands of people wheeling and dealing on everything from potatoes to padlocks. Keep a close eye on your valuables here – better yet, don't bring any.

Masks and other carvings can be purchased at the **craft market** [189 C2] facing the taxi rank at Rond-Point BDGL or (more expensive) in front of the Ihusi Hotel. At the other end of the shopping spectrum, and one of the best spots in town for elegant souvenirs, is **Kivu Nuru** [189 A5] (m 099 550 2550), a boutique with a super-stylish range of African-inspired clothing, jewellery and accessories.

The **bookshop** Librairie Lave Littéraire [187 F3] (m + 250 994 133614) has a useful stock of books (including Bradt guides!), newspapers, magazines, maps and more.

Le Chalet (page 191) has a little boutique that sells Kivu coffee, Virunga chocolates, cakes and souvenir T-shirts, and typical handicrafts including a large choice of masks. The spa at Lac Kivu Lodge (page 190) stocks European cosmetics and suncream, which you can't find elsewhere in town.

SPORTS AND ACTIVITIES Based at Le Chalet restaurant, **Kayak Kivu** (m 099 062 2714; f) rents out kayaks on the lake for US$15/20 per hour for a single/double kayak, or US$55/68 for the whole day.

The **Ihusi Hotel** (page 190) has a swimming pool which non-guests can use for a rather steep US$10. Tennis is also available there for a similar fee. The **Lac Kivu Lodge** (page 190) has a well-equipped gym and fitness centre with qualified coaches that offer individual training programmes. You can also swim in the lake here, or rent stand-up paddleboards for US$15 for 2 hours.

When security permits, **horseriding** is available at the dramatically located Malaika Lodge (m 099 862 4595; w malaikalodge.com), in Mushaki village, 40km from Goma in the hills west of Sake. Riding costs US$20 per hour, and there is also good accommodation (**$$**).

OTHER PRACTICALITIES International Visa and Mastercard can be used to withdraw US dollars from any of the numerous **ATMs** dotted around Goma, including at Lac Kivu Lodge and the Ihusi Hotel. Use an ATM within the bank (or in a hotel lobby), where possible, and always in daylight. US dollars are accepted everywhere, but only new bills (post 2009), in mint condition. Even a small pen mark on a note is enough for it to be rejected.

A **4x4 vehicle** can be hired, with driver (m 099 434 4805; e mbumamatari@ gmail.com; but see security advice, page 185) at US$100 per day.

There are several **pharmacies** along Rutshuru Road, stocked with some basic medications. Doing the circuit around the pharmacies looking for the one that has the medicine you need is a time-honoured tradition in Goma for sick visitors. As elsewhere in the DRC, if you are seriously ill or injured, seek medical evacuation as soon as you are fit to travel. **Hospitals** in Goma that meet international standards are:

CIMAK [186 B2] Clinique Internationale de Médecine Avancée au Kivu; 43 Av La Frontière, Q/ Katindo; m 085 504 4658; **f** CIMAK GOMA

HEAL Africa [189 B2] 111 Rue Lyn Lusi; m 081 312 7810, 099 712 9934; w healafrica.org. A Christian health-care & community development non-profit organisation hospital.

WHAT TO SEE AND DO In colonial times, Goma was a beach resort for well-to-do Belgians and, along the lakeshore, many old Belgian mansions survive. **Lake Kivu** is still an attraction, especially if you are interested in watersports such as paddleboarding or kayaking. Many visitors, though, are most interested in the nearby volcanoes and the impact of Nyiragongo's eruptions on the city. Check out the **destroyed cathedral** [187 F1] at the northern end of Boulevard Kanya Muhanga, once a large church that was flooded with lava. It's now an open-air space covered in graffiti, a pyramid rising from the black earth. If you follow the lava flow north (be careful of militia activity in or near the IDP camps), you'll eventually reach the city's edge and a large **lava field** which is unique in its own right – near the road north to Rutshuru is a large hill where the lava originally erupted, spouting from the ground several kilometres from the volcano. It was initially predicted to flow southeast into Gisenyi, but flowed almost directly south to envelop central Goma instead.

Situated on Mount Goma, above the port, the **Goma Volcano Observatory** [186 D2] (Observatoire Volcanologique de Goma, OVG; w virunga-volcanoes. org; ⊕ Mon–Fri) is responsible for monitoring the activity of Virunga's two active volcanoes, Nyiragongo and Nyamulagira, and for providing information on them to the local authorities. To visit the observatory, ask at the Virunga National Park office; contact details for the directors are on the observatory's website.

When the security situation permits, follow the road west out of the city and you will eventually encounter a turn-off to **Green Lake**, a beautiful small body of water in a volcanic crater. Near the lake are several pits where volcanic ash is being mined and turned into bricks. Westward are the **Mokoto Lakes**, four quiet bodies of water surrounded by lush green volcanic mountains – to reach the lakes follow the turn-off north from Sake. Keep heading west and you will arrive in **Masisi**, a popular spot for visiting indigenous Pygmy communities. There are also some beautiful villages filled with dairy farms, a rare sight in the DRC; this is where Goma's delicious cheese is made.

A few kilometres north out of Goma are hillsides of lush volcanic farmland and hundreds of wooden cabins built after the eruption of the volcano. Their black exteriors and aluminium roofs make them a striking backdrop against the lush green of the area. As you gain altitude, some striking views of the city can be had. This is also the beginning of **Virunga National Park** and the hiking trail leading to **Mount Nyiragongo**; see page 211 for details.

BUKAVU

Thanks to Sean Connolly, contributor to Bradt's guide to Rwanda, for his research in Bukavu, on which this section draws heavily.

In an almost incredibly scenic location along the hills at the extreme south end of Lake Kivu, the five green and densely populated peninsulas of Bukavu bend and stretch northwards into the lake at odd angles, revealing a surfeit of panoramic views around nearly every corner. Old colonial mansions dot the lakeside peninsulas, interrupted by winding dirt roads descending to the shore. The town was founded in 1901 and called Costermansville in honour of Paul Costermans, one of the original architects of the Congo Free State. It has seen some nasty combat during its time – in the late 1960s it was the site of battles between Moïse Tshombe's Katangese soldiers, Mobutu Sese Seko's regular army, and several hundred mercenaries led by Jean Schramme – this was the situation into which Dian Fossey (page 214), naively unaware of Congolese politics, found herself arriving. Bukavu was again caught up in battle during the late 1990s as the RCD ran through the city, and yet again in 2004 when Laurent Nkunda's troops staged minor attacks in the hills west of the centre. Yet on the surface it shows no real scars of combat or displacement.

Increasingly, several high-end hotels have taken up property beside the old mansions as Bukavu aims to regain some status as a lakeside resort, an escape from the busier environment of Goma. Their business comes from those tourists who take the plunge and cross here from Rwanda, or from those who take the *canôts rapides* from Goma. Bukavu was once the main commercial centre for the Kivus, but the lifestyle is a little more laid-back than in Goma. Its tropical abundance stands in sharp contrast to Goma's harsh, elemental feel. Bukavu's situation mirrors the north end of the lake with uncanny repetition. Just as with Goma, it sits directly on the Rwandan border, here facing the much smaller Rwandan town of Cyangugu (Rusizi), and it also enjoys access to a national park known for its gorilla tracking, Kahuzi-Biega, just a short drive out of town.

It's not unusual to hear residents declare Bukavu as the most attractive city in the DRC and, on the face of it, the city's stunning location and surprisingly easy charm make it quite difficult to take issue with the idea. So while it's often overshadowed by the notoriety and singularity of the northern lakeshore and its attractions, a visit to Bukavu would still be a highlight of any eastern DRC itinerary – it might end up as one of your favourite towns too.

GETTING THERE AND AWAY Note that if you arranged your visa through the Visit Virunga website, you must enter the DRC at Goma, as the email printout is not accepted in Bukavu (page 183).

By road Travellers coming from Rwanda should first aim for Cyangugu (Rusizi), from where it's a short motorbike taxi ride from the bus station to the border and an easy walk across the bridge into Bukavu. Another motorbike ride will take you to the city centre.

By boat For details of boats to and from Goma, see page 188. Tickets for all boats and *canôts rapides* can be bought at the port [196 A2]. Ihusi Express tickets are also available at the Ihusi filling station on Place de l'Indépendance [196 A3].

By air Bukavu's Kavumu Airport is 35km north of town, close to Kahuzi-Biega National Park. At the time of writing, there are no scheduled services; as ever in the DRC, the best way to check if there are flights is to go to the airport and ask there. If your budget permits, the Goma-based airline Busy Bee Congo (w busybeecongo. com) can arrange charter flights.

GETTING AROUND Bukavu begins at the Rwanda border crossing, at Cyangugu. To get to Bukavu from the border, you cross the bridge and walk up a hill to arrive at the far busier Congolese side of the river. Bukavu's main thoroughfare is on the westernmost of the five peninsulas jutting out into the lake: **Avenue Lumumba** houses the main seat of government for Sud-Kivu Province as well as most of the city's amenities. Continue west along the lake for the boat stations for Idjwi Island and Goma. The **Central Market** [196 C4] area is the crossroads of the city, where all routes meet, and is a useful point of reference.

The Roundabout and Place de l'Indépendance [196 A3] before the ports is where you can generally find **transport by road** north along the west coast of Lake Kivu. To get to Uvira, there are no minibuses – you need to hire a private jeep, or simply ask when (and from where) the next truck is leaving.

LOCAL TOUR OPERATORS
Tourist information The **Kahuzi-Biega National Park/ICCN office** [196 C4] (m 099 211 6464; ☐ Kahuzi Biega National Park; ⊕ 07.00–16.00 Mon–Fri) on Avenue Lumumba can arrange transport, permits and other practicalities for visits to the park and its surrounding attractions, including the Centre de Recherche en Sciences Naturelles and the Lwiro Primates Rehabilitation Centre (pages 202 and 203).

Tour operators All the larger hotels can arrange trips to Kahuzi-Biega and surrounds, and the Goma-based operators on page 190 can also arrange trips to Kahuzi-Biega, Bukavu and Idjwi Island. The following agencies are based in Bukavu and can arrange trips anywhere in the region, including Idjwi Island.

Agence Espérance w agenceesperance.net. Ardent promoters of sustainable tourism throughout the Kivus, they run an ecolodge on Idjwi Island.
Pole Pole Foundation w polepolefoundation. org. Community-based conservation group active in the region since 1992 & winner of the 2016

Prince William Award for Conservation in Africa. *Pole pole* means 'slowly' in Swahili.
Simi Trek m 097 682 0166, 081 968 4610; ☐ SimiTREKkivu. This Kahuzi-Biega specialist has a lodge 3km from the park & runs day & overnight trips there.

BUKAVU

For listings, see opposite

⊙ **Where to stay**

1	Agence Espérance..........E3
2	Amazone.........................B4
3	Hotel Begonias................G2
4	Hotel Elila.......................E3
5	Hotel Elizabeth................D4
6	Hotel Horizon...................E3
7	Lodge CoCo.....................E3
8	Orchids Safari Club..........E3
9	Prokamu Guesthouse........F2

✕ **Where to eat and drink**

10	Chez Maman Kinja..........D4
11	Cosmo Koweit..................E3
12	Karibu Café.....................E3
13	Salt & Pepper..................B2
14	Wendy's Bar....................F3

WHERE TO STAY *Map, opposite*

Exclusive

Orchids Safari Club [196 E3] (25 rooms, 4 suites, 4 apartments) Av Kahuzi-Biega 22–24; m 081 312 6467, +250 813 126467/784 444137; e info@orchids-hotel.com; w orchids-hotel.com. Set in a beautifully manicured hillside compound just above the lake, this secure, owner-managed lodge has lounge bar, good restaurant (**$$$**) with French & Congolese menu, conference facilities; lake access for swimming or kayaking. B/fast, Wi-Fi, kayak hire & gym use inc. All rooms en suite with good bathroom, TV, phone, safe, desk, private balcony with lake view; modern, luxurious, well-furnished, parquet flooring & nice bed linen; apartments have 1 or 2 bedrooms, living room, kitchen. **$$$$$**

Mid-range

Hotel Begonias [196 G2] (22 rooms, 3 suites) 63 Av de la Montagne; m 084 701 6035, 099 767 2121; w begonias-bukavu.com. Some 700m from the border; smart, business-oriented hotel; secure parking; Wi-Fi. Top-floor restaurant; conference facilities, large pool, spa & sauna. Good-sized, comfortable tiled rooms; all have balcony, some with fabulous views over lake. **$$$**

Lodge CoCo [196 E3] (8 rooms) m 099 870 7344; w lodgecoco.com. This small lodge has a safari lodge feel. Secure parking; 24hr electricity & Wi-Fi throughout; restaurant with Congolese, Indian & European menus (**$$**); pizzeria; bar. Live music every Fri; vehicles to Kahuzi-Biega National Park can be arranged. Characterful rooms with African décor, wooden furnishings, comfortably appointed with big beds, writing desk, flatscreen TV & nets; b/fast inc. **$$$**

Thrifty

Hotel Elizabeth [196 D4] (34 rooms) 134 Av Kalehe; m 099 323 3553; w elizabethhotelbukavu.com. Formerly called Hôtel de Goma, quiet hotel in lush garden that envelops the entranceway; secure. Good restaurant, conference room, popular bar with fabulous views over the city; terrace with views of villages in Rwanda, bar & grill menu. All rooms en suite, with TV, Wi-Fi, fridge with mineral water, coffee-making facilities, European & US sockets, desk; some have balcony. Premium rooms, suites &

apartments also have AC & safe. Rooms **$$–$$$**, suites & apartments **$$$$**

Hotel Elila [196 E3] (25 rooms) 21 Av Kabare, Q/ Muhumba; m 097 002 1132; w hotelelila. com. Secure parking, pool, climbing wall(!), restaurant, terrace bar, high-speed Wi-Fi. All rooms en suite with lake view; small but well maintained; AC, TV; some have private balcony. **$$–$$$**

Hotel Horizon [196 E3] (35 rooms) 4 Av de Goma; m 099 440 6270; f Hotel-Horizon-Bukavu. 2 buildings linked by a corridor; garden; children's playground; secure. 2 good restaurants with Congolese & international menus; b/fast inc. Rooms on upper floors have balconies & lovely lake views. All rooms en suite with TV & hot water. **$$–$$$**

Budget

Agence Espérance [196 E3] (3 rooms) Av Pangi; m 099 822 5588, +32 470 700531; e luc.henkinbrant@gmail.com. This charming family home makes for a comfortable base in Bukavu & it's an ideal place to get further information about the region, from owners Luc & Espérance who run an ecotourism information centre. There's a tranquil garden out back, a comfortable living room & Wi-Fi. Excellent meals are available on request. The rooms are bright, simple & homely, with net, desk & reading lamps. **$**

Amazone [196 B4] (32 rooms) Av Kindu; m 097 813 5121. Formerly the Lac Tanganyika hotel & still one of the most affordable hotels in Bukavu (from US$15 dbl). Some renovations have been made, but still no Wi-Fi; hot water is by request. Bar-restaurant serves economical dishes & snacks. Rooms are basic but have mosquito nets. **$**

Prokamu Guesthouse [196 F2] (12 rooms) 7 Av Masikita; m 081 636 3585; e hmukungilwa@ gmail.com. Run by the Catholic Diocese of Kasongo; elegant colonial-era building, hidden away behind an unmarked red gate near the German consul's residence. Simple, clean rooms set in peaceful, grassy garden right on the lake. B/fast inc, other meals may be possible by arrangement (the nearest restaurants are almost 1km away). Hot water on request; cold running water unpredictable. **$**

✖ WHERE TO EAT AND DRINK *Map, page 196*

Several of the hotels listed on page 197 serve excellent food, and there's also no shortage of standalone restaurants.

Karibu Café [196 E3] Off Av Muhumba; m 099 309 7044; f Karibu cafe/bar. Popular with Congolese & foreign patrons alike, this relaxed bar has plenty of garden seating, DJ nights & occasional theme parties, plus a reliably carnivorous offering of barbecue meals & brochettes. $$

Salt & Pepper [196 B2] Av de Nya-Wera; m 089 923 9072; ⏰ 10.00–midnight daily. Good menu of Indian, Chinese & other dishes, with plenty of vegetarian & vegan options. Bar turns into nightclub in evenings. $–$$

Chez Maman Kinja [196 D4] 114 Av Hippodrome, Nyalukemba; m 097 395 2327. Near the Place Mulamba roundabout, recommended for authentic Congolese home cooking; grab a plastic chair at one of the plastic tables here for goat, grills, *ugali*, *matoke* & more. Hotel rooms also available ($) – see w mamankinja.com for details. $

Cosmo Koweit [196 E3] Av Claire; m 085 157 1909; f cosmo.koweit.restaurant; ⏰ noon–21.00 daily. Popular buffet restaurant serves heaps of beans, greens, bananas, meat, fish, cassava, & more for under US$5. $

Wendy's Bar [196 F3] Av Geneviève; m 099 161 6901; ⏰ eves daily. Little more than a shack built from planks of wood with some tables in the yard, this rootsy local bar, also known as Chez Wendy, has become an unlikely hub for foreigners based in Bukavu & is a sure bet to get you started at w/ends. $

SHOPPING The perpetually busy **central market**, known as Marché Nyawera [196 C4], sells everything from machetes to makeup and is a sure way to get a feel for what really makes Bukavu tick.

For **art and souvenirs**, Le Likembe [196 C4] (m 099 776 2707; ⏰ 08.00–16.00 Mon–Fri, 10.00–15.00 Sat) has a dusty but interesting selection of carvings, bags, paintings, masks, wire-frame children's toys and the like; prices here are marked, but a bit of negotiation probably wouldn't hurt. There's also a good selection of carvings and masks at the front of the Orchids Safari Club (page 197).

OTHER PRACTICALITIES Several banks along the main street have **ATMs**, dispensing US dollars. Rawbank's ATMs also dispense Congolese francs if you want them. Use an ATM within the bank, where possible, and always in daylight. The best place to find moneychangers is near the Rwandan border, but keep your wits about you.

BUKAVU'S HIDDEN TREASURE

Hidden away behind an unmarked gate at Rue Kabare 25 in a compound belonging to Catholic Xaverian missionaries, the **Musée du Kivu** in Bukavu [196 E2] (m 099 867 5658; e barthelemykayumba@gmail.com) might be the world's worst-marketed museum, but its collections are a veritable treasure trove of Congolese art and artefacts. Pieces from some two dozen ethnic groups across the DRC are represented, with many items donated to the collections by regional chiefs and elders in order to safeguard them from destruction during the fighting in the east. It's as impressive as it is unexpected, and the knowledgeable curator, Barthélemy, gives thorough explanations (in French) of the origins and purpose of each object. It's officially open by appointment only, but Barthélemy is usually around and will accommodate walk-in visitors without problem. There's no charge for entry, but a donation is expected (and well deserved).

The **Orchids Safari Club** (page 197) has lake access and a little grassy patch for sunbathing at the bottom of their compound, and they're pretty relaxed about people heading down there to use it, even if they're not staying at the hotel. They would probably appreciate you buying a beer or two, though. The Hotel Begonias (page 197) charges US$5 per person for day use of their **swimming pool**.

KAHUZI-BIEGA NATIONAL PARK

About 30km northwest of Bukavu, the 6,000km² Kahuzi-Biega National Park is named for the two extinct volcanoes that dominate its skyline, mounts Kahuzi (3,308m) and Biega (2,790m), which constitute the two highest peaks of the Mitumba range. It has been a protected area since 1934 and a UNESCO World Heritage Site since 1980. Divided into two unequal sections linked by a narrow strip of forest, the park's eastern portion covers a habitat of largely montane primary forest between 1,800m and 3,300m in elevation, while the much larger western section of the park sees elevations drop to between 600m and 1,500m (except for Mount Kamami at 1,700m) and a habitat of low, forested mountains punctuated by deep river valleys leading west towards the River Lualaba.

Kahuzi-Biega has suffered several incursions in recent decades. In 1994, refugees from the Rwandan genocide took up residence within the park; three years later it became a hideout for rebel militias during the Second Congo War, leading to it being placed on the list of World Heritage Sites in Danger in 1997. At the start of this century, a spike in global mineral prices, particularly for the components of coltan, saw more than 10,000 miners move into park territory, which had long since fallen out of government control. Within a couple of years, the elephant population had disappeared entirely, while gorillas had been reduced by as much as 90%.

Since those threatening times, however, a small renaissance is taking place in Kahuzi-Biega, and, as in its more famous cousin Virunga National Park, recent years have witnessed impressive strides in terms of both management and conservation. Despite the years of turmoil, Kahuzi-Biega today remains the only place in the world where you can track the critically endangered eastern lowland, or Grauer's, gorilla (*Gorilla beringei graueri*). Their range includes the protected areas of Kahuzi-Biega and Maiko national parks, but their total population is estimated at only a few thousand, down from nearly 17,000 in the 1990s. In Kahuzi-Biega, 200–300 individuals are now thought to be resident in the park, according to the most recent census in 2015. Even if you don't want to go gorilla tracking, you can hike out to the Tshibati Waterfalls or summit Mount Kahuzi. For ornithologists, the park has been listed as an Important Bird Area since 2001, with a total checklist of 450 species that includes 42 Albertine Rift Endemics (including African green broadbill), more than any other protected area in the region.

GETTING THERE AND AWAY Before you leave Bukavu for Kahuzi-Biega, you must have a **park permit**. These can be bought at the ICCN office in Bukavu (page 195); see page 202 for prices. Gorilla tracking and other activities within the park boundaries start at the Tshivanga visitors' centre/national park headquarters (✪ 2°18'52.1"S, 28°45'34.2"E), which lies about 35km north of Bukavu along the N3, branching left after 10km at the village of Miti (✪ 2°21'18.2"S, 28°47'36.8"E). After you have picked up the obligatory rangers and guides at Tshivanga, there will be another drive to the trailhead. The drive to Tshivanga takes about 1 hour and there's no public transport, so a private vehicle is required. ICCN at the park office in Bukavu can organise transport for US$150 per day for a 4x4 (maximum five passengers). Simi Trek (page 195) charges US$70 per vehicle for the return transfer, and it's also possible to hire a private taxi in town for closer to US$50. All tour agents and most hotels can also arrange vehicles.

The **Centre de Recherche en Sciences Naturelles** (⊕ 2°14'21.6594", 28°48'44.604") and **Lwiro Primates Rehabilitation Centre** lie alongside each other about 45km north of Bukavu. To get there, follow the N3 to Miti, but instead of forking left for the national park, head right along the N2 for 14km, until you see the Lwiro turn-off signposted to the left. The centre is just under 3km from here. A toll – US$2.50 for saloon cars, US$5 for 4x4s – is levied between Miti and Kavumu, on the road to Lwiro and the airport.

WHERE TO STAY *Map, opposite*

The majority of people visiting Kahuzi-Biega do so as a day trip from Bukavu (some even cross into the DRC as a day excursion from the Rwandan town of Cyangugu), but the recent opening of a chalet complex at Tshivanga means it is now possible to stay inside the park. There are also several accommodation options between Bukavu and the park, and around Lwiro. Advance booking is required or strongly advised for all accommodation in the vicinity of the park.

Tshivanga Chalets (10 chalets) ⊕ −2.31544, 28.75891; m 097 405 1800. Situated next to park HQ at Tshivanga, this recently opened facility comprises 10 attractive stone-&-thatch chalets with fireplace, net, TV, cane furniture & private terrace. It is a great place to stay if you plan on doing multiple activities in the park. **$$$**

Simi Lodge & Snack-Bar (7 rooms) ⊕ −2.33120, 28.76322; m 097 682 0166, 081 968 4610; f SIMI – Lodge & Snack-Bar, SimiTREKkivu. Set in manicured gardens 3km from the park headquarters at Tshivanga on the RN3 from Bukavu, this small lodge has comfortable rooms, a terrace restaurant (which can also prepare meals for day visitors with advance notice) & charges US$70 per vehicle for a return transfer from Bukavu. B/fast inc. **$$**

Abbaye de la Clarté-Dieu (9 rooms) ⊕ −2.37689, 28.79529; m 099 059 9372; w ocso.org/monastery/clarte-dieu. This brick abbey of Trappist nuns sits in expansive, lovingly tended & pine-studded grounds alongside Lake Zebede, close to the village of Murhesa, some 2.5km before the turn-off at Miti coming from Bukavu & 10km from Tshivanga. In time-honoured Trappist tradition, the nuns make a variety of goods, including yoghurt, ice cream, honey, jams, candles & cookies. The well-kept guestrooms are often fully booked by church visitors. **$**

Cemucac Guesthouse (4 rooms) ⊕ −2.23866, 28.80752; m 099 071 5630, 097 436 0539; w lwiroprimates.org. This delightfully timewarped colonial villa, just opposite the Lwiro Primates Rehabilitation Centre (page 203), has a formal feel, with massive old furnishings, multiple fireplaces & heavy wooden doors with carved accents. The Primates Centre doesn't officially run it but is the most reliable contact for reservation. Rooms are simply furnished but have nets; 2 shared bathroom, 2 en suite. Meals are available with advance notice, at US$4 for b/fast & US$8 for lunch or dinner. **$**

Guesthouse Formulac (14 rooms) ⊕ −2.23476, 28.86087; m 085 283 7575, 089 955 1648; e cabwinejc@yahoo.fr, cabwinejc@gmail.com. Set about 4km from the main road along the shores of Lake Kivu in Ciranga village, this enjoyably old-style auberge, built in the 1930s as accommodation to the Formulac Hospital, is now administered by the Catholic Archdiocese of Bukavu. High-ceilinged rooms, set in a fetching porticoed stone-&-brick building on a bluff overlooking the lake, have nets & many have private terraces as well. Meals are available ($), along with cold beers & sodas. If they're full, there are further rooms available at the neighbouring Katana Nursing College. The guesthouse can also arrange boat transfers from here to Kashofu on Idjwi Island for about US$100. To get here, take the right-hand turn-off 1.2km north of the turning for Lwiro. B/fast inc. Some rooms share bathrooms, others en suite. **$**

Guesthouse de Lwiro (5 rooms) ⊕ −2.23919, 28.81424; m 085 095 3286, 097 436 0539. In the grounds of the Centre de Recherche en

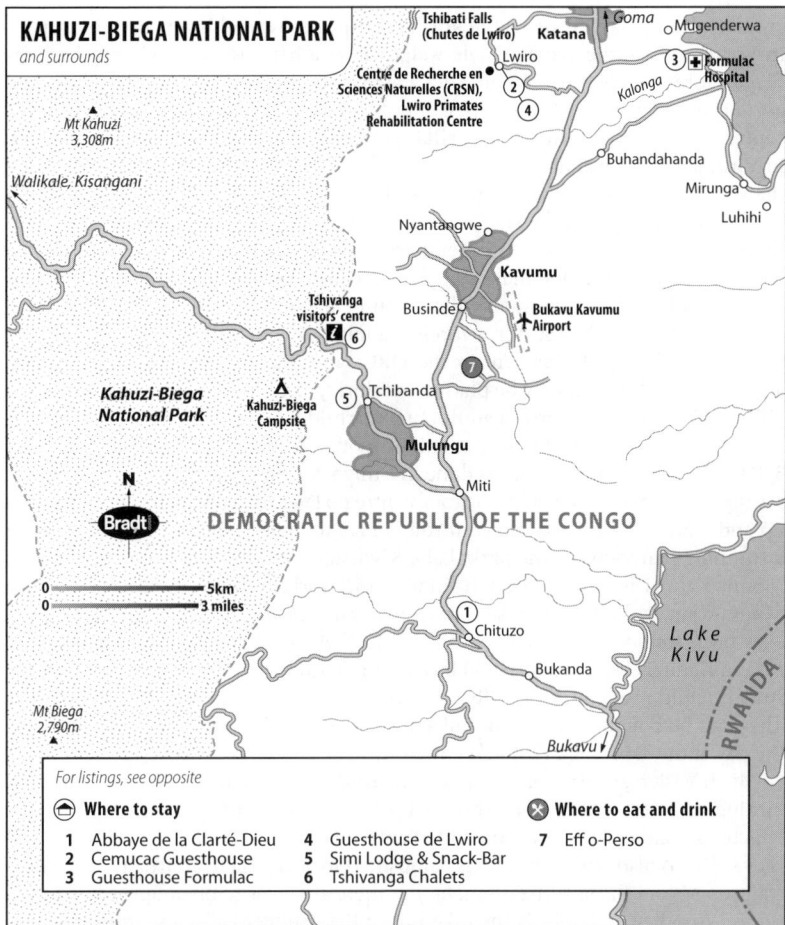

KAHUZI-BIEGA NATIONAL PARK
and surrounds

Tshibati Falls
(Chutes de Lwiro)   Katana   ↑ Goma   ○ Mugenderwa

Centre de Recherche en
Sciences Naturelles (CRSN),   Lwiro
Lwiro Primates
Rehabilitation Centre   ③ ✚ Formulac
Hospital

▲ Mt Kahuzi
3,308m

Walikale, Kisangani

Kalonga

Buhandahanda

Mirunga
Luhihi ○

Nyantangwe

Kavumu

Tshivanga
visitors' centre   Businde ○   Bukavu Kavumu
ℹ ⑥   ✈ Airport

*Kahuzi-Biega
National Park*   ⑤ Tchibanda

⚑ Kahuzi-Biega
Campsite

Mulungu

Miti

N   **DEMOCRATIC REPUBLIC OF THE CONGO**

Bradt

0 ___ 5km
0 ___ 3 miles

① Chituzo

Bukanda

*Lake
Kivu*

▲ Mt Biega
2,790m

Bukavu ↓

RWANDA

For listings, see opposite

🛏 **Where to stay**
1 Abbaye de la Clarté-Dieu
2 Cemucac Guesthouse
3 Guesthouse Formulac
4 Guesthouse de Lwiro
5 Simi Lodge & Snack-Bar
6 Tshivanga Chalets

❌ **Where to eat and drink**
7 Eff o-Perso

Sciences Naturelles, this mansion exudes colonial splendour. On the ground floor is a formal sitting & dining room centred on an enormous fireplace, wainscoted in dark wood & decorated with still-life paintings, all of which look to have changed little in the last 50 years. The cobbled-together rooms on the 1st floor are a let-down by comparison, but the beds are clean & have nets. **$**

❌ **WHERE TO EAT AND DRINK** *Map, above*
The guesthouses listed opposite can all arrange meals, but there are no supplies available in the park. Meals and supplies will likely become available with the opening of the chalets at Tshivanga.

Eff o-Perso m 099 031 9000; 🕐 24hrs. This large & well-signposted bar, restaurant, nightclub & swimming pool complex is set in a field 1km southeast of the main road, about 2km south of Kavumu. There are loads of garden tables for noshing on brochettes & swilling beer, plus an indoor dance club that goes at all hours, sometimes with live music. **$**

ACTIVITIES The biggest draw for visitors to Kahuzi-Biega is also the world's biggest primate – the eastern lowland, or Grauer's gorilla (*Gorilla beringei* *graueri*). It's the largest of all the gorilla subspecies (even bigger than its cousins in Virunga), and the average male weighs in at a hefty 160kg. Living in Kahuzi-Biega's forests between 2,100m and 2,400m above sea level, the few hundred gorillas thought to live in the park can be visited on treks from Tshivanga visitors' centre, and the practicalities of **gorilla trekking** here are broadly similar to those in Virunga or in Rwanda – trackers set out at 08.00, the mountainous hike to find the gorillas can take anywhere from 30 minutes to a couple of hours, depending on their movements, and visits last an hour. There are three habituated families in the park – Chimanuka with 19 members, Bonne Année with eight, and Pungwe with 22 – plus a solitary male called Mugaruka. It's possible to get **permits** in Bukavu without advance notice; these can be arranged at the ICCN office there and cost US$400/200/150 for a foreign adult/student/child; US$200/100/30 for an adult/student/child resident in the DRC (and many other African countries, although that discount may be phased out during the lifespan of this edition); and US$20/10/5 for a DRC citizen adult/student/child.

Other than gorilla trekking, activities on offer at the park include an ascent of 3,308m **Mount Kahuzi**, which is done in a thigh-burning, full-day, round-trip hike setting out from the Tshivanga visitors' centre no later than 09.00. It's about 4 hours up and 3 hours to get back down through lush montane forest which opens up to a stunning panorama of the park, Lake Kivu, and even Bukavu from the summit. Mount Kahuzi is also the only habitat in the world of the critically endangered Mount Kahuzi climbing mouse (*Dendromus kahuziensis*), of which only two have ever been found – 100m away from each other on Mount Kahuzi. **Permits** for Mount Kahuzi cost US$100/70/50 foreign adult/student/child; US$60/50/25 adult/student/child resident in the DRC; and US$15/7/3 Congolese adult/student/child. They can be bought at ICCN in Bukavu or, if you show up early enough, even on the day at the Tshivanga visitors' centre.

Much easier are the four new 3–4km **trails** – designated as marsh, cultural, birding or forest – cut near Tshivanga, or the 6km trail to Mount Bugulumiza, which takes about 3 hours return and offers fabulous views over mounts Kahuzi and Biega. This is also where the park's campsite is located. There aren't any functional trails up Mount Biega at the moment, but there are plans to open up a route in the future. Another highlight is the hike out to the Tshibati Falls, also known as Les Chutes de Lwiro. If you've already arranged your permit for this in Bukavu, you can head straight to Lwiro; otherwise, you'll need to pick up a ranger and guide at Tshivanga then get back in the car to reach the trailhead. The hike starts with a short trip through farms and fields before crossing into the park for another couple of hours until you reach the roaring falls at the end of a long valley. You can swim at the second waterfall. **Permits** for the waterfall or any of the trails cost US$35/25/15 foreign adult/student/child; US$25/15/10 adult/student/child resident in the DRC; and US$5/4/2 Congolese adult/student/child.

If you've had enough hiking and trekking for the time being, there are two compelling sights located just outside the park boundaries in Lwiro. The **Centre de Recherche en Sciences Naturelles** (CRSN; m 099 777 0616) is an enormous and majestic educational campus, replete with impressive ponds, fountains, archways, porticoes and spiral staircases. It was built in 1947 as part of IRSAC, the colonial Institute for Scientific Research in Central Africa. The scientists working at the CRSN include biologists, geophysicists and environmentalists; many have been at the CRSN for decades. Its magnificent library, with 7km of shelving, holds one of the largest collections in the DRC – thousands of books and academic journals, 350,000 biological specimens and almost 3,000 masks. The box on page 204 has

THE KAHUZI-BIEGA EXPERIENCE   *by Peter Eastwood*

I've been to Kahuzi-Biega four times in recent years, and loved every visit. I've now tracked gorillas there on six occasions, and having done the same thing in Uganda's Bwindi Impenetrable National Park (my first gorilla experience), there are a few things that I think make Kahuzi-Biega special.

First, there is the low number of visitors, which makes gorilla tracking in Kahuzi-Biega a very intimate experience. Secondly, although you'll be tracking at an altitude of 2,300m, these are not mountain gorillas but eastern lowland gorillas, which cannot be seen in the wild anywhere else in the world.

Thirdly, the tracking permit is far cheaper than it is in Rwanda and to a lesser extent Uganda. Finally, because the roads take you very close to the gorillas, you don't need to hike far to find them, and it is a lot easier going, as the vegetation isn't so impenetrable as it is at Bwindi.

We had incredible experiences each and every time we tracked gorillas at Kahuzi-Biega. On four trips, I was with other visitors that I'd brought to the park, and we had incredible family sightings every time. I think the longest we ever walked to find the gorillas was 30 minutes. In all cases, the gorillas seemed curious about our presence, as there aren't many visitors and they don't get overexposed to them. On one trip, we were specifically targeting deforestation, so we went to see the gorillas in an area deforested by local people. (Thankfully this has now been stopped, and the trees were coppiced, so will grow back quickly with protection.) Another time we went to see a single silverback who had lost one hand in a snare, resulting in the breakdown of his family group, which means he now lives a lonely life in a tea plantation – an incredibly sad story that highlights the reality of what we're trying to protect.

We also visited Lwiro Primates, which was thoroughly worthwhile. This vitally needed rehabilitation for chimps and monkeys is very close to Kahuzi-Biega and easily added to your day on the mountain. We were escorted by the chimp carers and managed to experience the close bond they have with the animals as well as gaining insights into how the various individual primates arrived at the sanctuary and their progress since arriving. It doesn't get many visitors, so it would pay to make advance contact so you are expected. There is accommodation there but we didn't stay over.

We felt safe and welcomed by all in Bukavu and Kahuzi-Biega. The staff at the park and at Lwiro Primates are desperate for tourists and were very welcoming, while the village children evidently enjoy the unusual sight of *wazungu* (white people) who aren't UN soldiers. Overall, this part of the Congo was nothing like I'd anticipated. I had expected to be greeted by a traumatised, war-torn population, but on the whole people seemed very cheerful and friendly despite the high level of poverty. I can't recommend a visit too highly!

a personal account of a visit to the CRSN. The admission fee is US$30 for foreign citizens, US$4 for DRC citizens.

Affiliated with the CRSN, and located next to it, **Lwiro Primates Rehabilitation Centre** (m 099 071 5630, 097 436 0539; w lwiroprimates.org) cares for chimps and monkeys that have been orphaned by illegal hunting and the bushmeat trade. Founded in 2002, it now takes care of more than 100 chimpanzees, as well as *by Katie Robinette*

About an hour's drive from Bukavu, past the airport and skirting Kahuzi-Biega National Park, is the small town of Lwiro. I might have even called it a village, with its dirt road and mud-straw houses, except that it has more (potential) tourist attractions than any one village could have.

From my base in Bukavu, we spent two weekends in a row in lovely Lwiro recently. First, we paid a visit to Lwiro's very own Research Centre for Natural Sciences. The fact that it was built in the 1940s and is still maintained and running is an inspiring example of tenacity in a country where, in the past few decades, the norm leans more towards pillage and decay. Thanks to recent funding donations and the hard work of the dedicated Lwiro scientists, this giant compound is still home to a diverse array of educational exhibits and natural science laboratories. We visited first a museum of local cultural artefacts – kitchen tools, hunting tools, musical instruments and, my favourite part, a showcase of chiefs' hats. We were told that the hat covered in buttons was indicative of the chief with the most power. Personally, though, I think the woven, feathered fedora is much more hip by today's standards.

Another tour highlight was the Biodiversity Centre – a taxidermy tribute to the many unique animals that call the Congo home, including a giant pangolin, which looked like the love-child of a pinecone and an anteater. From snout to tip of the tail, it was at least 6ft long. We also visited the ophiology lab, which sounds innocuous but was actually full of snakes – both dead and alive. On one side of the lab, the walls were lined with glass jars filled with thousands of dead snakes. On the other side, in glass cages, two huge vipers cuddled in a peaceful yin-yang, and a small but agitated cobra, hood taut, struck in the direction of anything that moved.

But forget high fashion, stuffed animals and feisty cobras. For me, the most stunning part of our tour was the library. The research centre maintains a gorgeous wood-panelled, spiral-staircased, double-decker library, complete with a card catalogue system, brass chandeliers and a massive fireplace. It reminded me of the library that Belle loved so much in the castle in *Beauty and the Beast*. The library is home to an eclectic mix of scientific and historical volumes, not all of which are particularly politically correct by today's standards, including *My Pygmy and Negro Host* and *My Dark Companions and their Strange Stories*. One jewel of a find was *How I Found Livingstone in Central Africa*, the 1911 publication of a travel book written by Henry Morton Stanley, one of the first European explorers to venture through the Congo.

The following weekend found us back in Lwiro, for a hike to Les Chutes de Lwiro – the Lwiro Waterfalls in Kahuzi-Biega National Park. The hike wasn't too long, but it took us through fields and forests, ending at two big, beautiful waterfalls. The mist from the crashing water made the whole area lush and muddy, and the water was surprisingly freezing cold when we dipped our feet in.

100-plus monkeys of 16 different species, including the inimitable owl-faced guenon (*Cercopithecus hamlyni*) and localised Allen's swamp monkey (*Allenopithecus nigroviridis*), with more arriving all the time. The spacious, well-kept enclosures (some as large as 3ha) and visibly dedicated staff would be praiseworthy in any location – to have kept it going here, during decades of war and turmoil, is almost miraculous. Entrance costs US$30 and includes a tour of the grounds (in English, Spanish or French) and a first-name introduction to whichever of the chimpanzees stops by to check out the new arrivals.

IDJWI ISLAND

Magnificently green and unrelentingly hilly (*idjwi* means 'voice' in the island's Kihavu language, for calling across the many valleys), the 285km² Idjwi Island sits at the centre of Lake Kivu, 40km long and nearly 30km wide at its largest, making it the second largest lake-island in Africa (after Ukerewe in Lake Victoria). It's a rustic place, meaning even more rustic than usual for the DRC, with very few vehicles and numerous tiny villages along the shore. It is a thin, mountainous stretch of territory best known for its pineapple and papaya plantations – and increasingly for its high-quality arabica coffee. There are also a few caves on the island in addition to some birdlife. Fishermen can be hired to take you along the shorelines and visit the small islands through lush and dense jungle, and tour the small villages.

The people of Idjwi have long been isolated from events on the mainland – sometimes intentionally. Local legend has it that the island was used as a place of exile in pre-colonial times, specifically for unmarried mothers cast out by their families. Banished from the mainland, the growing community of unattached women on the island unsurprisingly began to attract the attention of local fishermen. Either unable or unwilling to pay the dowries required to marry in their communities back on the mainland, the frisky fishermen would pitch up to the island from time to time and try their luck with the women there, until a number of them eventually settled down with partners and moved to the island themselves.

Some 40,000 Rwandan Hutus fled to Idjwi in 1994; they found refuge in the forests in the centre of the island, with deforestation following as they cut down trees for cooking and staying warm. Since then, however, security concerns on Idjwi have been minimal compared with the mainland, and you could easily spend a couple of days happily exploring the island's dozens of coves and tracks, hills and valleys, fishing and farming villages. There are even a few ruins: the island is home to a derelict mansion originally built by a Belgian prince and later used by Mobutu on his visits to the island. As getting around Idjwi can be quite challenging, you may find it useful to have a guide; any Goma- or Bukavu-based tour agency can arrange trips, but Agence Espérance in Bukavu (page 197) and Kivu Travel in Goma (page 190) both have links to the island and are particularly recommended.

GETTING THERE AND AWAY Almost all the boats that operate between Goma and Bukavu call at Idjwi Island. The best option is the public service (*vedettes*), which has part-route fares. One of the *vedettes ordinaires* has scheduled stops at Monvu and Bugarula (and at Kalehe on the mainland) on its way between Goma and Bukavu; in 2024, the fare from Bukavu to Monvu was US$15, from Monvu to Bugarula US$10, and from Bugarula via Kalehe US$15. This is a better deal than the Ihusi Express which, although it calls at Idjwi, charges the same US$50 for a one-way ticket to Idjwi as for a ticket all the way between Goma or Bukavu. The Ihusi Express always calls at Bugarula; it can also stop at Monvu, but only if a passenger has advised that they want to be picked up or dropped off there; so you

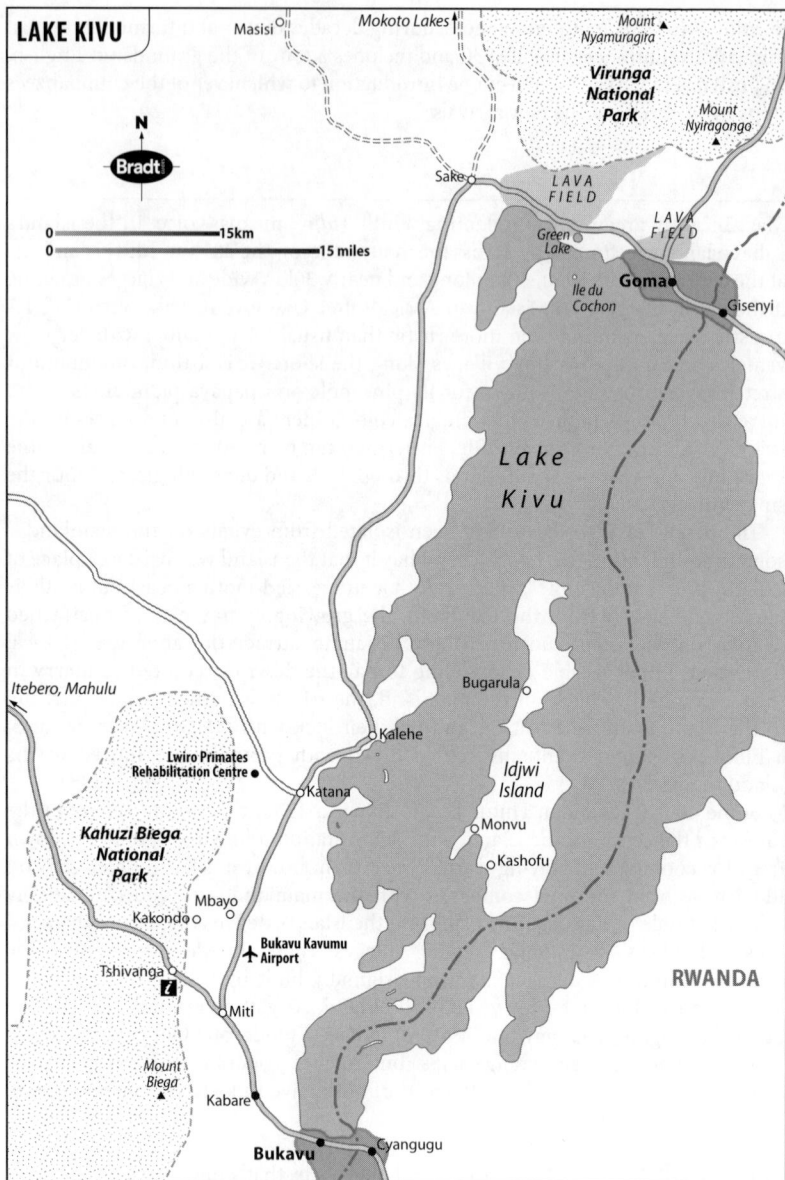

LAKE KIVU

N

Bradt

0 ——————— 15km
0 ——————— 15 miles

Masisi
Mokoto Lakes
Mount Nyamuragira
Virunga National Park
Mount Nyiragongo
Sake
LAVA FIELD
LAVA FIELD
Green Lake
Ile du Cochon
Goma
Gisenyi

Lake Kivu

Itebero, Mahulu
Bugarula
Kalehe
Lwiro Primates Rehabilitation Centre
Katana
Kahuzi Biega National Park
Idjwi Island
Monvu
Kashofu
Mbayo
Kakondo
Bukavu Kavumu Airport
Tshivanga
Miti
RWANDA
Mount Biega
Kabare
Bukavu
Cyangugu

must confirm this when buying your tickets. Reconfirming the day before would be a wise move as well. See page 188 for the operators' contact details.

On the island itself, there are no roads worthy of the name and only perhaps a dozen cars, so motorbikes are king; any guesthouse will be able to connect you with a driver. There are no banking facilities of any kind on the island.

WHERE TO STAY Idjwi Island is divided into two zones – Idjwi-Nord, with Bugarula as the main village, and Idjwi-Sud, with Monvu as the main village. Idjwi-Nord has a solar mini-grid, with storage, that supplies electricity to households, businesses, schools and health centres.

Idjwi-Nord

Hope Land (16 rooms) ✛ −2.05208, 29.05540; m 099 494 3307, 099 423 0238; e hopelandidjwi@gmail.com; ⬛ Hope Land Idjwi Hotel. On the lakeshore, less than 50m from the dock in Bugarula, this lovely resort is run by a couple of ophthalmologists. Built into a lush hillside facing the lake, plus a thatched bar-restaurant floating on the water. Conference room; 4x4 vehicle for hire. Camping in the gardens may be possible. Spotless rooms, all en suite with solar-powered hot water, nets & Wi-Fi; b/fast inc; some have balconies. **$$**

Oasis Lodge (10 rooms) ✛ −2.02731, 29.06230; m 099 218 9897, +257 7514 6350 (WhatsApp); w oasislodge-idjwi.com. Formerly Idjwi Ecolodge, Oasis is 4.5km north of Bugarula, set in landscaped grounds on the lakeside, with its own sandy beach. The Ihusi Express boat calls here. Bar-restaurant serves some of the finest meals on the island, using ingredients from its own permaculture garden; lakeside terrace. Kayaks & pedalos for hire. Guest accommodation in large waterside duplex or triplex thatched bungalows with either flush or compost toilets; some have lofted sleeping area. FB **$$**

Idjwi-Sud

Iko Idjwi Resort (4 rooms) ✛ −2.22746, 28.98651; m 099 971 1062, +1 240 606 1243; e iko.idjwi@gmail.com. Set on Île Mohembe, an emerald flyspeck of an island just off Idjwi's

southwestern coast, this sleepy resort has room for only 8 guests. Basketball court, barbecue facilities; activities on the lake can be arranged. En-suite rooms in main house, 2 bungalows connected by flower-lined paths. Advance reservations essential. FB **$$$–$$$$**

Congomani Guesthouse (12 rooms) ✛ −2.22815, 29.03088; m +250 991 758814; e fredkahmad2@gmail.com, mbakarobert@ yahoo.fr. This neat & green compound sits on the lakeshore just outside Kashofu village & offers somewhat basic rooms in the main house, plus a few smarter standalone chalets in large gardens. Also known locally as la maison blanche ('the white house') after its white walls, it serves generously portioned & well-priced meals (US$5 b/fast, US$10 other meals) & arranges pirogue excursions on request. A motorbike from the southern boat dock at Monvu should cost roughly Fc7,000. Electricity in the evenings, hot water on request. Some rooms with shared bathroom, others en suite. **$**

Paroisse de Kashofu ✛ −2.22410, 29.02416; m 099 762 2222, 099 773 8572. The attractive brick buildings of the Catholic church in Kashofu, in the far south of the island, date from 1936. A few very basic sgl & twin rooms are available for visitors. Meals are taken communally with the priests at set times. Older rooms set around central courtyard, with communal bathrooms; new block at rear has en-suite facilities. All have mosquito nets & solar power. FB **$**

UVIRA

Located in the extreme southeast of Sud-Kivu, most travellers who find themselves in Uvira (✛ 03°24.27 S, 29°08.90 E) will probably be arriving from or departing to Burundi. At the time of writing, the area between Bukavu and Uvira is very insecure, due to the presence of armed militias. If the Rwanda–Burundi border is open, it is much safer to use the Bukavu/Cyangugu crossing and avoid Uvira altogether. In more peaceful times, Uvira was a transport hub for this sparsely populated area, and was served by boats from Kalemie. It also has a rather pleasant beach on Lake Tanganyika, though if you want to swim, you'll be competing with the locals doing their laundry (and risking bilharzia).

WHERE TO STAY Uvira has a few hotels that cater to those who need to be here. Chief among them is **Hôtel de la Cote** (sgl/dbl **$$$**), which should have amenities that are normally hard to find in this region.

The Albertine Rift has been a boon for birdwatchers over the decades, and has the largest concentration of unique species in Africa. The Itombwe Mountains are in the southwestern hinterlands of Lake Kivu, comprising a huge green area in the region. West of the major north–south road corridor to Uvira, the undulating mountains are mostly uninhabited and covered by thick forests in highland areas (montane forest), along river streams, as well as bamboo forests.

Research here has revealed 83 unique montane forest species, half of the entire number found on the continent. A total of 563 different species have been found within the Itombwe Mountains, 43 of them endemic to this region. The Congo bay owl and Schouteden's swift are two birds that exist nowhere else outside Itombwe. Finding these species is unlikely for the casual visitor, however – they are only known from single samples collected over half a century ago. No surveys were done from 1960 until 1996, and even in 1996 the level of research completed was minor due to ongoing conflict.

Itombwe is not a protected area at the time of writing, although WWF is working with local communities to identify a potential reserve for the eastern lowland gorillas resident there. Birdwatchers should talk to ICCN in Bukavu about arranging a visit, though their expertise on birding is minimal. At the time of writing, the area is very insecure, due to the presence of armed militias. The closest village is **Kamituga** (✛ 03°03.18 S, 28°10.55 E) on the northwestern edge of the mountains. The most likely access point for visitors would be **Uvira** (page 207) on the border with Burundi.

VIRUNGA NATIONAL PARK

with thanks to Philip Briggs, author of Bradt's guide to Rwanda

NOTE *As was the case with many African national parks, Virunga National Park suspended tourist visits in March 2020 in response to the Covid-19 pandemic. Unlike most others, including Kahuzi-Biega National Park (page 199), Virunga has never reopened fully (Tchegera Island reopened briefly in 2022), because of the very dangerous security situation in the area. At the time of writing, the heavily armed M23 militia occupies much of the park. There is no immediate prospect of it reopening to tourism, although local tour operators had hoped (optimistically) that this might happen in time for the centenary year of 2025. It has therefore not been possible to update the information in this section.*

One of Africa's most biodiverse conservation areas, the 7,900km² Virunga National Park runs for more than 300km along the border with Rwanda and Uganda. It protects the entire Congolese portion of the Virunga volcanoes, Rwenzori Mountains and Lake Edward, and a habitat range encompassing glacial peaks, Afromontane moorland, high-altitude forest, lowland rainforest and open savannah.

It is Africa's richest protected area in terms of avian diversity, with an astonishing 706 bird species recorded (more than in the whole of neighbouring Rwanda), including several DRC or Albertine Rift endemics. A checklist of 208 mammal species contains 23 primates (including mountain gorilla, eastern lowland gorilla and common chimpanzee) along with species endemic to the DRC such as the okapi (page 6) and typical savannah-dwellers such as lion, elephant and buffalo.

Virunga National Park was established in 1925, and inscribed as a World Heritage Site in 1979. In its original incarnation as Albert National Park, it extended over just 200km², centred on the Virunga Mountains, but a series of boundary extensions over the next ten years meant it had more or less taken its modern shape by 1935. Since then, it has alternated between periods of conservation priority and high tourist volumes (notably during the late colonial era and over the 1970s and early 1980s) and periods of almost total neglect and abandonment. In 2010, after decades of being near-ungovernable, the park enjoyed an upsurge in fortune, one that saw the resumption of formal volcano climbs and of gorilla and chimp tracking, as well as the opening of a new upmarket lodge and tented camp in 2011. Sadly, hostilities in the region mean tourism at the park has been suspended for several lengthy periods since then, though tourist numbers rebounded impressively over the last sustained period when it was fully operational, with more than 6,000 visitors recorded in the busiest years.

The award-winning 2014 film *Virunga* raised the profile of the park considerably and brought to light some of the threats facing its future, including the distasteful but frighteningly possible prospect of oil drilling within the park. Along with the publicity generated by the film, pressure from local NGOs and civil society groups seems to have forced a moratorium on further exploration – the main investor pulled out in 2015 – but proposals to redraw the park's boundaries and place the drilling sites outside the park still retain support within the DRC government.

GETTING THERE AND AWAY Several local and international operators offer organised tours to Virunga National Park. These include those listed on pages 52 and 190, as well as the Rwandan operator Green Hills Eco-tours in Gisenyi (w greenhillsecotours.com). Accommodation, activities and transport within the park can also be booked through the website w visitvirunga.org or in person at the park's booking office in Goma (page 188).

WHERE TO STAY AND EAT *Map, page 210*
NOTE *Please note that information here reflects the situation prior to the closure of Virunga National Park in March 2020. None of the places listed below is open at the time of writing and it is possible that some have been destroyed by militia activity. However, should the park reopen during the lifespan of this edition, we expect that most if not all of these places will be restored to working condition.*

Of the options listed here, it's worth noting that Bukima Tented Camp, Lulimbi Tented Camp and Mikeno Lodge are considerably more expensive than almost anywhere else in the DRC, outside Kinshasa.

Bukima Tented Camp ⊕ −1.37989, 29.43434; w visitvirunga.org. Set at an altitude of 2,130m among cultivated fields bordering the national park, this upmarket tented camp is the ideal place to spend the night before gorilla tracking, as it is the starting point for visits to the groups living around Bukima. Mounts Karisimbi & Mikeno, the 2 tallest Virunga volcanoes, provide a dramatic backdrop, while panoramic views over the plains below include Nyiragongo smouldering on the horizon after dark. Each of the 6 standing tents is set on a shaded platform & comes with solar-heated shower, private terrace & wardrobe. Good meals & drinks are available. Bring warm clothes, as it can get cold at night (though the nightly campfires & hot-water bottles in your bed go a long way towards staving off the chill). **$$$$$**
Lulimbi Tented Camp ⊕ −0.51116, 29.67167; w visitvirunga.org. Lulimbi consists of 10 permanent tents set in the savannah alongside the Ishasha River, just a few kilometres south of where it flows into Lake Edward. It's about a 4hr

drive from the park headquarters at Rumangabo, though security concerns mean access is often more reliable by air or from the Ishasha border with Uganda. It's possible to spot waterbuck, elephant, buffalo & lion (among other wildlife) & there are plenty of hippos in the river. Guests can join chimp habituation walks & elephant monitoring patrols, as well as game drives & boat trips on the lake. **$$$$$**

Mikeno Lodge ⊕ −1.34263, 29.36275; w visitvirunga.org. Set at an altitude of 1,550m, this superb 12-room lodge stands alongside the park headquarters at Rumangabo, about 90mins' drive from Goma. Unlike any upmarket lodge in the Rwandan side of the Virungas, it is set in the heart of the rainforest, an environment teeming with monkeys & offering plenty of opportunities to birders. Accommodation is in large & stylishly decorated lava-block-&-thatch cottages, each with a king-size bed or twin beds, cosy sitting area with fireplace, en-suite hot shower & tub, & secluded private balcony. The raised dining & bar area has a large wooden balcony offering good views into the forest canopy. **$$$$$**

Tchegera Tented Camp ⊕ −1.64823, 29.11756; w visitvirunga.org. This exclave of the national park comprises a diminutive crescent-shaped island – the rim of a sunken volcanic caldera – situated in Lake Kivu just off the Bulenga Peninsula, some 12km from Goma. The 8 comfortably equipped standing tents are situated a few steps from the lakeshore & come with solar-heated showers. There are magnificent views from every corner of the startlingly green island, including across the water to the Nyiragongo & Nyamuragira volcanoes & their night-time blush. It's a great place to put your feet up after hiking in the park, & birders will have no trouble keeping themselves busy, but if you'd still like to get in a bit of a workout, there are paddleboards & kayaks available as well. **$$$$$**

Kibumba Tented Camp ⊕ −1.48399, 29.37274; w visitvirunga.org. Opened in 2017, this camp sits on a hilltop offering dramatic views to Nyiragongo from the open-sided fireplace lounge & bar. The 18 standing tents, set into a ridge leading back from the dining area, all have a private terrace overlooking the surrounding forest & come with solar-heated hot showers (quite welcome given an elevation just below 2,200m). The most budget-friendly option in the park, it represents excellent value for money, with

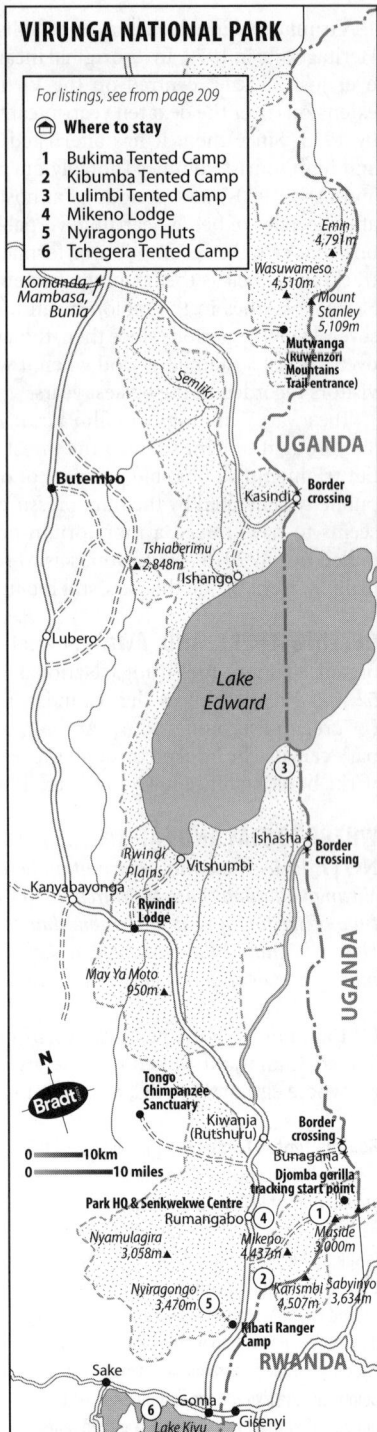

VIRUNGA NATIONAL PARK

For listings, see from page 209

⌂ **Where to stay**
1. Bukima Tented Camp
2. Kibumba Tented Camp
3. Lulimbi Tented Camp
4. Mikeno Lodge
5. Nyiragongo Huts
6. Tchegera Tented Camp

Emin 4,791m

Wasuwameso 4,510m

Komanda, Mambasa, Bunia

Mount Stanley 5,109m

Mutwanga (Kuwenzori Mountains Trail entrance)

Semliki

UGANDA

Butembo

Kasindi

Border crossing

Tshiaberimu ▲2,848m

Ishango

Lubero

Lake Edward

Rwindi Plains

Vitshumbi

Ishasha

Border crossing

Kanyabayonga

Rwindi Lodge

UGANDA

May Ya Moto 950m

Bradt

Tongo Chimpanzee Sanctuary

Kiwanja (Rutshuru)

Border crossing

Bunagana

Djomba gorilla tracking start point

0 — 10km
0 — 10 miles

Park HQ & Senkwekwe Centre
Rumangabo

Nyamulagira 3,058m▲

Mikeno 4,437m▲

Maside 3,000m

Nyiragongo 3,470m▲

Karismbi 4,507m

Sabyinyo 3,634m

Kibati Ranger Camp

Sake

RWANDA

Goma

Gisenyi

Lake Kivu

a level of service & meals comparable to its more expensive counterparts. **$$$$**

Nyiragongo Huts w visitvirunga.org. Perched at an altitude of 3,400m immediately outside the rim of Nyiragongo Crater, these 8 basic huts each contain 2 beds with waterproof mattresses but no bedding. A common drop toilet lies about 50m away. There are no cooking facilities & no food is provided, unless you arrange a packed meal with the park in advance. Use of the huts is included in the price of the Mount Nyiragongo hiking permit (page 213).

ACTIVITIES

Southern sector When the park is open, both gorilla and chimp tracking are available in the southern sector of the park, as is a stunning but tough hike to the top of Mount Nyiragongo, with its spectacular live lava lake. Permits for all activities can be booked online at w visitvirunga.org/shop, as can transport from Goma, along with applications for DRC visas. Permits and transport can also be booked in person at the park office in Goma (page 188). Permits are still normally available at short notice, except during the peak gorilla-tracking season (July–August), when the DRC's gorillas attract an overspill from Rwanda and Uganda. Advance booking may become necessary more often, especially with the US$1,100 price differential between here and Rwanda before Virunga closed.

Around Rumangabo Visitors to Mikeno Lodge (see opposite), which stands adjacent to the park headquarters, will find the surrounding forest offers plenty of opportunity for free primate viewing and birdwatching, whether from the small network of roads that encircles Rumangabo, or from the short walking trail that connects the lodge to the entrance gate. The most common **primates** here are the blue monkey, Rwenzori colobus and olive baboon, all of which are frequently seen in the lodge grounds or close to the main administration building in the headquarters. Wild chimps are also seen in the forest from time to time.

Birdlife is varied, and includes a wide range of forest specialists, most conspicuously perhaps Sladen's Barbet (a Congo endemic), white-headed wood-hoopoe, cinnamon-chested bee-eater, yellow-whiskered greenbul and grey-green bush-shrike. Other attractive forest residents that often draw attention through their calls include black-billed turaco, Ross's turaco, black-and-white casqued hornbill, double-toothed barbet, yellow-billed barbet, narrow-tailed starling and Sharpe's starling.

Set in a jungle clearing 5 minutes' walk from the lodge, the **Senkwekwe Centre** is the only facility in the world for orphaned mountain gorillas. It is named after the silverback Senkwekwe who was killed by gunmen, along with six other members of his group, in 2007. The 1ha enclosure has provided sanctuary to six orphaned gorillas including two females, Ndezi and Ndakasi, who survived the 2007 massacre. The orphans can be watched from several viewing platforms, but tourists are forbidden to enter the enclosure.

The **Congohounds** programme is also based at the park headquarters in Rumangabo, where specially trained bloodhounds and springer spaniels are used to patrol the park, tracking the scents of poachers and their contraband. Ask for a demonstration if you're staying at Mikeno Lodge – watching the bloodhounds track a ranger hundreds of metres based solely on a piece of ivory the ranger held is truly impressive, and even more so when you consider that the tracking done in the park will usually extend for kilometres, not metres!

Mount Nyiragongo A popular activity in Virunga National Park is the hike up the live volcano Nyiragongo, whose perfect cone rises above Goma and the

Since the 1990s, over 200 park rangers have lost their lives protecting wildlife in Virunga National Park. Many others have been kidnapped and mutilated. The perpetrators are the heavily armed militias who use the park as a hideout. With its sweeping forests for camouflage and abundant wildlife for poaching, the Virungas offer obvious attractions to the rebels. Hidden deep in the forests, they have easy access to all sorts of wildlife for both filling their own bellies and for ivory and other resources they can traffic to finance their activities; the fact that some of the animals they hunt are endangered species does not suppress their appetites.

Some 20 years ago, the park's Lake Edward was home to the world's most important hippo stocks. Then, there were almost 30,000 of them; now there are estimated to be just 300. The annihilation of the hippo population has been due to prolonged rebel activity around it. One Mai-Mai group planned the slaughter of the lake's hippos with military precision. During 2006, unchallenged and in broad daylight, fighters aboard motorboats, armed with AK47s, moved from pod to pod shooting hippos until, it is said, the waters of Lake Edward turned red with their blood. Meat and ivory (from the animal's long canine teeth) were then sold, with the profits used to purchase more arms. This was neither an unusual nor an isolated incident.

Such scenes might seem impossible to imagine happening in a national park elsewhere, but Virunga National Park is far from typical. Over 3,000 square miles of jungle, forest and savannah, and the wildlife within it, are protected against thousands of armed rebels by only 770 rangers. Little wonder that hippo, elephant and buffalo numbers in the park were able to fall so low.

Recognising the impossible odds stacked up against the rangers in their efforts to protect endangered wildlife, a collaborative initiative in 2007 between ICCN and several international wildlife organisations addressed them. Robert Muir, formerly Africa Director for the Frankfurt Zoological Society (w fzs.org), explained: 'In their work protecting wildlife in the Virungas, the rangers haven't lacked commitment or bravery – they've lacked training and tools. Our mission has been to help fill the gaps in the rangers' resources and provide practical support in the provision of training and equipment.'

The Virunga rangers now attend six months of pre-deployment training, including humanitarian aid, training in human rights and other legal aspects, combat tactics and advanced first aid. Only 50% of participants pass the training course. In 2022, the rangers conducted 4,500 patrols. Their work is supported by aerial surveillance. Better equipped and better trained, the Congo Rangers have more of a fighting chance than ever before. But they still face incredible risks. To fully protect the wildlife that inhabits the world's most dangerous national park, more men, more training and more equipment are needed. The families of fallen rangers receive pensions, free schooling and free health care from the national park.

Lake Kivu shore to an altitude of 3,470m. One of Africa's most active volcanoes, Nyiragongo's eruptions caused devastation in the 19th and 20th centuries, before the eruptions of 2002 and 2021 devastated the city of Goma. The hike to the top passes the subsidiary cone formed by one of the recent eruptions. At the top, sheer windswept cliffs plummet into the nested main crater, which is at least 600m deep and has an average diameter of 1.2km. At the heart of this immense natural cauldron, a circular lake of live lava bubbles, its surface pattern ceaselessly mutating as blackened crusts of magma collide, crumble and melt, spewing bright red flumes of molten rock tens of metres into the air. It is a thrilling, mesmerising spectacle, especially towards dusk, when the glowing lava eerily illuminates a swirling red mist – no less so because the violent heat of the lava lake contrasts so strikingly with the chilly windy conditions on the crater rim and with the more tranquil view south over the lights of Goma on the Kivu shore.

The standard trip runs overnight, with participants sleeping in one of the huts on the rim, which is highly recommended as the view of the lava lake is most spectacular at dusk and after dark. However, it is possible to hike there and back in a day, and a one-day trip can usually be organised upon request. Hikers should bring all the food and liquid they will need; there are no cooking facilities at the top and you should bank on at least 3–4 litres of water per person. The huts have mattresses, but it can be very cold and windy at the top; a sleeping bag is required, as is a good fleece and rain jacket, hiking boots or sturdy walking shoes, plenty of warm clothes (ideally including gloves), and a change of clothes in case of rain. Before Virunga National Park closed, tour operators offered options with packed meals and water, known as a 'half backpack', and meals, water and cold-weather gear (sleeping bag, jacket, etc), known as a 'full backpack'. A torch (flashlight), ideally a headtorch, is also essential; the light on your phone won't last overnight. Once on the edge of the crater, do step cautiously: in 2007, a tourist died after falling into the crater while taking photographs.

The hike starts at **Kibati Ranger Camp** (⊕ 1°34'08.2"S, 29°16'44.9"E), about 15km from Goma on the west side of the main road to Rumangabo. It is only 6.3km from here to the rim, but it is a steep climb, starting at an altitude of 2,000m and gaining more than 1,400m, and the ascent takes around 4–6 hours, depending less on your individual fitness than on the overall fitness of the party (all hikers on any given day are expected to stick together for security reasons), as well as how acclimatised they are to high altitudes, and the duration of the customary breaks at each of the four 'posts' along the route.

The first 2.5km, from Kibati to Post One, follows a flattish trail that is generally easy underfoot through an area of montane forest, and takes around 40 minutes. The second stage to Post Two (2,533m) is steeper: a 1.1km, 20–30-minute ascent of the scree-strewn southeastern slope of the dormant subsidiary cone created by the 2002 eruption. From here, it is slightly less than 1km to Post Three (2,762m), a 20–30-minute ascent along an old lava flow to the base of the main cone, which rises a daunting near-45° angle ahead. The toughest leg follows, gaining almost 500m over 1.3km, a 60–90-minute hike that brings you to Post Four (3,235m), site of a ruined old mountain hut. En route, the trail passes some active steam vents (emanating from what is presumably a subterranean magma flow connecting the main crater to the subsidiary cone), as well as running through some stunning fields of giant lobelia, and offering views over the 2002 crater to Lake Kivu. From Post Four, the breathlessly steep scramble up the final 400m of loose rocks leading to the crater rim should take 20–30 minutes.

When the park was open, up to 16 overnight volcano permits were issued daily, corresponding to the number of beds in the eight double huts at the rim, and these cost US$300 for foreign adults, US$175 for foreign children and US$90 for adult DRC citizens. Check-in at the Kibati Ranger Camp started at 09.00, which meant you needed to leave Goma about an hour earlier, and most hikers were back at the base by around 10.00 the next day. Porters could be hired to carry up to

15kg of luggage each. Individual hikers need to pay for transport between Goma and Kibati, which can be arranged through the park website or booking office in Goma. Transport can also be arranged through any tour operator in Goma. Budget travellers looking to save some dollars can get from Goma to the entrance by motorbike taxi. Even seasoned hikers tend to suffer some leg stiffness after the steep ascent, so Nyiragongo is best saved for after other activities such as gorilla or chimpanzee tracking, which will also give you time to adjust to the altitude.

Gorilla tracking Virunga National Park offers a mountain gorilla tracking experience comparable in quality and in most other respects to that of neighbouring Rwanda. Seven gorilla groups are habituated to tourist visits, with six permits being issued daily for larger groups, and four for smaller groups, creating a total availability of 36 permits daily. Ten of these permits apply to two gorilla groups based in the area around Djomba, which lies close to the Ugandan border and is most normally visited as a day trip from the Ugandan town of Kisoro (and falls outside the scope of this guidebook). Another 20 permits apply to four groups that are normally tracked from Bukima Tented Camp, which lies on the slopes of Mount Mikeno about 90 minutes' drive from Mikeno Lodge and twice that distance from Goma. There is now also one recently habituated group that can be tracked from near Kibumba Tented Camp (page 210).

Gorilla-tracking permits for Virunga National Park cost US$400 (or US$150 for DRC citizens), more affordable than the US$800 charged in Uganda, and far cheaper

DIAN FOSSEY

The eminent gorilla researcher Dian Fossey began her career in the Congo at probably the worst possible time to do so. During the incursions of white mercenaries into the east, the rise of Mobutu Sese Seko, and persistent tribal conflict across the region, she set up a small camp at the foot of Mount Mikeno in Albert Park (now Virunga National Park) where she conducted the research for which she became legendary. It was not long until she was detained, as Mobutu, having recently taken control of the army, began a crackdown on all foreigners inside the country assuming they were spies. Her camp was dismantled and she was taken down to Rumangabo, where she was held for two weeks. Reports of her treatment vary wildly, and so does the story of how she left the Congo – by her accounts she was denied permission to leave and escaped through Bunagana, aided by a friendly priest; by other accounts she was formally kicked out. At any event she spent less than six weeks in the country as the security situation disintegrated further.

She would begin her research again on the Rwandan side of Mount Mikeno. Her studies and the subsequent work of her foundation have done much to assist in the protection of Congolese gorillas, making a positive impact on conservation efforts in both Virunga and Kahuzi-Biega parks.

Most biographies of Dian Fossey deal in some depth with her time in the Congo during the 1960s. Her autobiography, *Gorillas in the Mist*, also turned into a movie starring Sigourney Weaver, touches on her initial difficulties in the Congo. Also worth reading is the *Dark Romance of Dian Fossey*, which spends a dozen pages explaining the factors that led to her leaving the country. It's also worth visiting the website of her foundation, the Dian Fossey Gorilla Fund International (w gorillafund.org).

than the US$1,500 asked in Rwanda. An even better deal was to be had from 15 March to 15 May and 15 October to 15 December, when low-season permits were available for only US$200. The experience is broadly similar to tracking in Rwanda, with the same 1-hour limit imposed on tourist visits, but the setting is a lot more remote and underutilised – indeed, there are still days when nobody goes tracking at Bukima. In addition, there is the option of overnighting at the magnificently located Bukima Tented Camp before you track, which really sets the tone for the adventure. For independent travellers, the logistics of reaching Bukima are more complicated than getting to Kinigi (the base for tracking in Rwanda) and transport costs are higher, but the increased price of permits in Rwanda means Virunga is now an unambiguously better choice for the budget-minded.

Chimp tracking Since 1993, the only chimpanzee tracking within Virunga National Park (when it is open) is with a habituated group resident near the park headquarters at Rumangabo. Tracking starts at 06.00 from Mikeno Lodge and, given the distances involved from any other accommodation, this means that participants are restricted to guests staying at the lodge. Hikers set out in groups of four or fewer, and time with the chimps is limited to 1 hour. Note that the chimps at Rumangabo will occasionally migrate in and out of tracking range, so visits are sometimes cancelled because of the chimps' movements; the Virunga park website indicates whether they're currently in the area or not.

Further afield The activities described previously all take place at the southern end of the national park, but there are many undeveloped attractions further afield, their potential unrealised because of decades of low-level war. A few dozen kilometres northwest of Rumangabo, Tongo is a 10km^2 block of medium-altitude forest isolated from other similar habitats by lava flows. Traversed by an 80km network of walking trails, Tongo was home to a community of around 35 chimpanzees first habituated by the Frankfurt Zoological Society (FZS) and opened to tourism in the late 1980s. Since 1993, apart from a couple of years between 2010 and 2012, Tongo has been closed to visitors because of security risks. Also in the Tongo forest are the Tongo Hippo Pools, where around 100 hippos lived in water so clear you could see them under the surface. It is likely, however, that the chimpanzees and the hippos have been poached to local extinction in the last three decades of conflict.

Northern sector Note that all areas of the northern sector of the park are off-limits to visitors at the time of writing.

Rwindi Plains The plains are a beautiful savannah surrounded by towering mountains to their west and east, and Lake Edward to the north. It feels like a slice of Katanga dropped on the far eastern border, with rolling grasslands and long periods of sunlight. Winding streams among the plains create ideal refuges for hippo populations. Lion, leopard and elephant also thrive here.

Poaching and rebel activity have taken their toll on populations in Rwindi. Animal populations that used to be in the thousands now are often in the hundreds. This is true for big game that is often targeted by illegal hunting, and the elephant population is said to hover around only 400 at the moment. Hippos are at dangerously low levels, a shocking decline as in the past streams were literally clogged with them. When the author first passed through, the area had massive antelope populations and the road was often blocked by groups of baboons.

There have been confirmed sightings of lions, but as they are nocturnal and the area is vast, seeing one is unlikely. Waterbuck, buffalo, jackal and warthog are also common in the area.

The plains occupy several hundred square kilometres and have dozens of vehicle trails criss-crossing the savannah. It is possible, when the region is safe, to head to **Vitshumbi** (⊕ 00°41.57 S, 09°22.26 E) to view bird and hippo populations in addition to plains animals. While hippo can sometime be seen along the river, Lake Edward is their usual haunt. Ishango tends to be a better option for viewing them, however.

On the road northwest towards Kanyabayonga the track winds up the mountains and provides an excellent panorama of the entire plains. There is a **plaque** here that commemorates the building of the road, replacing an old trade route used by caravans. The road was completed in 1931, and 2007 may have been the first time it saw any maintenance.

Practicalities The **Rwindi Lodge** is no longer in use and there are no plans to open it to tourists anytime soon. If it ever reopens, it has about a dozen private thatch bungalows that date back to the days of the Belgian Congo, and a main structure where meals could be served, as well as a bar and pool.

Mount Tshiaberimu Incorporated into Virunga National Park in 1938 and once called Kiavirumu or 'mountain of the spirit', this is a unique ecological zone in the Albertine Rift – and the most important area of flora in the hills west of Lake Edward. The lowland vegetation of bamboo forest gives way to deep coniferous foliage and patches of flowers at higher altitudes. This 2,848m mountain southeast of Butembo, with views of Lake Edward, is a beautiful sight in its own right in the impressive eastern ranges along the border. However, most importantly it is the home of mountain gorillas, one group of which was habituated to human presence in 2001. At last count there were 22 gorillas and one was born in 2006 – he was called 'Musomboli', Swahili for 'Voter', as he was born in August that year when DRC voters were going to the polls.

As is often the case in the DRC, the gorilla population here has taken a nosedive in recent decades. The original survey of gorilla populations here in 1931 put their numbers at 20,000 – while widely considered to be an overestimation, the reduction in numbers is still drastic. A 1963 survey which counted 80 individuals seems more realistic. This major depopulation is more unfortunate than usual since the gorillas of this mountain boast unique features; research is ongoing as to whether they are lowland gorillas, proper mountain gorillas or a unique subspecies. They have even been given their own scientific name, *Gorilla gorilla tshiaberimuensis*. The altitude of their habitat is above 2,800m; it is considered the smallest isolated gorilla population in the world.

Good news does exist in Tshiaberimu, however, as a decade's worth of conservation efforts have led to the local population, the gorilla's biggest threat, reducing their incursions into the remaining wilderness. The gorillas were originally identified as being at risk in 1995, when they numbered only 17. Tourism has been established as a primary goal to drive home the value of these creatures to the economic well-being of the surrounding population in addition to retaining their natural heritage.

Practicalities Mount Tshiaberimu can be reached from a winding road southeast of Butembo. The central taxi stand is also a good place to hire out a car for the day, and should cost around US$50. The road is not good, however, and it will likely be easier with motorbikes – the distance is only a few dozen kilometres, so it shouldn't be too painful. First you need to reach the village of **Burusi**, then 12km later follow a connecting road to reach the base camp called **Kalibina** where there is some basic accommodation. There is also a winding road for 46km here along Lake Edward from Ishango, though this will take longer and transport is not as easy to find.

At the foot of the mountain there is an ICCN station where permits are sold, for US$250 a day. As usual this includes a guide and armed guards. They only accept six visitors each day, and prior bookings can be made in Beni or Ishango.

Ishango (✛ 00°08.14 S, 29°36.10 E) Following the River Semuliki southward along a road from the Beni–Kasindi border into Virunga National Park, you arrive at the quiet northern shores of Lake Edward. This area was not caught in nearly as much combat as the southern coast, though in recent years has still had problems with rebel activity. It is known as a prime spot for birdwatching, as several species migrate here at various times of the year. Lake Edward is one of the few places in the DRC which still has a population of hippos. Avoid swimming, however, as hippos are aggressive; there are also crocodiles in the lake.

The countryside around Ishango is home to many of the animals that can be seen in Rwindi, including forest elephants, antelopes and baboons. Some of the more common birds are eagles, herons, cormorants, storks and pelicans. When the skies are clear there are great views of the mountains that line the western shore of Lake Edward, as well as the Rwenzoris to the north. Fishing tours are also popular here, or another option is to visit the village of **Kiavinyonge**, immediately west of Ishango (✛ 00°09.08 S, 29°33.17 E), where the villagers go out every morning on their boats. The archaeological site of Ishango is where the 'Ishango Bone', with its mysterious engravings, was discovered (page 15).

Practicalities Ishango is reached from **Kasindi** (✛ 00°02.33 N, 29°42.52 E) on the Ugandan border, and is along a 30km road south from the main road to **Beni**. From Beni it is quite feasible to reach here as well, but via motorbike, unless walking the 30km from the main road sounds like fun – there is usually a minibus service direct to the border from Beni. The **Ishango Lodge** is run by ICCN and has about eight bungalows; at the last check it was open for business. They charge US$50 per person for a visitor's permit, and the lodge is US$25 per night. Check in Beni before you make the trip, however, as there are problems with armed militias around Ishango.

THE RWENZORI MOUNTAINS

The Rwenzori range is Africa's most mysterious. Generations of explorers passed them by without noticing them, as they are often shrouded in cloud. It was not until 1888 that Henry Morton Stanley, at the foot of the mountains on a clear day, noted them in European records.

The Rwenzoris are not volcanic. They were created by the Albertine Rift, tectonic plates pushing up against each other in Africa's Great Lakes region. These are the only mountains in Africa with glaciers. The continent's other highest peaks, Kilimanjaro and Mount Kenya, see regular snowfall, but permanent icepacks elude them. In the Rwenzoris you ascend above the cloud cover to a different world entirely – strange primeval vegetation grows to unreal sizes in the higher elevations. Often-frozen lakes provide freshwater streams to villages below. Unique birdlife is in abundance across the mountainsides. And some of Africa's most difficult climbs are on Mount Stanley (Mont Ngaliema).

The range has been well developed for tourism, and is seeing a resurgence in interest due to its proximity to the Ugandan border and a well-marked trail to two of its peaks. The highest peak, Margherita, is still very much for experienced alpinists, however.

HISTORY The Rwenzoris were the famous 'mountains of the moon' that traders from ancient times spoke of when arriving in Egypt from sub-Saharan Africa. Ptolemy included them in his map of Africa during the 2nd century CE; they were widely considered to be the source of the Nile River until the mid 20th century.

The range was first spotted by people in Henry Morton Stanley's company when they passed through the region in April 1888, during the so-called 'Emin Pasha Relief Expedition' (Emin Pasha was the governor of an Ottoman-Egyptian province that bordered the northern shores of Lake Albert). Two members of the expedition saw the glaciers of the range in the distance after assuming them to be unusual clouds. They recorded the mountains and reported them to Stanley. Until this time, the existence of the Rwenzoris had been doubted by Western Africanists.

It was not until the following year, when the surviving members of Stanley's expedition returned to the region, with Emin Pasha and his followers, that an attempt was made on one of the summits. Emin Pasha and Stanley's military commander, William Grant Stairs, began the climb in June 1889. They started from Katuba, but lacked the proper equipment to reach the summit, and turned back at 3,200m.

In 1891, Emin Pasha returned with the eminent German naturalist Franz Stuhlmann, to explore the region west of Lake Albert. As part of this expedition, they confirmed the existence of the glaciers and ascended Mount Stanley. They had a camp at the base of the mountains, in the valley of Butahu, which they nicknamed the 'Camp of Bottles', referred to in local languages as Kampi ya Chuba. It remains a visiting point to this day. They left a bottle here, and subsequent visitors added to the collection.

In 1906, the Duke of Abrizzi, an Italian, came well prepared with a team that made the first ascents of Margherita. The first attempt from the Belgian side of the mountains did not come until 1932, when a scientific team led by Count Xavier de Grünne arrived. It was on this expedition that the entire range was finally surveyed.

Tourism was big on the Zairian side of the border throughout the Mobutu period, but Mai-Mai rebels moved in during the late 1990s, which essentially shut down the tourist business. They are still there.

ORIENTATION The Rwenzori Mountains run along a south–north axis which forms the border between Uganda and the DRC. The range consists of six major mountains, with Mount Stanley (its official name is Mont Ngaliema) being the highest and most important for visitors from the Congolese side. Mount Stanley itself has several smaller ridges; from south to north: **Mugule** (4,450m), **Wasuwameso** (4,510m) and **Moraine** (4,350m), which can be visited en route to the main peak, **Margherita** (5,109m), Mount Stanley's highest point. Other peaks on Mount Stanley, from north to south, are **Albert** (5,087m), **Alexandra** (5,091m), **Moebius** (4,916m), **Elena** (4,968m), **Savoia** (4,971m), **Elizabeth** (4,928m) and **Philip** (4,920m). On a clear day, all are visible from Wasuwameso or Moraine.

The trail up to the peaks is well marked, and reasonably well maintained. It takes three days to reach the **Kiondo Hut**, where the trail splits, to continue to either Wasuwameso ridge for some spectacular views of Mount Stanley and its peaks, weather permitting, or to head east for a day to **Moraine Hut** (4,495m), which passes by some frozen lakes and, while about 100m lower than Wasuwameso, gets closer to Peak Margherita. This is also the staging ground for heading out to the glaciers.

THE TRAIL From the ICCN station at **Mutsora** (1,700m), the first day's walking is through dense scrub forest typical of the lowlands of the Albertine Rift. Huge trees covered in moss begin to envelop the trail as it winds along the valley of the Butahu River, crossing numerous streams as they flow into the river from their originating points along Mount Mugule. It takes roughly 5 hours to reach the first hut, **Kalonge** (2,138m). From the hut there are striking views of the valley to be had.

Continuing onward across another major stream, the Nwamwamba, the trail runs into numerous steep sections, covered in mud and roots and vines, the entire region teeming with thick moss of many colours. The lowland bamboo forests give way to massive heather trees, and the temperature begins to shift drastically as the trail finds its way into the cloud systems that continually blanket the mountains and where the humidity rises significantly. Unique birdlife begins to emerge, and the day ends when arriving at **Mahangu Hut** (3,310m). This is generally considered the hardest part of the trail, and should take around 5 hours. There is usually fresh water available here from the mountain streams.

From Mahangu the trail continues north into the cold alpine air, and it can often get blocked by snowfall. The route is covered with huge roots of the heather trees and ascends sharply. It is along this stretch of trail that the heather trees shift to the strange, huge flowers that the Rwenzori range is known for. It's a curious botanical wonderland of beautiful saturated colours, massive foliage of species that most people would assume could only grow as large as a palm and certainly not at these altitudes. This is also where the trail ascends above the near-permanent cloud cover, and the entire region becomes enrobed in a moist fog. Water can be heard flowing under the moss. After about 4 hours you come to the **Camp of Bottles** (4,030m), the historic staging ground for ascents in the region. Another hour's hiking onward reveals the next hut, **Kiondo** (4,200m), and the trail splits from here. The nights get mighty cold from here on and the hut is often blindsided by high winds. The hut has a beautiful view of **Lac Noir** (Black Lake; 3,757m) to the southeast, down the mountain. There are also great views of other peaks in the region: Alexandra, Moebius, Elena and Savoia.

From Kiondo it is most common to continue the ascent north to **Wasuwameso** (4,510m), only an hour or so along the trail, and take photos of Peak Margherita before descending back to Kiondo – or rushing back to Mahangu, as Kiondo can be an uncomfortable place to spend the night.

If you have a bit more time, from Kiondo you can continue northeast – crossing a glacier and following the trail along the often frozen lakes, **Lac Vert** (Green Lake; 4,157m) and **Lac Gris** (Grey Lake; 4,253m). This route requires winter climbing gear – ice-axes, crampons and the like. Part of the trail is quite slippery and requires hanging on to a cable that's been installed. Some guides might not be experienced with this stuff: make sure yours is. The vegetation dissipates into dirt, a clear alpine trail, with the massive flowers seen only a few hundred metres below now disappearing to be replaced mostly by lichen. The hike should take around 3 hours to the final hut, **Moraine**, a small and beat-up old cabin that visitors dread staying in. There is also room for camping on the shores of Lac Gris, which could be a better option provided you have a tent to pitch. This can be done in a round trip for the day, finishing again at Kiondo, or if you're really quick about it, spending the night in Mahangu. The descent from Mahangu to Mutsora should take only a full day.

Beyond Moraine are the permanent glaciers, as well as the climbing routes to reach Peak Alexandra and Peak Margherita, which are definitely not intended for hikers. The permanent glacier begins at about 4,800m, an hour's hike from the

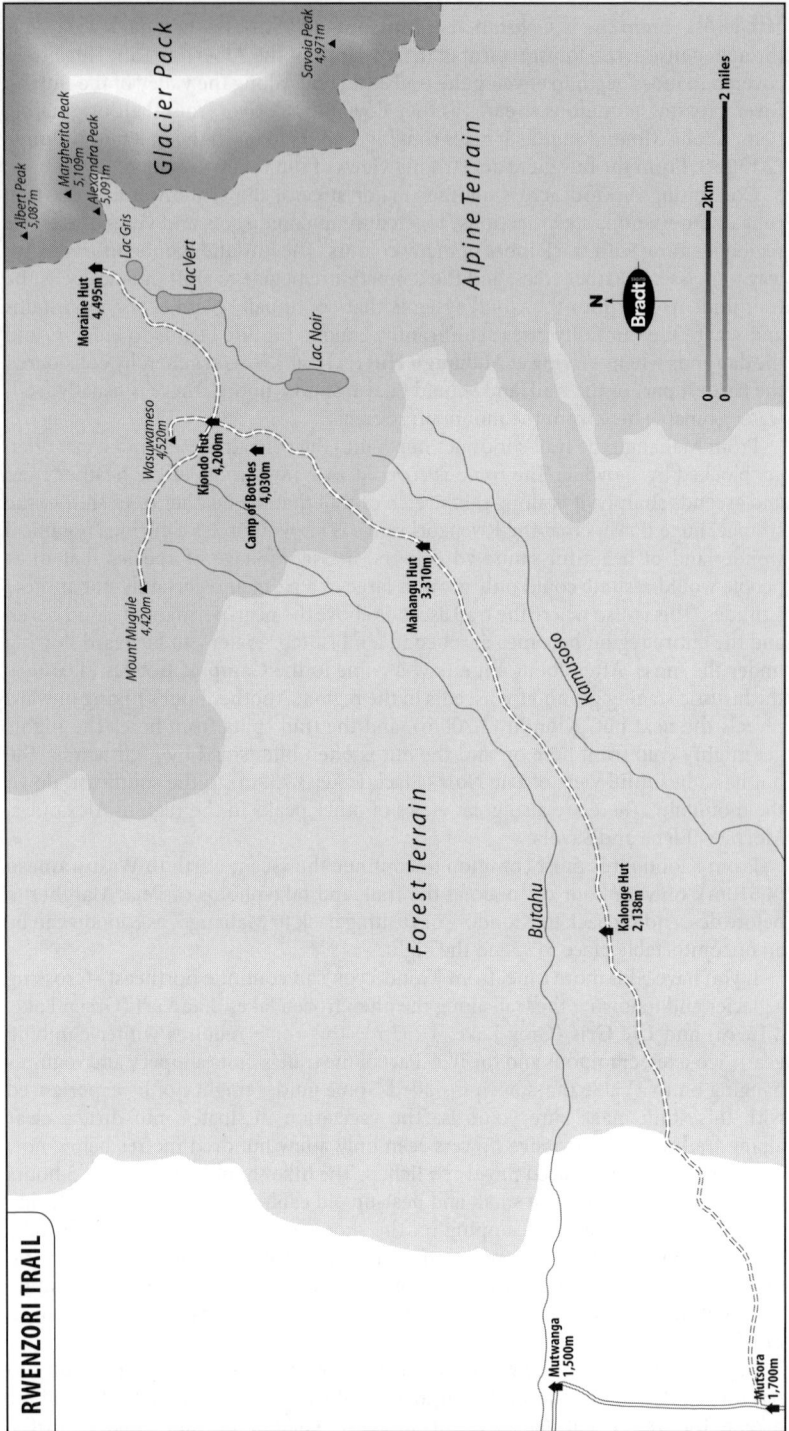

RWENZORI TRAIL

Glacier Pack

Albert Peak
5,087m
▲ Margherita Peak
5,109m
▲ Alexandra Peak
5,091m

Savoia Peak
4,971m ▲

Lac Gris

Lac Vert

Moraine Hut
4,495m

Lac Noir

Wasuwameso
4,520m ▲

Kiondo Hut
4,200m

Camp of Bottles
4,030m

Mount Mugule
4,420m ▲

Alpine Terrain

Mahangu Hut
3,310m

Kamusoso

Forest Terrain

Butahu

Kalonge Hut
2,138m

N

Bradt

0   2km
0   2 miles

Mutwanga
1,500m

Mutsora
1,700m

220

Moraine Hut. Continue north along the base of Peak Alexandra, with Peak Albert coming into view. Between Alexandra and Albert is the Congolese route to Peak Margherita, by all accounts harder than the Ugandan route. It is also possible to continue east between the Alexandra and Moebius peaks to reach Margherita from the Ugandan side. From Moraine to the peak is another two days' hiking.

PRACTICALITIES From Beni or Kasindi you must get to the village of **Mutwanga** (⊕ 00°20.27 N, 29°44.59 E) at the foot of the mountains and then continue a few kilometres up a vanishing and rocky route to the ICCN station at **Mutsora** (⊕ 00°19.03 N, 29°44.45 E). Mutsora is seeing an infusion of money which includes funds for major renovations to their once-dilapidated offices as well as several bungalows at the foot of the mountain. From here you can buy a permit at US$300 per person for the ascent. This should include a guide, though they'll probably want some tips later on, and it's unlikely they will speak English. The huts have fireplaces and bunk beds, though Kiondo and Moraine are in desperate need of some maintenance. If you can bring some plastic to hang over the windows, which are often broken, it will make your sleeping much easier. Bring a mummy-style sleeping bag.

Naturally, if you are doing any hiking off the main trail, such as making an attempt on Peak Margherita, you'll need to bring all of your own equipment – as you may have guessed, there is no mountaineering store in either Mutwanga or Beni. If you are going to spend any serious time on the mountains, I recommend picking up the book by Henry Osmaston, *Guide to the Rwenzori: Mountains of the Moon*. Also take a detailed elevation map with climbing routes, if you can find one.

RUTSHURU

The district of Rutshuru, filling the corner between the border of Uganda and Virunga National Park to the west, is one of the most lawless and dangerous districts of the DRC at the time of this update. In the 2023 polls, it was one of only three districts in the entire country where the elections were not held because of the security risk, to voters and polling staff alike. The largest village you pass through, if it ever becomes safe to pass through, is Kiwanja, a simple one-road town with large trucks parked on the roadside in the evenings, and sprawling suburbs of dirt trails and mud huts stretching into the jungle. It's also a good place to catch a minibus further north to Kanyabayonga, Lubero and Butembo, or east to Bunagana.

Near Kiwanja are the **Rutshuru Falls**, buried in the jungle on a turn-off from the main road to Goma, just past the road east to Bunagana. At 30km north on the road to the Rwindi Plains Lodge is the volcano of **May Ya Moto** (950m), whose underground geothermal activity has created some **hot springs** along the river to the right of the road – boiling mud rather than a relaxing spa experience.

WHERE TO STAY AND EAT For lodging, the best rooms in town, with en-suite bathrooms and running water, are just past the park checkpoint at **Busanza Guesthouse** (10 rooms; sgl **$**, camping **$**). **Hôtel Grefamu** (**$**) at the north end of town just off the main road is the oldest place in town and certainly looks like it. Rooms are basic but have mosquito nets and either shared or en-suite bathrooms, with running water for US$10 more. Across the street is **Hôtel Kathatha** (22 rooms; sgl **$**) with no en-suite bathrooms. They have three double rooms (**$**) and three apartments (**$$**). There is also a restaurant here, and another one a short distance to the south, with fish dishes. Finally the **Centre d'Accueil Protestant** has more simple rooms (sgl **$**), and if you get there on a Saturday, there is usually a wedding going on – try to be the guest of honour and get a free drink.

BUNAGANA (✛ *01°17.57 S, 29°35.47 E*)

This small village at the foot of a volcano could be your first taste of the DRC, if you have arrived here for gorilla trekking. It's certainly nothing spectacular, little different from the frontier on the other side, criss-crossed with dirt roads and barely any vehicles compared with the relative affluence of Uganda. Hopefully you've stocked up on supplies on the other side of the border; the only things to buy in Bunagana are charge cards for a mobile phone, and fresh fruit.

WHERE TO STAY AND EAT Just past the border crossing, **Chez Mama Kennedy** (6 rooms; **$**) has basic single rooms with a shared washroom. They can also cook up some simple meals, and arrange transport up to the trekking sites. If you follow the road west towards Kiwanja the nearby Protestant church in the village of Tshengerero has purchased a **campsite** on the right-hand side of the road, easily noticed by its concrete signage out front. It's in the middle of rolling hills with basic washrooms and a restaurant, and should charge less than US$10 for an evening.

BUTEMBO

Butembo is one of the DRC's most affluent towns, surrounded by almost nothing; an oasis of prosperity in the mountains of the east. New office blocks have gone up along the wide thoroughfare that cuts through town, and beautiful new mansions fill the suburbs, with green hills and even, on occasion, well-maintained lawns. Shining new vehicles dot the otherwise motorcycle-clogged streets of the town; shops are filled to the brim with sandals and luggage, clothes and cheap electronics from Indonesia. The reason for all this prosperity is mining.

As far back as the 1920s, there was a gold mine in Butembo. Nowadays, the city's wealth comes from illegal artisan mining within the northern sector of Virunga National Park – gold, still, but also the components of coltan, used by almost all of us in our phones and computers. Those exploiting these resources are armed militia groups, mainly the Islamist ADF. The minerals pass through Butembo and other border towns, from where they are smuggled into Rwanda or Uganda. The profits finance the ADF's weapons, but also the new mansions and cars in Butembo.

GETTING THERE AND AWAY Butembo is served by minibuses from Goma and Beni, although note that this road, the N2, is very dangerous. M23 fighters control several towns along it, including, as of June 2024, **Lubero**. If you want to visit Butembo, it is much safer to fly. At the time of writing, Busy Bee Congo (**w** busybeecongo. com) operates four flights a week between Goma, Butembo and Beni. As ever in the DRC, the best way to check whether flights are operating is to go to the airport and ask there.

WHERE TO STAY Butembo has several hotels, mostly in the thrifty and budget price ranges.

Hôtel Butembo (26 rooms) 100 Av Président de la République; **m** 099 877 7924. Right in the city centre, but set back from the main road, quieter than one might expect from the location. Secure parking, free airport pick-up, large bar-restaurant with Congolese menu. Electricity early mornings & evenings; 24hr hot water, theoretically. Hotel buildings set around a courtyard & tropical gardens, with animal statues here & there. Rooms tiled & clean; some share bathrooms, others en suite. **$–$$**

BENI

Situated in a lowland region of the Great Rift Valley that divides the DRC from its eastern neighbours, Beni's surrounding countryside shows hints of the deep Ituri rainforest which envelops the region just a few dozen kilometres north. It's not as cold as Butembo or Lubero, with warm nights that can be spent in a few nightclubs around the city.

This is the northernmost city of the province of Kivu-Nord. Before the security problems that continued to plague eastern DRC at the time of writing, it was one of the most tourist-friendly towns in the country and, in the past, it saw plenty of visitors plying the overland route around Virunga National Park and onward into Uganda. Beni is an easy place to navigate, with a single north–south road where visitors can find pretty much everything they may want.

GETTING THERE AND AWAY At the time of writing, Busy Bee Congo (**w** busybeecongo.com) operates four flights a week between Goma, Butembo and

WHERE T-SHIRTS GO TO DIE

An interesting detail of the DRC's hinterlands is the millions of cast-off pieces of clothing that have made their way to a final resting place of sorts deep in the jungle. Since their country receives large shipments of aid from the wider world, the Congolese dress themselves in the gifts given to them – which more often than not are the pieces of clothing that no-one wants.

It becomes obvious that these people do not know, or even care, what may appear on their shirts and clothes. This may seem surprising in a country where so many people pay close attention to their appearance, but the DRC's poorest cannot even indulge in that luxury.

In Beni some years ago I encountered a younger fellow wearing a Home Depot shirt, intended as a uniform for employees there; it had a patch stencilled on to it, proudly sporting the name 'Matt'. His name was, indeed, not Matt; and he had no idea what Home Depot was in the first place. It was simply a clean shirt, one he bought at the market, for a low price.

Numerous other relics of Western culture pop up on the backs of the Congolese: television shows from the 1980s (*Alf*, anyone?), strange Christian festivals held around the world, excess volunteer shirts for any number of random organisations; shirts from rock bands that have come and gone, shirts from bankrupt businesses. Their meanings can be bizarre reminders of the global intervention that has always been a hallmark of the Congo Free State, and sometimes they can be an inadvertent reminder of how impoverished many millions of Congolese are. At a refugee camp in Bunia I spotted a man wearing a Nine Inch Nails shirt that on the back read 'Now I'm Nothing'.

Poke around at local market stalls and you'll find cast-offs from parts of the world that one might never associate with the DRC. Ask the people where they got them, and they may simply shrug. It's clothing, and since most of them can't read English, the colours and patterns are far more important than whatever it may mean to a random foreign visitor passing through.

Beni. As ever in the DRC, the best way to check what flights there are, and when, is to go to the airport and ask there. Cetraca, which used to serve Beni, suspended its operations in 2024 after its latest accident.

Shared taxis to Butembo take about 2 hours. Minibuses to Bunia leave at sunrise (06.00).

⌂ WHERE TO STAY

Albertine Hôtel Beni (28 rooms) Bd Nyamwisi; m 097 086 8032. 10mins from airport; secure. Has pool, good restaurant, terrace bar, gardens; electricity at set times, hot water; Wi-Fi; gym, pool table. Good-sized, comfortable, en-suite rooms, at various price-points; b/fast inc. **$$–$$$**

Centre d'Accueil Protestant 28 Av Atsongia; m 099 431 3440. Basic but clean rooms, in bungalows set in gardens. Water tank, hot water on request, electricity in evenings. B/fast inc, set lunch (**$**) can be ordered. **$**

ITURI

In the far northeastern corner of the DRC, Ituri is a rolling region of lush rainforest barely penetrated by civilisation. Living in and around the dense jungles are communities of the indigenous Pygmy people. Villages and even towns are connected only by footpaths. And if they have survived the depradations of armed commercial poachers, there are many iconic animals. Ituri conjures up dreams and myths of the deep African rainforest, and it lives up to these expectations in many ways. From the air, you can see how undeveloped the countryside is, compared with other agrarian regions in Africa. Winding along the battered dirt trails on a motorbike, surrounded by towering trees, is a highlight for the adventurous traveller.

Yet Ituri has a long and sad history of conflicts – see page 36 for background to the so-called Ituri Conflict. The deep forests are full of heavily armed militia groups who are responsible for most of the poaching and mining that goes on there, the proceeds of which pay for their weapons. They burn down villages that stand in their way and kill villagers just for belonging to a different ethnic group. Thousands of people have fled and survive as best they can in refugee camps or precarious housing in the cities. The province has been under a 'state of siege' (*état de siège*) since 2021 (page 41).

CANNIBALISM

Cannibalism has, perhaps, been one of the most insidious things to emerge from the darkest equatorial jungles since the end of the Congo wars and the escalation of the Ituri Conflict. In a nation where the powers of sorcery and magic are still very much believed by the vast majority of the population, killing an adversary and eating a part of their flesh can be seen as inheriting the power of your enemy. Both Hema and Lendu tribal warriors have engaged in this ritualistic cannibalism, as have other militia groups in eastern DRC.

The indigenous Pygmy communities of Ituri, largely removed as participants in the conflict, have been targeted from all sides. Human Rights Watch has reported on several cases of cannibalism in eastern DRC and interviewed numerous witnesses to cannibalistic acts. Field workers from Médecins Sans Frontières have also confirmed cases of cannibalism. In peacetime, cannibalism was largely unknown across the rainforest; it seems to be more of a tactic to instil fear. Perhaps it also gives the perpetrators a sense of power and invincibility within Ituri's harsh conflict.

BUNIA The original Belgian settlement in the area was a fort, at Irumu, to guard trade routes from Stanleyville to British East African interests. Large mines built in the mountains made Irumu obsolete and administrative power shifted to Bunia. During the colonial period, the town developed a sound infrastructure. Then the Second Congo War brought the start of Bunia's, and Ituri's problems. As the Ituri Conflict raged, anyone who could afford to leave the city did so.

Bunia appeared briefly on the international stage in June 2003 when French paratroopers landed there, in one of many attempts to stop the bloodshed. A large army of paparazzi followed them into the city, celebrating the arrival of military force, then departed almost the same afternoon. Roads into the city were closed, and soldiers and armoured personnel carriers patrolled the streets, to ensure that the town remained disarmed – a way to ensure that those who sought safety in Bunia would not be subject to violence. In 2004, the UN's mandate was expanded to allow its peacekeepers to intervene to protect civilians. Bunia was a shell of its former self, but it saw a resurgence of activity with UN and NGO staff coming and going.

Bunia's airport became a stage of operations for the entire Ituri mandate. The refugee camps became larger, enveloping the surrounding hills. Thousands of tarpaulin huts grew from the grass, Toyota Land Cruisers filled with tired-looking European aid workers followed, and the deep scars that the Hema and Lendu had inflicted on each other began a very slow healing process. Yet the city centre was abandoned, a stretch of empty buildings and dirt roads. The daily activity among thousands of unemployed refugees was watching UN white armoured personnel carriers roll through town in a display of authority.

The UN peacekeepers had some success in removing the threat to Bunia's citizens, but conflict in Ituri broke out again in 2017 and is ongoing. Bunia now has thousands of internally displaced people, surviving in camps on its outskirts, to deal with. The UN is planning its withdrawal from Ituri by the end of 2024; international humanitarian organisations, which include UNHCR, WFP and Caritas, are unlikely to be leaving any time soon.

Getting there and away As ever in the DRC, the best way to check what flights there are, and when, is to go to the airport and ask there.

Minibuses for Beni and Butembo leave at sunrise (06.00). You can also get shared taxis to Mahagi on the Ugandan border. There may also be regular minibus services to Kisangani, at least in the dry season when the road is reliably passable.

Where to stay

Bunia Executive Lodge (30 rooms) 5 Rue Pacifique, Q/ Bankoko; m 081 321 3253; w bunia-executivelodge.com. Very close to airport, in quiet, secure area. Secure parking; airport pick-up, car hire available. Rooms set around central garden with good-sized pool; conference facilities, restaurant with Congolese & international menu; free Wi-Fi throughout. B/fast inc; room service available. Also has duplex apartments & 3-bedroom villa with kitchen (**$$$$**). All rooms well maintained

& comfortable, en suite with toiletries; AC, flat-screen TV, fridge or mini-bar, complimentary water. **$$–$$$**

Ituri (11 rooms) Bd de la Libération; m 099 551 2070, 081 292 1280. A big orange building with internal courtyard, partly grassed & planted with flowers. 24hr electricity & hot water, theoretically; no Wi-Fi. No restaurant, but reception will order meals in from a nearby restaurant; b/fast inc, on terrace or in room. Simple rooms, en suite, TV. **$**

MOUNT HOYO RESERVE (✤ 01°15.00 N, 30°00.00 E) This was once the centrepoint of Ituri's tourist industry in the times of Zaire and the Belgian Congo, a beautiful geographic masterpiece where the tall mountains of the Albertine Rift Valley collide with the majestic rainforests of the province. The indigenous Pygmy communities in the region of Mount Hoyo were said to be some of the least sullied by outside societies, remaining steadfast to their ancient traditions and lifestyle.

Rampant tourism in the 1980s to see the 'Last of the Pygmies' wrecked much of this, as the indigenous communities learned to capitalise on foreign visitors. Further incursions from local traders who introduced tobacco and alcohol made these communities more interested in bartering for external substances than living in a traditional manner. It was no longer a 'real Pygmy experience' but a watered-down, sanitised version of what was expected of them by visitors who were paying a lot to see what the brochures promised them.

Since the 1990s, all this has changed. Foreign troops rolling across the region, intense tribal conflict, and now the occupation of the forests by armed militias have made it almost impossible for the indigenous communities to survive at all. The reserve is completely out of bounds to visitors for the foreseeable future.

This is unfortunate as, whatever the depredations of the ADF rebels, the Mount Hoyo Reserve will still have natural wonders. There are numerous **caves**, buried among jungle vegetation and winding streams. These caves were used frequently in the 19th century to hide from Arab slave traders. The best known are **Maria Theresa**, with two large stalagmites nicknamed Adam and Eve for their two white free-standing columns, and **Matupi**, with a series of rooms and some unique rock formations. The reserve also has a waterfall called **Escaliers de Venus**, or Stairways of Venus, so named because the water flows down over rocks that appear to be steps. It used to be possible to ascend the mountain itself, over two days; a guide (and maybe some security) would be necessary in future, as the trail will not have been maintained and is probably impossible for an outsider to find.

Getting there and away Mount Hoyo Reserve is southeast of **Komanda** (✇ 01°21.56 N, 29°45.48 E), and you head east on a road just before the town. There was once a lodge at the entrance to the reserve offering some rooms and assistance to visit all of the sights, though continuing conflict has kept it closed. Park permits could be obtained at the ICCN office in Beni.

Appendix 1

LANGUAGE

FRENCH Tenses and pronunciation can be a problem for the beginner in French – but making errors with regard to these does not mean people will misunderstand you. Some Congolese themselves will often throw in words from their native language when the mood hits them.

The letter 's' is often seen at the end of words but pronounced softly, if at all, unless the next word starts with a vowel. This goes the same with 'x' and 'z', for example '*veux*' is pronounced 'veu' and '*Allez*' is said as 'Allay' as the 'ez' ending on a word is said as an 'ay' sound.

Accents are common in written French, with the acute accent (*l'accent aigu*) (angling upwards from left to right, as in 'é') and the grave accent (*l'accent grave*) (angling downwards from left to right, as in 'è') being most common. The *aigu* is pronounced with an 'ay' sound so *café* is pronounced 'caf-ay'. *Grave* accents lengthen the sound of the accented 'e', so for example *mère* rhymes with *chair*.

The cedilla (*la cédille*) is a little curve below letter 'c', such as in *Français*, and simply means that the 'c' should be given an 's' sound. So *Français* is pronounced 'Fran-say'. Without the cedilla, 'c' is hard before 'a' (café), hard before 'o' (Congo), hard before 'u' (cuisine) and soft (so an 's' sound) before 'e', 'i' and 'y'.

Negation of a verb or other word is preceded by a *ne* and followed by a *pas*. So while one would say *je mange* to say 'I eat' the negative would be *je ne mange pas* for 'I don't eat'.

Finally, the French spoken in the DRC has a Belgian flavour; for example, you may well hear people using *septante* for 70 (*soixante-dix* in standard French) and sometimes even *nonante* for 90 (instead of *quatre-vingt-dix*).

Greetings/salutations

Hello	*Bonjour*	Thank you very much	*Merci beaucoup*
What is your name?	*Comment appellez-vous?*	Excuse me	*Excusez-moi/ Je m'excuse*
Goodbye	*Au revoir*	You're welcome	*Je vous en prie* (formal)
My name is…	*Je m'appelle…*		
How are you?	*Comment ça va?*		*Je t'en prie* (informal)
I am fine	*Je suis/vais bien*		
Please	*S'il vous plaît*	Yes	*Oui*
Thank you	*Merci*	No	*Non*

Common phrases

How much?	*Combien?*	Where are you going?	*Vous allez où?*
I don't understand	*Je ne comprends pas*	Let's go!	*Allons!*
Where is…	*Où est…*	I would like…	*Je voudrais…*

I think…	*Je pense…*	I know/I don't know	*Je connais/*
I want/	*Je veux/*		*je ne connais pas*
I like/I don't like	*J'aime/je n'aime pas*	I don't have	*Je n'ai pas*
It's possible/	*C'est possible/*	When?	*Quand?*
it's not possible	*ce n'est pas possible*	Help!	*Au secours!*
I do not want	*Je ne veux pas*		

Common words

airport	*aéroport*	hunting	*chasse*
animals	*animaux*	jail	*prison*
arrested	*arrêté(e)*	juice/orange juice	*jus/jus d'orange*
bananas	*bananes*	lake	*lac*
beef	*viande de boeuf*	lunch	*déjeuner*
beer	*bière*	man/woman	*homme/femme*
bill/receipt	*facture*	market	*marché*
bird	*oiseau*	medication	*médicament*
boat	*bâteau*	money/change	*argent/monnaie*
border	*frontière*	mosquitoes	*moustiques*
breakfast	*petit déjeuner*	motorcycle	*moto*
bridge	*pont*	mountain	*montagne*
bus	*l'autobus*	nausea/to vomit	*nausée/vomir*
car	*voiture*	park	*parc*
cave	*grotte*	passport	*passeport*
chicken	*poulet*	police	*police*
church	*église*	rain	*pluie*
cliff	*falaise*	river	*fleuve*
coffee	*café*	route	*itinéraire*
country	*pays*	security	*sécurité*
diarrhoea	*diarhée*	sick/ill	*mal/malade*
dinner	*dîner*	springs	*eau de source*
doctor	*médecin*	store	*magasin*
embassy	*ambassade*	street	*rue*
expensive/inexpensive	*cher/pas cher*	sun	*soleil*
fever	*fièvre*	taxi	*taxi*
fish	*poisson*	tea	*thé*
forbidden	*interdit*	ticket	*billet*
4x4 truck	*quatre par quatre*	toilet	*toilette*
friend	*ami/copain,*	truck	*camion*
	amie/copine	vaccination card	*carte des*
gorilla	*gorille*		*vaccinations*
health	*santé*	war	*guerre*
hill	*colline*	water	*d'eau*
hospital	*hôpital*	waterfall	*chute*
hotel	*hôtel*		

Numbers

0	*zéro*		5	*cinq*
1	*un*		6	*six*
2	*deux*		7	*sept*
3	*trois*		8	*huit*
4	*quatre*		9	*neuf*

10	*dix*		40	*quarante*
11	*onze*		50	*cinquante*
12	*douze*		60	*soixante*
13	*treize*		70	*soixante-dix/septante*
14	*quatorze*		80	*quatre-vingt*
15	*quinze*		90	*quatre-vingt-dix/nonante*
16	*seize*		100	*cent*
17	*dix-sept*		500	*cinq-cent*
18	*dix-huit*		1,000	*mille*
19	*dix-neuf*		10,000	*dix mille*
20	*vingt*		½	*moitié*
30	*trente*		¼	*quartier*

Time and dates

Monday	*lundi*	Friday	*vendredi*
Tuesday	*mardi*	Saturday	*samedi*
Wednesday	*mercredi*	Sunday	*dimanche*
Thursday	*jeudi*		

morning	*matin*	day	*jour*
noon	*midi*	week	*semaine*
afternoon	*après-midi*	month	*mois*
evening	*soir*	hour	*heure*
today	*aujourd'hui*	What time is it?	*quelle heure est-il?*
tomorrow	*demain*	five o'clock	*cinq heures*
yesterday	*hier*	next week	*la semaine*
now	*maintenant*		*prochaine*
later/late	*plus tard/en retard*		

Countries

Australia	*Australie*	England	*Angleterre*
Austria	*Autriche*	France	*France*
Canada	*Canada*	Germany	*Allemagne*
Central African	*République*	Ireland	*Irlande*
Republic	*Centrafricaine*	Japan	*Japon*
Congo Republic	*République du*	New Zealand	*Nouvelle Zélande*
	Congo	Scotland	*Écosse*
DRC	*République*	South Africa	*Afrique Du Sud*
	Démocratique	Spain	*Espagne*
	du Congo	United States	*États-Unis*

NATIONAL LANGUAGES The DRC has four 'national languages': Kituba, Lingala, Swahili and Tshiluba. Please note that words in the African language vocabulary list that begins on page 231 have been split with hyphens to indicate where stress should be placed when speaking.

Lingala Lingala was originally developed as a 'military' language, or rather one that was used only by officials of the Belgian Congo. Over time, it became the lingua franca along the banks of the River Congo, where there was no common tongue between tribes. It has traditionally been the language of the Congolese army, although Swahili is becoming more widely spoken even in the army, and of Congolese music. There are slight differences of dialect, but the version used by TV presenters and so forth is a standardised language. As Lingala has developed, numerous words have been adopted from French or even Portuguese.

Swahili The same Swahili used across East Africa will work fine in eastern DRC, with very little difference in local words or accents. Plenty of interchange between visitors has made the language reasonably uniform the closer one gets to the eastern border. However, the Swahili used in central DRC can be jumbled with words from Lingala or Tshiluba, along with anything in French that might come to mind faster than Swahili.

Kikongo The Kikongo language is descended from the ancient language of the Kongo Kingdom (page 16). A variant of it, Kituba, is spoken in the Republic of the Congo.

Tshiluba The two cities where Tshiluba is mainly spoken are Kananga and Mbuji-Mayi, with minor variations between the dialects. I have included the versions normally used in Mbuji-Mayi, the largest Tshiluba-speaking city.

African language vocabulary

Greetings/salutations

English	Lingala	Swahili	Kikongo	Tshiluba
Hello	M-bo-tay	Jam-bo	M-bo-tay	Mo-yee
Goodbye	Ken-de-kay Ma-la-mu	Kwa-he-ree	Koo-en-da M-bo-tay	Noo-sha-la M-bee-pa
How are you?	San-go Nee-nee?	Ha-bar-ee?	Yin-ka Moo-tin-doo?	Ma-loo Kay?
I am fine	Ma-la-mu, Mu-le-see	Nu-zuri	Bay-to Kay M-bo-tay	Bim-pa, Twa-sa Kee-dee-la
Please	Pa-la-do	Ta-fa-da-lee	Lem-voo-ka	Oo-fwee-la Loo-say
Thank you	Mee-lee-see	A-san-tay	Ma-ton-do	Twa-sa Kee-dee-la
You're welcome	Lee-kam-bo-tay	Ka-ree-bu	Kee-ma Ve	Ka-kway-na Bwa-loo
Yes	Ee-yo	N-dee-yo	In-ga	Ee-yo
No	Tay	Ha-pa-na	N-ka-too	To

Common phrases

How much?	Bo-nee?	N-ga-pee?	In-kwa?	In-ga?
I don't understand	Na-Yo-Kee-Tay	See-fa-ha-mu	Moo-noo Ba-koo-sa Ve	Tshay-na Hgoo-voo-a To
Where is...?	Wa-pee...?	Wa-pee...?	Wa-pee Kee-see-ka?	N-ten-ee?
When?	Tayn-go?	Lee-nee?	In-kee nTay-ngo	Dee-ba Kay-ee?
foreigner (white)	mon-de-lay	mu-zun-gu	—	Mu-to

Numbers

0	zee-ro	se-fu-ree	nee pa-va-la	ee-nee-zay-oo-goo
1	mo-ko	mo-Ja	mo-see	oo-moy
2	mee-ba-lay	m-bee-lee	zo-lay	ee-bee-dee
3	mee-sa-to	ta-too	ta-too	ee-sa-too
4	mee-nay	n-nay	ee-ya	ee-na-yee
5	mee-ta-no	ta-no	ta-noo	ee-ta-noo
6	mo-to-ba	see-ta	sam-ba-noo	ee-sam-bom-bo

7	n-sam-bo	sa-ba	ni-sam-bwa-dee	moo-an-da moo-tay-kay-ta
8	mo-am-bee	na-nay	na-na	moo-an-da moo-koo-loo
9	lee-bwa	tee-sa	eev-wa	tshee-tay-ma
10	zo-mee	ku-mee	koo-mee	dee-tay-ma
11	zo-mee na mo-ko	ku-mee na mo-jo	koo-mee mo-see	dee-koo-mee n-oo-moy
12	zo-mee na mee-ba-lay	ku-mee na m-bee-lee	koo-mee zo-lay	dee-koo-mee n-ee-bee-dee
13	zo-mee na mee-sa-to	ku-mee na ta-too	koo-mee ta-too	dee-koo-mee n-ee-sa-too
14	zo-mee na mee-nay	ku-mee na n-nay	koo-mee ee-ya	dee-koo-mee n-ee-na-yee
15	zo-mee na mee-ta-no	ku-mee na ta-no	koo-mee ta-noo	dee-koo-mee n-ee-ta-noo
16	zo-mee na mo-to-ba	ku-mee na see-ta	koo-mee sam-ba-noo	dee-koo-mee n-ee-sam-bom-bo
17	zo-mee na n-sam-bo	ku-mee na sa-ba	koo-mee sam-bwa-dee	dee-koo-mee moo-an-da moo-tay-kay-ta
18	zo-mee na mo-am-bee	ku-mee na na-nay	koo-mee na-na	dee-koo-mee moo-an-da moo-koo-loo
19	zo-mee na lee-bwa	ku-mee na tee-sa	koo-mee eev-wa	dee-koo-mee nee tshee-tay-ma
20	n-too-koo mee-ba-lay	ish-ir-in-ee	ma-koo-mee zo-lay	ma-koo-mee a boo-dee
30	n-too-koo mee-sa-to	thay-la-thee-nee	ma-koo-mee ta-too	ma-koo-mee a sa-to
40	n-too-koo mee-nay	a-ro-bay-nee	ma-koo-mee ee-ya	ma-koo-mee a na-yee
50	n-too-koo mee-ta-no	ham-see-nee	ma-koo-mee ta-noo	ma-koo-mee a ta-no
60	n-too-koo mo-to-ba	see-tee-nee	ma-koo-mee sam-ba-noo	ma-koo-mee a sam-bom-bo
70	n-too-koo n-sam-bo	sa-bee-nee septanet	ma-koo-mee sam-bwa-dee	ma-koo-mee nee moo-an-da moo-tay-kay-ta
80	n-too-koo mo-am-bee	the-ma-nee-nee	ma-koo-mee na-na	ma-koo-mee nee moo-an-da moo-koo-loo
90	n-too-koo lee-bwa	tee-see-nee	ma-koo-mee eev-wa	ma-koo-mee nee tsee-tay-ma
100	n-ka-ma mo-ko	mee-ya	n-ka-ma	loo-ka-ma
500	n-ka-ma mee-ta-no	mee-ya ta-no	n-ka-ma ta-noo	ka-ma ee-ta-noo
1,000	n-ko-to mo-ko	el-foo	dee-fun-da mo-see	tshee-hoo-noo
10,000	n-ko-to zo-mee	ku-mee el-foo	ma-foon-da koo-mee kee-tee-nee mo-see na zo-lay	

Time and dates

Monday	Mo-sa-la Mo-ko	Joo-ma-ta-too	Kee-loom-boo Ya Loo-ndee	Mu Dee-moy-ee
Tuesday	Mee-sa-la Mee-ba-lay	Joo-man	Kee-loom-boo Ya Zo-lay	Mu Dee-bee-dee
Wednesday	Mee-sa-la Mee-sa-to	Joo-ma-ta-no	Kee-loom-boo Ya Ta-too	Mu Dee-sa-too
Thursday	Mee-sa-la Mee-nay	Al-ham-ee-see	Kee-loom-boo Ya Ee-ya	Mu Dee-na-yee
Friday	Mee-sa-la Mee-ta-no	El-joo-ma	Kee-loom-boo Ya Ta-noo	Mu Dee-ta-noo
Saturday	Mo-ko-lo Mwa M-pu-so	Joo-ma-mo-see	Kee-loom-boo Ya Sa-ba-la	Mu Dee-sam-bom-bo
Sunday	Ee-yen-ga	Joo-ma-pil-ee	Kee-loom-boo Ya Loo-min-goo	Mu Dia-loo-min-goo
today	le-lo	le-o	loo-boo	lay-loo
tomorrow	lo-bee	ke-sho	m-ba-see	ma-la-ba
yesterday	lo-bee	ja-na	ma-zo-no	ma-kay-lay-la
now	see-ko-yo	pa-pa	may-loo may-loo	m-pee-djay-oo

233

Appendix 2

GLOSSARY OF NAMES AND ACRONYMS

GLOSSARY OF NAMES

Albertville	Former colonial name for Kalemie.
Antoine Gizenga	Leader of the rebel government in Stanleyville in 1961; also prime minister from 1960 to 1961.
Avikat	Aviation Katangaise, air force and air cargo company of independent Katanga state from 1960 to 1961.
Bakwanga	Former colonial name for Mbuji-Mayi.
Bantu	General ethnic group to which most tribes in central Africa belong.
Banyamulenge	Tutsis who settled in eastern Congo. Though ethnically the same, they are differentiated from Rwandan Tutsis.
Cabinda	Small exclave of Angola wedged between the two Congos.
Christoph Gbenye	President of the Lumumbist-loyal government of Stanleyville, 1965–67.
Congo Reform Association	First humanitarian organisation to protest against the atrocities in the Congo Free State, 1898–1906.
Coquilhatville	Former colonial name for Mbandaka.
Costermansville	Former colonial name for Bukavu.
Cyrille Adoula	Founder of the MNC; Prime Minister of Congo-Léopoldville 1961–64.
Diogo Cão	Portuguese explorer and the first European to encounter the mouth of the River Congo.
Dona Beatriz	See *Kimpa Vita* (opposite).
Elisabethville	Former colonial name for Lubumbashi.
Ernest Wamba Dia Wamba	Politician who led splinter group of the RCD called RCD-ML, based in Kisangani.
Etienne Tshisekedi	Leader of Zairian opposition party the UDPS. Prime minister under Mobutu Sese Seko and Laurent Kabila.
Évolué	Belgian programme of assimilation for the Congolese, whereby they were rewarded for becoming more European.
Federal State of South Kasai	Secessionist region of the DRC, with capital at Mbuji-Mayi. Independent from 1960 to 1961.
Gaston Émile Soumialot	Political leader of the Simbas from 1965 to 1967.
Gécamines	State-owned mining corporation of the DRC, formerly UMHK.
George Washington Williams	African-American historian who first documented atrocities against the Congolese by Belgians.

HMS *Congo*	First steam-powered warship commissioned to navigate up the River Congo.
Interahamwe	Extremist Hutu militias aimed at murdering Tutsis. Fled into eastern DRC from Rwanda in 1994.
Jadotville	Former colonial name for Likasi.
James Kingston Tuckey	British explorer who made first attempt to navigate up the River Congo, in 1816.
Joseph Kabila	Son of assassinated Laurent Kabila and former president of the DRC.
Joseph Kasa-Vubu	First president of the Congo Republic (Léopoldville) from 1960 to 1965.
Katanga	Former province of the DRC, independent from 1960 to 1963. Further fracture from 1960 to 1961 as North Katanga seceded.
Kimbanguists	Religion founded by Simon Kimbangu in the Belgian Congo in 1940s.
Kimpa Vita	'Congolese Joan of Arc'; reunited Kongo Kingdom in 1700. Also referred to as Dona Beatriz.
King Léopold II	Belgian monarch who engineered the creation of the Congo Free State.
Kongo Kingdom	Nation that dominated the Congo regions from 1400 to 1665.
Laurent Désiré Kabila	Rwandan- and Ugandan-backed leader of the AFDL and head of state of the DRC from 1997 to 2001.
Laurent Nkunda	Rebel general of RCD-Goma faction operating in the Nord-Kivu region.
Léopoldville	Former colonial name for Kinshasa.
Luluaborg	Former colonial name for the city of Kananga.
Lusaka Peace Accord	1999 peace agreement aimed at ending the Second Congo War (page 34).
Mai-Mai	Jungle rebel groups in the eastern DRC.
Mbanza Kongo	Original capital of Kongo Kingdom, in present-day Angola. Renamed to São Salvador by the Portuguese.
Mike Hoare	Irish mercenary of the 1960s who conducted a number of operations in Congo-Leopoldville.
Mobutu Sese Seko	Head of state of the DRC from 1965 to 1997.
Moïse Tshombe	Leader of secessionist Katanga state from 1960 to 1963. Later appointed Prime Minister of Congo-Léopoldville.
Nicolas Olenga	Military leader of the Simbas from 1965 to 1967.
Nyiragongo	Large volcano near Goma, which last erupted in 2002.
okapi	Rare animal found only in the northeastern DRC, most closely related to the giraffe.
Operation ARTEMIS	European force that arrived in Ituri Province between May and September 2003.
palm wine	Common alcoholic drink in the Congo.
Patrice Lumumba	First prime minister of the Congo Republic in 1960.
Paulis	Former colonial name for Isiro.
Ponthierville	Former colonial name for Ubundu.
Port Francqui	Former colonial name for Ilebo.
Portuguese Congo	Former colonial name for Cabinda.
Pygmy	Indigenous peoples living in Congo rainforests.

São Salvador	See *Mbanza Kongo* (page 235).
sapeur	Man who practises *la Sape*, a subculture defined by elegant, flamboyant clothing and mutual respect.
Shaba	Traditional name for Katanga Province; name used in Mobutu's Zaire from 1969 to 1997.
Simbas	Leftist rebels in eastern Congo during the mid 1960s.
South Kasai	Secessionist province of Congo-Léopoldville from 1960 to 1961. Folded back into Congo-Léopoldville and divided into two modern-day provinces, Kasai Occidental and Kasai Orientale.
Stanley Falls	Former colonial name for Boyoma Falls (near Kisangani).
Stanley Pool	Former colonial name for Malebo Pool (shores of Kinshasa and Brazzaville).
Stanleyville	Former colonial name for Kisangani.
Thysville	Former colonial name for Mbanza-Ngungu.
Tippu Tip	Arab-African trading magnate of the 19th century who assisted Henry Morton Stanley in his explorations of eastern Congo. Claimed eastern Congo from 1884 to 1887.
William Henry Sheppard	African-American missionary who documented atrocities against the Congolese people at the end of the 19th century.

NAMES AND ACRONYMS FOR CONGO-KINSHASA

DRC, Democratic Republic of the Congo, République Democratique du Congo, RDC, RD Congo, DR Congo, Congo-Kinshasa

Obsolete names: Congo Free State, Belgian Congo, Colonie Belge Du Congo, Congo Belge et Ruanda Urundi, Congo-Léopoldville, People's Republic of the Congo, Republic of the Congo, Zaire

GLOSSARY OF ACRONYMS

ABAKO	Association Des Bakongo. First political party to form in the Belgian Congo, led by Joseph Kasa-Vubu.
ADF	Allied Democratic Front. Ugandan rebel group that was used as Uganda's reason to invade eastern DRC in 1998.
AFDL	Alliance des Forces Démocratiques pour la Libération du Congo-Zaire, or Alliance of Democratic Forces for the Liberation of Congo-Zaire. Laurent Kabila's Rwanda- and Uganda-backed rebellion that marched on Kinshasa in 1997.
AIA	Association Internationale Africaine. Humanitarian organisation created by King Léopold for the African people.
AIC	Association Internationale du Congo. Private holding company created by King Léopold for securing assets in the Congo under his name.
AMP	Alliance pour la Majorité Présidentielle, or Alliance for the Presidential Majority. Kabila's former political party.
ANC	Armée Nationale Congolais. Reformed army of 1960s Congo-Léopoldville.
AU	African Union. Formerly called AEC and OAU.
CNL	Conseil National de Libération. Lumumbist party that took Stanleyville in 1964; engineered the Kwilu Uprising.
ECC	Eglise du Christ au Congo. Federation of Protestant church groups in the DRC.

FARDC	Forces Armées RD Congo. Current name of national army in the DRC.
FAZ	Forces Armées Zaïroises. Mobutu Sese Seko's regular army forces.
FDLR	Forces Democratiques de Libération du Rwanda. Rwandan Hutus based in eastern DRC who fought against the Rwandan-backed RCD.
FLEC	Frente para a Libertação do Enclave de Cabinda. Separatist organisation in Cabinda enclave.
ICCN	Institut Congolais pour la Conservation de la Nature. Congolese parks management board.
LRA	Lord's Resistance Army. Fundamentalist rebels fighting against the Ugandan government with rear bases in northeastern DRC.
MLC	Mouvement de Libération Congolais. Ugandan-backed group in the northern DRC that fought against Kinshasa in the Second Congo War.
MNC	Mouvement National Congolais. Political party in 1950s Belgian Congo, led by Patrice Lumumba.
MONUC	Mission de l'Organisation des Nations-Unies en République Démocratique du Congo, or Mission of the UN in the DRC. Second UN mission in the DRC from 2000 to 2010; then renamed to MONUSCO.
MPLA	Movimento Popular de Libertação de Angola, or Popular Movement for Liberation of Angola. Had training camps in Congo-Brazzaville throughout the 1960s.
NGO	Non-governmental organisation.
ONUC	Operation des Nations-Unies au Congo. Operation of the UN in the Congo. First UN mission in the Congo, from 1960 to 1964.
RCD	Rassemblement Congolais pour la Démocratie, or Rally for Congolese Democracy. Broke into three factions: RCD-Goma; RCD-K/ML (based in Kisangani); and RCD-National. Dispersed at the end of 2003.
RPF	Rwandese Patriotic Front. National army of Rwanda that invaded eastern Congo.
UDPS	Union pour la Démocratie et le Progrès Social. First opposition party permitted in Zaire, led by Etienne Tshisekedi, father of the current president of the DRC.
UMHK	Union Minière du Haut Katanga. Belgian mining company that operated in Katanga Province from 1906 to 1966, then nationalised and renamed Gécamines.
UN/UNESCO/ UNHCR/UNICEF	United Nations/United Nations Educational, Scientific and Cultural Organisation/United Nations Humanitarian Commission for Refugees/United Nations International Children's Emergency Fund.
UNITA	União Nacional para a Independência Total de Angola. Angolan rebels who held rear bases along the Angola–DRC border. Abandoned armed struggle and participated in electoral politics after the death in 2002 of its leader Jonas Savimbi.
UPDF	Ugandan People's Defence Force. Ugandan regular army that invaded eastern Congo.

Appendix 3

FURTHER INFORMATION

BOOKS
History There is no shortage of books on Zaire and the Democratic Republic of the Congo, and many of them illustrate wonderfully the coloured and often brutal history of the country.

Edgerton, Robert *The Troubled Heart of Africa: A History of the Congo* St Martin's Press, 2002. A straightforward account of the Congolese timeline, and probably easier to read on bumpy dirt roads than some thicker and more academic accounts of Congolese history.

Enwall, Beverly *Mbote, Mondele: The Story of the Democratic Republic of Congo* Asgaard Viking Editions, 2011. A history of the DRC extracted from the diaries of numerous officials, journalists and missionaries who worked in the country.

Gourevitch, Philip *We Wish to Inform You That Tomorrow We Will be Killed With Our Families: Stories from Rwanda* Picador, 1999. So much of what happened in the country at its transformation from Zaire to the DRC was a direct result of what occurred in Rwanda. Even now in the Kivu provinces with Interahamwe, understanding the battle between Hutus and Tutsis is critical to understanding why the eastern part of the country continues to be in turmoil. This book does a fine job in explaining the Rwandan genocide.

Hinde, Sidney Langford *The Fall of the Congo Arabs* Methuen & Co., 1897, and Bibliobazaar, 2009. A historical account of the skirmishes between Belgian forces and Arab slave traders in the eastern Congo Free State, and the events surrounding them that eventually led to them leaving the region.

Hochschild, Adam *King Leopold's Ghost* Mariner Books, 1999. Perhaps most famous among the books on the DRC, and most pertinent to understanding the long-running conundrums of the country. It documents the early decades of the Congo Free State, how such an unimaginable place began to form and later exist under the Belgian monarch's rule.

Kennedy, Pagan *Black Livingstone: A True Tale of Adventure in the Nineteenth Century Congo* Penguin, 2002. Chronicling the life and times of William Henry Sheppard.

Lewis, Jerome *The Batwa Pygmies of the Great Lakes Region* Minority Rights Group International, 2000. Lewis describes the history of the Batwa Pygmies in the Great Lakes region of eastern DRC, Uganda, Burundi and Rwanda, and the pressures faced today by what are believed to be the region's earliest inhabitants. An informative 32-page report, also available as a PDF from w minorityrights.org.

Liebowitz, Daniel and Pearson, Charles *The Last Expedition: Stanley's Mad Journey through the Congo* W Norton, 2006. This book does a great job of chronicling Stanley's last voyage up the River Congo to Sudan.

Manning, Olivia *The Remarkable Expedition* New York, Atheneum, 1995. A reissued account from 1947 of the events connected with the rescue of Emim Pasha by Henry Morton Stanley.

Marchal, Jules *Lord Leverhulme's Ghosts: Colonial Exploitation in the Congo* Verso, 2008. A heavily researched exploration of labour practices in colonial Congo. Introduction by Adam Hochschild.

Nzongola-Ntalaja, Georges *The Congo: From Leopold to Kabila* Zed Books, 2002. At the more academic end of things is this fine account delving deeper into the details of the DRC's history. If you need solid clarification of cause and effect throughout the country's history, this book is where to find it.

Prunier, Gérard *Africa's World War: Congo, the Rwandan Genocide, and the Making of a Continental Catastrophe* Oxford University Press, 2011. A detailed and formal account of the precursors and the outcome of the war in the DRC. Includes a chapter on putting the war into context, and what it means in a national, continental and global perspective.

Stanley, Henry Morton *In Darkest Africa: Or the Quest, Rescue and Retreat of Emin Governor of Equatoria*, Volumes 1 & 2. Stackpole Books, 2001. Stanley's own record of his last disastrous journey into the Congo, an expedition to rescue Emin Pasha following an uprising of Sudanese Muslims in Equateur Province.

Stanley, Henry Morton *Through the Dark Continent: Volume 2* Dover Publications, 1988. On the theme of the scramble for Africa. Stanley's accounts – his direct writings of this time, uncoloured by present knowledge – of the journey down the River Congo are an interesting look at the exploration of a region where no other European had visited.

Stearns, Jason *Dancing in the Glory of Monsters: The Collapse of the Congo and the Great War of Africa* Public Affairs, 2011. A well-written and well-researched account of the DRC from the fall of Mobutu, to the beginning of its 1996 war, to the present.

Turnbull, Colin M *The Forest People* Jonathan Cape, 1961 (and later reprints by different publishers). A compassionate and absorbing account of the time the author spent among the Pygmies of the Congo's Ituri Forest. He describes the history, background, lives, families, hunting, illnesses, quarrels, love affairs, music and traditional ceremonies of these ancient peoples.

Wrong, Michela *In the Footsteps of Mr Kurtz* Harper Perennial, 2002. For a fine documentation of the final years of Mobutu's regime, written in an easy-to-read style it provides a good account of how Zaire's vast riches were shuttled away by an African dictator while the people of this vast and rich nation were left, again, to fend for themselves.

Economy

Carmody, Padraig *The New Scramble For Africa* Polity Press, 2011. Gives a broad overview of the economic pressures and growth in African countries that is defining the beginning of the 21st century on the continent. Plenty of details on the situation in the DRC.

Eichstaedt, Peter and Hill, Lawrence *Consuming the Congo: War and Conflict Minerals in the World's Deadliest Place* Lawrence Hill Books, 2011. A detailed account of the internal factors and global powers still involved in shaping the modern Democratic Republic of the Congo's economy.

Grignon, Francois, Nest, Michael and Kisangani, Emizet François *The Democratic Republic of Congo: Economic Dimensions of War and Peace* Lynne Rienner Publishers Inc, 2006. An academic paper exploring the connection between the DRC's economic structure and how it relates to the constant conflict that the country has suffered.

Matamba, Tumba Bob *The Development of the Democratic Republic of the Congo: Promises, Bankruptcies, and Challenges* Trafford Publishing, 2011. Written by a local Congolese academic and businessman, it provides a solid account of the DRC's challenges to achieve prosperity.

Nest, Michael *Coltan* Polity Press, 2011. Probably the most articulate and well-researched resource on the illegal trade of coltan, and its relation to the economy of the DRC.

Miscellaneous

Butcher, Tim *Blood River: A Journey to Africa's Broken Heart* Random House, 2007. A modern-day journalist follows Henry Morton Stanley's original overland voyage from Kalemie to Boma.

Conrad, Joseph *Heart of Darkness* Penguin Books, 2000. For fiction, no-one should visit the Congo without having read this famous account of Conrad's own journey down the River Congo. It is often cited as the first great literary work of the 20th century.

Duffy, Kevin *Children of the Forest: Africa's Mbuti Pygmies* Waveland Press, 1995. An exploration of Pygmy culture.

Hergé *Tintin in the Congo* Egmont Children's, 2005. On a lighter note is this book, a great read, if not entirely politically correct, and he is still the most famous cartoon character to visit the Congo.

Makelele, Albert *This is a Good Country: Welcome to the Congo* Authorhouse, 2008. A historical record of writings by a variety of Congolese contributors on their history since independence.

Naipaul, V S *A Bend in the River*, Picador, 1979. Although the river and the town at its bend are never mentioned by name, the book is set in Kisangani and is a brilliant fictionalisation of the turbulent politics of the newly independent (and also anonymous) country.

Roome, William J W *A Traveller in the Congo – A Historical Sketch of a Traveller's Experience in Africa* Read Books, 2011. A reprint of a turn-of-the-20th-century travel journal of the Congo.

Stewart, Gary *Rumba on the River: A History of the Popular Music of the Two Congos* Verso, 2004. A full exploration of the roots of Congo music can be found in this book, an excellent reference for music past and present that best defines the 'Congo' sound.

Che Guevara in the Congo

Guevara, Ernesto 'Che' *The African Dream: The Diaries of the Revolutionary War in the Congo* Patrick Camiller (trans), Grove Press, 2001. As a primary source, his diaries have been translated into English in this book.

Galvez, William *Che in Africa: Che Guevara's Congo Diary* Ocean Press, 1999. Easier to read, this book chronicles his time in eastern Congo and how he got there.

Gleijeses, Piero *Conflicting Missions: Havana, Washington, and Africa, 1959–1976* University of North Carolina Press, 2002. Most detailed historically is this book, which is heavy on Cuba's involvement with Angola but indispensable reading for the finer details of Che Guevara and Cuba's power plays across both Congos in the 1960s.

Villafana, Frank R *Cold War in the Congo: The Confrontation of Cuban Military Forces, 1960–1967* Transaction Publishers, 2009. A detailed account of Cuban involvement in both Congos throughout the 1960s, for both Western and communist interests.

Wildlife guides

Kingdon, Jonathan *The Kingdon Field Guide to African Mammals* Christopher Helm Publishers, 2003. For detailed descriptions on mammals seek out this excellent book. A little bit obsessive with smaller mammals, which is perhaps good, but unlikely one will get the chance to observe these creatures up close too often in the DRC. Nonetheless it's one of the best English-language field guides for wildlife enthusiasts. It's a bit unwieldy and perhaps a better choice for travelling with is the shorter version, *The Kingdon Pocket Guide to African Mammals* (Princeton University Press, 2005).

Sinclair, Ian *Birds of Africa South of the Sahara* Princeton University Press, 2004. This birding guide comes highly recommended and covers all the species that can be seen in central Africa. It includes a representative drawing of every bird species recorded on the continent along with diagrams of their migratory range.

Stuart, Chris and Stuart, Tilde *Southern, Central, and East African Mammals* New Holland Publishers, 1992. With information on where to find common species within the confines of 'Zaire', meaning it's a little outdated these days but still a solid resource for those looking for wildlife in the DRC.

Survival guides If you're working for an extended period of time in the DRC and don't have any training or experience in a rather volatile tropical region, I definitely recommend first of all attending a basic survival course for tropical wilderness. As well, having a few books around to refresh your memory is always handy.

Pelton, Robert Young *Come Back Alive* Doubleday, 1999. A solid and entertaining read on the subject which covers pretty much everything one may encounter on Congolese soil, if only in basic detail.

Randall, Jeff and Perrin, Mike *Adventure Travel in the Third World: Everything You Need to Know to Survive in Remote and Hostile Destinations* Paladin Press, 2003. More robust details on economically underdeveloped nations survival skills such as bribery and hiring armed guards can be found in this detailed guide.

Werner, David *Where There Is No Doctor* Macmillan Education, 1993. An excellent medical field guide that has easy-to-read instructions on basic medical care when facilities don't exist, how to recognise symptoms, and provide treatment in remote regions.

WEBSITES

Agence Congolaise de Presse w acp.cd The national press agency, in French; a good source of news from all over the DRC.

Africa Confidential w africa-confidential.com. Well-researched analysis and reporting on African politics. Some articles by subscription.

All Africa w allafrica.com. Collects all online press releases for African nations, sorted by country.

Congo Mines w congomines.org. Supported by The Carter Center, a portal for information on the industrial mining sector in the DRC.

International Crisis Group w crisisweb.org. Decent summary of the DRC conflict, with ongoing analysis and reports.

Global Security w globalsecurity.org. Well-maintained site that provides a decent breakdown of the continuing conflict in the DRC, with a large amount of background information available.

Human Rights Watch w hrw.org. Numerous operatives on the ground make their reports well researched and highly illuminating. They have provided continuous coverage on atrocities across the eastern DRC.

Radio Okapi w radiookapi.net. The most reliable source of all aspects of news about the DRC, in French; the website of Radio Okapi, the United Nations' radio station, which broadcasts across the country, in French and the four national languages.

FILMS

The African Queen (1951) John Huston, Director. Starring Humphrey Bogart and Katharine Hepburn. Bogart won his only Oscar for the performance, and the Africa scenes were shot entirely near Ubundu, just south of modern-day Kisangani.

Masters of the Congo Jungle (1959) Henry Brandt, Director. Documentary depicting the struggles inherent in the Belgian Congo. Portions narrated by Orson Welles.

The Nun's Story (1959) Fred Zinneman, Director. American film starring Audrey Hepburn, concerning the fictional account of a Belgian nun working in the Congo.

Gorillas in the Mist (1988) Michael Apted, Director. Starring Sigourney Weaver. Fictional retelling of the life and times of Dian Fossey, with her initial difficulties of researching mountain gorillas in the Congo.

Mountains of the Moon (1989) Bob Rafelson, Director. Chronicles the story of Richard Francis Burton and Jonathan Speke as they search for the source of the Nile, and encounter the Rwenzori Mountains.

When We Were Kings (1996) Leon Gast, Director. Detailed documentary of 'The Rumble In The Jungle', Muhammad Ali and George Foreman's Kinshasa fight in 1974.

Mobutu, King of Zaire (1999) Thierry Michel, Director. Documentary exploring the life and times of Mobutu Sese Seko.

Lumumba (2000) Raoul Peck, Director. French drama exploring the murder of Patrice Lumumba.

Congo River (2005) Thierry Michel, Director. Explores the history and entire length of the River Congo from source to mouth.

Katanga Business (2009) Thierry Michel, Director. Documentary about the mining industry in Katanga Province. Thierry Michel is a Belgian documentarian who has specialised in the Democratic Republic of the Congo. His films are in French but include English subtitles.

Virunga (2014) Orlando von Einsiedel, Director. Documentary about brave park rangers risking their lives to protect mountain gorillas.

Index

Page numbers in **bold** indicate major entries; those in *italic* indicate maps.

INDEX OF ADVERTISERS